Diamond Greats

Diamond Greats

Profiles and Interviews
with 65 of Baseball's
History Makers

Rich Westcott

Meckler Books
the trade division of
Meckler Corporation

The author would like to express his appreciation to the following for providing the photographs for this book:

A special thanks to Allied Photocolor of St. Louis, Missouri, George Brace Studio of Chicago, Illinois and Jim Rowe of Berwyn, Illinois for supplying many of the pictures.

Also, thanks to the Baltimore Orioles, Boston Red Sox, Chicago Cubs, Cincinnati Reds, New York Yankees, Philadelphia Phillies, Pittsburgh Pirates and St. Louis Cardinals, and to *Baseball Hobby News*, Mrs. Jennie Betts, George Case, Jack Russell, Mickey Vernon, Whitey Witt and Tony Zonca.

FIRST EDITION

Library of Congress Cataloging-in-Publication Data

Westcott, Rich.
    Diamond greats.

    1. Baseball players—United States—Interviews.
I. Title.
GV865.A1W47   1988   796.357'092'2 [B]   87-24023
ISBN 0-88736-220-6

Meckler Books, the trade division of Meckler Corporation, 11 Ferry Lane West, Westport CT 06880
Meckler Ltd., Grosvenor Gardens House, Grosvenor Gardens, London SW1W 0BS, UK

Printed on acid free paper.

Manufactured in the United States of America.

To Lois,

who is not only my wife and mother of my four great children,
but also my best friend...
for caring and for always being there when help is needed.

Contents

Acknowledgments

A book of this kind is not produced easily. For one thing, it takes the cooperation and assistance of a number of people.

Foremost, of course, are the subjects themselves—the players who so generously contributed their time, their stories and in many cases the hospitality of their homes. Without exception, these men have willingly and with warmth and vigor returned to the days of yesteryear to recall those nearly always happy times when they performed as major league players.

It can be honestly said that not a single man featured in the pages of this book was anything but a gracious interviewee. To a man, these former players have opened up their hearts and their memories, and cheerfully allowed an outsider a beautiful and very special glimpse of baseball history that most people never see.

To these men, who have contributed immeasurably to this book, I am deeply indebted, not only because they gave so much of themselves, but because they allowed me the enjoyable privilege of sharing and reliving their experiences with them.

I am also grateful to *Baseball Hobby News* and its editor, Frank Barning, without whom this book would not exist. It was Barning who originally consented to publish my interviews with former players, and who since then has published most of those found on the following pages.

His interest in these works and the encouragement he has provided over the years have been most helpful.

Last but hardly least, I wish to thank my wife, Lois, for her invaluable work as a typist, proofreader and general editorial consultant. Her willingness to pitch in with unyielding determination assured that the completion of this book would be possible.

Introduction

There are many reasons that professional baseball is such a colorful and enduring sport. But of all the reasons that come quickly to mind, none has had more bearing on the rich history of the game than the players themselves.

More than records and statistics, more than legendary teams, more than ball parks overflowing with character, the players are the ones who have given substance to the National Pastime and make it the magnificent attraction that it is.

Some have been national heroes; some have commanded no more attention than a solitary line in a box score. All, however, were big leaguers. And they not only helped to shape the game, they formed its very backbone.

Diamond Greats is a look at some of these men, their careers and the contributions they have made to the special game called baseball.

Many threads unify the 65 players profiled on the following pages. Foremost, they all performed with admirable skill and were men of noteworthy achievements.

Whether they were Hall of Famers, Most Valuable Players, batting champions, Cy Young Award winners, fielding leaders, or stolen base champions, all accomplished certain levels of proficiency that raised them well above the levels of ordinary players.

Virtually every player led his league in one category or another at some point during his career. Many also performed extraordinary feats or took part in history-making events. All have been baseball stars of some magnitude, and as such have played significant roles in the evolution of the game.

The careers of these players range from the early 1900s to the 1980s. Although their experiences vary, they have one other thing in common: all loved the game of baseball.

Personal interviews with these players, done over a period of six years, have taken me on a fascinating journey through baseball history. From the peerless recollections of Whitey Witt to the animated pronouncements of Ted Williams, from a look at the momentary brilliance of Don Larsen to a view of the relentless durability of Gaylord Perry, the excitement of having baseball history relived right before my eyes has been an experience that could never be duplicated.

This book has been carefully divided into a series of categories, including sections on members of baseball's Hall of Fame, Most Valuable Players, champion hitters and outstanding pitchers. The section ''The Old Guard'' deals with players who performed mostly in the 1930s or earlier. ''Men of Special Distinction'' features players who performed historic feats that rank among the most memorable events in the history of the game. Finally, ''Solid Performers, One and All'' focuses on players who, although they may not have been among the top stars of their eras, were outstanding, everyday players who performed valiantly during their careers.

The stories these players have told represent a living history of the game of baseball. It is hoped that their recollections and the stories of their deeds will not only help to accentuate the accomplishments of these fine players, but also will serve as a contribution that will help to preserve the rich lore of baseball.

This group of players ventured into areas where only a relatively few have tread. And they did not tread lightly. They played hard, they played with passion, and they played to win. They enjoyed their careers, and they were thankful that they were given the talent to be baseball players.

Most of all, though, they played exceptionally well.

—Rich Westcott

Hall of Famers

Luke Appling—
Old Aches and Pains Could Hit

At an age when most men have yielded long ago to the temptation of retirement, Luke Appling slows down only long enough to salute the pleasures of a good life.

Appling is approaching 80. But for him, age is no barrier to activity. He is a man whose abundant energy is matched by a *joie de vivre* that refuses to be extinguished.

Recognition of that condition occurred in 1984 when Appling's employer, the Atlanta Braves, named him their batting coach. Several years later, Appling was still going strong, traveling the minor league circuit as the Braves' roving hitting instructor.

It has been a marvelous career for the former Chicago White Sox shortstop who was elected to the Hall of Fame in 1964. Over that period, there is little in the game that Appling has not either seen or done.

As a player, Appling put in 20 years in the big leagues—all with the Chisox—winning two batting championships and ranking as one of the game's finest shortstops.

He finished his career with a lifetime batting average of .310, which included nine straight seasons over .300 and only two seasons in which he hit under .300 as a regular.

Appling was the first White Sox player to win a batting title when he led the league in 1936 with a .388 mark. That is the highest average ever attained by an American League shortstop. He won the crown again in 1943 with a .328 average.

Luke hit over .300 14 times as a regular. In 1947, his .306 average was the sixth best in baseball history for 40-year-old players. He followed up with .314 and .301 averages the next two years.

Nicknamed ''Old Aches and Pains'' because of his career-long habit of proclaiming physical discomforts, Appling ended his playing career in 1950 with 2,749 hits. Primarily a singles and doubles hitter, he socked only 45 career home runs. Luke collected 1,116 RBI and scored 1,319 runs.

Although there were better fielders, Appling's longevity helped to place

3

him among the all-time defensive leaders at his position. Only Luis Aparicio (2,581) played in more games at shortstop than Luke (2,218). Appling ranks second on the all-time list in doubleplays (1,424), fourth in assists (7,218), fifth in chances (12,259) and seventh in putouts (4,398).

He led American League shortstops in putouts once, in assists seven times (a major league record) and in errors five times. His career fielding average was .948.

That's not really such a bad record, considering Appling started life as a lefthander.

"As a boy, I was a lefthanded pitcher," the High Point, North Carolina native reveals. "Later, I wanted to play shortstop, so I switched to throwing with my right hand. When I got to high school, I figured I could pitch left-handed and play shortstop righthanded. But my coach wouldn't let me, so that was the end of that."

Appling claims that his only baseball aspiration as a youth was to play for the local semipro team.

"I was just a country boy," he says. "I didn't know anything about professional baseball. The only time I had any contact with professional baseball was when I went to college in Atlanta. I'd sit in a tree outside the ballpark and watch the Crackers play."

It didn't take Luke too long to get inside the park. After just two years at Oglethorpe University, he was signed to a contract by the Crackers, then a member of the Southern League. Luke hit four home runs in his final college game.

During his two years at Oglethorpe, Appling distinguished himself as a splendid all-around athlete. He was a three-sport star, which included play-ing football against his father's wishes.

"Back home, I played semipro football until my daddy caught me," Appling recalls. "He put a stop to that. But then when I got to Oglethorpe, I just decided to see if I could play some football there.

"I wound up being a 60-minute man. I was a 162-pound fullback on offense and linebacker on defense. We had a pretty good team. In fact, in 1929 we beat Georgia, 13–6."

Appling's collegiate career was shortened by his signing with the Crackers. But after hitting .326 in 104 games in 1930, his stint with the Crackers was short-lived, too. Atlanta sold him to the White Sox at the end of his first minor league season.

The 5' 11", 190-pound infielder made his major league debut at the end of 1930. He spent the next season as a reserve, then moved into the starting lineup in 1932.

For the next 18 seasons, a broken leg in 1939 and military service in 1944 were the only causes for Appling's absence from the regular lineup. He played with injuries and aches and pains, including a 27-game stint with a broken finger.

Through it all, Appling weathered a series of weak White Sox teams.

Luke Appling.

In his 20 seasons—only nine other players have spent more years with one team—Luke played on only five first division clubs. None finished higher than third place. Collectively, Appling's Pale Hose finished 298 games under .500.

Surrounded by such mediocrity, Appling stood out like a lighthouse in a hurricane. He was named the major league's All-Star shortstop by *The Sporting News* in 1936, 1940 and 1943. He played in four All-Star games.

The shiniest year in Appling's glittering career came in 1936 when he tore up American League pitching to a .388 tune. That year, Luke poled 204 hits, passing the 200-hit mark for the only time in his career. He also drove in 128 runs and scored 111, the only time he broke 100 in each category.

Appling beat out some prime talent to win the crown. Behind him in the race were: Earl Averill (.378); Bill Dickey (.362); Charley Gehringer (.354); and Lou Gehrig (.354).

Luke had one five-hit game and six four-hit games. He finished second to Gehrig in the voting for most valuable player.

When he won his second batting title, there was less competition at the top. Behind Luke's .328 was Dick Wakefield with a .316 mark, followed by Ralph Hodgin (.314) and Doc Cramer (.300). No one else hit over .300.

During his career, Appling was a notorious foul ball hitter. He could hit foul balls at will, and once put 23 straight fouls into the stands.

"I did it just for fun," says Appling of his proclivity for slicing souvenirs to the paying customers. "It was something I could do well. I'd do it to devil the other team sometimes."

If he played today, Appling thinks he would be even better at that practice. "The balls are twice as lively as they were when I came up," he says.

"But that's not all that's changed. The uniforms are better. The infields are better. The umpiring is better. The game has changed a lot.

"I still have one of my old gloves," he adds. "You should see the difference between that and the gloves they use today. The gloves we used were a lot smaller. With the gloves they have now, they shouldn't ever miss a ball.

"I enjoyed playing when I did, though," Appling says. "As for the money, we didn't get that much, but it doesn't bother me what the players get today."

Appling has made many stops along the baseball trail since his playing days ended.

He managed in the minor leagues for Memphis, Richmond and Indianapolis, has been a coach for the Detroit Tigers, Cleveland Indians, Baltimore Orioles, Kansas City and Oakland Athletics and the Chicago White Sox, has been a scout for Oakland and managed briefly in 1967 at Kansas City.

During his time with the Athletics, he became a close friend and admirer of former Oakland owner Charley Finley.

"I more or less introduced Finley to the game," relates Appling. "I knew his dad in Chicago. He was a federal marshall. One time, I got Charley four tickets to a game. The seats were right by the dugout, and he was thrilled. The next time I saw him—which was many years later—he was the owner of the A's.''

During his tenure with the A's, Appling worked with Reggie Jackson, Rick Monday, Sal Bando and many others when they were coming up through the club's system in the 1960s. In recent years, he performed in similar fashion with young Atlanta hitters such as Dale Murphy, Bob Horner, Glenn Hubbard and Bruce Benedict.

Appling has been with the Braves since the early 1970s, working much of that time as a minor league batting instructor. His summers have been spent entirely on the road, traveling from one minor league team to another.

Luke doesn't complain about his schedule, but it does limit his domestic duties as well as his chances to pursue such activities as answering his fan mail.

''I am working every day, on the road all season,'' he says. ''By the time the season's over, I have three big boxes full of letters. It takes me all winter to get through them, but I try to answer every letter I get.''

He does it with the same energy that he displayed as one of baseball's greatest shortstops.

Lou Brock—
Stolen Base King

There have been batters who have turned the art of hitting into a fine science. And there have been pitchers who have made the technique of throwing the ball an exact study.

But few players ever regarded the stolen base as anything more than a simple play based on a little guile and a lot of speed. Watch the pitcher, take your lead, and streak down the basepath with flurry of speed and a flashing of spikes.

To Lou Brock, though, stealing a base was always more than that. Stealing a base was an act performed with the precision of a fine watch. There was no element of chance; stealing a base was a calculated move that was based on a thorough understanding of all the factors involved.

As baseball's all-time base-stealing champion, Brock is to the stolen base what Ted Williams is to hitting. Both raised their specialties to such levels of perfection that they become sciences unto themselves.

Brock, of course, was not just a base-stealer. The 1985 electee to the Hall of Fame was also a hitter of considerable repute, his 3,023 hits making him one of only 15 players in baseball history to have hit safely more than 3,000 times in a career.

The lefthanded left fielder from El Dorado, Arkansas, had a batting average of .293 during his 19-year big league career with the Chicago Cubs and St. Louis Cardinals. He hit 149 home runs, 486 doubles and 141 triples, and drove in 900 runs while scoring 1,610.

A member of five National League All-Star teams and three pennant-winners—his .391 World Series batting average (34-for-87) is the second highest in big league history for players appearing in 20 or more games—Brock hit above .300 eight times, including his final season when he hit .304 at the age of 40.

"I always enjoyed hitting," Brock says. "It was not the same as stealing a base. Hitting and stealing are two different worlds. But I enjoyed setting up the pitcher when I was at the plate.

"Getting my 3,000th hit," he adds, "was the crowning point of my

Lou Brock.

career. It was the star on the crown, and I enjoyed that better than any other milestone.''

Despite a career filled with excellent hitting—as a regular, he batted below .270 only twice—Brock, who prides himself in being a ''five dimensional'' player who could hit, hit with power, run, field and throw, was most noted as a base-stealer. With good reason, too.

He stole more bases (938) than any player in modern baseball history. Eight times he led the National League in steals. And in 1974 he set the all-time single-season record—since broken by Rickey Henderson—with 118 stolen bases.

Brock approached the art of base-stealing with the same intensity that a race-car driver approaches a race. He explored every angle, familiarized himself with every possibility.

He studied anatomy and applied that knowledge to reading the pitchers' movements. He took movies of pitchers and other stolen-base artists. He kept charts and statistics and in later years used computers to assist him.

''In base-stealing,'' Brock says, ''it's not how fast you can run, but whether or not you can read the pitchers and understand the movable parts of the body. If, for instance, a righthanded pitcher is going to throw to first, do you know the first thing that moves when he goes from his stretch to the throw? It's his butt. So, if you watch that, you'll be able to tell if he's going home with the pitch or to first.

''The pitcher is the only man who can stop a base-runner. It's so simple, yet so complicated.

''I learned so much from the camera, too,'' Brock continues. ''In spring training, I would shoot pitchers' moves. Then I would study the pictures.''

Brock also studied and talked with other base-stealers.

''Maury Wills was probably the foremost authority on the subject,'' he says. ''I also talked with Luis Aparicio. But knowledge was really hard to get because so few people really knew anything about base-stealing.''

Early in his career, after he had been traded from the Chicago Cubs in 1964 to the St. Louis Cardinals with two minor leaguers for pitcher Ernie Broglio and two others in one of baseball's most lopsided trades, Brock sought St. Louis resident Cool Papa Bell, the legendary speed merchant from the Negro League.

''The first time I met him, I didn't know it was him,'' Brock says. ''Then I put the word out that I wanted to see him again, and he showed up one day and we talked. I really had to squeeze it out of him. But finally, he started to tell me stuff that you would never find in books, even today. Stuff like how to read a pitcher so the hitter is at an advantage. It was incredible.''

From his discussions with base-stealers, Brock learned, among other things, that, depending on where the weight is placed on their feet, pitchers throw in various ways and with various speeds. ''What you know about each pitcher,'' Brock declares, ''dictates how far off the base you can take a lead. It almost develops into a formula.''

Brock, like all base-stealers, says you steal on the pitcher, not the catcher.

The catcher is only as good as the pitcher and how well he holds the runners. Take Johnny Bench. He had an arm like a cannon. But the Cincinnati pitching staff always seemed to have the attitude of "We want you to run because Bench will throw you out." So they never held you on the base. That being the case, why take a 12-foot lead when you can take a 16-foot lead? You know what a difference that four feet makes? Even with Bench, they never caught me.

Developing the proper attitude is also necessary for a base-stealer, Brock says.

"You've got to have a passion for the art," he says. "It's a love affair. When you're in love with something, you have no fear. You combine that with arrogance, and you have a person who can beat a pitcher every time.

"Arrogance is important," Brock adds. "But you can't have it until you have knowledge. And you only get knowledge by intensive study.

"A base-stealer always has to think action," Brock continues. "Each stolen base is a challenge. You are being challenged to a duel. You have a reputation, but the pitcher says, 'You won't do it on me,' and it becomes a contest. As a base-runner, you have to project a certain amount of arrogance which says, 'Don't mess with me or I'll take the base.' "

Brock says he decided to take the upper hand with pitchers early in his career after the Los Angeles Dodgers' Sandy Koufax hit him with a pitch.

"There were unwritten laws that said when to steal and when not to," Brock says. "Who put them in, I don't know. But if you broke one of the rules, you became a shooting gallery next time you came to the plate.

"One day I had stolen a base, and the next time up, Koufax nearly broke my shoulder with a pitch. That was the last straw. After that, I decided nobody is going to dictate to me when to steal a base. It's either going to be my game or their game. Before long, the whole concept became erased."

Ironically, Brock didn't think of himself as a base-stealer in his early years in organized baseball. As a young player, he was more noted as a long-ball hitter.

"Coming out of college (Southern University in Baton Rouge, Louisiana), I had always hit third, fourth or fifth," he recalls. "I didn't even realize I was fast. I didn't find that out until I was in the big leagues."

When Brock joined the Cubs at the end of the 1961 season—after just one season in the minors—he was a raw youngster with undetermined skills.

"I didn't know what kind of player I was going to evolve into," he says. "In fact, I spent the first three years trying to decipher where I was. It was only after I was traded to the Cardinals that I realized I could steal bases.

"Johnny Keane was the manager. He asked me, 'Can you steal?'

"I went around to everybody I could find and asked them, 'How do you steal bases?' But the knowledge just wasn't there. The first time I was going to steal, I got picked off. It was all trial and error for me that year. The key for me was the confidence the manager had in me."

After stealing only 40 bases in his first two years in Chicago—and hitting just .263 and .258—Brock stole 43 bases and hit .315 in 1964, helping the Cards to the NL pennant. The next year, his count moved up to 63. Then in 1966, it went to 73 and Brock won the first of four straight stolen base crowns.

By then, he had purchased his first movie camera, and was deeply immersed in the study of the stolen base.

"No question, by 1966 I figured the sky was the limit," says Brock. "By that time, I had taken all the guesswork out of stealing bases. It had become a science with me, and I continued to learn the rest of my career."

Brock went on to set a number of stolen base records, including most seasons with 50 or more stolen bases (12). Meanwhile, his batting average hovered around the .300 mark nearly every year.

One of his best all-around years came in 1967 when he hit .299 with 21 home runs while leading the league in runs scored (113) and stolen bases (52). Another especially solid season occurred in 1971 when Brock led the league with 126 runs and 64 steals while hitting .313.

Along the way, there were some negative figures, too. Lou was often among the league leaders in strikeouts, and fanned often enough that he currently ranks fifth on the major league's all-time list. He also led National League outfielders in errors seven times, and was caught stealing 295 times during his career—both major league records.

On the other hand, Brock hit into only 114 doubleplays in 10,332 at-bats. Four times he had more than 200 hits in a season, once hitting in 26 straight games. He stole four bases in one game twice. And three times he broke up no-hitters—once against the Atlanta Braves' Denny Lemaster in 1967 and twice against the San Francisco Giants' Jim Barr in 1973 and 1975.

Brock's finest season came in 1974 when at the age of 35 he broke Wills' all-time single-season stolen base record of 104, set in 1962. While swiping 118 bases, Brock hit .306 and was named the National League's and the major league's Player of the Year by *The Sporting News*.

Unlike the way it would seem, Brock says it was not a particularly grueling effort to set the record.

"I only had to run 30 to 35 percent of the time I was on base," he says. "I didn't have many bruises. One time a tendon slipped off my knuckle when I was sliding, but that was about the only injury I had. I think the demand and the stress would be tougher on a player today than they were on me."

Brock always played well under stress, as evidenced by three outstanding World Series performances. After hitting .300 in the 1964 series, Brock went wild in 1967 and 1968, hitting .414 and .464, respectively, and stealing seven bases in each. In the '67 Series, he also hit a titanic 450-foot home run in the sixth game in an 8–4 loss to the Boston Red Sox.

Brock, whose number 20 has been retired by the Cardinals, still resides in St. Louis where he is engaged in a number of activities. He owns several companies, including some retail shops at airports around the country, serves as a spokesman for Major League Baseball and the Equitable Life Insurance Co., and has dabbled in broadcasting with both the Cardinals and Chicago White Sox.

Brock has also designed a program in which he conducts three-day, one-on-one seminars with major league base stealers. Among his pupils have been Vince Coleman of the Cardinals, Steve Sax and Mariano Duncan of the Dodgers and Kirby Puckett of the Minnesota Twins.

"Base-stealing is a concept, just like hitting and throwing," he says. "Big league clubs don't teach base-stealing as a concept, so that's what I am trying to get across."

The apex of Brock's brilliant career arrived in 1985 when he was inducted in the Hall of Fame. It was an occasion that left Brock overflowing with pride.

Lou Brock demonstrates his classic running style as he steals another base.

"I had no idea what would happen," he says of the day he was inducted.

In fact, I'm still trying to digest it. When you stand at that podium, the history begins to hit you. You think of all the people who stood there, and you look to your left and to your right, and you see all those great players sitting there. Standing up there and being able to take my place among the greatest players who ever played major league baseball—all of the sudden, it hits you, and your knees just turn to jelly. It was the proudest moment of my life.

Bill Dickey—
Possibly Baseball's Greatest Catcher

The game of baseball has not been heavily endowed with great catchers. In the long and marvelous history of the game, only 10 men who
have played the position have reached such high levels of achievement that
they have been placed in the Hall of Fame.

No doubt, that is because catching is the most demanding position on
the diamond. Invariably, if teams find someone who can handle himself ade-
quately behind the plate, that is sufficient. The man need not be a good
hitter, too.

Bill Dickey, on the other hand, could handle himself expertly behind
the plate as well as alongside of it. It didn't matter whether he was using
a glove or a bat, Dickey was equally adept with either piece of equipment.

Dickey is generally regarded as one of the two best catchers who ever
played the game. There are some who will cast a vote for Mickey Cochrane
as the best, but Dickey does not lack support for his candidacy.

His credentials certainly justify such an elevated status. During a 17-year
career with the New York Yankees that extended from 1928 to 1946, Dickey
compiled a lifetime batting average of .313. He had 202 home runs and 1,209
RBI, and in 13 seasons as a regular, he hit over .300 10 times.

Bill, who was elected to the Hall of Fame in 1954, took part in 18 World
Series'; eight as a player and 10 as a coach. (He also managed the Yankees
in 105 games in 1946.)

He retired from baseball after the 1960 season and, for the next 17 years,
worked as a salesman for Stephens, Inc., a large investment banking firm
in Little Rock, Arkansas.

Dickey, who was born in Louisiana but moved to Little Rock when he
was 15, worked at that position until he was 70. Until he was in his late 70s,
he still maintained an office at Stephens, going there regularly to answer
his mail.

"I've been keeping busy just doing the things I want to do," says the
ex-catcher whose lifelong reputation as a real gentleman is not diminished

when you meet him in person. "We have a lake house, and I do a lot of fishing and golfing.

"I don't have much contact with baseball. I watch a good deal of baseball on television, but I don't see the Yankees as much as I'd like to. Of course, I went to the Hall of Fame inductions to see our two Arkansas boys (George Kell and Brooks Robinson) taken in."

It surprises him somewhat, but Dickey gleefully reports that he receives some 200 letters a week from baseball fans. "I think most of them come from being in the Hall of Fame," he says. "But I don't mind. I sign everything with a SASE.

"I love to sign for kids who want autographs for themselves. But I hate it when people want a bunch of things to sign or when the same people keep writing back three or four times. They're just trying to get you to sign so they can sell them. I don't like that."

Dickey says he maintains a special room at his home for his many pictures and trophies. He also has one of his mitts and a Yankee cap, but no uniforms or cards.

Although he was one of baseball's greatest catchers, Dickey views that appraisal with characteristic modesty. "I consider it an honor to be mentioned with men like Cochrane, Hartnett, Campanella, Berra and Bench," he says. "I'd take any one of them. But I don't think you can really pick one of us over the others."

While his entire professional career, including two and one- half years in the minors, was spent as a catcher, Dickey did not start out at that position as a boy. He was originally a pitcher.

"My father and brother played on a semipro team," he says. "I was the batboy. Even as a boy, I loved to play. At first, I was a pitcher; I became a catcher in my last year of high school."

Following his high school graduation, Dickey joined a semipro team and earned $10 a game. "I had no idea of ever playing professionally," he says. "I was going to go to college."

After one year at Little Rock College, he signed a pro contract in 1925 with the Little Rock Travelers. His salary was $300 a month, he recalls. "My room and board came to $3 a week and that included having a lady do my laundry."

Dickey joined the Yankees at the end of the 1928 season. The following year, he became the club's regular catcher. Over the next six years, his lowest batting average was .310.

Dickey's finest year at the plate was 1936, when he hit .362 with 22 home runs and 107 RBI. The next year, he hit .332 with career highs in home runs (29) and RBI (133).

As good a hitter as he was, Bill was equally brilliant as a receiver. One of his most spectacular achievements came in 1931 when he went the entire season without a passed ball.

"I loved to make a great defensive play," Dickey recalls. "I'd rather do that than hit a home run."

One of his greatest defensive plays, he remembers, occurred when he leaped out to catch a sidearm fastball delivered by Johnny Murphy that was 10 feet away from the plate.

"One of the things I prided myself on was having quick hands," he says. "I got to the point where a pitcher couldn't cross me up."

Bill Dickey.

Bill also prides himself in having been able to tell where a foul ball would land in the stands without turning his head. He could, he says, see a foul ball come off the bat.

By his own admission, Dickey did not always have an accurate throwing arm. "I was gifted with a good arm," he says, "but it was a little erratic."

To cure his wildness as a young catcher, Bill went to center field and practiced hitting a spot on the wall. He threw for 20 minutes every day.

The method worked, because few baserunners took liberties with Dickey's arm. In fact, he is in the record book for having gunned down three runners in one inning in a game in 1929.

"It wasn't as tough with baserunners then," he says. "There weren't as many guys who stole as much as they do now. But it doesn't make any difference who the runner is. If he's held on base by the pitcher, he can't outrun the ball from the catcher.

"On the other hand," he adds, "the hardest play for a catcher is to catch a wild pitch from a man who can't hold a runner on base.

"The best situation for a catcher," he says, "is to work behind the plate when a good pitcher is on the mound. I liked to catch guys with great stuff."

Among those he puts in that category with the Yankees were Waite Hoyt, Red Ruffing, Lefty Gomez, Tiny Bonham and Herb Pennock, who Dickey claims had the "greatest control of any pitcher I ever caught."

Of opposing pitchers, Dickey rates Lefty Grove and Bob Feller as two of the best he ever faced. "Grove was the fastest," he says, "although Ruth once told me that Walter Johnson was even faster."

Mention of Ruth brings a twinkle to the eyes of the great ex- catcher. "He was a legend then, and he still is," Dickey says. "He was real good with kids and easy to get along with. He was also a real good outfielder. I liked him a lot. And he helped me a lot, too. They used to talk about how the veteran players wouldn't help young players. Well, Babe helped me when I came up. He helped me with my balance and with my pitch selection."

Another player of whom Dickey speaks fondly is Lou Gehrig. "He was one of the greatest who ever lived, both as a person and as a player," he says. "He was the kind of guy who won ball games all by himself. Why, you can't imagine anybody scoring the number of runs and driving in the number of runs that he did. He would usually account for 300 or more runs in a season."

Dickey, whose younger brother, George had a brief career as a catcher with the Boston Red Sox and the Chicago White Sox, played on some of the greatest baseball teams ever assembled. From 1936 to 1943, the Yankees won seven pennants and six World Series' in eight years. Eliminate their one losing Series (1942 to St. Louis) and the Yanks lost only five World Series games during that stretch.

"I think probably the 1932 club (which with Ruth and Gehrig won the American League pennant by 13 games over the Philadelphia Athletics who had won the pennant the last three years) was the best one," says Dickey.

"But the 1936 through 1939 clubs, when Joe DiMaggio had come along, were also very sound ball clubs. The late 1940s-1950s teams when we won five straight World Championships ranked up there, too."

Having appeared in so many World Series', it is hard for Dickey to pick his most memorable one. "As long as we won, I was happy," he says.

"I enjoyed all of them," he adds, "but I guess one of the ones I enjoyed the most was in 1943." In that Series, Bill's last as a player, he hit a two-run homer off Mort Cooper to give the Yankees a 2-0 victory in the deciding game.

Dickey says he didn't make a lot of money during a career which included 13 consecutive years in which he caught 100 or more games. His highest salary was $25,000.

"In 1936," he remembers, "I hit .362 and was paid $12,500. I had to hold out for two weeks the following spring to make $15,000.

"The players today," he adds, "make a lot more money. But they don't have as much fun as we had. We had more fun and there were no arguments and no scandals in the newspapers.

"I think I played at the right time. I played with a lot of great ballplayers, many of them Hall of Famers. It was a wonderful era. I consider myself lucky to have played then.

"Playing with the Yankees during that time," he adds, "was special, too. You can't put a finger on it. Fans from all over the country looked up to the Yankees more than they did to other players.

"The crowing achievement for me," he says, "was getting elected to the Hall of Fame. That's the ultimate for a ballplayer. When I was a kid, I didn't even know there was a Hall of Fame."

More than 30 years after his selection, though, Dickey not only epitomizes what the Hall of Fame is all about, he stands at the summit of his catching peers.

Bobby Doerr—
Premier Second Baseman of the 1940s

In the 1940s, when the Boston Red Sox were tearing apart American League pitching with as awesome a batting order as was ever posted, one of the steadiest contributors to that attack was the club's second baseman, a sturdy Californian with a name that in part came from a famous American general.

Robert Pershing Doerr was that rare combination of good power-high average-slick fielding second baseman. Others on the Red Sox may have been more prominent and earned more money, but none was more eminently linked with the Bosox than Bobby.

During a 14-year major league career that was spent entirely in Boston, Doerr established himself as one of the premier second baseman in baseball. Bobby was rewarded for his efforts with election in 1986 to the Baseball Hall of Fame.

At the top of his career, Doerr formed a devasting punch with Ted Williams, Dom DiMaggio, Johnny Pesky and later Vern Stephens, Al Zarilla, Billy Goodman, Birdie Tebbetts and Walt Dropo. Particularly in the late 1940s, when the Red Sox won one pennant and lost two others by the scant total of two games, Doerr and his teammates had no equals as a regular lineup.

There were many good second basemen in that era, but in the American League, there were two who ranked far above the others: Bobby Doerr and Joe Gordon of the New York Yankees and later the Cleveland Indians.

The easiest way to start an argument back then was to invite comparisions between the two. Invariably, no doubt because of his New York affiliations, the flashy Gordon usually commanded the most attention. In reality, though, he had nothing over Doerr.

Bobby's statistics (Gordon's are in parentheses) compared favorably. His career batting average was .288 (.268) in 1,865 (1,566) games. Doerr had 2,042 (1,530) hits, 1,247 (975) RBI, scored 1,094 (914) runs and hit 223 (253) home runs.

Doerr, however, was not just a solid hitter. An outstanding fielder who

Bobby Doerr.

glided smoothly after ground balls, Bobby led American League second basemen in fielding percentage five times (to Gordon's none), in double plays five times and in putouts four times. At one point, he held the major league record at his position for consecutive errorless games (73) and consecutive errorless chances (404).

In 1944, *The Sporting News* named Doerr the American League's Most Valuable Player. A year earlier, Bobby had captured the nation's attention when his three-run homer at Philadelphia's Shibe Park gave the American League a 5–3 triumph in the first All-Star game played at night. It was one of nine All-Star teams for which Doerr was chosen.

That home run off of Johnny Vander Meer still ranks as one of Doerr's most memorable days in baseball.

"In those days, the All-Star games were just like the World Series," he says. "They were real big. Hitting that home run was a great thrill."

So, too, was winning the 1946 American League pennant, the only time the Bosox were able to get to the top during their powerhouse days of the 1940s.

Ultimately, that pennant set the stage for what would become for the Red Sox and their fans several years of utter frustration. Despite their great hitters, the Red Sox lost the 1948 pennant in a one-game playoff with Cleveland, and the 1949 flag by one game to the Yankees. They trailed New York by four games in 1950.

"Not winning pennants in 1948, 1949 and 1950 was a great disappointment," says Doerr. "But we just didn't have the pitching. In 1946, we had good pitching, with Dave Ferriss, Tex Hughson and Mickey Harris. All three got sore arms in 1947 (when Boston finished 12 games behind New York), and after that we never had the two or three real good pitchers we needed. If any one of those fellows hadn't been hurt, we would have won the pennants."

Doerr thinks the best of those Red Sox teams was the 1950 club, which had a league-leading team batting average of .302 and also led the circuit in team fielding. That year, Stephens and Dropo each drove in 144 runs to tie for the league lead; Billy Goodman won the batting championship as a utilityman, and the lowest batting average in the regular lineup was Doerr's .294. Unfortunately, Mel Parnell (18–10) was the only big winner on the pitching staff. The club finished in third place, behind the Yankees and Detroit Tigers.

"That was one of the real good hitting clubs of all-time," Bobby remembers. "We had a club that was full of fine hitters (six starters hit above .300), but again, we didn't have the pitching."

As a hitter, Doerr had many fine seasons, only once batting below .270. He hit .318 in 1939, .325 in 1944 and .309 in 1949.

In 1948, he hit 27 home runs, collected 111 RBI and had a .285 average. Two years later, he had an equal home run total while driving in 120 runs and batting .294.

Doerr, who never played any position in pro baseball except second base, drove in more than 100 runs six times in his career. No game, however, matched the one he had on June 8, 1950, when he drove in eight runs.

Bobby's career home run total is the second highest in the American League for a second baseman (Gordon is first) and the fourth highest for that position in the major leagues.

To date, he and Williams have the fifth-highest home run totals in American League history for two teammates. Between 1939 and 1951, the two combined for 549 round-trippers.

Doerr and Williams went way back together. In 1936, when Bobby was in his third year of professional baseball as a member of the San Diego Padres, Ted appeared with the Pacific Coast League (PCL) team for a tryout. Doerr remembers the occasion well.

"He hit about six or seven balls out of the park," Bobby recalls. "I thought to myself, this guy's a ballplayer. He had that good stroke even then."

Williams was signed to a Padres' contract, played a year with Doerr and eventually wound up with the Red Sox in 1939, two years after Bobby's arrival.

By the time he reached the majors in 1937, Doerr had stacked up some impressive credentials. Originally signed to a pro contract at the age of 16 after he and Mickey Owens, later a big league catcher but then a shortstop, teamed to win the California American Legion championship, Doerr began his pro career in 1934 with Hollywood of the PCL.

The following year, at the tender age of 17, Doerr hit .317 for Hollywood. A year later, he hit .342 at San Diego and, along with teammate George Myatt, was purchased by the Red Sox.

Doerr played in 55 games the next season for Boston, then in 1938 became the club's regular second baseman at the age of 20. He hit .289 that year, and fielded almost flawlessly alongside shortstop-manager, Joe Cronin.

"Going to the majors at that point was a tremendous experience for a young kid like me," Doerr says. "I got to break in on a team that had Jimmie Foxx, Cronin, Lefty Grove and Pinky Higgins. And I played against men like Lou Gehrig, Al Simmons, Joe DiMaggio and Charley Gehringer.

"Gehringer was my boyhood idol. I couldn't wait to see him when I got to the majors. I wasn't disappointed. He was so great.

"The pitchers were great, too. Bob Feller was real tough. So were Johnny Allen and Mel Harder. When I first got to the big leagues and saw all those great pitchers, I thought to myself, 'I don't know if I can make this or not.' But, as you play more, you begin to adjust."

Bobby adjusted beautifully. Except for one year (1945) in the military service, he was as good if not better than any second sacker of his era.

Along the way, Doerr posted some outstanding numbers. For instance, in 1939, he registered 13 assists in one 10-inning game. In 1942, he participated in 132 doubleplays, which ranks seventh on the American League's all-time list. And in 1949, he and Stephens took part in a combined total of 262 twin-killings, the fourth-best mark in major league history.

Doerr retired as a player after the 1951 season and returned to his home in Oregon. "For a whole year," he says, "I just fished and tended my 125 head of cattle. I had been playing professional baseball since I was 16, and I was tired. Plus, I had hurt my back; so it was time to get out."

Although his career was over at the relatively young age of 33, Doerr left the game with no regrets.

"What would I have done if I hadn't played baseball?" he asks. "I know what I would've done. I would've worked for the telephone company like my dad and brother did.

"I dreamed of playing baseball from the time I was a little kid. I grew up during the Depression, and we lived near a playground. All I did was play baseball.

"Through baseball, I got to go all over the world. I went three times to Germany, to South America, to Korea. All the nice places I've been, and the nice things I have—I have a place on a river where I can fish any time I want—I would never have had without baseball."

Doerr stayed out of the game until 1957, when he returned to the Red Sox as a scout. In 1967, he moved up to the coaching lines with the parent club, staying until 1969.

Big guns in the Boston Red Sox' hitting attack in 1946 included (from left) Bobby Doerr, Johnny Pesky, Dom DiMaggio, Ted Williams and Rudy York.

In recent years, Doerr was a batting coach for the Toronto Blue Jays. Later, he worked on a limited basis with Toronto at spring training, in the minor leagues and the instructional league before retiring.

The fit-looking Doerr in the last few years has spent much of his time on his 120-acre ranch in Junction City, Oregon.

He still sees some of his old Boston teammates, and he plays in several old-timers' games each year.

Doerr says he receives many letters from fans. "Some of them are pretty cute, the way they ask you to sign an autograph," he says. "I'm flattered that they ask me. It's nice that kids have that interest, and it's great for baseball. I know when I was growing up, I used to have pictures hanging all over my walls. The only thing that annoys me is when players don't sign."

Bobby has a number of items from his playing days, including the glove with which he set the errorless fielding record in 1948. He also has bats signed by Babe Ruth, Ty Cobb, Ted Williams and Joe DiMaggio, some baseballs from special occasions and many autographed pictures.

They are all reminiscent of another era. It was an era when no second baseman stood any taller than Bobby Doerr, the anchorman of the Red Sox' infield.

Bob Feller—
A Notch Above the Rest

B etween the late 1930s and the early 1950s, major league baseball was endowed with one of the most superb collections of pitchers ever assembled. Future Hall of Famers abounded, and there was a rich supply of outstanding pitchers toiling just below the level of immortality.

Of all the great hurlers of the period, though, one pitcher stood a notch above the rest. He was a pitcher with a consistently better record in that era than anyone else. He could throw a baseball at least as fast as any pitcher ever did, and he had a terrifying curve and just enough wildness to make him absolutely awesome.

His name, of course, was Bob Feller. And not only was he the king of his day, people had no difficulty using his name in the same sentence as those of such bygone legends as Walter Johnson, Cy Young and Christy Mathewson.

Although he worked for Cleveland Indians teams that were usually less than great, Rapid Robert was a true superstar. He was the glamor boy of major league moundsmen in the 1940s. He attracted huge crowds whenever he pitched and, when he signed a contract for the unheard of sum of $80,000, he was by far the game's highest-paid hurler. In fact, only Ted Williams and Joe DiMaggio had higher salaries.

During his career, which extended from 1936 to 1956, Feller posted a record of 266-162. He had a 3.25 lifetime earned run average and he registered 46 shutouts. Bob struck out 2,581 batters, walked 1,764 and gave up 3,271 hits in 3,827 innings. His strikeout total ranks 14th on the current all-time list, and his walk total is third.

The Hall of Famer—the first graduate of American Legion baseball to gain entry into the Cooperstown shrine when he was elected in 1962—was a 20-game winner six times: 1939 (24-9); 1940 (27-11); 1941 (25-13); 1946 (26-15); 1947 (20-11) and 1951 (22-8). He pitched three no-hitters and 12 one-hitters, a major league record. He led the American League in strikeouts seven times, in wins six times, and in innings pitched and complete games five times.

Bob Feller.

Many of his records have been broken, but when he was pitching, Feller's name was sprinkled throughout the record book. Among his most spectacular feats, in 1938 he became the first modern player to strike out 18 players in a nine-inning game (against the Detroit Tigers). And in 1946 he set the major league mark for strikeouts in a season with 348.

Unquestionably, Feller would have gone on to far greater heights had he not missed nearly four seasons during World War II. Bob was in the U.S. Navy when his career would have been at its apex.

Today, Feller won't dwell on what could have been. From all indications, he is a man of the present, and that includes an extremely busy schedule, much of which is spent doing promotional work for the Indians.

He spends a considerable amount of time traveling, doing public relations work for the team, meeting with the news media and fans. In the spring, he also works as a pitching instructor with the Indians' minor leaguers.

"I really enjoy this kind of work," says Bob, who also attends 50 to 60 games each season. "I've been doing it since 1980. There isn't that much money in it. I could be making more elsewhere. But I'm happy. Things are going well for me."

In recent years, a number of Feller's personal items, particularly uniforms, have found their way into baseball collectors' hands. "I have sold some things," Feller says, "not because I wanted the money, but because I didn't want the stuff anymore. I've kept the stuff that has sentimental value. The rest is kind of like a used car. If you don't care for it, you might as well get rid of it."

Much of Feller's memorabilia has been donated to the Baseball Hall of Fame and to the Ohio Hall of Fame. "It's spread around quite a few different museums," he says. "But I still have quite a bit myself."

The great righthander worked 15 years in the insurance business following his retirement from baseball. Then he was employed in sales for two different hotel chains before rejoining the Indians.

It has been more than 50 years since Feller and his rocketing fastball exploded onto the baseball scene. In 1936, Bob was just a 17-year-old farm boy from Van Meter, Iowa. The Indians spotted him, and signed him to a contract for $75 a month. Feller went directly to the majors, never spending a day in the minors.

"I had wanted to be a big league player since I was a little kid about five years old," Feller recalls. "I didn't care about the money when I signed. All I wanted was the opportunity to play."

Stories of Feller's boyhood development as a pitcher soon surfaced. Reporters learned that Bob's father had started him throwing behind the family barn when he was just three years old. Later, the youngster would combine his farm chores with baseball, a practice that proved highly beneficial to him later as a pitcher.

"My dad," Feller remembers, "put up some lights and fenced in an area behind the barn, and we began having catches. We did it every night when I was little. I also did all of the jobs around the farm. It was hard, manual labor, but it developed my body, made me good and strong, and I think had a lot to do with why I could throw a baseball so hard.

"I also did a lot of work on a punching bag," he adds. "I was very active physically. I played a lot of basketball. And in the summer I played on two or three different sandlot baseball teams."

As a 17-year-old right off the farm, Feller posted a 5–3 record in his first big league season. Within two years, he had become one of the league's top hurlers, and by the age of 20 had his first 20-win season.

In 1940, Feller was one of the leaders of the "Cry Baby Rebellion," a name given at the time to a revolt the Cleveland players staged against their manager, Ossie Vitt. A threatened players' strike in protest of Vitt's managerial tactics failed to materialize.

That year, Feller was the first American League pitcher to toss a no-hitter on opening day, beating the Chicago White Sox. He went on that season to register a career high 27 wins.

Feller, who was named to six American League All-Star teams, had

Two of baseball's greatest pitchers, Bob Feller (left) and Cy Young, swapped secrets before a 1947 game in Cleveland.

what he considers his finest season in 1946, his first full year in the majors since 1941. That season, Bob set his one-season strikeout record (since broken by Nolan Ryan), was the winning pitcher in the All-Star game, had a 26-15 record for a sixth place club, and pitched his second no-hitter, this one against the New York Yankees.

Two years later, with a record of 19-15, Feller teamed with two 20-game winners, another future Hall of Famer, Bob Lemon and rookie Gene Bearden, to pitch the Indians to their first American League pennant since 1920.

Feller got his long-awaited chance to play in a World Series when he started the opening game against the Boston Braves. Bob and Johnny Sain hooked up in one of the great pitching duels in World Series history, Feller yielding just two hits and the Braves' righthander giving up four.

The Indians lost, 1-0, when pinch-runner Phil Masi scored from second on a single by Tommy Holmes in the bottom of the eighth inning. Moments before he scored, Masi had been called safe on a pickoff attempt in which Feller reeled and threw to shortstop-manager Lou Boudreau, sneaking in behind the runner.

"That was a real controversial play," Feller says, recalling how Boudreau screamed in protest of umpire Bill Stewart's decision. "Masi was out by three feet."

Feller got another chance to pitch in the Series with the starting assignment in the fifth game. But he took the loss in that one, too, after getting knocked out during a six-run, seventh-inning Boston uprising in a game which the Braves won, 11-5.

By the early 1950s, Feller had lost some of the blinding speed from his fastball, which earlier in his career had been clocked at nearly 100 miles per hour. But he had developed an assortment of other pitches, and he continued to baffle opposing hitters.

He had his last great season in 1951 when he posted a 22-8 record, which included his third no-hitter, a whitewash of the Tigers.

Feller was 13-3 in 1954 as the Indians won another American League pennant. That year, Bob belonged to what is sometimes cited as the finest pitching staff ever to play for one team. It included three future Hall of Famers, Feller, Lemon and Early Wynn, plus Mike Garcia, Hal Newhouser, Art Houttemen, Don Mossi and Ray Narleski. Feller did not make an appearance in the World Series that fall.

Bob, who retired in 1956, says he played in an era when baseball was truly a pleasant undertaking. "We had good camaraderie among the players, and there was more loyalty then and a lot less confusion.

"There were 50-some minor leagues and only 16 major league teams. Only the very top-notch players made the majors. Obviously, there's a difference today. There are some fine players, but there are fewer top-notch ones."

There are ever fewer who could be put on the same level as Bob Feller, the fireballing righthander of one of baseball's finest eras.

George Kell—The Finest
Third Baseman of His Day

When George Kell walks into a visiting ballpark these days, people not only recognize him, often they've been standing there for a while waiting for him to arrive.

It didn't used to be that way for Kell, despite the fact that he's a former American League batting champion. But times have changed for the ex-third baseman.

The reason, of course, was his induction in 1983 into the Hall of Fame.

Since Kell walked through the portals of baseball immortality, life for the once-great American League slugger has undergone some substantial changes.

"It's something you have to go through to know what it's all about," Kell says. "But it certainly has made life different for me. Right before I was inducted, Al Kaline told me that going into the Hall of Fame would be followed by the greatest year of my life. He said it would change my entire life."

And Kell's partner on Detroit Tiger telecasts and now a fellow Hall of Famer was entirely correct.

"The first thing that happened," relates Kell, "was that I received about 500 congratulatory letters. Then people started writing for my autograph. I was getting, 40, 50, 60 letters a day, many of them with pictures. I saw some pictures I never saw before.

"For the last couple of years," Kell adds, "the fan mail had been terrific. It's so much more than it used to be. That's been a major change since my induction."

But there have been others. Kell can't walk into a restaurant now, especially in Detroit, without being recognized.

"They never used to recognize me before," he says, even though he's received plenty of public exposure through more than 25 years in the broadcasting business, first on network television and since 1968 doing Tigers radio and TV coverage. "But there's something about going into the Hall of Fame that changes the situation. I'm not any better of a person, and I certainly haven't become a better ballplayer. But once you go in, people perceive you differently.

"When I was on the road with the Tigers, people never used to recognize me," Kell continues. "Now, everybody knows who I am, and they wait at the stadium gates to see me."

When each new group enters the Hall of Fame, Kell claims they go through the same changes he did. But it's hardly the kind of thing any of them would dare to complain about.

Rather, induction into the Hall of Fame is the most rewarding and emotionally uplifting experience a baseball player can have. No one stated that more clearly than Kell himself when he was enshrined.

"You can't possibly know the feeling inside of me unless you've been at this podium," he told a hushed audience. "This is a very emotional moment for an old ballplayer like me. I stand here in awe."

And more than a few have stood in awe of George Kell, too. In his 15-year major league career, Kell complied a lifetime batting average of .306 with 2,054 hits, 881 runs and 870 RBI. Throughout the late 1940s and early 1950s, he was the American League's premier third baseman, hitting over .300 eight straight years and leading the league in batting in 1949 with a .343 mark.

"During the season, I really wasn't thinking about the batting title," the five-time American League All-Star relates. "I was just trying to do the best job I could. I had no plans for a batting title.

"Even on the last day of the season, I wasn't thinking too much about it," Kell continues. "Ted Williams and I had been nip and tuck all year, and we went into the last game with both of us having a chance to win it.

"I was seated next to Hoot Evers on the bench before the game," and he said, 'You're going to win it.' We were playing the Cleveland Indians, and I hit a double and single off of Bob Lemon. Later, I struck out against Bob Feller who had come in in relief.

"Williams, it turned out, went hitless. But I didn't know I had won until I walked in the clubhouse and they called down from the radio booth to tell me. It was a big thrill."

Kell wound up beating Williams by less than one point. With both hitters finishing with .343 averages, the statisticians had to go to the fourth decimal place to determine the winner.

The following year Kell recorded a .340 average, but this time lost the batting crown to another Boston Red Sox player, Billy Goodman, who hit .354. A utilityman, Goodman played in just enough games (110) to get enough at-bats (424) to qualify for the title.

"I should have won that year, too." laments Kell, who led the league with 641 at-bats, 218 hits and 56 doubles. George also led the league in hits (191) the following year while batting .319 and finishing third behind the Philadelphia A's Ferris Fain and Chicago White Sox' Minnie Minoso in the batting race.

Finishing among the league leaders in batting was an event that Kell

George Kell.

practiced regularly. In 1946, the year that the Washington Senators' Mickey Vernon won the title, Kell was fourth with a .322 mark. The following season his .320 placed him fifth behind Williams' league-leading average.

By that time, Kell, whose brother Skeeter played for the 1952 A's, was firmly entrenched with the Tigers after getting what he calls his "biggest break."

George broke into the major leagues with the downtrodden A's late in the 1943 season after leading the Inter-State League with a .396 at Lancaster. Kell had spent four seasons in the minors.

"When I got to the majors, I felt like I was in over my head," he says. "The A's had Al Simmons as a coach, and some of the other greats like Bing Miller and Jimmy Dykes were around. They all tried to change my stance at the plate. Mack said, 'Leave him alone. He's hit everywhere he's played. He'll hit up here, too.' "

Kell was the A's regular third baseman in 1944 and 1945. Although he had respectable years, his marks (.268 and .272) provided little suggestion of what was to come.

Early in the 1946 season, with the A's in need of a lefthanded-hitting outfielder and with Hank Majeski waiting in the wings to play third, Kell was traded to the Tigers for Barney McCoskey.

"I didn't want to leave Philadelphia," Kell remembers. "I felt very comfortable there.

"Mr. (Connie) Mack called me, and said, 'I'm going to send you to a good ballclub. You're young and you can play, and some day you're going to thank me for this.

"I didn't know what I was getting into," Kell recalls. "But although the trade was a surprise, it certainly turned out all right."

McCoskey, although an excellent hitter, arrived with a bad back. He hit .354 after joining the A's in 1946 and .328 and .326 the next two years. But by the end of 1948, he was through as a regular.

Kell, called by Mack one of the five best players he managed in that era, went on to a banner career, which extended through 1957. He was traded from Detroit to the Boston Red Sox in the spring of 1952 in one of the biggest trades in major league history. Nine front-line players were involved in the swap with Kell, Evers, Dizzy Trout and Johnny Lipon going to Boston for Walt Dropo, Bill Wight, Fred Hatfield, Johnny Pesky and Don Lenhardt.

George stayed with the Red Sox until they swapped him in the spring of 1954 to the Chicago White Sox for Grady Hatton and $100,000. He hit .312 for the Chisox in 1955, then went to the Baltimore Orioles the following year where he finished his career in 1957.

Kell, who hit .297 in his final year, eventually moved to first base in 1957 to make way at third for another Arkansas native, Brooks Robinson. Ironically, the two marched into the Hall of Fame the same day.

If Kell has any regrets, it is that he never got a chance to play in a World Series. And, he wouldn't have minded playing more seasons in Boston than he did.

"If I had to do it all over again, I would sure like to have played more in Boston," he says. "What a place to play. I was a pull-hitter, and with that left field wall, it was really nice to play there.

"Of course, Detroit was great," he adds. "It was a great place to play, great place to raise a family. We had great teams; it was just a terrific place to be."

Kell is an affable man, extremely direct and with no pretense about him. He is justifiably proud of his baseball accomplishments, but equally humble, as illustrated by a line in his acceptance speech at Cooperstown.

"I suspect that George Kell has taken more from the game than he could ever put back," he said.

That is a point that could be argued either way.

Al Lopez—
Outstanding in Two Careers

Over the years, one of the many irrefutable truths that has emerged in baseball is the old axiom that good players don't make good managers.

The game is littered with examples to support that postulate. Conversely, the majority of baseball's finest pilots have been men who have risen from the splinters of obscure benches, lowly reserves who have used their inactivity as players to develop a keen knowledge of the game and its many subtleties.

There are, of course, exceptions to every rule. And in this case, none is more conspicuous than Al Lopez, a superb player and possibly an even more superb manager.

Lopez parlayed the teachings of a 19-year career as one of the game's most talented catchers into a 17-year career as one of the games most successful managers. The combination of the two earned him a place in the Hall of Fame in 1977.

The seventh son of nine children of immigrant parents from Madrid, Spain, Lopez rose from the sandlots behind the cigar factories in Tampa, Florida, to a 50-year career in professional baseball. Along the way, there was little that Al either didn't see or didn't do.

As a player during a career spent between the years 1928 and 1947, most notably with the Brooklyn Dodgers, Boston Braves and Pittsburgh Pirates and briefly with the Cleveland Indians, Lopez was not only one of the finest defensive catchers of his and all other eras, he was the most durable man ever to go behind the plate.

Lopez caught in 1,918 major league games, until recently an all-time major league record. Twelve times he caught more than 100 games in a season. He led National League catchers in fielding three times, once going a whole season (1941) without a passed ball.

Al finished with a career batting average of .261 with 1,547 hits. Not a power hitter, he managed only 52 career home runs while collecting 652 RBI.

As a manager, Lopez posted a 1,414–1,017 record with the Indians and

Al Lopez.

Chicago White Sox. His won-lost percentage (.581) is currently ninth best in baseball history and his wins rank 13th on the all-time list.

Lopez won two pennants and his teams finished second 10 times. Only two of his teams finished out of the first division.

In Lopez' case, there was a direct correlation between the years he spent as a player and the years he spent as a manager.

"One of the main things that helped me later on as a manager," Lopez says, "is that as a player I was a catcher. I was also captain of most of the teams I played on. I think catchers should make good managers because they are the ones who direct the whole game. Everything is right there in front of them.

"I was fortunate, too," Lopez adds, "in that I played under six managers—Wilbert Robinson, Max Carey, Casey Stengel, Bill McKechnie, Frankie Frisch and Lou Boudreau—and all of them are in the Hall of Fame.

"Robby was a good manager. I was fortunate to break in with a man like him. All the players loved him, and he liked all the players and had their respect.

"Casey had one great trait. He liked to develop young kids. He was great with young players. He didn't manage any differently when he was with the Yankees years later. He just had better material.

"Carey liked to run a lot. Of course, he was an old base-stealer himself. He was good with young kids, too. McKechnie was great with pitchers and was a great defensive manager. Frisch was offensive-minded.

"I learned something from all of these men. And when I became a manager myself, it helped me quite a bit to have played for them."

Lopez was destined to play in the big leagues almost from the time he was a youngster growing up in Ybor City, the Spanish section of Tampa.

"I had an older brother who was a very good baseball player, and I always tried to be better than he was," says Lopez, who still lives in Tampa. Now he lives in a handsome house that backs onto Tampa Bay. "I was always a catcher, even as a kid. In those days, we didn't have masks or chest protectors. I used to get all banged up."

Lopez was playing on the sandlots of Tampa when he started to attract some attention.

"My team was in the playoffs. I was 16," he remembers. "I happened to have a good series. A newspaper man from the local Spanish paper came up to me and asked me if I'd like to play for the Smokers (Tampa's minor league team in the Florida State League).

"I said, 'Sure.' So he gave me a note to take to the manager. He said I could find him in a local pool hall. I went to the pool hall and found him and gave him the note. He said, 'You want to sign a contract?' I didn't even know what a contract was. He said, 'How much do you want?' I said, 'I don't know.' So he said he'd give me $150 a month. I thought that was great. I would've signed for $100. All I wanted to do was play."

At that point, Lopez had an advantage over most youngsters. As a 16-year-old, he had caught the legendary Walter Johnson.

"The Washington Senators used to train in Tampa," Lopez recalls. "They'd just bring in their regulars and a couple of minor leaguers. They never had any more than three catchers, so they were always looking for local boys to catch batting practice. They paid $35 a week.

"Well, hell, I'd have done that for nothing. So I got the job. I caught batting practice by the hour. Washington won the pennant that year. They had a great team that not only included Walter Johnson, but they had Stan Coveleski and Firpo Marberry.

"One time they let me catch Johnson in an exhibition game. He pitched five innings. I didn't know if I could catch him, but I managed to do it. Before the game, he said, 'Hey, kid, don't call too may curveballs.' He didn't have much of a curve, but he could sure throw hard.

"After that game, I figured, if I could catch Johnson, I could catch anybody. That really helped give me confidence."

A confident 16-year-old Lopez joined the Tampa Smokers in 1925. He spent most of the next five seasons in the minors, posting some fine averages (.315 in his second year at Tampa, .326 at Macon and .327 at Atlanta). In 1928, the Dodgers purchased his contract for $10,000. After joining Brooklyn for the end of the 1928 season, Lopez stuck with the Dodgers in 1930.

Known then as the Daffy Dodgers, a nickname that paid homage to the crazy antics of the club and some of its players, Brooklyn always seemed to have a handfull of respectable performers. But it never ranked among the frontrunners of the National League.

"When I got there, I thought they were a pretty good ball club," Lopez recalls. "Babe Herman was a helluva player, especially as a hitter. Dazzy Vance was a great pitcher. He had a tremendous curve and he was fast. He was as good as anybody I've ever seen. I'd put him in a class with Grove, Alexander and Dean. And we also had Lefty O'Doul, another helluva hitter.

"Robby said he wanted me to learn the league. So he sat me on the bench for the first couple of weeks of the season. Then he put me in, and I never came out."

Lopez hit .309 in his rookie season, a career high.

"That was the year Bill Terry hit .401," Al says. "(John) McGraw complained that the ball was too lively. The next year, Terry dropped all the way down to .349. They did something to the ball. I think that was a mistake."

By 1931, Lopez was so firmly entrenched that he not only kept another promising young catcher on the bench, but at the end of the season the Dodgers traded the talented backstop away. Ernie Lombardi went on to a Hall of Fame career, himself, most of which took place with the Cincinnati Reds.

Lopez played with the Dodgers through the 1935 season, winning a fielding title and hitting .301 in 1933, earning his first of two spots on the

NL All-Star team in 1934 and once even accomplishing that rarest of feats—
an unassisted doubleplay by a catcher.

Traded to the Boston Braves, Lopez played into the 1940 season in Bean-
town. He was then swapped to Pittsburgh. In 1941 with the Pirates, he had
one of the greatest seasons with the glove, playing in 114 games without a
passed ball. That year, he made the All- Star team again.

By then, Lopez had also established himself as the games' most durable
catcher.

"Catching was always very easy for me," Lopez says. "I had good legs,
and I was very comfortable back there. I played a little bit at second and
third base, but catcher was the place I liked to be.

"To be a catcher, you better like baseball. You have to like it more than
anything. Of course, a catcher has to be thinking all the time. The most
important thing, though, is that the pitchers have to have confidence in him.
They have to have the confidence that the catcher is going to call the right
pitches.

"I never had any major injuries," Lopez adds. "I had all my fingers
broken at one time or another, but I never missed much time. In fact, I
probably could've caught more if I had cared about records. But in those
days, records and averages didn't mean everything, like they do today. To
us, the big thing was winning."

As a player, Lopez did not play on too many winning clubs. The second place finish of his 1944 Pirates was the highest any of his teams ever
placed. Next came the third place finish of the 1932 Dodgers.

As a manager, though, it was a different story. By the time he had been
traded to the Indians for the 1947 season, Lopez was moving resolutely in
the direction of managing.

"I had been thinking about it, and I decided I wanted to try it," Al
says. "It was kind of a challenge. I had managed when Casey got thrown
out of games, and I was anxious to see what I could do on my own."

After spending a year as a backup catcher with the Indians, Lopez asked
club president Bill Veeck for his release. Veeck obliged, and Lopez found
himself a job the following season as the skipper of the Pirates' Indianapolis
club in the American Association.

Lopez' first team finished first and won 100 games.

He stayed two more years in Indianapolis, finishing second each time.
After the 1950 season, Veeck asked Lopez back to Cleveland to pilot the
Indians.

It was not an easy assignment. Boudreau, Lopez' manager with the
Indians in 1947, was an extremely popular figure in Cleveland, had piloted
the Tribe to a World Series victory in 1948 and had the club in the thick
of the pennant races the succeeding two years. But Veeck, incurring the wrath
of local fans, had traded his playing-manager to the Boston Red Sox following the 1950 season.

"The fans weren't too happy," Lopez recalls of his arrival in Cleveland. "Boudreau was a great favorite. Some of them didn't like me replacing him. I got some nasty letters."

In his first three years in Cleveland, Lopez drove the Indians home second each time. Then in 1954, the Indians ran away with the American League pennant while winning 111 games (an American League record for a 154-game season), finishing eight games ahead of the second place Yankees.

Although they lost the World Series in four straight games to the New York Giants, the '54 Indians left an indelible mark on baseball history.

"It was one of the greatest teams of all time," Lopez says. "There used to be a saying that to win the pennant you had to beat the second division teams. Well, we beat the Boston Red Sox that year 20 of 22 games, and they were a great first division club.

"I don't think we lost over two games in a row all year. Of course, I think we had one of the greatest pitching staffs ever put together. We had three future Hall of Famers—Bob Feller, Bob Lemon and Early Wynn. We had Mike Garcia, who had as good a year as any of them. We had a great bullpen with Ray Narleski and Don Mossi. We had Art Houtteman and Hal Newhouser, who did a great job for us.

"Plus, we had a great all-around team. We had some outstanding hitters in Al Rosen, Larry Doby and Bobby Avila. It was a great team to manage. It was just a case of sitting down and letting the pitchers do their jobs. They'd hold the other club, so all we'd need were a few runs."

The '54 Indians were upset in a World Series that was memorable because of the sensational catch made in center field by the Giants' Willie Mays on a drive off the bat of Vic Wertz and by the pinch-hitting heroics of New York's Dusty Rhodes, whose two home runs and seven RBI in six at-bats had a part in three of the four Giants' wins.

"In every Series, there's always a player who steps forward and stands out," Lopez analyzes. "In this case, it was Rhodes. He just played great ball. I don't think Mays' catch had any effect on us. He even said it wasn't one of his greatest catches. I think what got us more than anything was that we just hit a slump all at once, and the Giants played some great ball and made some great plays."

After their 1954 season, the Indians finished second twice more under Lopez. Then, following the 1956 season, Al abruptly resigned from the team.

"The last week of the season, we were fighting for the pennant and playing the Yankees in Cleveland," Lopez remembers. "For one game, we had 5,000 people in the stands. After the game, I made the statement that if we ever had a bad year, it was really going to be tough drawing fans. I said, I thought I ought to get out of there.

"On top of that, Rosen had gotten hit in the nose by a batted ball. The fans booed him when they were taking him off the field. I said the fans were bush. I shouldn't have said that, but I was mad."

Lopez quickly got a job with the White Sox, and after two second place finishes, he led Chicago to a pennant in 1959. The Chisox lost, four games to two, to the Los Angeles Dodgers in the World Series.

"That was a good team, but you had to manage more than you did with the Indians," Lopez says. "The White Sox were a real good defensive team—much better than the Indians. But we didn't have the hitting. We had to scratch for runs and steal bases. The team was built around speed and defense with guys like Nellie Fox and Luis Aparicio."

Lopez had three more second place finishes with the White Sox before health problems forced him to retire at the end of the 1965 season. But Al was back to manage in Chicago in mid-1968 after the White Sox fired Eddie Stanky.

"They asked me to come back because they really needed help," Al says. "It was a bad ball club. They were in last place. I finished the year, then went back the next year. But I had stomach problems and back spasms, so I figured I'd better get out."

Lopez left the team after 17 games of the 1969 season. He stayed with the club in an advisory capacity for several years, and then retired to a life of leisure in Tampa where he plays golf nearly every day, and where the local stadium—site of Reds' spring training games and the Tampa minor league games—is named after him.

In 1977, Lopez received the biggest honor of all when he was named to the baseball Hall of Fame in Cooperstown.

"I never had any idea that would happen," Lopez says. "I didn't think my name had been brought up before. But being inducted was just a great feeling. It's what every one in baseball wants, and I just really appreciated it. It was the highlight of my career."

Lopez looks back on that career, and finds many other things in which he takes pride.

"Playing was more fun than managing," he says. "I enjoyed playing very much and hated to sit on the bench as a player. I think I contributed to every club I was on. We always tried to win, and some of the clubs had pretty good success, although I wish we had gone to a World Series.

"I thought I had an interesting career. I couldn't ask for any more. In fact, I wish I could do it all over again.

"I guess the biggest secret to being a successful manager," he continues, "is to have discipline on the team. You have to respect the players, and the players have to respect you. If you can get that, you can get discipline.

"The toughest part of disciplining players is dealing with the substitutes and nonregular pitchers. They're the guys you have to worry about. You have to keep them in a good frame of mind.

"The next most important thing is how you handle the pitching staff. You have to do that right. I was always very fortunate. I had two great pitching coaches in Mel Harder at Cleveland and Ray Berres at Chicago."

Would Lopez rather be remembered as a player or as a manager?

"It's nice to be remembered as both," he says. "And I'm happy to have had the opportunity to do both."

It was an opportunity that few have had. Even fewer have been as successful.

Johnny Mize—
The Big Cat Was a Big Clouter

An inspection of the batting record of Johnny Mize, one of the more renowned sluggers of the 1930s and 1940s, produces two reactions.

One is respect. Mize posted some highly impressive figures during his 15-year major league career.

The other reaction is amazement. How did it take the Hall of Fame selection committee so long to induct this feared slugger into the Valhalla of the baseball gods?

During his big league career (Mize spent three years at the height of his career in the military service in World War II), Johnny was one of the premier hitters in baseball with a lifetime average of .312 2,011 hits, 359 home runs and 1,337 RBI.

He was the National League batting champion in 1939 when he hit .349, and he led the league in home runs in 1939 (28), 1940 (43), 1947 (51) and 1948 (40)—the latter two years in a tie with Ralph Kiner. Mize also led the league in RBI three times (1940, 1942, 1947), in runs scored in 1947, in triples in 1939, in doubles in 1941 and in slugging percentage in 1938, 1939, 1940 and 1942.

Mize reached double figures in home runs 13 straight years; he hit above .300 nine straight times; he drove in more than 100 runs eight times; he scored more than 100 runs in five different seasons; and once he had more than 200 hits.

Clearly, Mize has a batting record that could be the envy of all but a few of the game's foremost hitters. During a career with the St. Louis Cardinals, New York Giants and New York Yankees, the muscular lefthanded slugger had few equals when it came to striking fear into the hearts of opposing pitchers.

Although he retired after the 1953 season, having led the American League in pinch-hits his final three seasons, Mize was not elected to the Hall of Fame until 1981. It was, of course, a well- deserved honor, even if it did come late.

"It certainly was an honor," recalls the soft-spoken former first baseman,

Johnny Mize.

"but it came 28 years after I stopped playing. After waiting that long, getting elected kind of loses the luster."

Although Mize tried to minimize the attention that was directed his way in the years immediately following his election, he has in recent years been much more kindly disposed toward the extra attention he now gets as a Hall of Famer.

John has become one of the most sought-after ex-players on the baseball card show circuit. His willingness to appear at shows to sign autographs has resulted in requests for his services throughout the country. Often he travels to shows with his former Cardinals teammate and pal, Enos Slaughter.

"Other than that, though, my life hasn't really changed much since I was elected," Mize says. "I'm still doing everything the same as before."

Which is to say that John is taking life easy in Demorest, Georgia, a sleepy little village of about 1,000 people tucked in the northwestern tip of the state. Now well into his 70s and partly hobbled by creaky knees, Mize's life is a far cry from the glamorous career he once led as a member of nine National League All-Star teams, five American League World Championship teams and three of *The Sporting News'* Major League All-Star teams.

Mize, who broke into baseball as an outfielder in 1930, hit .329 in his rookie year with the Cardinals in 1936—the same year that Joe DiMaggio and Bob Feller made their major league debuts. From that year through 1947, Mize put together nine straight .300 seasons, including ones with averages of .364, .337 and .349 following his rookie year.

Six times during his career, Mize hit three home runs in one game—a major league record that still stands. As accomplished as he was as a hitter, Johnny was also an outstanding fielder. In 1947, he led National League first basemen in assists while tying a Giants' club record in fielding for first basemen with a .996 percentage.

It was in 1947 that Mize staged his greatest season, leading the league in RBI (138) and runs scored (137), tying for the lead in homers and hitting .302. That year, the Giants, with Mize, Willard Marshall, Walker Cooper, Bobby Thomson, Bill Rigney and Sid Gordon, had one of the most awesome slugging crews ever assembled on one team. Although the club finished in fourth place, it set a major league record with 221 home runs for the season.

Johnny, whose nicknames included "Big Jawn" and "The Big Cat," played six years with the Cardinals before being traded for two nondescripts to the Giants in 1942. He was sold to the Yankees during the 1949 season, becoming a part-time first baseman and one of the game's top pinch-hitters. In five seasons with the Yankees, Mize played in five World Series, hitting .286. His best production was in the 1952 Series against the Brooklyn Dodgers when he hit .400 with three home runs.

Mize was a giant of a man then, standing 6' 2" with a listed playing weight of 215, and he is still a huge figure who, aside from his white hair, looks fit enough to step up to the plate on a moment's notice. An avid golfer and college football fan, particularly of the University of Georgia team, Johnny lives with his wife in the town where he was raised.

After leaving baseball, he spent two years in New York City where he had a radio show. Then he lived in Florida for a number of years. Among other things, he operated an orange grove for 10 years, and also worked as a recreation director in St. Augustine before returning to Georgia. He has two children, one a school teacher and one a banker.

Mize, who as a youth played on a high school and a junior college team simultaneously, looks back at his long and successful career in baseball with a strong sense of satisfaction. But his quiet, unassuming manner seems to prevent him from getting too excited about his exploits. "I know one thing," he says. "I was born 30 to 35 years too soon."

How well would he handle today's pitchers? "There's really no way of telling," he says. "The ball's a little livelier now, and with the artifical turfs, a lot of routine ground balls are going as hits. But today's pitchers are better, so it's hard to say how I'd do.

"When you're hitting," he adds, "you can hit any pitcher. When you're not hitting, you don't hit any of them, even the bad ones. All of them gave me trouble from time to time."

The Big Cat no longer maintains a close connection with baseball, although he attends some Old Timers' games, goes on some of the junkets for Hall of Famers and, of course, attends the collectors' shows.

"I hadn't really known about baseball collecting until I'd been out of baseball for a while," he says. "Now, I'm getting some old pictures of myself (from autograph seekers) that I didn't even know about."

A first cousin of the wife of Babe Ruth, Mize says he didn't save many items from his playing days. "I've got a few bats hanging in the rafters of my barn," he says. "I also have a bat that belonged to Babe Ruth, and a watch of his."

During his playing days, Mize occasionally drew comparisons between himself and Ruth. Both were big men who swung the bat from the left side and who hit with considerable amounts of authority.

John didn't have the statistics that the Babe did. But he had an outstanding record. It placed him among the elite hitters of his day.

Brooks Robinson—
The Game's Best Gloveman at Third

It is an idelible image: Brooks Robinson dives to his right toward the foul line, with his body fully extended, skids across the dirt on his stomach, squeezes the ball as it smacks into the glove on his outstretched arm, scrambles to his feet, and fires to first ... just in time to rob another batter of what appeared to be a certain hit.

The play is over in a matter of seconds, but the memory of that sequence may last forever. Making a diving, backhanded stop of a shot whistling down the third base line is one of the most spectacular plays in baseball, and Robinson executed it as though it was a special science that he, alone, had perfected.

For 23 years, Robinson performed countless repetitions of the play as the third baseman for the Baltimore Orioles. He did it in meaningless games and he did it in the big games, such as the 1970 World Series when all of the civilized world finally learned what Baltimoreans had known for years—that Brooks Robinson was purely and simply the best fielding third baseman who ever lived.

His fielding earned Robinson, who retired after the 1977 season, an admission ticket into the Hall of Fame. During his career, Robinson won 16 Gold Glove awards, and is the major leagues' all-time fielding leader at third base with a remarkable .971 percentage.

Surprisingly, Robinson has retained only one of those Gold Gloves. "I've given all of the others away," he says. "I thought my mother should have one, so I gave one to her. I've given the rest of them to other people in my family and to various friends."

Robinson, an extremely personable fellow, also reveals some other interesting things about himself. For one, despite being a righthanded thrower and batter, he writes with his left hand. And, unlike some players who have difficulty making the transition to private life when they retire from baseball, Brooks moved out of the spotlight with relative ease.

He has a number of professional interests in the Baltimore area, and, he says happily, is able to spend much more time now with his wife and

Brooks Robinson.

four children in their home in Lutherville, Maryland, a town which also houses Johnny Unitas and a number of other present and former Orioles and Colts.

"I don't miss playing at all," Robinson claims. "At first, I thought I would, but I can honestly say that the last few years have been as pleasant as any years have ever been for me.

"I played so many games," adds the man who played more games (2,870) than any third baseman in major league history, "that I just completely lost interest. When you play and play and play, it finally gets to you. I couldn't wait to get out and do other things."

One of the things Robinson is doing is serving as color man on the telecasts of Orioles home games for WMAR–TV in Baltimore, a post he has held for 10 years. Brooks works about 60 games a season.

He acknowledges that that contact with the game has helped him make the switch from player to ex-player. "I would have hated to say, 'That's it; I'm never going to see another game after I retire,' " Brooks explains. "The television job has allowed me to stay in touch with baseball while not having to play it anymore."

Another of Robinson's interests also keeps him around the game. Five years ago, he and a lawyer friend opened a consulting business, which caters to athletes and people in communications. The company represents them and helps them handle their personal finances.

"We saw a real need for this kind of agency," says Robinson. "There are so many guys getting bad advice today. No matter who you are, you need some help."

Robinson also has a third job. Since 1964, he's been involved in training and public relations work for Crown Petroleum Company, and its 300 Baltimore-area stations.

In the past, Brooks owned a sporting goods business and a restaurant, which he ran from 1960 to 1971 with ex-first baseman and former general manager Eddie Robinson (no relation to Brooks).

Brooks says that he keeps in touch with many of his former teammates. He talks frequently by telephone with his close friend Dave McNally in Billings, Montana, and with Boog Powell in Key West, Florida. And he often sees Jim Palmer and Mark Belanger, fellow neighborhood residents in suburban Baltimore.

When he began, he wouldn't have dreamed he was going to have such a successful career as a third baseman. A native of Little Rock, Arkansas, where his boyhood idol was Stan Musial, Robinson was originally signed by the Orioles as a second baseman.

As an 18-year-old in 1955, he hit .331 in his first year of pro ball at York (Pennsylvania) in the Piedmont League. He went to Baltimore at the end of the season, and for the next two years was up and down between the Orioles and the minors. In 1958, at the age of 22, Robinson took over as the Birds' regular third baseman.

What followed was a big league career that stands as a monument to longevity and to stability. Brooks went on to play more years (23) with one club than any player in baseball history. Only five players (Jim McGuire, Eddie Collins, Bobby Wallace, Ty Cobb and Pete Rose) played more years in their careers than Robinson, and his total number of games played is exceeded only by Hank Aaron, Cobb, Musial, Carl Yastrzemski and Pete Rose.

Brooks, a noted clutch-hitter, finished his career with a .267 batting average, which included 2,848 hits and 268 home runs. He had 1,357 RBI.

A member of 18 All-Star teams—he was the game's most valuable player in 1966—Robinson enjoyed his greatest season in 1964 when he hit .317 with 28 home runs and a league-leading 118 RBI (all career highs). Brooks was named the American League's MVP that year.

It was at the hot corner, though, that Robinson placed his strongest

Brooks Robinson strikes a familiar pose—making another sensational defensive play at third base.

stamp on the game of baseball. Playing well off of the third base line, a tactic that was permissible because of the great range he had to his right, Brooks forced alterations in the batting styles of players who would do anything to avoid hitting the ball his way. The net result was usually a bonus for Orioles pitchers.

Robinson holds 10 major league fielding records for third basemen, including career records for most putouts (2,697), most assists (6,205), most chances (8,902) and most double plays (618). Eleven times, he led American League third basemen in fielding, another record.

Brooks' most glorious moment as a fielder occurred in the 1970 World Series against the Cincinnati Reds. It was the third of four fall classics in which Robinson participated, but it was the one he and most baseball fans will never forget.

During the five-game series, won by the Orioles, Robinson came up with one spectacular play after another. Sprawling in the dirt, snatching a blistering shot, then leaping to his feet to throw out the hitter, Brooks had Cincinnati batters thoroughly frustrated.

"I never had five games in a row like that," recalls Robinson, who also hit .429 in the Series and led the Orioles with two home runs and six RBI. "In fact, that was the most unbelievable two weeks I ever had. You could go months without having chances to make plays like those."

As a result of the plays, Robinson was showered with attention from the news media. And, because of the national attention a World Series gets, his prowess at third base registered all over the country.

Orioles fans, of course, were less impressed. Having seen it all before, they'd known for years that nobody could play third base like Brooks.

Enos Slaughter—Nobody
Played the Game Any Harder

In an era when greed, arrogance and nonchalance are words synonymous with the definition of all too many professional athletes, Enos Slaughter is a forceful reminder that it wasn't always this way.

Spend some time with the former star outfielder, and it is obvious that he is a man of great vitality, possessing none of the characteristics that make many of today's players so obnoxious and so drab. Clearly, Slaughter enjoys life and being with people, and he savors every moment of his long and storied baseball career.

In the same manner in which he played, Slaughter, the gregarious North Carolinian who was nicknamed "Country," delivers spicy comments and tells lively stories about his career, under a full head of steam. He is refreshingly outspoken and as colorful a personality now as he was as a player.

During a 19-year big league career, nobody played harder than the hustling ex-captain of the St. Louis Cardinals. To Slaughter, the game always deserved and always got his best effort.

"It was a thrill just to be able to go to the ballpark all those years," he says. "There was only one way to play. I always figured that if you couldn't go out there and hustle for two and one-half hours, you ought to find another job."

In 13 seasons with the Cardinals, beginning in 1938, plus two stints and five years with the New York Yankees, halves of two seasons with the Kansas City As and a few games in 1959 with the Milwaukee Braves, Slaughter hustled to a lifetime batting average of .300, driving in 1,304 runs and scoring 1,247 more. A candidate for 3,000 hits had his career not been interrupted by three years in the Air Force during World War II (he finished with 2,383 hits). Enos was a member of seven All-Star teams and a participant in five World Series—two with the Cards and three with the Yanks.

The crowning achievement of his superb career came in 1985, when Slaughter was rewarded with election to the Hall of Fame. It is an honor richly deserved by a man who could run, throw, field and hit and who, during his career, drove in 50 percent of the runners who were in scoring position when he was at the plate and who struck out just 538 times in 7,946 career at bats.

"It was an honor to get in," he says, while wondering why it took so long for his election.

Aside from that lengthy and unpardonable oversight, Slaughter remains loyal to the game. "I love the game of baseball, and I feel very fortunate to have played it," he says. "My heart and soul were in the game. I always took care of my health, and I could do everything they asked me to do."

Probably the most widely remembered play in Slaughter's career was his dash from first to home on Harry Walker's hit to left-center to score the winning run in the seventh game of the 1946 World Series against the Boston Red Sox. The picture of Enos sliding across the plate as Boston catcher Roy Partee waited up the line for shortstop Johnny Pesky's tardy throw is etched forever in the minds of baseball fans of that era.

"To me," Slaughter recalls, "that was just another play. It was just heads up baseball. Our manager, Eddie Dwyer, had told me earlier that with two outs I should try to score if the opportunity came along.

"I was stealing second when Walker hit the ball, which was off a pitcher named Bob Klinger. When I got to second, the ball hadn't hit the ground, yet. I said to myself, 'I can score.' I just kept running. I could've walked across the plate."

Although Pesky hesitated when he got the relay from center fielder Dom DiMaggio, then turned the wrong way for making a throw to the plate, Slaughter doesn't blame the shortstop for as much of a blunder as most people did at the time. Enos prefers to place some of the blame with the other Red Sox infielders for their failure to let Pesky know what was happening behind his back. He allows, however, that maybe they tried to do that, but couldn't be heard above the noise of the crowd.

Regardless, Slaughter remembers every detail of the play, just as he recalls all of the other fine points of his career. He can reel off his statistics as well as any computer, and he recites with ease the lineups of teams he played with and against.

With relish, he tells about certain experiences—such as the time an orange was dropped on his head as he was catching a drive against the wall in Yankee Stadium in the 1942 World Series, or the time he hit .498 in an armed services league peppered with major leaguers in 1943.

"I'll tell you something I never told anybody before," Slaughter confides. "I almost never made it to the big leagues. I was almost released in 1935, my first year in the minors."

The man who would become one of the most exciting players of his or any other era explains that as a raw 19-year old, he ran flat-footed because he didn't know the proper way to run. His Class D manager, Billy Southworth, spotted that and told the young player, "Kid, if you don't improve your running, I'm going to have to release you."

Enos Slaughter.

"They showed me how to run on my toes," recalls Slaughter. "I practiced that for three straight days. Learned to do it right, and that's what kept me in the game for 25 years. In fact, when I was 41 years old and playing for Kansas City, I was timed going from home to first at 3.6 seconds. That ranked in the top 25 in the American League."

Southworth, Slaughter discloses, also was responsible for instilling in him the need to hustle. "One day," says Enos, "I came in from the outfield and stopped running when I got to the third base line. I walked the rest of the way to the dugout. When I got there, Billy says, 'Kid, if you're tired, I'll get somebody else to play for you.' From that day on, I always hit the top step of the dugout running, both coming in and going out."

He didn't make much money during his career, but that neither bothered Slaughter then, nor does it now. He signed his first minor league contract for $75 per month. Two years later, when he hit .382 at Columbus, Ohio, and was the most valuable player in the American Association, Enos received $150 per month. He was up to $700 per month by his second year with the Cardinals—a season in which he led the National League in doubles. But Slaughter says he never made more than $25,000 a year in the big leagues. Yet, he led the league in hits in 1941 with 188 and in RBI in 1946 with 130, and he hit a sparkling .336 in 1949—third best in the circuit.

"I know they make a lot of money today," Slaughter concedes, "but I don't begrudge then. As far as I'm concerned, I'm just thrilled to have played in the era I did. We had communication, the guys jelled, they spent time together. They were the best of people then, and none can take their places.

"There are some good players today," he admits, "but the teams in the '40s and '50s had 25 good players. When I played, if you didn't hit .300 they'd tell you to go back to the minors to learn how to hit.

"The game of baseball is the easiest thing in the world to play. But players today don't look at it that way."

Although he criticizes modern players and managers who rely on platooning, insisting that he "made his living hitting lefthanders," the left-handed swinging Slaughter claims that the hardest pitcher for him to hit was a righthander, the Dodgers' Carl Erskine. "I got my hits off him but he caused me as many problems as anybody," Enos says. "He had a real good, live fastball and two tough curveballs."

He doesn't have to tangle with such pitchers anymore, but Slaughter still takes an active role in old-timers' games. He was even seen sliding head first into second base in one such game a few years ago. Always the warhorse, he insists he'd do it again today, too.

Slaughter's last formal contact with baseball was a seven-year stint from 1970 to 1977 as head baseball coach at Duke University. Slaughter's teams, hampered, he says, by the absence of scholarships, hovered around the .500 mark during his reign.

Most of Slaughter's time today is spent on his 240-acre farm in Roxboro, North Carolina, near the place where he was born and where as a boy, he milked cows before school and caught rabbits with his dogs on the way home.

"I'm just enjoying life, taking life easy.," says Slaughter, who arises before 6. a.m. each morning and works all day on the farm. The father of four daughters ranging in age form 13 to 30, Slaughter produces some 12,000 pounds of tobacco each year, and raises a few cattle. He does most of the work himself.

When he's not hustling around his farm, Slaughter retreats to a lakeside cabin in the North Carolina mountains to hunt and fish. Even when he's in the middle of the lake, all alone in his boat with just a fishing pole for company, baseball, the game he loves, is never too far from his thoughts.

Ted Williams—
Baseball's Consummate Hitter

It does not seem possible that Ted Williams is nearly 70 years old. It feels like just yesterday that The Splended Splinter, one of the last of the true American sports heroes and the idol of millions, was being acclaimed the greatest natural hitter in the history of baseball.

Pinch me if I'm dreaming, but have the last 30 or 35 years passed that quickly?

Ah, they must have. For now we see Ted, still splendid but no splinter, grey spots flecking his black, curly hair, and no longer the menacing figure who once terrorized opposing pitchers and occasionally the press and fans.

He is still the same free spirit, still the same outspoken, rugged individualist with charm and a touch of mystique that allows him to dominate a room. Perhaps, though, he has mellowed with time.

Regardless, he is still the one and only Ted Williams, #9 of the Boston Red Sox, the same guy worshipped by little boys throughout the land during a career that went from 1939 to 1960 and that reached the summit with his election to the Hall of Fame in 1966.

For the sake of those too young to revel in the wonders of this marvelous player, let it be said that Ted Williams was simply the game of baseball's most perfect hitter. With a swing that was technically correct in every detail, he ravaged American League pitchers to the beat of a .344 lifetime average, which included six batting championships and the game's last .400 mark, a .406 in 1941.

Among the galaxy of impressive records, Williams has the sixth highest lifetime batting average in major league history, and he ranks second in slugging average (.634), ninth in home runs (521) and ninth in RBI (1,839). Had he not missed nearly five years during the peak of his career, serving in first World War II and then the Korean War, his records might be unapproachable.

After signing a pro contract with his hometown San Diego club as a fresh 17-year-old, Williams interned for three years in the minor leagues— all in Triple A. In his last year, he tore apart American Association pitching

Ted Williams.

at Minneapolis with league-leading totals in average (.366), home runs (43), RBI (142) and runs (130).

Brought up to the Red Sox for the 1939 season, Williams served notice immediately that he would be one of baseball's premier hitters with a .327 batting average and a league-leading 145 RBI. There was no sophomore jinx for this fellow. Ted piled up a .344 mark in 1940, then the next year cracked the fabled .400 circle. That year, he won his first home run crown with 37 four-baggers.

Over the next five seasons (with Williams missing three full seasons during that time), Ted's average never went below .342 the figure he registered in 1946 after returning from the War and a grueling stint as a Navy combat pilot.

Despite another one and one-half years in the service in the early 1950s and another partial season because of a broken arm, Williams continued his batting onslaught the rest of his career. In 1957, at the age of 39, he won his fifth batting title with a .388 average. He came back the following year with a .328 mark to win still another batting crown.

Meanwhile, Williams was named the American League's Most Valuable Player in 1946 when he led Boston to the only pennant of his era while hitting 38 homers, driving in 123 runs and scoring 142. In 1949, he won his second MVP when he led the league with career highs in home runs (43), RBI (159) and runs (150) while hitting .343.

Altogether, Williams collected four home run crowns, and led the league in RBI four times, in runs scored six times, in doubles twice, in bases on balls eight times and in slugging percentage nine times.

Williams both scored and drove in more than 100 runs eight straight times and nine times altogether. He drew 100 walks or more in 11 different seasons.

He was named to the American League All-Star teams in 15 different seasons and was *The Sporting News* Major League Player of the year five times.

As he has always been, Williams is the consummate authority on the art of hitting a baseball. He will talk on the subject—as well as on fishing—for hours, critiquing and demonstrating the fine techniques of the very special science of placing a bat against a speeding baseball.

His theories, he says, began to develop as a teenager in San Diego.

"I had an Arky Vaughan bat, and I had a Bill Terry bat before that," he says. "If there was any player I leaned toward when I was 13 or 14, it would've been Terry. I used to go in my backyard at night, by myself, with my Bill Terry bat.

"I didn't even think about swinging like Terry. But I would say, 'I'm in the Polo Grounds. Here's a ball, high, inside.' Boom. Right field. 'Here's a ball. Low, inside.' Boom. Left-center. I'd swing and swing—with no ball—and I'd think about it.''

The more he thought, the more the theories evolved that someday would be put to use in a major league uniform.

The most important asset a hitter can have, he says, is not the 20-15 vision that he had, or precision timing, or strong wrists or coordination. "The biggest innate talent that a good hitter is always blessed with," he says, "is the ability to put the bat on the ball.

"That's what Willie McGee of the Cardinals has. He doesn't have great style or great technique. In fact, he looks lousy as a hitter. But he's got that ability to get the bat on the ball. Plus, he runs like a reindeer. He's got a different kind of style than anybody I ever saw leading the league in hitting. And that's not meant to take anything away from McGee. He's a hard-working little guy, a good player."

To Williams, who remains involved with baseball as a hitting instructor in spring training for the Red Sox and as an occasional roving minor league hitting coach during the season, style is extremely important.

"There are some great athletes today, guys who can roll and tumble and dive and run and throw. But I don't think there are as many stylish hitters and not quite as many good hitters today. They don't know that little game like the older hitters. The reason is, they haven't played as much. But there are some guys like Brett, Schmidt, Carew, Hernandez—and you can keep naming guys, Boggs is another—who are good hitters."

Will any of them become the first player since Williams to hit .400?

"I think somebody will," Ted says. "Two guys have come reasonably close in recent years (Carew with a .388 in 1977 and Brett with a .390 in 1980). I think it's going to be done again; you're darned right.

"Boggs," Williams adds about the Red Sox third baseman, "has certainly proved he can get the bat on the ball. He does it as good as anybody.

"They're going to find a way to pitch to him a little better. But that park helps him in Boston because he hits inside-out."

How would Williams, a Florida resident who also has a summer home in Canada and a boys' camp in Massachusetts, hit today?

"I don't know," he says forthrightly. "I've thought about it. I can't tell you how the pitching is because I don't hit against it."

Ted says he had enough trouble with pitching in his own day.

I could name 20 pitchers who were tough on me. Lemon, here's one for you—Willis Huddlin, Ford, Feller, Newhouser. There were a lot of guys who gave me trouble. There was a guy with the Browns. I can't think of his name. He was a lefthander. Pheew. Boy, I hated to hit against him. He had a good curve and he was herky-jerky, and you didn't know where the ball was going. Then there was Raschi, Reynolds, Page. Trout was tough, too, although I could usually hit him.

Williams hit opposing pitchers often enough, however, to supply himself with many memorable moments during his storied career. But one of the highest points was in the 1941 All-Star game in which his home run off Claude Passeau gave the American League a 7–5 victory.

"I was a young kid coming into that game," he says. "And bam! I won the game in the bottom of the ninth inning with two away and two runs behind and two men on base. It was a big thrill for me.

The textbook swing of Ted Williams was without flaw.

"But my last home run (a 450-foot, eighth inning blast in his last time at bat) was a big thrill. It did a little something different to me. I felt it a little bit more.

"Then I hit some home runs late in the season that I got big charges out of. For example, in 1948, I beat the Yankees two games late in the season. I hit a two-run homer against Lopat, then I hit a two-run homer against Reynolds the next day that knocked them out of the pennant.

"Of course," he adds, "I remember sometimes when I was lousy, too. Some guy said to me, 'Did you ever get in a slump?' I thought, Oh, boy, Oh, boy."

Williams says he thinks today's salaries are "great," and that he does not condemn modern players for their free agent hopscotching.

"I wouldn't criticize any player for taking the free agent route," he says, "because the name of the game is to make dough. If a player's with a club that doesn't feel like he's worth what another club does, it's certainly his prerogative to say, 'I'm going to play over there.'

"I don't know if I would've ever become a free agent. It's very possible that playing for a fellow like Tom Yawkey, if you deserved to get $1 million, you'd get $1 million. If you were a $100,000 ballplayer, you'd get $100,000. If you were as good as anybody in the league, you got as much as anybody in the league. Probably, if you played for Yawkey and the Red Sox, you wouldn't have to worry about being a free agent."

Although he insists that baseball is in a healthy state at present, Williams is troubled by the diversions that are either luring young athletes away from the game or distracting those who are in it.

"I'm sure this is close to being right," he says. "Hitting a baseball is as hard or harder than anything else in sports. I'm the first guy who said that, and I think it's right.

"And if that is true, you need more hours, more dedication, more opportunity and you have to have innate ability. Putting them all together, you still have to develop your talent. But even with all these attributes, it's harder for a guy today to try to duplicate the great hitters of a while back because he hasn't played as much.

"You've got more emphasis on school. You've got more vacation time. You've got travel. You might want the kids to go to Europe for the summer. You've got TV all the time. You've got more sports, some just as lucrative. You've got tennis, you've got golf, you've got boating. Some guy might be a helluva ballplayer, but he might also be a football or basketball player. So he gets diverted.

"You've got nine million things going on that keep you from having that complete dedication and the chance to spend as many hours going in that one direction that you need.

"When I was growing up, the only thing I could do was hit. Hit. Hit. Hit."

The Old Guard

Dick Bartell—
A Fiery Competitor with Talent

No one can ever say that shortstop is a position for shrinking violets. Good shortstops hustle. They plan with take-charge aggressiveness. They're cocky. They scrap, they claw, they fight. They get their uniforms dirty by the third inning. You can't be laid back and play a good shortstop.

In the overall scheme of things, shortstop is a postion that requires more than talent. It is just as important for a shortstop to be a leader and a fiery competitor.

There aren't many like that these days. Once upon a time, there were, though. The land was filled with fiery shortstops who found nothing inappropriate about busting an onsliding opponent in the chops or flinging a baseball toward the bridge of his nose.

None performed this role any better than Dick Bartell, a fiercely competitive little rooster who plied his trade at shortstop for 18 big league seasons.

Bartell was nicknamed Rowdy Richard. It was with good reason. He was as fiesty as they came, and he had what was once described as "one of the scrapiest dispositions in the majors."

A 5'9", 160 pounder, Bartell also had talent. He had a lifetime batting average of .284, slamming 2,165 hits, including 442 doubles and 79 home runs. He was a good base-stealer, and a player who always drew numerous walks. And he was a fine fielder with excellent range, who often led the league's shortstops in various defensive categories.

A Chicago native who grew up and still lives in Alameda, California, Bartell reached the majors in 1927 with the Pittsburgh Pirates. By the time he retired in 1946, he had also played with the Philadelphia Phillies, New York Giants, Chicago Cubs and Detroit Tigers.

He played well for all of them. Bartell had six seasons when he hit over .300. He led National League shortstops in doubleplays four times and putouts and assists each three times. He played in three World Series'. And he was the starting shortstop in two All-Star games, including the first one in 1933.

At a time when talented shortstops were plentiful in the big leagues,

Bartell was as well-equipped as any of them, a good-hitting, good fielding player and a sparkplug who wouldn't give an inch to the opponent.

"I guess you could say I had a pretty satisfactory career," Bartell says. "I know I enjoyed every minute of it. I always went out and gave 110 percent."

He gave so much, in fact, that Bartell was frequently embroiled in battles with opponents. He had some memorable brawls, including ones with Leo Durocher, Bill Jurges and Van Mungo.

"The most memorable battle I was ever in, though, was a free-for-all we had in St. Louis while I was with the Giants," Bartell says. "There was a lot of friction between the Cardinals and the Giants. Dizzy Dean always pitched against Carl Hubbell. Nobody ever scored before the fifth inning. If you did, it was a miracle.

"One day we were playing, and we had the lead and Dean was getting madder and madder. He knocked down six straight batters. Finally, Jimmy Ripple dropped a bunt down the first base line, and everybody started out of the dugout. Fights were breaking out all over the place. There were five or six fights going on at once. It was so bad, even the police wouldn't come in to break it up.

"When they finally got it stopped, and we went out on the field, the fans threw so many bottles at us, it took us an hour to clean up the field so we could finish the game."

That was earning your money the hard way. Bartell says he never earned that much, anyway. His highest salary was $20,000. But that was okay. Dick was more interested in playing baseball than becoming a millionaire.

"Baseball was in my blood," Bartell says. "I came from a family of baseball players. My dad was an outstanding second baseman. He had once made an unassisted triple play, and he never let me forget it. My dad's brother was also a fine player, and I had two brothers who were good players, too.

"As a kid, I practiced all the time. I was always practicing. My first year in high school, I was a second baseman. I wanted to be a second baseman like my dad. But the coach switched me to shortstop. So I quit the team. I didn't want to play shortstop.

"I came home, and my dad said, 'You're going to play,' and I said, 'No, I'm not.' We went back and forth. Finally, he grabbed me by the seat of my pants and took me back to the ball field. He marched me up to the the coach and said, 'Here's your shortstop.' It turned out to be the best move of my life."

When he finished high school, Bartell signed a contract with the Pirates. His first year's salary was $2,500.

"I had three college scholarships offered to me," Bartell says. "A lot of major league clubs wanted to sign me, too, including the New York Yankees. But my dad was a close friend of Joe Devine, a Pittsburgh scout, and he said, 'I don't care if the Yankees offer you 10 times more, you're going to sign with the Pirates.'

Dick Bartell.

"That turned out to be a disaster. Barney Dreyfuss owned the team, and he was the toughest guy in the world to play for. He wouldn't spend a dime extra if he had to."

Bartell spent the 1927 season in the minors, then came to the Pirates at the end of the year. It was just in time to go to the World Series where he watched in awe as the Yankees, with Murderers' Row at its zenith, battered his club in four straight.

"Before the first game, they put on a show in batting practice like we never saw before," Bartell recalls. "They were hitting shots on top of the stands. That had an effect on the Pirates. They were scared stiff."

Dick spent the 1928 season with the Bucs as a reserve infielder, hitting .305 in 72 games. Then he took over the regular job at short in 1929 and hit .302.

"After that, I figured I'd get a substantial raise," he says. "But Dreyfuss wouldn't give it to me. So I held out for 30 days. Finally, Dreyfuss' son, Sam, who was a good man, not like his father, signed me to a contract."

In 1930, Bartell hit .320 while collecting a career high 75 RBI.

"Toward the end of the season, I asked for a $5,000 raise," Dick remembers. "Barney was furious with me. You'd have thought I'd asked him for a blood transfusion. After that, he did all sorts of things to get me, including saying that I overspent my meal allowance by $2.50. He took that out of my salary.

"I went to him, and told him he couldn't do that. He grabbed me by the shirt and started yelling and hollering. I was just getting ready to deck him, but he was an older man, so I backed off. He said, 'Get the hell out of here. You're fined and suspended for the rest of the season.'

"I went to Judge Landis about it, but he said he didn't have any jurisdiction over something like that. So I went home, and that winter Dreyfuss traded me to the Phillies. Even though they were a last place ball club, I was tickled to death. It was just great to get away from Barney."

Bartell quickly asserted himself in Philadelphia. The downtrodden Phils were weak and lethargic, but the energetic shortstop began pumping life into the club, and was soon not only being called "Pepperpot" by the local writers, but was also named captain of the team.

Bartell hit .289 in 1931. He followed that with seasons of .298, .271 and .310, twice scoring more than 100 runs, a feat he achieved only three times in his career.

In 1932, Bartell helped the Phillies finish in fourth place, the only time between 1918 and 1949 that the club placed in the first division. He was one of six starters to hit above .300 that year.

The following season, he became the National League's first All-Star shortstop when the two leagues met for the first time. Although he went 0-for-2 and the American League won, 4-2, Bartell still remembers that game at Chicago's Comiskey Park with great pleasure.

"It was a great thrill to be selected to the first All-Star game," he says.

"And it was a great thrill playing in the game. It was an experience that nobody can ever take away from me."

That same year, Bartell also accomplished another noteworthy feat. In a 7–1 Phillies' win over the Boston Braves, he hit four consecutive doubles to tie a major league record currently held by 19 players.

"After I hit the fourth double, the game was stopped, and I was given the ball," Bartell recalls. "I didn't even realize what I was doing until they brought it up."

Except for the 1932 season, the Phillies had little success in the standings, regularly inhabiting the lower levels of the National League. It was sometimes a chore to come to the ball park, especially when it was seedy old Baker Bowl. But Bartell persevered.

"I just went out and played and gave it all I had," Bartell says. "Sometimes I'd go home at night after playing hard all day. We'd lost, 10–4, or something like that, and I'd be bleeding. I'd say, 'I'm just not going to keep this up.' But I'd be back the next day ready to go all over again.

"I always liked to hit," Bartell adds. "I suppose I inherited some of it. I used to work hard at fielding and I'd watch the other shortstops, but hitting just came naturally. I had about the same stance all my life, although I changed bats sometimes.

"I think you can say, when I got two strikes on me, I did one thing you don't see today. I'd choke up on the bat about two inches. I always made it a practice to protect the plate.

"There were some tough pitchers back then," Bartell adds. "The Dean brothers, Hubbell, Hall Schumacher, Dazzy Vance. I remember my first episode as a major league player was against Vance. I said, 'He doesn't look so tough.' I went out and struck out three times.

"I remember facing Bob Feller in 1936. He was just a rawboned rookie. The Cleveland Indians and New York Giants came north together from spring training. Feller was with them, and the first time he pitched against us, he was as wild as a March Hare. He struck three or four of us out, but everybody was choking up on the bat. He had a great curve and a real good, live fastball. I was just happy to get a walk."

Bartell relates how he would deal with certain kinds of pitchers.

"When somebody threw you spitballs or knocked you down, you'd try to hit the ball up the middle through the box," he says. "That would be the hitter's way to retaliate."

Bartell figured he was a long-term fixture with the Phillies, but his calculations were wrong. Following the 1934 season, he was traded to the Giants for four players and $50,000. None of the four players who came to the Phillies was a significant contributor to Philadelphia fortunes.

"Gerry Nugent, who was the Phillies' owner, had said to me, 'Dick, I feel sorry for you. Here I am trading everybody away out of necessity, and they are going to other clubs to make more money than I can pay you. You'll be the last one to go.'

"He told me that I was his franchise, his whole team. 'When I trade you,' he said, 'it will mean that I am going bankrupt.' "

One year after Nugent made those statements, Dick was the starting shortstop on a Giants team that would soon win a National League pennant.

"Bill Terry had told Horace Stoneham that if he got me, he would win the pennant the following year," Bartell says. "Stoneham said there wasn't a player in the world worth $50,000. He said to call the deal off. But Terry made it anyway, and one year later, in 1936, we won the pennant.

"Terry was sharp," Bartell adds. "I saw him take a club one year with players who were mostly through, and he manipulated that team and kept it in contention all season. He was an outstanding manager."

The year 1936 was one in which Bartell also had his most memorable achievement as a Giant. It happened during the World Series, when Dick's home run led the Giants to an 8–1 win over the Yankees in the opener at the Polo Grounds.

"It was a tremendous thrill just to be in a World Series, but it was a bigger thrill to hit the home run that put us ahead," Bartell says.

"When I hit that homer, I had one thought on my mind. In fact, I almost missed first base. I had to go back and tag it. I kept thinking all the way around the bases that my dad had an enlarged heart, and he was at the World Series, although the doctor had told him he couldn't go. But my dad said his son was in the World Series, and he was going. He told the doctor he was flying. The doctor said, 'That's even worse.'

"The only thing I had on my mind when I hit that home run was, 'My God, my dad is going to have a heart attack. I couldn't wait to get to home plate to see if he was all right. When I got there, there he was, jumping up and down, waving his hat and yelling, 'That's my son, Dick Bartell.' What a relief it was to see him whooping it up. "

Bartell played four seasons with the Giants, hitting .262, .298, .306 and .262. New York won another pennant in 1937, the year that Dick was voted to start in his second All-Star game. That year, he was also named the shortstop on *The Sporting News'* Major League All-Star team.

Along the way, Bartell, who in 1937 had the rare feat of hitting two grand slam home runs in one game, also picked up the nickname Rowdy Richard.

"I had held out one spring," Bartell remembers, "and Stoneham said, 'Come down (to spring training) and we'll talk about it.' I told him if he paid my transportation down, I'd come. When I got there, I finally signed. A sportswriter from New York, Gary Schumacher, said, 'Would you mind if I say Rowdy Richard signs?' He used it, and it became a kind of trademark. I guess I was a rowdy, though."

After the 1938 season, Bartell was traded to the Cubs as part of a six-player deal that had Jurges coming to the Giants. Dick stayed one year in the Windy City, hitting .238, and was then swapped to the Tigers.

Hitting .295 in 1940, Bartell helped the Tigers to the American League pennant, but for the third time in his career, his team went down to defeat in the World Series (the Giants had lost twice to the Yankees and the Tigers bowed to the Cincinnati Reds).

Early in the 1941 season, Bartell was abruptly released by the Tigers. He was signed a few days later by the Giants. That year, Dick collected his 2,000th major league safety while hitting .303 for New York.

Dick played two more seasons with the Giants, then was drafted into World War II. He rejoined the Giants as a player-coach in 1946, but played in only five games.

"I was primarily a third base coach for Mel Ott," Bartell says. "He didn't want me anywhere but there. The only time he played me was when he ran out of players."

The Giants released Bartell after the season. Dick spent the next three years managing in the minor leagues. He returned to the majors in 1949, working from then until 1955 as a coach with the Tigers. During the 1956 and 1957 seasons, he was a coach with the Reds.

Leaving baseball after that, Bartell spent the next six and one-half years as a salesman for a creamery. Later, he owned a liquor store for 10 years.

Although he is now retired, Bartell is still active. In 1987 he and writer Norman Macht teamed up to publish a book called *Rowdy Richard,* an account of Bartell's days in the National League.

Dick has also been mentioned often as a strong candidate for the Hall of Fame. So far, however, his selection has not occurred.

"I think I belong," he says. "I know if you go on statistics, mine speak for themselves. I should get in on my merits. If I don't make it, I don't make it. But I think I was an asset to baseball."

And, he quickly admits, baseball was an asset to Bartell.

"It made me what I am today," he says. "Everything I have, I owe to baseball. I feel I was lucky to have the career I had. Some of it was pretty tough, but I enjoyed every minute of it."

Huck Betts—
Pitcher in Baseball's Golden Era

It was just after World War I had ended, and the young man from Delaware had been released from the service. While casting around for a job, he had spent the summer pitching for a college team in Dover.

A friend who delivered mail knew Philadelphia Phillies owner William Baker. One thing led to another, and Baker asked the young pitcher to Philadelphia for a tryout.

Soon afterward, the pitcher left his home in Millsboro, Delaware, and headed for Baker Bowl. A little while later, the big league career of Walter (Huck) Betts was born.

Betts parlayed that trip into a professional baseball career that went from 1920 to 1935, including 10 years in the big leagues, the first six of them with the Phillies.

A relief pitcher during most of his career with the Phillies, he later became a starter for the Boston Braves. His career record shows 61 wins and 68 losses with an earned run average of 3.93 in 307 games. Betts worked in 1,366.1 innings giving up 1,581 hits, striking out 323 and walking 321.

A 5'11" 170-pound hurler during his playing days, Betts performed in an era sometimes referred to as "The Golden Age of Baseball." Although neither the Phillies nor the Braves of those years was very golden—the Phils finished in eighth place eight times between 1919 and 1930—Betts is one of those rare gems whose vivid memories of that era help to give baseball history its rich luster.

He was 91 years old when he died in 1987 while still living with Jennie, his wife of more than 60 years, in the same house he built soon after his playing days ended. His age made him one of the oldest living former major leaguers, and his treasure chest of fascinating stories made him one of the most interesting.

Huck—who was given his nickname by Phillies' Hall of Fame shortstop Davey Bancroft because of his resemblance to Huckleberry Finn—played with such other Phillies luminaries as Eppa Rixey, Lee Meadows, Cy Williams, Casey Stengel, Bob Muesel and Johnny Mokan. His first manager was Gavvy Cravath. He roomed with Russ Wrightstone and later Jimmie Wilson and sometimes double-dated with the fun-loving Stengel.

"There was never much pressure playing on those teams because we got beat most of the time," Betts recalled. "But we had some good players. Some of those fellows could play real well. Only trouble was, Baker always

Huck Betts.

had financial problems, and he would always sell a player or two to pay the debts. Of course, he usually got a good price for them."

Betts was a raw recruit when he joined the Phillies in 1920. He had no minor league experience.

"I had always played as a kid," he recalled. "When I got bigger, I could throw the ball pretty good. We played a lot of sandlot ball.

"When I was about 11, I went with our high school team, which was going to play another school. We went by boat. The Millsboro pitcher couldn't get the other side out, so I said, 'I'll pitch.' I got 'em out, but coming home on the boat, it was cold, and my arm got all stiff. It's been crooked ever since."

With his crooked arm, Betts became an infielder, and played there through most of his high school career. Then he went to a college in Dover, which later became Wesley College, where he returned to the mound.

"We had pretty good success," he said. "Won all our games. But then I got drafted in the Army. I didn't play any more because I came down with the flu—that was during the epidemic in 1918—and then I got pneumonia and was unconscious for five days."

The Army finally sent Betts home. Once there, he was contacted by the coach at Wesley and invited back to pitch. Wesley (then called WCI) lost only one game, then won the league playoffs when Betts pitched a no-hitter against a team from Milford.

"After that," he said, "I played for a town team. We played pretty near ever day.

"It was at that point that Baker asked me up for a tryout. It was the end of August, 1919. They kind of liked me, and wanted me to sign. But I saw I didn't belong there. I was afraid if I went up there at the end of the season, I didn't have much of a chance of making a good showing. I would just get disgusted.

"So I said, 'No, I don't think I want to sign.' I said, 'If you want me to go to spring training next season and start fresh, I would be glad to do that.'

"That's what they did. And next spring I went to Birmingham, Alabama, where we trained. A couple of pitchers had sore arms. Finally they got down to me, and they kept me on the roster. I didn't have any experience, so I just stayed in the bullpen all the time. I wound up staying there for six years. It was hard to get out of there if you weren't a starter."

When he joined the Phillies in 1920, Betts was a member of a staff that was headed by Rixey, Meadows and George Smith. Betts worked in 27 games that year, posting a 1–1 record.

"That was Bancroft's last year on the club," Betts recalled. "He had made it known that he wasn't going to play for the Phillies anymore because he knew that John McGraw wanted him for the Giants. So one day, he just came off the field and hit Cravath, the manager, in the face with his glove. 'That's the last game I'm going to play for you.' he said. A little while later, the Phillies traded him to the Giants."

Betts, meanwhile was trying to hang on, learning all he could about the art of big league pitching.

"When I joined the Phillies, the pitching coach was Jesse Tannehill, an old pitcher himself," Huck recalled. "He taught me how to throw a screwball. I developed it pretty good. In fact, I even learned to throw an underhanded screwball later on. I also threw a curve, a fastball and a slow curve. I was a control pitcher. I always thought that you lose a lot of strength in your arm when you strike men out all the time. I'd rather let 'em hit it. Get 'em out on two or three pitches."

One game in which Betts got 'em out quickly that year was his first start in the big leagues.

"I had Boston beat 1-0 in the ninth inning," he remembered. "Wrightstone was playing third base. A fellow named Powell led off the ninth for Boston. I whispered to Wrightstone, 'Don't get back too far. This fellow might bunt on you.' Sure enough, Powell laid down a bunt and beat it out. They took me out of the game, and put in Bill Hubbell. He lost the game, 2-1.

"The first game I won in the big leagues," Betts added, "was against Pittsburgh. I won, 4-2, in 12 innings against a fellow named Ponder."

Betts was pitching most of the time out of the bullpen. He relieved in 30 of the 32 games in which he pitched in 1921 when he posted a 3-7 record. In both 1922 (1-0) and 1923 (2-4), he spent part of the season back in the minors.

"In 1923, the Phillies wanted Heinie Sand to play shortstop," said Betts. "He was at Salt Lake City. The team there wanted me, so they told the Phillies they could have Sand if they sent me out to Salt Lake City. I went out there for part of the season."

Betts came back and posted 7-10 and 4-5 records in the next two years with the Phillies. But pitching at Baker Bowl with its short right field wall was never easy.

"It was a real tough place to pitch," Huck remembered. "An ordinary fly to right was a home run.

"Straight away center was very deep. In fact, our clubhouse was in center field, and the visiting clubhouse was a floor below it. We had a swimming pool in our clubhouse. I remember one time Hughie Jennings—he was a coach then—came in after a game. There was a lost of steam, and you couldn't see too well. He jumped into the pool, but there wasn't any water in it. Hughie landed right on his head.

"I remember the bleacher seats were open." Betts added. "The gamblers used to sit out there and bet on games. They were about the only ones who came. If we had 500 at a game, it was a big crowd.

"But Baker Bowl was all right. With my pitching style, I had pretty good success there. It was a small park, like the Polo Grounds and the park in Boston, but I always thought from a fan's standpoint, the closer you are to the game, the better it is. It made the game more interesting.

"I went with my son to Veterans Stadium a few years ago, and I remember thinking to myself, 'Boy, is this a big difference from where I played.' It was a long walk to the park, and everyone was rushing past you in a hurry. At Baker Bowl, you got off a street car and you were just about inside the ballpark.

"Of course, as a player, I was always glad to be on the road. You got tired of playing at Baker Bowl. There was no excitement. Nobody was ever there. It wasn't much pleasure."

One road game that Betts distinctly recalled was a contest in Brooklyn.

"We had lost 11 games in a row," he said. "We stopped at Brooklyn but all our trunks had gotten lost. We had no uniforms, no nothing. We went out in Brooklyn's away uniforms with different shoes and gloves, and we beat them. Then darned if we didn't get home and lose 12 straight."

As a reliever, Betts found that he "didn't have much chance to win many games." But he would never give in to hitters, even if it meant throwing at them.

"I threw at 'em, sure. I did," he said. "Sometimes I meant to hit 'em, too. They'd hit the ball back at you and laugh at you. It was different in those days. The catchers even had signs to give to you to throw at a batter.

"We wouldn't let a hitter dig in. If he did, we used to say, 'We'd turn his cap around.'

"Jimmie Wilson was my roommate for a while, but later on when we were on different teams, he took advantage of me. I hit him right in the temple. Pitchers were mean back then. You couldn't let the batters get the edge on you."

Even if it meant throwing an occasional spitball?

"No, I never thought much of the spitball," said Betts. "I didn't throw it. When you had a spitball pitcher in the game, it was hard for the infielders to throw the ball in a hurry. They never knew where it was going. Players would always hesitate after they got the ball when a spitball pitcher was throwing. It didn't look good, either. And it wasn't sanitary."

Betts said one of the toughest hitters he faced was Chick Hafey, a Hall of Famer who played for the Cardinals and Reds. "He didn't swing, he'd slap at the ball," Huck said.

"One of the best hitters I ever faced, although I usually could get him out, was Rogers Hornsby. One time we played six games in four days. Twice I went in with the bases loaded and struck Hornsby out. But once he hit a ball off me clear over the clubhouse—or at least a little to the right of it— at Baker Bowl. He stood so far away from the plate that you thought he couldn't reach a pitch on the outside. But you better not throw him one there."

During his career with the Phillies, Betts played for several different managers, the last of whom was Art Fletcher, who had come from the Giants in 1920 in a trade for Bancroft. Betts, as well as a number of other players, didn't get along with Fletcher.

"One year, Cy Williams hit .308 and they gave him a $1,500 raise," Betts recalled. "The next year, his average went down to .293, but he hit 41 home runs. They docked him $1,500. Fletcher wrote a letter to Baker. He said, 'Don't give in to him. He'll sign anyway.'

"The year Williams hit 41 home runs, Fletcher wouldn't take him on a road trip the last four games of the season because he didn't want him to have more home runs that year than Babe Ruth. Ruth and Williams wound up the season tied.

"My last season with the Phillies," Betts said, "Fletcher talked against giving me a raise. Every time I made a point with Baker, Fletcher would talk against me. We had a big argument, and he never played me the last month of the season.

"He told me, 'I'm going to send you where it's hot,' I said, 'Any place is better than being with you.' "

Betts was sold in the winter of 1925 to Ft. Worth. He refused to report the next spring, and wound up being sold to St. Paul where he played the next five years.

In 1930 in a game at Indianapolis, he pitched St. Paul to a 1- 0 win in the first night game in organized baseball.

In 1931, Betts won 22 regular season games and two playoff games at St.Paul, and was purchased by the Boston Braves. Manager Bill McKechnie turned Betts into a full-time starter, and for the next three years, Huck went 13-11, 11-11, and 17-10. In 1933 he was third in the league in ERA with a 2.79.

One of his most satisfying games was in 1932 in his first game against the Phillies.

"I beat the Red Sox in the first game of the Boston City Series," he recalled. "Four days later, I started in New York and beat the Giants, 7-1. Three days later, I beat Brooklyn, 3-2, then I beat Brooklyn back in Boston, 2-1. A few days later, we came into Philly, and I beat the Phillies in Baker Bowl, 3-0. I felt more delighted about winning that game than any I ever won."

One other game that gave Betts great pleasure, though, was in 1933 when he beat the Giants' Carl Hubbell, 2-1. The Braves' runs ended Hubbell's streak of 45 1/3 scoreless innings of pitching, a major league record that still stands.

Arm trouble finally brought an end to Betts' career after the 1935 season, the same year that Babe Ruth retired from the Braves. Betts returned to Millsboro where he eventually built and operated a movie theater for 32 years.

Betts, who was elected to the Delaware Hall of Fame in 1980, had two children, four grandchildren and four great-grandchildren.

He also had the satisfaction of knowing that he played major league baseball in an era that may historians rate as the best in baseball annals.

Art Butler—
Played with Greats and Near Greats

The story of Art Butler is a fascinating saga of one man's travels through the major and minor leagues.

It is enough that Butler roomed with Honus Wagner, played with Rogers Hornsby, was managed by Miller Huggins, and was a close friend of Jim Thorpe.

Of perhaps even greater significance, however, is the fact that before he died in 1985 at the age of 98, Butler was the oldest living former major leaguer.

A lifetime resident of Fall River, Massachusetts, Butler had a 22-year professional career. He played in the majors from 1911 to 1916, breaking in with the Boston Braves, then spending two years with the Pittsburgh Pirates and three with the St. Louis Cardinals.

A utility infielder during most of his big league career, Butler was the Cardinals' regular shortshop in 1914 and 1915. His lifetime batting average was .241.

The ex-infielder, who was known in his day as an extremely smart player, was one of 23 major leaguers to come from Fall River, a city of about 95,000 that sits on the Rhode Island border. The list includes names such as Dick Siebert, Buss Gibson, Jerry Remy and Mark Bomback. Many of them reached the majors with the help of Butler, who called them "his boys" and who over the years took a personal interest in promising players in the area.

Artie's own pro career began with a minor league team in Fall River. Because of a hearing defect as a boy, Butler was unable to finish high school, and, instead, entered baseball.

"I always had Nap Lajoie in mind," he said. "He played in Woonsocket (Rhode Island) near my home. He was a cab driver. I figured, if a cab driver could become a ballplayer, why couldn't I?"

Butler became not only a ballplayer, but a well-traveled one. Along with the three major league teams for which he played, he also had an extensive minor league career. After leaving the majors in 1916 following a shoulder separation, Artie played for an assortment of American Association and

Art Butler.

International League clubs, including St. Paul, Milwaukee, Kansas City and Buffalo.

Butler's major league career, though unspectacular, had, nonetheless, a number of highlights. One was a two-out, ninth inning single which spoiled a no-hit bid by the Philadelphia Phillies' Grover Cleveland Alexander.

"My greatest thrill in baseball was when I came to the major leagues, and in my first ballgame, we happened to be playing the New York Giants. Christy Mathewson was pitching. I happened to get a base hit that helped to win the game. Christy Mathewson was one of the greatest pitchers in baseball."

Butler also claimed he got the first hit at Braves Field while he was playing for the Cardinals. "They were dedicating the new park, and that day, 50,000 attended," he said. "There were 40,000 in the seats and 10,000 in the outfield. I was playing second base, and the crowd seemed like it was only 10 feet away."

During his career, Butler won a couple of unusual prizes. One was an Oakland automobile in 1926 when he was playing for Albany (New York). "They claimed I led the whole country in fielding," he said. "So they gave me a car.

"I also won a horse in Kansas City. The vice president of the club, a retired horse dealer, gave a horse to the leading hitter on the team. The horse was imported from England. It was a white elephant to me because I had no place to put him. It was a beautiful horse, but I sold it at an auction."

Butler conceded that playing baseball in his day was a tough way to make a living. "It was a hard life," he said. "Any profession is tough, but it was especially hard in baseball where you're performing before thousands of people every day. You're tense. There's tension and worry, and there's always somebody waiting on the bench to take your job.

"We played for peanuts," he added. "But it was enough to keep us from crying poverty."

When asked his highest salary, Butler quietly demured. "Ballplayers never quote their salaries," he said. "That's the first rule in the book. I would never tell anyone, even my own folks. But I had a good contract. It was in the thousands of dollars."

In addition to playing conditions and low salaries, Butler remembered other aspects of the game as being hard on the players. Particularly difficult to deal with were the assortment of beanball pitchers with which a batter had to cope.

"There were plenty of pitchers who threw at you intentionally," the old National Leaguer said. "I was hit twice, once in the face. My nose landed on the left side of my face. They pushed it back and taped it up. Instead of going to the hospital, that was it. Today, you're scratched or you run into a fence, and they take you off the field on a stretcher.

"Also, I was hit once on the temple when I was with Bridgeport," Butler continued. "I was hitting—they couldn't get me out that year. The only way they could stop me was to get me away from that plate. So, they aimed for my head. Beanball Johnson, they called him around the league, hit me in the temple.

"I went home for a week. They said I had a fractured skull. I wasn't taken to the hospital. I just went to the dressing room, and dressed on my own. That night, I was never so sick in all my life. My face turned black, blue, yellow—the color of a rainbow. I must have had blood clots."

Butler had fond memories of his pal Honus Wagner with whom he played on the 1912–13 Pirates. "He took a liking to me when I joined the ballclub, and he had me as a roommate," Artie recalled. "Naturally, we became friendly. We used to eat our meals together. He didn't chum around with the oldtimers."

> He liked to attend Western pictures. Whenever there was a Western, we'd go to see it. One time, we're in Hot Springs, Arkansas, and we were at a silent picture. Honus was always chewing tobacco. He chewed Bull Durham. He kept spitting on the floor. The floor was slanted. We were sitting three rows behind the piano player, who was in the orchestra pit. Pretty soon, the orchestra pit was getting flooded with tobacco spit. I told Honus, "Don't spit on the floor anymore or we'll get fired out of here."
>
> Honus was a real gentleman. He could get along with anyone. He never fought with anybody, never got mixed up in a rhubarb.

Another future Hall of Famer with whom Butler was friendly was Rogers Hornsby. In fact, Hornsby later insisted that Artie was one of three men who helped him become a great hitter.

Butler claimed that his contribution was mostly psychological. "I inspired him," he said.

Artie remembered when Hornsby came up to the Cardinals in 1915. "He joined us with a dollar suitcase and a few shirts in his bag. But he had weaknesses. All he thought about was gambling. His hobby was shooting craps and horses.

"When he first reported to the club, we were at practice. He wanted to hit, but the other player's wouldn't let him. They told him to go shag flies in the outfield. He said, 'I'm no shagger, I'm a hitter.' He wouldn't go out and shag balls, as rookies were supposed to do. But I felt sorry for him. When it was my turn to hit, I was playing regularly, so I'd tell him to hit for me. The other players couldn't say anything.

"He was the greatest natural hitter in baseball history," Butler asserted. "But he had a weakness of (catching) pop flies. He always told his manager that pop flies were for outfielders, not infielders. He had trouble catching them."

One of Butler's best friends in baseball was Jim Thorpe. "When we were in the International League together, we used to sit—he and his wife and my wife—outside the hotel and reminisce. Not once did he ever mention anything about the medals that were taken away from him. He'd talk about everything else.

"In baseball, he had a weakness on defense, and that's the reason he didn't stay too long in the majors. He was a pretty good hitter. His average shows that. But even though he was the greatest athlete in Olympic history, he was weak in running bases. He was a very nice guy, though. We used to talk and talk and talk baseball.''

Having played with or against, either in the majors or minors, many of baseball's early superstars, Butler had no trouble picking an all-time team. It is:

Outfield: Babe Ruth, Ty Cobb, Tris Speaker

First Base: George Sisler

Second Base: Nap Lajoie (''my favorite ballplayer'')

Shortstop: Honus Wagner

Third Base: Rogers Hornsby (the position he played most in his early years with the Cardinals)

Catcher: Mickey Cochrane

Pitchers: Walter Johnson (RHP), Lefty Grove (LHP)

Extra Man: Joe Jackson

Although he didn't put any modern players in that group, it's not because he looks down on present athletes. ''They're just humans, like we were,'' Butler said. ''They're no better, no worse.

''Everything else (in the game) has changed,'' he added. ''Take the gloves. I call them butterfly nets. I played next to Honus Wagner and then I replaced him, and I never saw him dive for a ball. I never saw any of the old-timers dive for a ball that was hit in the hole. They couldn't do it because they didn't have the glove to do it with. The ball would't stay in the glove. That's why you never saw anybody catch with one hand.

''I'm in favor of the ballplayers getting what they can in salaries, today,'' he added. ''With television, the club owners are capitalizing. They're getting more money than they can handle. The players just want a share of that. But I don't think it (the high salaries) will last too long. It's unusual for ballplayers to get paid more for six months of playing ball than the President of the United States gets.''

Baseball was Butler's life, even decades after he stopped playing.

''I love it,'' he said. ''I love baseball. And when I look at the games on television, I often think of things I would do that they're not doing today. They don't double steal. There's no unexpected steals. When I played, they never knew what I was going to do when I got on the bases.

''The fences are so close today. They pay big wages for hitting home runs. That affects the batting averages. Instead of practicing to become .300 hitters, they're swinging for the fences. And the fans are educated to the home run. I would never think of hitting a home run if I was playing.''

In 454 games in the majors, Butler hit just three home runs. He had 311 hits in 1,289 at bats in the majors. His highest average was .280 in 1913 with the Pirates.

After his big league career ended, Butler played 12 more years in the high minors. Throughout that period, he usually ranked among the top hitters and fielders in his league.

Doc Cramer—
A Star in Many Ways

Turn the pages of baseball history, and the likes of Roger (Doc) Cramer do not appear with any regularity.

He was a rare breed, this former American Leaguer—a solid outfielder who could hit, run and field, who seldom sat out, and who crammed as much into one colorful career as humanly possible.

Over a 20-year period, Cramer virtually did it all—playing for pennant-winners, World Series champions, All-Star teams, capturing league titles in a variety of categories, playing with some of the great stars of the game, and in the end setting some records that still stand.

He finished with a lifetime batting average of .296, spread over three decades from 1929 to 1948. Playing with the Philadelphia Athletics, Boston Red Sox, Washington Senators and Detroit Tigers, Cramer unloaded 2,705 hits in 2,239 games, scoring 1,357 runs, driving in 842 and hitting 396 doubles, 109 triples and 37 home runs.

Seven times he led the league in at-bats, a major league record, and nine times he came to the plate at least 600 times in a season, also a major league record. He led the league in hits in 1940 and in pinch hits in 1947, and he was first among outfielders in putouts (1936, 1938), doubleplays (1936) and fielding (1945).

Cramer hit .300 or above eight times during his career, three times getting 200 or more hits. He was selected three times for the American League All-Star team.

Probably the finest season in his remarkable career was in 1932, his first year as a regular with the A's. Cramer hit .336, joining with Al Simmons (.322) and Mule Haas (.305) to give Philadelphia an outfield of all .300 hitters.

That year, Cramer had 28 and 22 game hitting streaks. He also had a game in which he went 6-for-6 and a doubleheader in which he had eight hits (in 10-at-bats).

It was all part of a glorious career that began quite innocently while Cramer was playing in a sandlot game along the New Jersey coast. Doc, one of the few players ever to come out of the Jersey seashore, is a lively octogenerian now who lives not far from the town in which his professional career was launched.

"I was playing with Beach Haven," he recalls. "It was a Sunday afternoon. They didn't have Sunday ball back then in Philadelphia, so Jimmy Dykes and Cy Perkins of the A's had come down to the seashore.

"They saw me playing, and asked me if I'd come up to Shibe Park for a workout. They wanted me to be there that Wednesday. I told them I couldn't make it.

"But I did get there after a while," Cramer adds. "Connie Mack signed me right then. He took me into his office, and said 'We've got Ty Cobb, Tris Speaker, Zach Wheat, Al Simmons, Mule Haas and Bing Miller playing in the outfield. You beat one of those fellows out, and you've got a job.' "

After contemplating the impossibility of such a task over the winter, Cramer found himself assigned in 1929 to the Class D Martinsburg, West Virginia, club in the Blue Ridge League.

"I had an awful good year," Cramer remembers. "I started as a pitcher, but Mr. Mack sent the word down to switch me to the outfield. I wound up hitting .404 (which led the league) and had a 12-1 record as a pitcher."

At the end of the season, Cramer made an incredible jump all the way to the big leagues, appearing briefly with the A's. The following year, he reported to Philadelphia's spring training camp.

"Coming up to the A's was sort of scary," Cramer recalls, "because I was just a big, old country boy. It was different then than it is now. You could never hit with the regulars in batting practice, for instance. You'd walk up there to hit, and one of them would say, 'You hit in the morning.'

"Some of the veterans gave us a real hard time. Some of them were good to you, too. Eddie Collins was a coach. He was a big help. So was Bing Miller.

"You just had to show those guys you could play. If you couldn't show them you could play, you just didn't play. That was it."

Cramer showed the A's he could play so well that the defending World Champions kept him on the opening day roster in 1930. But Doc was soon sent down to Portland of the Pacific Coast League.

"They had sent me up to pinch-hit in a game in Washington," Cramer says. "The count went to three and one. I was supposed to take, but I missed the sign and swung. I popped up.

"On the train coming back to Philadelphia that night, Mr. Mack came into the dining car. He waved me over, and told me to sit down with him. Then he said, 'You're going to Portland tomorrow morning.' He added, 'Do you know why you're going there?' I said, 'No.' He said, 'To learn the signs and to learn how to field.'

"I said, 'No, I'm not going.' He said, 'Yes, you are.' We went back and forth, yes, you are; no, I'm not. But I was on the train to Portland the next day. I had a good year there, too, so I didn't mind it too much."

Doc Cramer.

After hitting .347 at Portland, Cramer came back to the A's at the end of the season. This time, he remained with the club until the end of 1936.

Cramer was a reserve on the A's 1931 pennant-winning team, and appeared twice in the World Series as a pinch-hitter. The second time up, he batted against spitballer Burleigh Grimes with the bases loaded, two outs and the A's trailing, 4–0, in the ninth inning of the seventh game. Cramer roped a single and drove in two runs.

"Mr. Mack sent word down the bench for me to come up," Cramer recalls. "He said, 'You're going to hit for Walberg.' I said, 'All right.' But to tell the truth, I was scared to death.

"I went up to hit, and every pitch Grimes threw was a spitball. I kept fouling them off. Finally, I got a hit and two runs scored. But they were the only runs we got. We lost the game and the Series to the St. Louis Cardinals.

"Old Burleigh could throw some spitballs," Cramer continues. "He could throw that pitch two ways. He'd throw it sidearm, and it would break right in on you. Or he'd throw it overhand, and it would come up and just drop, like you'd drop something overboard off a boat.

"The spitball was something like a knuckleball only it broke quicker. I think it was the toughest pitch to hit."

Despite their losing the Series, four games to three, the A's of 1931 were, in Cramer's opinion, one of baseball's greatest teams.

"They were the best I ever played on; in fact, the best I ever saw," he says. "They had Lefty Grove, George Earnshaw and Rube Walberg. All won over 20 games that year. Then they had Waite Hoyt, Eddie Rommell and Jack Quinn. We'd go into a four-game series and Grove, Earnshaw and Walberg would pitch the first three games. It didn't matter who pitched the last one.

"But that team didn't just have good pitching. It had good power, too. Mickey Cochrane, Jimmie Foxx, Al Simmons. It was a real thrill playing with those guys, especially when I got to hit ahead of them."

Grove, Cramer claims, was the fastest pitcher he ever faced, but probably not the toughest—at least for him to bat against.

"Ted Lyons was," he says. "He had everything, and could throw any pitch right where he wanted to. He'd never throw at you; at least, not at your head. He'd throw at your feet. He'd holler at you, tell you to skip rope.

"Feller was fast, but I could hit him," Cramer continues. "Grove could throw harder. I'll never forget the time we were playing in Yankee Stadium. Quinn was pitching, and we had the Yankees beaten, 3–0. They got a run, then they got three on with nobody out in the ninth inning. The old man brought in Grove. In 10 pitches, we were in the clubhouse.

"He struck out Babe Ruth, Lou Gehrig and Tony Lazzeri. Lazzeri fouled off one pitch. I was in center field, looking right down Grove's arm. He was fabulous. He didn't have a curve. All he had was a fastball. Everybody knew what they were going to hit at, but they still couldn't hit him."

In 1932, Cramer was installed as the A's regular right fielder. The following year, though, Mack moved him to center field.

"That was a funny thing," Cramer recalls. "I had played right at Portland, and Bob Johnson played center there. We came up at the same time, and then he was moved to left and I played center. I still don't know why that happened.

"Playing center field was a lot different then," Cramer adds. "They play a lot shallower today. We were taught that you couldn't let a ball hit the bottom of the fence. They told us, 'Give a guy a single, but don't give him a triple.' Today, they play a lot of singles into triples. You see that happening all the time."

Cramer was not only an outstanding fielder with a strong arm, he was considered an excellent base-runner for a man of his size (6' 2", 185 pounds). He got the nickname, Flit, from his A's teammates because of his speed.

Doc, who attracted that nickname from his boyhood job, driving a local doctor around town in a horse and buggy, had seasons of .336, .295, .311 and .332 as an A's regular. While the club plunged in the standings as Mack sold off his established stars, Cramer emerged as one of the team's standouts and a big local favorite.

In 1934, Cramer hit for the cycle, and a year later he had his second six-hit game. That made him and the Cardinals' Jim Bottomley the only modern major leaguers to hit safely six times in one game twice in their careers.

Cramer, somewhat of a cutup as a player, especially when it came to performing practical jokes and squashing eggs on the head of his buddy, Ted Lyons, was also establishing a reputation as a player who rarely missed a time at bat.

Three striaght years with the A's he led the American League in at-bats (tying a major league record that he would match again several seasons later). Eventually, Cramer would reel off 13 consecutive seasons in which he never appeared at the plate less than 540 times.

"I never got hurt," he says. "The only time I ever got hurt was when I broke my collar bone one year. Lou Gehrig hit a ball—it had been raining and the field was wet—and I dove for it. I caught the ball, but my shoulder snapped. It came right out through my shirt."

In 1935, Cramer was named to the major league All-Star team by *The Sporting News*. That year, he hit .332, fourth highest in the league while collecting 214 hits.

Doc rarely poled a home run; his career high for one season being eight in 1933. In fact, later in his career, he did something no American League player has ever duplicated; he came to the plate 500 or more times five different years without a home run.

"I was a line drive hitter," he says. "I didn't hit many home runs. When I did hit one, it was usually a line drive. I never got many bases on balls, either. I was a first-pitch hitter. Anything I could reach, I'd swing at."

At the end of the 1935 season, the now downtrodden Athletics rewarded Cramer for his excellent year by trading him to the slightly better Red
Sox. In Boston, Doc rejoined some of his ex- A's teammates-particularly Foxx,
Grove and Walberg—while continuing as one of the league's most solid,
everyday players.

After a .292 season, Cramer put together years of .305, .301, .311 and
.303 for the Bosox. Again, he was a member of an all-.300 outfield, this time
joining in 1938 with Ben Chapman (.340) and Joe Vosmik (.324).

"Actually," says Cramer, "when Wes Ferrell was pitching, we had just
about an all-.300 hitting lineup. We had Foxx (who won the batting championship that year with a .349 average), Joe Cronin, Pinky Higgins."

Only second baseman Bobby Doerr (.289) and catcher Gene Desautels
(.291) hit under .300.

Before Cramer left the Red Sox, the club had added another .300 hitter, a fresh kid named Ted Williams.

"Ted was a good boy," Cramer recalls. "You could tell he was going
to be a helluva hitter. I had the job of teaching him how to field. That was
a hard job. I wasn't a teacher, but I'd take him out to the outfield, and they
would hit ground balls to him. One would go through his legs, another would
hit him in the chest. I'd try to tell him how to overcome those problems.

"We were out there one day. Two or three he caught, and two or three
he didn't. Finally, he said, 'The hell with it. They're not going to pay me
for this. They're going to pay me to hit'. And so he did."

Boston traded Cramer in 1940 to Washington, and Doc spent the 1941
season in the nation's capitol with Mickey Vernon, Cecil Travis, George Case
and Buddy Lewis. After hitting .273, he was swapped to the Tigers.

Cramer had one more .300 season (1943). In 1945, at the age of 40,
he not only hit .275, he also led American League outfielders with a .991
fielding percentage.

That year, while World War II raged toward a conclusion, Detroit won
the pennant and then took the World Series from the Chicago Cubs in seven
games. Cramer hit .379 in the fall classic.

"I had a good Series," he acknowledges, "but the caliber of baseball
wasn't like it was before the war. We had to use almost anybody we could
find. Everybody was going to war. But we had some good players. And when
the war finally ended, we got Hank Greenberg and Virgil Trucks back, and
Greenberg hit a home run to win the pennant."

Cramer spent two more full seasons in a reserve role with the Tigers,
then retired soon after the start of the 1948 campaign. Rather than linger
on the baseball scene, he returned to his home along the Jersey coast, and
resumed his old vocation as a carpenter.

"I was a carpenter before baseball, and I went back to being one after
baseball," he says.

Today, Cramer watches baseball on television, talks on occasion to former teammates and once in a while wonders whether or not he will ever attract enough votes to get into the Hall of Fame.

There are many people who think he should be in it already.

"If I go in, all right," he says. "If I don't, all right, too. I've made

Two of the top Boston Red Sox hitters in the mid-1930s were Roger Cramer (left) and Jimmie Foxx.

up my mind not to commit myself. But in accordance with what they've put in there, yes, I think I should be in.

"But I'd never—like Rizzuto and some of the others—go out and beg to go in. I know a lot of them have gone out and hollered about getting in. I wouldn't do that. But I'll tell you one thing. They'd better put me in while I'm alive because there's no point in going in after I'm dead."

His record clearly states the case. There is no point in leaving him out.

Doc Cramer was an outstanding, all-around player who put in 20 big league seasons and collected close to 3,000 hits. His kind do not pass this way often.

Tony Cuccinello—
A Great Way to Spend a Lifetime

Sixty years is a long time to spend doing anything. But for Tony Cuccinello, there couldn't have been anything better than the nearly six decades he spent connected with the game of baseball.

Now approaching 80, Cuccinello leans back, tilts his ever-present baseball cap to the rear of his head, and wonders, where did the time ever go?

"Those years sure flew by," says the man who had what he calls "a wonderful career" in a game he so obviously loves. "I wouldn't trade them for anything. And I'd go right back and do them all over again, too, if I could."

It's easy to see why. During his long connection with baseball, Cuccinello drew paychecks as a player, coach, minor league manager and scout, the combination of which provided him with a career that was as interesting as it was varied.

A big league infielder for 15 seasons between 1930 and 1945, Tony was a member of the first National League All-Star team in 1933. He was almost the oldest man ever to win a batting title in 1945. And he had numerous memorable games, both at the plate and with the glove during his years with the Cincinnati Reds, Brooklyn Dodgers, Boston Braves, New York Giants and Chicago White Sox.

A scrappy, hustling competitor, Cuccinello played with and against many of the game's greatest players and under some of its finest managers. And when he was through playing, he became a highly respected coach, spending from 1949 to 1969 with the Reds, Cleveland Indians and White Sox.

A 5' 7", 160-pound mighty mite, Cuccinello hit a highly respectable .280 in the majors. He drove in 884 runs and scored 730.

Despite his small size, Tony could hit the long ball on occasion. He poled 94 home runs, including a high of 14 in 1934. His specialty, though, was hitting doubles. Cuccinello smacked 334 two-baggers during his career, 11 straight times hitting 20 or more in a season and five times going over 30. His career high was 39 in 1931.

"I was pretty much a line drive hitter," Cuccinello says. "I was a good

93

hit and run man. I hit mostly fifth or sixth in the lineup. I watched the way the big guys hit, and because I was small, I figured the best thing for me to do was just meet the ball. So that's how I hit my whole career. I was a contact hitter. It worked out pretty well."

Cuccinello was also extremely adept with the glove. He led National League second basemen in doubleplays four times, in assists twice and in putouts once. At one point, he held the NL record for most doubleplays (128) in one season by a second baseman. His 10 assists in a 22-inning game in 1939—while playing third base for the Braves—were just two short of the major league record.

"I could always field pretty well," Tony remembers. "It just came naturally to me. As a kid, my brothers would hit grounders to me. We'd use a taped up old bat, and we'd play all day."

One of Tony's other brothers, Al, also had a brief sojourn in the majors. He played in 54 games in 1935 for the Giants. In one game that season, Al and Tony, then with the Dodgers, hit home runs. Brothers have hit homers in the same game only eight times in baseball history—the last time being in 1974 when Graig and Jim Nettles homered for the New York Yankees and Detroit Tigers, respectively.

Tony and Al and the other young Cuccinellos formed their initial connections with baseball on the sandlots of Astoria, Long Island. "Eventually, I started playing in a semipro league in New York City," Tony says. "At the time, I was still in high school."

Despite his age, Cuccinello was good enough to attract the attention in 1926 of a neighbor, who happened to be a catcher for the Syracuse team in the International League. "He asked me to go with him to a workout with Syracuse, which was playing that day in Jersey City," Tony recalls. "I cut school to go.

"After the workout, they offered me a contract. I couldn't sign it because I was only 16. So my older brother signed it for me, and I joined the team.

"In my first game, they let me pinch-hit in the ninth inning. I got a double. Then the next fellow up singled. I stumbled rounding third and fell down. I didn't score. Boy, was that embarrassing.

"I stayed with Syracuse for about two months and had three hits in my only four times up. Then they farmed me out to Lawrence, Massachusetts, which was Class B."

After hitting .283 at Lawrence in 1926, Tony was offered a promotion the following season to Topeka, Kansas.

"To be honest, I didn't even know where Topeka was," he recalls. "I didn't want to go there. I asked to be sent back to Lawrence, and they obliged. I had a good year there (hitting .310), and the next year I was assigned to Danville of the 3–I League (where he again hit .310). Branch Rickey saw me playing there, and that fall he bought me for Columbus in the American Association."

In 1929, Cuccinello hit .358 at Columbus with 20 home runs and 111

Tony Cuccinello.

RBI. He led the league in hits (227) and doubles (56). That was enough to write his ticket to the big leagues.

Tony's contract was purchased by the Reds, and the following spring he took over as the starting third baseman in Cincinnati.

"I'll never forget my first game," Cuccinello says. "It was against the Pittsburgh Pirates. I got a hit in my first time at bat. It came off a pitcher named Remy Kremer."

He recalls:

> I hit well the first month of the season, then I went into a slump and they took me out of the lineup. Harry Heilmann was with the team, and I asked him to help me out. He worked with me for about three weeks. He found out I was lifting my head and taking my eye off the ball. I was hitting the ball back to the pitcher all the time. They finally put me back in the lineup, and, My God, I started to hit again. I finished with a .312 average (with 10 home runs and 78 RBI).

Shifted to second base the following year, Tony hit .315 while collecting 39 doubles and 93 RBI, a club record for second basemen until broken by Joe Morgan. He also led the league's second sackers in putouts, assists, errors and doubleplays. And, in one of his most memorable games, he lashed six hits in six consecutive at-bats, including two doubles and one triple.

"Sidney Weil was the owner of the Reds back then," Cuccinello remembers. "In my first year with the club, he gave all the players blank contracts and let them fill in the numbers. My second year there, he didn't do that. He wanted to give me the same amount of money. I held out."

Having thus earned the disfavor of management, Tony found himself packing his bags at the end of the '31 season. In a blockbuster trade, Weil shipped Cuccinello and two others to the Dodgers for Babe Herman, Ernie Lombardi and Wally Gilbert.

It turned out to be a good move for Tony. Not only did he get to return to his native New York, he became a teammate of Al Lopez. The two would strike up a lifelong friendship.

Cuccinello also came into contact with Casey Stengel, one of many prominent managers for whom he worked.

"I had played for Dan Howley in Cincinnati," Tony says. "He was a natty dresser; always came to the ballpark wearing spats. My first manager in Brooklyn was Max Carey. He wanted everybody to do the things that he did as a player, which was impossible. He was a Hall of Famer.

"I had played under Burt Shotten at Syracuse. He was a real good manager. So were Bill McKechnie and Jimmy Dykes, who I later played for. McKechnie never played for the big inning. He always played for one run, always going along with just what he had.

"Stengel wasn't like the others. He was a good manager and he really knew baseball. He especially helped the young boys. He would let the veteran players alone. But any time you did something good he'd let the whole club know about it. A lot of people thought he was a clown. But he was a good baseball man. I really liked him."

At Brooklyn, Cuccinello had four respectable seasons, his best coming in 1932 when he hit .281 and in 1935 when he batted .292. In 1933, he was chosen for the first All-Star game, and made an appearance as a pinch-hitter.

It was a good period for Tony, and for baseball. Even though the 1932 Dodgers with a third place finish were the only first division club on which he played in his entire National League career, Cuccinello performed, he thinks, in the best of times.

"Baseball was at its peak in the 1930s," he claims. "A lot of people say that baseball in the period from 1925 to 1935 was in its prime. To me, that's right. You really had to be good to play then. Why, they used to send guys who hit .320 and .330 back to the minors because they couldn't field.

"The hitter who really made an impression on me was Rogers Hornsby. When I was a kid I used to go to the Polo Grounds to watch him play. I idolized him, I thought he was one of the best hitters in baseball history. Nothing phased him. They used to knock him down, and he'd come back and knock the pitchers off the mound with line drives up the middle."

Cuccinello adds:

> There were a lot of great pitchers around then. Charlie Root, Dizzy Dean— they were tough as hell. They'd throw under your chin. You had to protect yourself all the time. Hal Schumacher was a good pitcher. Dazzy Vance was on his way out, but he still had a helluva curve. Eppa Rixey, I played a little with him. What a competitor he was. If you made an error, he'd bawl you out right there on the field. And Carl Hubbell. He wasn't a pitcher; he was a thrower. I didn't have much trouble with him, but a lot of other guys did.

After the 1935 season, it was time for Cuccinello to move on again. The Dodgers shipped him, Lopez and two others to the Braves in an ill-conceived deal that netted the Bums two players (Ed Brandt and Randy Moore) who proved of little consequence in Brooklyn.

Tony played a little more than four seasons in Boston. His first year there, he had one of his best seasons in the majors when he hit .308 and drove in 86 runs. In one game that year, he hit two doubles in one inning.

In Boston, Cuccinello also eventually teamed with a player he considered to be the finest of many outstanding shortstops with whom he played during his career.

"Leo Durocher was a good fielder and we set a doubleplay record together in Cincinnati," says Cuccinello. "And Lonnie Frey was good at Brooklyn. But the best I ever played with was Eddie Miller. What a shortstop he was. He was one of the best fielders I ever saw in all my years in baseball. On the force at second, he would say to me, 'Where do you want the ball?' I'd tell him, and he'd put it right where I asked him. He was brilliant."

Tony was brilliant himself in a game in 1939. He reeled off 10 assists in a 22-inning game while playing third base.

"It was my first game back after knee surgery," he says. "Dick Bartell had slid into me at second, and my knee was all torn up. I had been out for two months. Finally, I told Casey I was ready to play. He put me in, and I played the whole game. After that game, I had to take two days off before I could play again.''

Still hobbled—as he would be the rest of his life—by the knee injury, Cuccinello was traded by the Braves to the Giants early in the 1940 season. He finished the year in New York, then retired so he could accept a job as manager of Jersey City in the International League.

Tony piloted the club to a fifth place finish in 1941. He was set to return in 1942, but a call from Stengel, the Braves' manager, changed his plans.

"He wanted me to be a player-coach," Cuccinello recalls. "I got my release from Jersey City and went to Boston. I threw batting practice, coached third base and pinch-hit."

Cuccinello was released at mid-season the following year, so he could sign with the White Sox who were desperate for players. It was, of course, wartime then. Because of chronic laryngitis, a condition he had endured since he was a child—he had lost his voice at one point for three years—Cuccinello was not drafted into the military service.

For one and one-half years, he was a reserve infielder for Chicago. But in 1945, Cuccinello's playing time increased and he was often stationed in the regular lineup at third base.

He hit like a demon. For five months, Tony led the league in hitting. He was nearly 38 years old.

"I went into September hitting .335," Cuccinello recalls. "But I didn't have the 400 at-bats that were necessary to qualify for the batting title. So Dykes, my manager, would play me seven innings every day, then take me out.

"It came down to a race between me and Snuffy Stirnweiss, the Yankees' second baseman. With two days to go, I was leading by two points. But our last two games were rained out. And in his last game, Stirnweiss hit a ball to third base that was booted, but they gave him a hit. He wound up beating me by one point .309 to .308."

Had he won the title, Cuccinello would have been the oldest batting champion in baseball history.

"It was a big disappointment, not winning," he says. "When you're second, they don't put your name in the record book.

"I wasn't going to play anymore, though," he adds. "My legs were bothering me. Before the season ended, I already had my release in my pocket. Mr. (Chuck) Comiskey thanked me for the job I did, and I moved on."

Out of baseball in 1946, Cuccinello became manager of Tampa in the Florida State League in 1947 and led the team to a second place finish and 104 wins. The following year, he joined his friend Lopez as a coach at Indianapolis.

Cuccinello moved back to the big leagues in 1949 to begin a three-year stint as a coach with the Reds. Then in 1952, he rejoined Lopez, who was, by then, manager of the Indians.

Tony was a coach for Lopez throughout the former's tenure as manager of the Indians and White Sox. After Lopez retired at the end of the 1965 season, Cuccinello went to work for two years with Mayo Smith and the Detroit Tigers. He and Lopez were reunited in 1969 when Al returned briefly to manage the White Sox.

That was Tony's last year in uniform. Although he had never played for a pennant winner, he had been a coach in three World Series—1954 with the Indians, 1959 with the White Sox and 1968 with the Tigers.

Cuccinello, who years earlier had moved to Tampa, was a scout in that area for the Yankees until retiring from the game in 1985.

Today, Tony lives down the street from Lopez, his buddy and regular golf partner. He has a room full of pictures and a head full of memories.

"I guess the only thing I really regret is that I never managed in the big leagues," he says. "I turned down four jobs as manager. I said I would manage if they could get somebody else to go around to all the speaking engagements. I didn't graduate from high school, and I just never felt I could get up in front of a group and speak.

"Other than that, it was a career that was very satisfying. I enjoyed every minute of it. I don't think you could ask for a better way to spend a lifetime."

Bill Jurges—
Good Field, Good Hit Shortstop

In the days when shortstops had to hit more than their weight to remain in the big leagues, no matter how well they could field, Bill Jurges ranked among the leaders of his profession.

He was a good field, good hit shortstop who played in the majors for 17 years. A high-spirited battler, Jurges helped the Chicago Cubs to three pennants in the 1930s and later anchored a sturdy New York Giants' infield.

Jurges played at a time when his National League contemporaries at shortstop were people such as Arky Vaughan, Leo Durocher, Dick Bartell and Lonnie Frey and later Marty Marion, Pee Wee Reese, Eddie Joost and Eddie Miller. All could field and all could hit.

If you check the descriptive material on the back of his 1941 Play Ball baseball card, you will see that Jurges was called "the most valuable shortstop in the National League."

Such praise was hardly the whim of some hyperbolic copy writer. That particular year, Jurges hit .293, his second highest average in the majors.

In 1939 and 1940, Jurges was a member of the National League All-Star team. He led National League shortstops in fielding percentage four times, and still holds the World Series records for most putouts in a six-game series (16 in 1935) and most double plays in a four-game series (five in 1932).

During a career that began in the majors in 1931 and ended in 1947, Jurges had a lifetime batting average of .258. He had 1,613 hits with 721 runs scored and 656 runs batted in.

It was not solely as a player, though, that Jurges achieved distinction. He also served in the big leagues as a coach, scout and briefly as manager of the Boston Red Sox.

After spending more than 50 years in baseball, Jurges retired and took up residence in Largo, Florida. It takes little prompting for memories of his storied career to come pouring out.

"I was there when Babe Ruth supposedly pointed out the home run he was going to hit in the '32 World Series," Jurges says, "and I was there when Gabby Hartnett hit his home run into the darkness in '38.

Bill Jurges.

"With the Ruth homer, Tony Lazzeri said later that Ruth always did that (pointed). We were riding him pretty good from the bench. After we got two strikes on him, Gabby, who was catching, said that Ruth waved and said. 'That's only two strikes.' Everybody thought he was pointing to center field.

"I remember the pitch he hit. It was a little outside. I swear it went through (pitcher) Charlie Root's legs and then over the center field fence.

"As for the Hartnett home run (which defeated the Pittsburgh Pirates and helped the Cubs to the National League pennant), the umpire had said that would be the last inning. It was getting dark, but you could still see the ball. Mace Brown threw Hartnett a hanging curve."

Jurges was also present for another famous incident in baseball history. But he claims that the incident was misinterpreted.

> The Giants and the Dodgers had their offices close together, and all the sports writers always hung around the two offices, looking for stories. One day, Bill Terry came into the Giants' office, and saw the big crowd standing around. "For crying out loud, isn't Brooklyn still in the league?" he said. He didn't mean it in a derogatory way. He was just saying "How come nobody's over at the Dodgers' office?" But it was taken the wrong way, and because of it, Brooklyn got mad and later knocked the Giants out of the pennant.

Jurges easily recalls how he entered professional baseball.

"I was brought up in Brooklyn," he says. "I wasn't a Dodger fan, I just liked baseball, although I liked the Dodgers' Zack Wheat. I was playing semipro ball in Long Island and working in a bank. I had a good job there. A fellow asked if I would be interested in playing professional baseball. I talked to my folks, and they said it was okay, so I signed with Manchester, (New Hampshire) for $250 a month.

"I signed as an outfielder. In 1927, I went to spring training in Manchester, and it was cold as hell. Snow was on the ground. They had three regular outfielders. I could see I wasn't going to play, so I started fooling around shortstop. The manager asked me if I could play there, and I said, 'Sure.' So that's how I became a shortstop in professional ball.

"My second year at Manchester, I hit over .300 (.332) and was named the New England League MVP. Then Manchester sold me to the Cubs for $5,000."

Jurges played the next two years in Reading (Pennsylvania) in the International League, then broke in with the Cubs in 1931.

"My starting salary was $4,000," he says. "Rogers Hornsby was the manager. My first game, he sent me in to pinch hit. I got a two-base hit off a lefthanded pitcher from Brooklyn.

"But I wasn't a regular right away," Jurges adds. "In fact, in 1932, I still wasn't starting. I finally said, 'If I don't play, I'm going to quit and go back to the bank.' Early in the season, though, our regular shortstop, Woody English, broke his thumb. They put me in, and I stayed there for the next seven years."

Over that period, Jurges was a mainstay in the Cubs' lineup. His best years were in 1936 when he hit .280 and in 1937 when he had a .298 mark with a career high 65 RBI.

Bill was the sparkplug of a powerful Cubs infield that had Charlie Grimm, then Phil Cavarretta at first, Billy Herman at second and Stan Hack at third.

The Cubs had outstanding teams then, a point that was reflected in their winning pennants in 1932, 1935 and 1938.

"We lost all three World Series, '32 and '38 to the Yankees and '35 to the Tigers," Jurges says. "The Yankees were terrific. They beat the hell out of us (four games to none both times). But we made out all right. We got Series shares of $3,800 in '32, $4,100 in '35 and $4,400 in '38.

"I guess I remember the '35 Series the best," Jurges adds. "I was the clown of the Series. I made an error on a ball hit by Goose Goslin that lost one game (Game #4, 2-1). Then Tommy Bridges struck me out with a man on third in the ninth inning of the last game (won by Detroit, 4-3). I can still see that big curve ball of his coming up to the plate and exploding."

Jurges also clearly remembers the third game of the 1932 Series. "I had a chance to go 4-for-4, but I hit a line drive to left that was caught by Ruth in my last trip to the plate." Jurges hit .364 in that Series.

Perhaps Jurges' fondest memory, though, came during a regular season game in 1933.

"It was the greatest day of my life," he says. "It was the day I got married. I got married in Birdsboro, Pennsylvania, and then took a train to Philadelphia where we were playing a doubleheader at Baker Bowl. I went 7-for-8, handled about 14 or 15 chances without an error and stole a couple of bases."

Another pleasant memory for Jurges also occurred during those early years with the Cubs.

"Hartnett, Augie Galan and I used to hang around with a fellow who broadcast Cubs' games for a radio station in Des Moines, Iowa," he says. "We always called him Dutch, then, although you probably know of him as Ronald Reagan.

"One night we were in spring training in California, and we were all supposed to get together, but Dutch didn't show up. Finally, he got there around 10, and told us he had been to Hollywood to take a screen test. He wore glasses then, and we all kidded him. 'You, take a screen test? As ugly as you are?'

"Well, he told us he had signed a contract with a movie company for $275 a week. And that was the end of Dutch as a broadcaster. He was a terrific guy to be around, though. He didn't smoke, or drink, and he didn't cuss.

"I still hear from him once in a while," Jurges adds. "He called me when my wife of 51 years passed away in 1984."

During his playing career, Jurges was more noted as a solid, sure-handed fielder than he was as a hitter.

"I was a good, natural fielder," he says. "And I worked at it." I didn't work at hitting. After a shoulder injury in 1937, I couldn't hit the high pitch.

"I got hurt sliding into home," he recalls. "I was on third and a fly ball was hit to Vince DiMaggio. Incidentally, I always thought he was a better center fielder than Joe. I tagged up, and slid home, but my arm was caught in back of me. I tore up my shoulder, and it was never right after that. In fact, it still hurts. At the time, I was leading the league with a .340 average. That's the year I wound up with a .298."

A year later, Jurges' friend Hartnett took over at mid-season as Cubs' manager. "I was offered the job," says Bill, "but I turned it down. Hartnett had been with the club for 17 years. I wouldn't have felt right taking the job that belonged to him.

"After he got the job, he said to me, 'As long as I have the ball club, you'll be with me.' So what's he do? Right after the World Series, I was the first player traded. He sent me to the Giants along with Ken O'Dea and Frank Demaree for Dick Bartell, Gus Mancuso and Hank Leiber."

Jurges hit .285 his first year with the Giants, then two years later batted .293. That year (1941) he slugged nine consecutive hits, one less than the National League record.

In 1942, Jurges tied a major league record for fewest chances in an extra inning game when he had no plays in 11 innings.

Bill played for the Giants through 1945 when he was released. In 1946, he went to spring training with the Boston Braves, but was again released. He hooked on with the Cubs, and spent his last two seasons in Chicago.

After his retirement, he opened a miniature golf course and a driving range in Alexandria, Virginia. But after running that for a couple of years, he returned to baseball. He had a stint as an infield instructor for the Braves, helping to mold a young Eddie Mathews into a big league third baseman. Then he managed in the minor leagues, at one point piloting a Cleveland Indians farm club in Cedar Rapids, Iowa, where he had a young pitcher named Ray Narleski.

Jurges joined Charley Dressen as a coach with the Washington Senators in the mid-1950s. Then on June 28, 1959, he was named manager of the Red Sox. One year later, he was fired, also on June 28.

"It is very important for managers to get a ball club with players on the way up," Jurges says. "On that club, most of them were on the way down.

"Ted Williams was terrific, though," he adds. "He was wonderful. He's a real man's man; never lied, never BSed you."

After the Red Sox job, Jurges moved to the Baltimore Orioles as a scout. While there, he says, the Orioles vetoed a trade proposed by Dodgers' manager, Walter Alston, of Sandy Koufax, Johnny Podres and John Roseboro for Gus Triandos and others.

Jurges then worked as a special assignment scout for the New York Mets,

Houston Colt 45s, Washington Senators-Texas Rangers, Seattle Pilots and
Oakland A's. He was also a supervisor for a while for the major league
scouting bureau. While with Houston, he had a lot to do with developing
the fielding skills of a young Joe Morgan.

He sees today's players as being considerably different from the ones
of his era.

"Today, the ballplayers on the whole aren't as good, although the pitching's better," he says. "The pitchers have more deliveries, and there's
always a fresh pitcher out there. Years ago, they only had one relief pitcher
on a team.

"All a pitcher had then was a real good fastball and a curve ball. And
they were meaner. Some of them would throw at you to kill you.

"In my day," he adds, "Dizzy Dean was one of the toughest pitchers
I had to face. He could throw hard, but his best pitch was a slider. Diz had
a great assortment of pitches. But Paul (Dean) could throw harder than Diz.

"Another tough pitcher was Tex Carlton, a sidearmer with the Cardinals and later the Cubs. Dazzy Vance, Carl Hubbell, Freddie Fitzsim-
mons, Hal Schumacher, Jesse Haines, they were also tough. Van Mungo
threw the hardest of any of them, but he had no breaking stuff.

"Personally," Jurges continues, "I think the artificial turf has taken
away from the game. A bad hop was always part of the game. Now you don't
get them.

"Pittsburgh's field was always like concrete in front of home plate
because of the Waners. They could bounce a ball up in the air and beat
it out. That Paul. He could use the bat.

"The best looking hitter I've seen in recent years," adds Jurges, "was
(Roberto) Clemente. But of the players today, about five percent of them
are superstars, 55 percent are decent major league players, and 40 percent
of them are just a little above Triple A.

"And they have the owners over a barrel. It used to be that the owners
took advantage of the players. Now it's the opposite. But I don't begrudge
the present players and the salaries they're getting. More power to them.
I wish I was at that point in my career, although I do think that there's going to come a time when all sports are going to be priced out of the market.

"In my day," Jurges concludes, "most of us were just crazy about
baseball. We just loved to play. All I ever wanted to do was play baseball.
And once the game started, all I wanted to do was win.

"I don't think they feel that way anymore."

Johnny Moore—
Hard-Hitting Outfielder

He was the Philadelphia Phillies' best hitter in the late 1930s.
He was the Chicago Cubs' center fielder over whose head sailed the home run ball that Babe Ruth supposedly pointed out in the 1932 World Series.

And he was the Boston Braves' scout who signed future Hall of Famer Eddie Mathews.

His name is Johnny Moore, and he had a distinguished career in baseball that spanned nearly 50 years.

During his nine-year big league career, Moore had a lifetime average of .307. From 1934 through 1937, he put together successive batting averages of .330, .323, .328 and .319 for the Phillies in what was one of the most dismal periods in the club's history.

Although the Phillies finished in seventh place three times and in eighth once during that period, Moore provided a rare spark of talent, leading the team in hitting three times.

A native of Waterbury, Connecticut, Moore lives today in Bradenton, Florida, with his wife of more than 60 years, Rita. Johnny spent virtually all of his working life in baseball. After retiring as a player in 1945, he was employed until 1971 as a scout, first for the Boston-Milwaukee-Atlanta Braves and then for the Montreal Expos.

The Moore home is sprinkled with momentos of Johnny's career. The customary bats, balls, books and assorted pictures are in evidence.

A cabinet in the living room contains the best testament to Moore's career—a stack of scrapbooks, full of pictures and clippings from John's playing days.

Moore's playing career spanned 22 years as a pro. His best years, though, were in Philadelphia.

John landed with the club in May, 1934, in a trade with the Cincinnati Reds. At the time, Jimmie Wilson was the Phillies manager.

"Jimmie and I were good friends," Moore recalls. "But I didn't expect him to do me any favors. I still had to produce."

Johnny Moore.

And produce he did. In his first year with the Phillies, Moore hit .343 for the team while ending the season with a .330 batting average (16 games with the Reds). He drove in 98 runs and hit 11 homers.

The following season, Moore upped his home run production to 19 while batting .323 with 93 RBI. He had 16 homers, 68 RBI and a .328 average the next year.

Moore played his first two years in Philadelphia in right field, which meant he had to deal with the short (280 feet) but high right field fence at Baker Bowl. By the time Johnny joined the Phillies, Baker Bowl was a decrepit bandbox that was falling apart and was the laughing stock of the rest of the National League.

"It was about to fall down," Moore remembers. "The playing field was in bad shape. The whole park was in bad shape."

Playing right field required special techniques. "Telegraph poles held up the fence," Moore says. "If a ball hit the fence, it would drop straight down. If it hit a pole, it would bounce all the way back to the infield. I knew where every pole was, so I could tell how to play each ball that was hit out there.

"We always seemed to have good hitters in those days," Moore remembers. Dick Bartell, Pinky Whitney, Ethan Allen, Lou Chiozza and Dolph Camilli were all good, steady ballplayers and good hitters. Chuck Klein came back to the Phillies later on, and he was a good, strong powerhitter.

"The trouble was, we never had any pitching. Our pitching staff always had a lot of holes in it. And our defense wasn't up to par, either. We'd always get a lot of runs, but so would the other team."

The one damper on Moore's Philadelphia experience occurred after the 1937 season. John hit .319 that year, but for reasons never fully explained to him, he was sold that winter to the Los Angeles Angels, then of the Pacific Coast League. Imagine that happening today!

"They often sold players when they needed money," Moore says. "Gerry Nugent (the owner) never had much money, and they often had to economize because they weren't winning and pulling big crowds. Most of the time, they never got more than one or two thousand at a game. I remember one year, I asked Nugent for a raise, and you'd think I asked him for the franchise.

"They needed money, so they sold me to Los Angeles. I was really disappointed. I had heard that Brooklyn was interested in me, but I guess Los Angeles offered more money."

Thus, Moore, just short of becoming a 10-year man in the majors, returned to the minors where his career had begun 14 years earlier. It was a career that Johnny had started building as a child.

"I thought of nothing else but baseball," he says.

At the age of 14, Moore entered a trade school to learn tool and die making. He became a certified practitioner in that trade and along the way also played semipro baseball and basketball.

One day, Moore was offered a job with a major tool and die company in Waterbury. He could work as well as play on the company's baseball and basketball teams and live in a company- owned house. "I thought Santa Claus had come," Moore recalls.

An outstanding basketball player, Johnny played against the original Celtics and other top teams. But his real love was baseball. Soon, Moore attracted the attention of pro scouts. A New Haven scout saw him play on a day in which Moore hit a home run ball out of a park, a feat previously matched only by Babe Ruth.

"He said, 'How'd you like to go down to New Haven and play?' " Moore says. "I'd have paid him to let me go."

The team was owned by George Weiss, later to gain prominence as a general manager of the New York Yankees. Moore put in two and one-half seasons with New Haven, another with Waterville (New Hampshire) and one with Reading (Pennsylvania), then in the International League, where he hit .328.

The Cubs, who had bought Moore's contract from New Haven, called him up at the end of the 1928 season. He stayed with Chicago the following season, a year in which the Cubs won the National League pennant. The players, Moore recalls, got a losers' share of $2,100 after bowing four games to one to the Athletics.

With an outfield of Hack Wilson, Riggs Stephenson and Kiki Cuyler, Moore had no chance to crack the starting lineup. The Cubs sent him to Los Angeles in 1930 where he hit .342 that year and .366 the next before being recalled late in the season.

Moore became the Cubs' regular center fielder in 1932. He hit .305 and Chicago went to the World Series again, this time against the Yankees.

It was that Series that Babe Ruth, according to some accounts, pointed to the spot to which he was going to hit a home run. The ball flew into the right-center field stands over Moore's outstretched glove.

"I ran as far as I could to the fence," Johnny recaps. "I can't say whether Ruth pointed or not. Our pitcher, Charlie Root, denied it. I know both teams were really razzing each other. Our bench was really riding Ruth, and he was answering them right back."

Moore's manager with the Cubs was Joe McCarthy. "I'd put him as one of the all-time greats," John says. "He was also a fine man. When I first came up, I was a little scared. But he really put me at ease."

After the 1932 season and the Yankees' sweep of the Cubs in the Series, Moore was traded to Cincinnati. He played with the Reds for just over one season before he was swapped to the Phillies.

John's biggest day in baseball came a few years later. In a game in 1936, he hit three straight home runs and collected six RBI in a game against the Pittsburgh Pirates.

"I had a shot at four home runs," Moore says. "The first three balls I hit were high flies over the right field wall. The fourth time up I hit the ball harder than the other three, but it was a line drive that was caught at the base of the fence.''

Moore remembers hitting the homers against a pitcher named Cy Blanton. Obviously, Blanton does not rank among the toughest pitchers John faced.

"The toughest would've been Carl Hubbell," Moore says. "I'd also put the two Deans in there with Van Mungo, Charlie Root, Sheriff Blake, Dazzy Vance and Paul Derringer. Mungo and Dizzy Dean were the fastest.

"Of course, a lot had to do with the backgrounds you were hitting against in those different parks. Wrigley Field had all those white shirts in center field for a background, and that was very hard to hit with. Sportsman's Park also was a solid mass of white.''

After the Phillies sent him to Los Angeles, Johnny played eight seasons in the Pacific Coast League. He hit above .300 seven times, including a league-leading .331 in 1941.

Moore never complained about his minor league status. But curiously, he was never called back to the majors until the Cubs beckoned at the end of the 1945 season. Moore appeared six times as a pinch-hitter.

After his playing days ended, Moore was hired by John Quinn as a scout for the Boston Braves. Eventually, Moore became supervisor of the whole western territory for the club as it moved from Boston to Milwaukee to Atlanta.

Moore prides himself as having been the scout who signed Hall of Famer Eddie Mathews for the Braves. John inked the third baseman to a $6,000 bonus contract after his high school graduation.

In his scouting career with the Braves, Moore also signed players such as Del Crandall and Max Surkont. He was also the scout who originally signed Tom Seaver to a $40,000 bonus contract with the Braves. The Braves lost Seaver on a rules technicality.

Moore, who signed more than 200 players, altogether, joined the Expos and his old friend John McHale in 1968. He was assigned the duty of setting up and running Montreal's West Coast scouting system. Moore retired from the Expos and from baseball in 1971.

After his retirement, Moore and his wife, parents of three children (one son played briefly in the Braves' farm system), traveled for several years before settling permanently in Florida. John, a three-handicap golfer, became a top player in the local seniors circuit, once beating his old nemesis Derringer in a playoff for the Sarasota championship.

The Moores now live in a handsome retirement community. John plays a little shuffleboard, but most of his neighbors are unaware of his background as a baseball player.

Imagine what they're missing!

Jack Russell—
Standout Relief Pitcher

Take a career that lasted 15 years, add in a couple of pennant winners and the chance to play with and against some of baseball's all-time greats, and it becomes obvious that the big league tenure of Jack Russell was as enjoyable as it was interesting.

Russell may not be one of the household names of the game, but he put together a career that went from 1926 to 1940, and for a while was regarded as one of the top relief pitchers of his day, working in an era before the bullpen had the attention it does now.

In a well-traveled career, the righthanded Russell played for the Boston Red Sox, Cleveland Indians, Washington Senators, Detroit Tigers, Chicago Cubs and St. Louis Cardinals. Playing mostly for second division teams, he appeared in 557 games, posting an 85–141 lifetime record with a 4.47 earned run average.

Russell, however, did play for two pennant winners—the 1933 Senators and the 1938 Cubs. In fact, he was pitching in the game in which Gabby Hartnett hit his legendary homer into the darkness to help the Cubs to the National League pennant.

"Tony Lazzeri pinch hit for me," Russell recalls, "and he drove in the tying run. A few innings later, Hartnett hit the home run off of Mace Brown of the Pirates to win it. It was so dark, Hartnett had trouble finding second base."

Russell, now into his 80s, is still an active businessman, heading an oil supply company he founded in Clearwater, Florida. An avid golfer, he won the American Seniors Amateur Golf Championship in 1961 in his first year of eligibility, and was second in the tournament twice.

A native of Paris, Texas, Russell began his professional career in his hometown in 1925.

Russell recalls:

> My parents didn't want me to play pro ball. But we had a Class D club in town, and they wanted to sign me to a contract. I said I couldn't because my mom and dad wouldn't let me. But right before the deadline for signing, I met them in the post office. They said they wanted to sign me for $300. I

told them I had to finish school, and could only play on Saturdays and Sundays, and I had to have a car to get to the away games.

I don't know where I picked up that stuff. I was just trying to get them to refuse me. But they didn't, and that year I won seven games.

By then, the scouts were watching Russell, who had originally learned the rudiments of pitching from former big league hurler Dickie Kerr, also a Paris resident.

Russell remembers:

When Kerr was with the White Sox, he worked out with our high school team before going to spring training. He showed me how to pitch. He showed me the proper motion, taught me how to throw a change of pace. He even taught me to back up throws. Back then, pitchers never backed up the bases. But I learned a lot from Kerr, which is why I stayed in the big leagues so long. They figured, this guy knows what it's all about.

The Red Sox figured that, too, purchasing Russell's contract for $2,000.

"At first, I didn't hear from anybody," Russell says. "Finally, when spring training was approaching, I got a letter from (Red Sox owner) Bob Quinn. He told me to pick up a train ticket at the railroad station, and go to New Orleans for spring training."

Although only a raw recruit, Russell made the Red Sox squad that spring. That season, he pitched in 36 games, posting an 0–5 record.

Over the next few years, Russell alternated between starting and relieving. Boston finished out of last place only once during Russell's time with the Bosox, but Jack broke into double figures in 1928 with 11 wins (14 losses). Two years later, he led the league in losses with 20.

After the 1928 season, Russell decided to petition Quinn for a raise. Jack held out for a salary of $10,000, which was double the amount that Quinn had offered.

In the midst of the holdout, Russell got a note from Quinn. "I finished in last place with you," it said, "and I can finish in last place without you." Russell quickly signed for Quinn's figure.

While he was still pitching for Boston, Russell had what he considers to have been the finest game of his career. It came against the mighty Philadelphia Athletics, three-time American League pennant winners between 1929 and 1931.

"We were playing in Braves Field," Russell recalls. "I was pitching against Lefty Grove, and we both had a shutout going into the ninth inning. I gave up a home run in the ninth to Mule Haas, and we lost, 1–0. I wound up with a two-hitter. I didn't win, but it was the best game I ever pitched."

Early in the 1932 season, Boston traded Russell to Cleveland. "That year, I beat Washington six times," he recalls. "At the end of the season, Luke Sewell and I were traded to the Senators."

Russell's first year in Washington was also the first year for the new Nats' manager Joe Cronin. The young skipper moved Russell to the bullpen

Jack Russell.

full-time, and Jack responded by leading American League relievers with 13 saves and 11 wins. Overall, he had a 12-6 record. And Washington won the pennant, but lost to the New York Giants in the World Series, four games to one.

Russell pitched in three games in the Series, taking the loss in the fifth and final game when he gave up a 10th inning home run to Mel Ott. "That ball hit off the glove of our center fielder, Fred Schulte, and dropped over the three-foot fence for a home run," Russell remembers.

"The game I remember the most was the first game," Russell adds. "We opened at the Polo Grounds. Carl Hubbell started for the Giants and Lefty Stewart pitched for us. I came in in relief in the third inning."

Russell scattered four hits over five innings, holding the hard-hitting Giants without a run. But the four runs yielded by Stewart held up to give New York a 4-2 victory.

Jack gave up no hits in two-thirds of an inning of relief in a 2-1 Washington loss in the fourth game, then gave up four hits in four and two-third innings of relief in the fifth game in which Ott's homer gave the Giants a 4-3 victory.

Russell recalls:

> The funny part about the Series was that right before it started, I had gotten some good advice from an old friend, Herb Pennock. "I see you're going to be in the Series," he said. "You'll find the Series is easy to pitch in. Just get the ball over the plate, and they'll swing at it. They're all anxious to hit. It's not like the regular season where they might try to work you for a walk. In the Series, everybody wants to hit."
>
> I had a good sinker ball and we had a helluva good infield with Joe Kuhel at first, Buddy Myer at second, Cronin at short and Ossie Bluege at third. They made a lot of doubleplays. So I did what Pennock said, and it worked—at least until Ott came up in the last game.

In 1934, Russell led the league in games pitched (54) and again in saves with seven. Although the Senators tumbled all the way to seventh place, Jack had by then earned the distinction of being one of the top relievers in the league. Even Babe Ruth said so.

"I have seen Russell several times while he was serving so well in the speciality which has staged him as the best relief pitcher in our league," Ruth wrote in his syndicated newspaper column.

The admiration was mutal. "Ruth hit some home runs off me," Russell recalls. "You had to be real careful with him. I tried to keep the ball down. I threw him a lot of sinkers because he uppercutted everything. Our second baseman always played short right against him.

"Most umpires wouldn't give you that low ball," Russell adds, "because they couldn't bend over to see it because of the big chest protectors they wore."

Another hitter Russell respected was Detroit second baseman Charley Gehringer.

"Gehringer was about the toughest batter I faced," Russell says. "I was bruised all over from getting hit by line drives from him."

Russell left Washington in the 1936 season, moving back briefly to the Red Sox before going on to Detroit for one season. Then he wound up with the Cubs in 1938, and with a 6-1 record out of the bullpen helped Chicago to the World Series.

Jack pitched in two games in the Series, which the Cubs lost in four straight to the New York Yankees.

He worked one more season with the Cubs, then moved to the Cardinals where he finished his career in 1940.

By then, Russell had been a part-time resident of Clearwater since 1935, the year he began his oil business. After retiring as a player, he coached high school football and plunged into amateur golfing circles. Eventually, he won numerous local championships and became president of the Florida Men's Amateur Golf Association.

Active in local civic affairs, Russell also became a city commissioner. In that position, he led a drive to build a first class spring training facility in his adopted city.

The Phillies had spent spring training in Clearwater since 1947, but played in a dilapidated, wooden stadium. Through Russell's efforts, a new stadium was opened in 1955.

Russell attended the dedication cermony, and was stunned to learn that the stadium was to be named after him.

"When I heard them announce that that was going to be the name of the stadium, I was absolutely dumbfounded," he recalls. "It just left me speechless."

Today, Jack Russell Stadium is still the spring training home of the Phillies and a monument to a former ballplayer and civic leader whose career took many interesting turns.

Whitey Witt—
A Rich Career Among the Greats

In a region noted for its rich baseball history, one of the Philadelphia area's most precious treasures is surely an elderly gent named Whitey Witt, and ex-big leaguer whose career began with the Philadelphia Athletics back in 1916.

The quiet, country lane which bears his name provides the only conspicuous testimony to his presence. He lives peacefully and without celebration deep in the farmlands of South Jersey. His is not a household name in baseball circles, but if you looked it up, you would find that Whitey Witt, one of the oldest living ex-major league players, had an excellent career that was as fascinating as it was remarkable.

In 10 years in the majors, Witt had a lifetime batting average of .287 with 1,195 hits in 1,139 games. Regarded as one of the fastest men of his day, the 5'7" center fielder was an outstanding leadoff batter, a fine hitter and owner of one of the game's best batting eyes. What's more, he was an excellent fielder.

In a five-year stretch between 1920 and 1924, the lefthanded-hitting Witt piled up successsive batting averages of .321, .315, .297, .314 and .297.

The numbers, however, tell only part of the story. Witt, a star player for the A's between the club's championship eras, was the first New York Yankee player to bat in Yankee Stadium. He was one of Babe Ruth's best friends, and one of the few players who could hit Walter Johnson.

In fact, Witt whose name was originally Ladislaw Waldemar Wittkowski, had a career built around Hall of Famers. He played for Connie Mack and Miller Huggins, roomed with Nap Lajoie and Zack Wheat, was there when Lou Gehrig broke in, and was good friends with Ty Cobb, Mickey Cochrane and Goose Goslin.

When Witt talks about this group, he does so with relish, lacing his recollections with anecdotes that make it seem as though they just happened. Despite his years, Witt is remarkably spry, as evidenced by his fondness for golf, a sport he plays sometimes as often as three times a week, usually shooting right around his age.

Whitey Witt (courtesy, Whitey Witt).

It has been more than 60 years since Whitey pulled on a big league uniform. But the charm and color of his era are still evident in his conversation.

In his career with the A's, Yankees and Brooklyn Dodgers, Witt played in what is often considered to be the golden era of sports. A native of Orange, Massachusetts, he came to Philadelphia as a shy, 19-year-old with no minor league experience, beginning his career with the A's as a shortstop.

"I went right from high school to the A's," he says proudly. "I was going to a boarding school in Barre, Vermont, and playing in the White Mountain League. That was a summer league with teams sponsored by the big resort hotels in New Hampshire and Vermont. Most of the teams were made up of college boys from places like Harvard, Yale and Dartmouth who had summer jobs at the hotels.

"I was hitting over .400 while playing for St. Johnsbury. A scout was following me. One day, I got a telegram from Connie Mack asking me to meet him in Boston.

"All I had on my mind was to play ball, so I went down to see him. When I got there, he said, 'We've been following you. I'm going to give you a two-year contract, and you'll get paid whether you make it or not.' He gave me a $5,000 bonus and I got a $1,800 salary. I came from a poor family with no money and I was right out of high school, so I thought I had it made."

Witt reported to the A's the next season, and soon found himself the team's regular shortstop. His second base partner and roommate was Lajoie.

"Connie Mack had just broken up his club," Witt recalls. "After he won the pennant in 1914, he sold off all his great players. Then he stocked the club mostly with college boys.

"We trained that year in Jacksonville, Florida. I'll never forget it as long as I live. Here I was just 19 years old and I had made the grade.

"Lajoie was the most graceful infielder I ever saw," he adds. "His career was done by the time I got there, but he helped me an awful lot. He took me under his wing. None of the others helped me, but he sure did"

In his rookie season, Witt led American League shortstops in errors with 78. The A's finished last, a feat they duplicated every season from 1915 through 1921.

"We had some pretty good players," Witt says. "Guys like Stuffy McInnis and Joe Dugan, my roommate later on. We had Rube Oldring in left, Wally Schang was there as a catcher, and we had Joe Bush pitching.

"But it was hard playing on those teams. You're losing all the time. It was no fun. When I got to the Yankees, it was so much different. We were always up in the race, and it was easy to play ball.

"I wasn't very good as a shortstop," Witt adds. "But I could hit, so Connie Mack kept me in the lineup."

Witt hit .245 his first year and .252 his second season. Before he got to play his third year, he was drafted for World War I, the first player, he says, pulled out of the big leagues for active duty.

"When I came back (in 1919), Connie Mack put me in the outfield," Witt says. "That's where I played the rest of my career."

Although he played briefly at second base in 1919, Witt wound up in left, then moved to right a year later. He lifted his average to .267 the first year back from the Army, then put together two strong seasons of .321 and .315.

During the winter of 1921–22, Witt petitioned Mack for a raise.

"I had played five years for Connie Mack, and I hit awful good for him," Witt says. "The last year, I played in all 154 games. By then, I was living right here where I do now. I had bought the place in 1921—Mack had let me borrow $2,000 for the mortgage. I went up to his office five different times to ask for a raise. Finally, he said, 'I'm either going to give you a $500 raise or I'm going to keep you out of baseball.'

"Now, that was after I'd played all those years for him. That really got under my skin. I took the raise, but I wasn't too happy.

"That spring, we trained in Eagle Pass, Texas. We played all our exhibition games against the Cardinals because they trained in Texas, too.

"One day, I'm playing right field. It's only a week before the season is to open, and it's pouring rain. I'm standing in water up to my ankles, I'm soaked to the skin and I'm mad as hell for not getting any more money.

"The winning run's on base, and the ball comes to me. Instead of throwing it to third, I just threw it over the catcher's head into the grandstand. The run scored, and we lost the game.

"Afterward, Mack calls me over, and he says, 'I'm going to get rid of you. Where would you like to go?' I didn't care.

"So the Yankees bought me—I heard it was for $15,000.

"I didn't want to leave the A's. I had hit good for them, and I had the farm in South Jersey. I had three or four thousand dollars in the bank. But it turned out pretty good, going from a tailender right into the World Series with Babe Ruth and that bunch.

"I didn't report to the Yankees right away," he adds. "I got there three or four days after the season had opened. They said, 'Where the hell have you been?' I told them I had taken a little vacation. I went to Atlantic City.

"Miller Huggins was the manager. He was a nice guy. He had been a player, so he understood. He said, 'Look, it's going to cost you more to live in New York than it did in Philadelphia.' And he gave me a $1,500 raise.

"Right away, I started to hit like hell. The Yankees put me right into the lineup because that was the year that Commissioner Landis had suspended Babe Ruth and Bob Meusel for playing in post-season exhibition games the year before. The Yankees needed outfielders."

Installed as the Yankees' center fielder, Witt hit .297 in 1922 while leading the league with 89 walks. After Ruth and Meusel returned from their six-week suspensions, Whitey became the anchorman, playing between the two lumbering sluggers.

"I had to cover a lot of ground between those two guys," Witt says. "But I was fast. I had run the 110 in 10.2 second in high school, and I could do the 220 in 23 seconds. They were pretty good times for those days."

Witt ended his first season with the Yankees with bandages on his head, but a smile on his face.

"Right at the end of the season, we went into St. Louis for a three-game series with the Browns. We were both fighting for the pennant, so there was a big crowd, and they had the field roped off.

"In the first game, I was going after a fly ball, and somebody threw a Coca Cola bottle that hit me right in the head. Knocked me out, and they carried me off the field bleeding on a stretcher.

"I didn't play the next game, which we lost, but I came back in the third game with my head all bandaged, and I got a hit in the eighth inning that won the game and the pennant."

The Yankees lost for the second straight year to the New York Giants in the World Series in five games. But the following year, the club's luck changed.

It all began in the season opener when, on April 18, 1923, the gates were opened to Yankee Stadium. The first Yankee hitter to bat in the new ballpark was leadoff man Witt.

"It really didn't feel any different. It was just another ball game," recalls Witt. "I felt a lot more shaky my first time up in the World Series. But I got a hit and two walks in that game. I was the first Yankee to get a hit and to score a run in Yankee Stadium. Babe Ruth hit the first home run."

From there, with Whitey hitting .314, the Yankees went on to win the pennant and capture their first World Championship. In the Series, they beat the Giants, four games to two. Witt's two doubles, a single and sacrifice fly accounted for two RBI in the fourth game, won by the Yankees, 8–4.

"Each Yankee player got $3,132.50 for the winner's share," remembers Witt. "I'll never forget that. They didn't give rings to us, either. They gave us solid gold watches.

"I got six hits in that Series," recalls Witt. "It's a great thrill to play in a World Series. But it was a bigger thrill for me just to play with my dear beloved Babe Ruth."

Had he still been alive, Ruth would be the same age as Witt. The two were inseparable friends, on and off the field, and when the Bambino died in 1948, Witt stood by his casket at the viewing in Yankee Stadium for five hours.

"Babe Ruth always considered me one of his best friends," Witt recalls. "I loved the guy.

"There was a lot of jealousy on our club. Some guys were always knocking Ruth, calling him a big bum and so forth. Wally Pipp was one of them, and they had a helluva fist fight once.

"I always said to those guys, 'Why do you knock him? He's our meal-ticket.' We would have been nowhere without him.

"Ruth hit the ball better than anybody," Witt adds. "And he was a helluva nice guy. He loved kids; he loved to visit hospitals; he loved the women. He always had a big bankroll with him.

"Babe never drank as much as people said he did. He ate a lot. But he didn't drink any more than you or me.

"In my book, there were two great ballplayers, Babe Ruth and Ty Cobb. They were the two greatest of all-time.

"Ruth had color. Cobb was spectacular. Everything he did was spectacular.

"I'll never forget when I played shortstop for the A's and Cobb would be on second. After every pitch, he'd run about halfway to third, and dare the catcher to throw the ball. If he threw it back to second, Cobb would be on third.

"When I played for the A's, Connie Mack always had pre-game meetings. He would get up and say, 'Today, we're playing Ty Cobb.' He would never say, 'The Detroit Tigers,' it was always 'Ty Cobb.' He'd say, 'Always throw the ball two bases ahead of Cobb.'

"One day, I'm playing left field and the ball comes out to me on one hop. Cobb leaves second, but he gives me the impression he's going to stop at third. He's just going along nice and easy. I took the ball, and threw it to the plate. I caught Cobb by about 20 feet. He never even slid."

In Witt's last year with the Yankees, the club had a rookie first baseman named Lou Gehrig. Whitey has vivid memories of the young slugger.

"To me, he was more valuable to the ball club than Ruth because he was very consistent," Witt says. "He never struck out, and he could drive in runs. He always got the bat on the ball.

"The most consistent hitter I ever saw, though," volunteers Witt, "was Joe Jackson. He was the best pure hitter. And he was a real graceful player. He and Lajoie were both very graceful and both great hitters."

The best pitcher Witt says he ever came up against was Dutch Leonard, the old Boston Red Sox and Detroit Tigers lefthander.

"I always figured he was going to hit me right in the ribs," Whitey says. "He was a sarcastic guy, too. I never liked batting against him.

"Now, Walter Johnson, if you look back, you'll find I hit very good against him. He had a speedball that would knock the bat right out of your hands. But I was a punch-hitter. I could get the bat around on him. I bet I hit .400 against him.

"Connie Mack used to say, 'Today, we're playing Walter Johnson. I want you boys to watch how Whitey hits against him.'

"Johnson didn't have a good curve. It wouldn't break much. But he had one of the greatest arms God ever put on a man. His speedball came up, and it looked like a golf ball coming at you. If he hit you, he'd have killed you.

"One time, we were down in Washington and both clubs—the Senators and Yankees—were leaving town at the same time. I went down to the railroad

station, and I'm walking along the platform. Both clubs were headed to the
dining car to eat dinner. A window was open, and who's sitting there but
Walter Johnson. He hollered out, 'Hey, Whitey. Come here. I want to talk
to you.' So I go in and have dinner with him.

"He says, 'There are three guys in the American League that I can
not get out. Eddie Collins, Eddie Murphy and you.' I thought that was a
great honor, coming from the best pitcher in the American League.

"Some other pitchers were easy to hit; some were tough," Witt adds.
"But I always figured I could hit any of them.

"Hitting was my main asset. I could field and I could run. I had a good
arm, too, at first, but something hit me in the shoulder after two or three
years in the big leagues. It straightened out pretty good to the point that
I could throw a ball from the outfield to second base. But usually in the
big leagues, if you can hit, they want you in that lineup. And since I could
hit, I was in that lineup every day."

One pitcher who Witt hit with spectacular results was Howard Ehmke.
In 1923, Ehmke, hurling for the Boston Red Sox, pitched a no-hitter against
the A's. In his next outing, he had another no-hitter going in the late innings against the Yankees. Witt ended Ehmke's big bid for double no-hit fame

*Bob Meusel, Whitey Witt and Babe Ruth made up the outfield of the 1922 and 1923
New York Yankees.*

when he bounced a single off the third baseman's chest. The ball then hit the Yankee third base coach, and Witt beat it out for a hit.

Whitey wrapped up his career with the Yankees after the 1925 season, moving on in 1926 to the Dodgers where he roomed with Zack Wheat.

"Zack was an Indian, you know," says Witt, "and he was good friends with Jim Thorpe. The two of them could sure drink. Thorpe would come to the hotel room, and they would polish off a fifth of whiskey in one evening."

After he left the big leagues, Witt played for three years in the minors, spending one season each in San Francisco, Kansas City and Reading (Pennsylvania). At the end of the 1930 season, he retired from professional baseball.

From 1933 until 1971, Witt owned and operated a tavern and package store in South Jersey. For a while, he also managed and played for a semipro team in the area, while palling around with ex-Washington and Detroit great, Goose Goslin, a neighbor in South Jersey.

Eventually, Witt sold the bar. For many years, he spent his winters in Florida and his summers playing golf and going to race tracks in the Philadelphia area.

Whitey sometimes returns to old-timers games at Yankee Stadium, but he finds himself astounded by modern baseball conditions, especially the salaries. His highest pay as a big leaguer was $9,000.

"The salaries today break my heart," he says. "Those guys don't deserve that kind of money. If I was playing today, I'd be one of those $300–$400,000 players.

"The game itself hasn't changed that much," he adds. "The ball was just as lively when I played as it is today. And the pitchers are no different.

"The only difference is, when I played you could throw a spitter. We never heard of a sinker or slider. It was all speedball, curve. Ed Cicotte was a great pitcher, and he had an emery ball. He kept a sheet of it hooked on his belt. The ball would sail on you."

But Whitey Witt, the little leadoff batter with the short stroke, could still hit it.

Most Valuable Players

Dick Allen—Controversial Slugger
with Tape-Measure Clouts

There were players who were bigger, players who were stronger and even a few who probably had more talent. But few ever hit a baseball as hard or as far as Dick Allen.

With the sleek body of a racehorse, muscles that rippled and wrists built like coiled springs, Allen hit some of the game's most prodigious clouts during an often brilliant, often stormy career that left an indelible mark in five cities.

It was a career that lasted 15 years in the big leagues, including two stints with the Philadelphia Phillies and terms with the St. Louis Cardinals, Los Angeles Dodgers, Chicago White Sox and Oakland A's.

It was a career in which Allen compiled statistics that could be construed as Hall of Fame caliber. And it was a career in which Allen's injuries and controversies often overshadowed his magnificent talent.

He hit .292 during his career with 1,848 hits and 351 home runs. Allen collected 119 RBI and scored 1,099 runs.

He won the two home run crowns, an RBI title, Rookie of the Year and MVP awards, and three times was the league leader in slugging average. Six times he hit more than 30 homers in a season, and he had seven years above .300.

Despite a nearly unanimous lack of support, there are some people who think Allen's numbers should have earned him a place in the Hall of Fame. The former slugger isn't one of them.

"I'm not disappointed (about not being elected)," Allen says. "It's never interested me much."

What does interest Allen these days are race horses, good friends and having the freedom to control his own life.

Allen hardly looks any different now than he did during the latter part of his playing days. He is still a free spirit, too, whose outspoken tendencies were ahead of their time when he played and who is not reluctant to speak his piece today.

Traces of bitterness that punctuated much of his baseball career

127

sometimes creep into his conversation. But his frequent smiles and ready humor suggest that he has mellowed, that he is no longer the angry man of baseball.

"I guess I was always kind of a Jesse James without guns," he says, looking back on a career dotted with suspensions, disappearances, run-ins with managers and incidents such as his fight with Frank Thomas, badly cutting his hand on the headlight of a car, writing messages in the dirt at first base, and sitting alone in the dugout while the Phillies celebrated their first division title.

"But I've matured. I'd like to let bygones be bygones. I'd like to think now that I had a swell career, both in Philadelphia and elsewhere.

"It was better the second time in Philadelphia than the first," he adds. "The first time, I left with a lot of bitterness . I said I'd never return. Then I did. I guess it goes to show that a lot of times we say things that we really don't know how they're going to turn out."

Allen still cherishes his independence, though. "Even now," he says, "there are certain things I will do and certain things I won't do."

Having good friends is important to him, too. "I'd rather have good friends," he says. "When I played, some of my best friends were members of the ground crew, parking lot attendants, people like that. Other people never understood that."

Allen's time is mostly taken up now with training race horses, some of which he and his brother, Hank, own, at Santa Anita in Los Angeles, California, where Dick now makes his home. He gets up early and goes to bed early, spending long hours with the four-legged friends who have replaced his baseball teammates.

That is not to say that baseball is completely removed from Allen's mind, although he's only been to a few major league games since his retirement in 1977.

"My oldest boy played in college (Bowie State in Maryland), and I watched him," Allen says. "And I do follow Mike Schmidt. He and I have a lot in common.

"I've never really lost touch with the game. But there's a lot of stuff I don't understand, like what's going on with all the drugs, the agents, things like that. It seems like everybody's mind is on everything but playing the game."

Allen says he has saved nothing from his playing days, in part because a fire destroyed his house when he was still living in Pennsylvania. "But I never really treasured those things anyway," he says. "Material things never meant much to me. A World Series ring would have been the only really important thing, and not having one, I'd have to say is my biggest disappointment in baseball."

He says he would welcome the chance to return to the game if "the right opportunity" came along. "Not to bring any racial thing into it," he says, "but where is there for a black guy when he gets done playing? There are very few coaches' jobs, very few managing jobs and forget the front office.

Dick Allen.

"So, you tend to turn to race horses. They're athletes. But that's the only thing there. That's kind of sad."

There was never anything sad about the way Allen hit a baseball. Starting with his days as a youth in Wampum, Pennsylvania, Dick generated boundless excitement with his bat.

An all-around athlete in high school—he was an All-State player in baseketball and led his team to two state titles—Allen signed with the Phillies in 1960 for an estimated $70,000 bonus, the highest amount paid a black player up to that point.

After four seasons in the minors, Allen, one of three brothers to make the big leagues, joined the Phillies at the end of the 1963 season following a year at Little Rock, during which he led the International League in home runs and RBI.

Originally a shortstop, Allen had been converted to second base, then to the outfield. But after coming to the Philies, he was switched to third base.

By that time, Allen was already having problems. He had been bothered by the racial attitudes and abuse in Arkansas and by the Phillies' unwillingness to give him a $50 raise after he hit .329 the previous year at Willamsport. A meager salary as a rookie in Philadelphia added to his discontent.

In his first full year, however, Allen ran away with the National League Rookie of the Year honors, hitting .318 with 29 home runs while becoming only the sixth NL player in history to have 200 or more hits as a rookie. He led the league in runs scored (125) and total bases (352). He also led league hitters in strikeouts and third basemen in errors (41).

That year, the Phillies had a six and one-half game lead with 12 games left to play, and blew the pennant after losing 10 straight.

"We really had a good team," laments Allen. "Probably one of the best I ever played on. We played well all season. We just came up a little short."

In the ensuing years, the same could not be said of Allen's bat. Although the man whose first name had migrated from Richie to Rich to Dick—he signs autographs in each of the three now—over the years continued to have trouble with his fielding and with striking out (he set a National League record with 150 in 1965), his overall hitting was outstanding.

After a .302 average in 1965, he hit .317 with 40 home runs and 110 RBI in 1966. Following a .307 season in 1967, his average fell, but Allen's home run production continued as big as ever with titanic blasts occurring regularly.

All the while, though, Allen's nonplaying problems were mounting, and management's and the fans' patience with him was diminishing.

"A lot of things weren't told. They couldn't be told," Allen claims. "I was put on the spot back then a lot of times.

"It seemed everything I did was magnified. When I came, they were drawing 6-7,000 fans. Then they started drawing 26,000, so, naturally, they were going to keep things boiling because it was going to fill seats."

Despite his drawing power, Allen was finally traded in 1969 after two managers—Gene Mauch and Bob Skinner—had lost their jobs over feuds with him. Even the trade was controversial. The Phillies sent Allen, Cookie Rojas and Jerry Johnson to the St. Louis Cardinals for Tim McCarver, Curt Flood, Bryon Browne and Joe Hoerner. But Flood refused to report to the Phillies, eventually testing baseball's reserve clause all the way to the U.S. Supreme Court. The outcome led to the eventual institution of free agency.

The Phillies got Willie Montanez in Flood's place, and Allen went on a cross-country path that led him to one-year stops with the Cardinals and Los Angeles Dodgers before landing with the Chicago White Sox in 1972.

Reunited with a long-time family friend, Chuck Tanner, manager of the White Sox, a rejuvenated Allen led the American League in home runs (37), RBI (113) and slugging average (.603) while hitting .308. After the season, he was voted the league's Most Valuable Player, one of only 11 players ever to have won both Rookie of the Year and MVP honors in their careers.

"It was a very enjoyable season," Allen recalls. "I liked being with Chuck Tanner. You could talk things over with him."

Allen hit .316 the following year with the White Sox, then .301 in 1974 while again leading the league in home runs with 32 and slugging average with .563.

The next spring he was traded to the Atlanta Braves. Allen refused to report, and the Braves wound up trading him back to the Phillies along with Johnny Oates for minor leaguers Jim Essian and Barry Bonnell.

"Coming back the second time was one of my fondest memories," Allen says. "I got a standing ovation before I even took a swing. It's just a shame that I wasn't in the best physical condition. But the team finally got a pennant, and they deserved it."

Allen played two years in Philadelphia, but his batting production was well below that of his previous seasons. After averaging 30 home runs a season in his first 11 years, he hit only 12 with a .233 average in 1975 and 15 with a .268 mark the next year.

Released after the 1976 season, Allen joined the Oakland A's and played with them for one season before retiring.

Except for brief assignments as a spring training batting instructor with the Texas Rangers in 1982 and with the Chicago White Sox in 1986, Allen has stayed away from baseball and the spotlight since his retirement. He says he has no regrets about his career.

"I don't think I'd change a thing," he says. "If you play without injuries, that would mean you weren't playing hard.

"I never thought about what I could've done," he adds, in answer to a suggestion that under different circumstances he might have scaled greater heights as a batter. "I like to think there were some other things in the game that this old body could do besides hit the long ball."

It is the long ball, though, for which he is best remembered. And the vision of balls flying off of his bat and disappearing over distant barriers is one that refuses to disappear.

Phil Cavarretta—
Hometown Hero of the Cubs

There was a time, long ago, when the Chicago Cubs were one of the elite teams of the National League. A perennial pennant contender whose presence sometimes graced the World Series, the Bruins of 40 and 50 years ago were always tough, colorful teams stocked heavily with multi-talented players.

One of the finest of that group was Phil Cavarretta.

A player of many dimensions, Cavarretta was a hard-working, inspirational athlete, an outstanding hitter and an excellent fielding first baseman. He played for the Cubs from 1934 to 1953, and during those 20 seasons no player at Wrigley Field was more popular.

Phil was a hometown boy who joined the Cubs at the tender age of 18. He went on to play for pennant winners in 1935, 1938 and 1945, captaining the club in his later years and eventually becoming its manager.

The National League batting champion and Most Valuable Player in 1945, Cavarretta finished his 22-year major league career in 1955 with the Chicago White Sox. His final figures showed a lifetime batting average of .293 with 1,977 hits, 95 home runs, 920 RBI and 990 runs.

"I always felt I was a Pete Rose-kind of player," Cavarretta says. "I always hustled, always played hard and gave 100 percent.

"I was a line drive hitter. I tried to hit the ball where it was pitched. I wasn't a power-hitter. I used to bunt, drag, anything to get on base."

A trim, dapper gentleman today with dark good looks, Cavarretta lives in Palm Harbor, Florida. After spending his entire working life in baseball, he retired from the game in 1980.

Cavarretta still watches as much baseball on television as he can, reads everything about the game that he can get his hands on, appears at old-timers games and visits the nearby spring training camps in Florida.

"I miss the game, I really do," he says. "I enjoy retirement, but after all those years, it's hard to get baseball out of your system. I miss the people most of all."

And the people—especially those in the Windy City—miss him, too.

When he held down first base for the Cubs, Cavarretta was the darling of the masses—a local boy with matinee-idol looks who played the game with enormous skill.

His was a success story that could have been written in Hollywood. "Originally, I played softball with that 16-inch ball," Cavarretta recalls. "Then I started playing baseball, and I took a liking to the game right away. When I got to high school, my interest in baseball really took off."

Although he was one of the top high school players in Chicago, Phil had one problem. "I came from a very poor family," he says. "My parents could hardly speak English. It was during the Depression, and my dad had no job. It was up to me to go out and try to make a buck."

Phil, a pitcher and first baseman at the time, discussed the situation with his high school coach. The coach got the youngster a tryout with the Cubs. Manager Charlie Grimm liked what he saw, the Cubs signed Cavarretta and the rest, as they say, is history.

Phil Cavarretta.

The young lefthander was assigned to Peoria (Illinois) of the Central League, but after a month the league folded. Cavarretta was reassigned to Reading (Pennsylvania) of the New York-Pennsylvania League. In 85 games, he hit .308 before being recalled by the Cubs at the end of the season.

"I was a Cub fan all my life, and now all of a sudden, I was a Cub, myself," Cavarretta recalls. "Even when I was a kid, I always wanted to play for the Cubs. We used to sneak onto the el and ride to Wrigley Field. A policeman would let us jump the fence to get in.

"Sometimes, the Cubs gave out duffle bags to the kids. You would go around the ball park, filling them up with trash. Then they would let you in to the game for free.

"I remember watching Hack Wilson, Riggs Stephenson and guys like that. I used to stand outside the park and watch them come out. A couple of years later, I was playing with those guys.

"And Billy Herman—I took a real liking to him. He was one of my favorites. Now, here I was, not only on the same team with him, but we became roommates."

Cavarretta was a shy 18-year old when he first reported to the Cubs at the end of the 1934 season. "I was supposed to join the club in Boston," he says. "I hardly knew where Boston was.

"I didn't talk much. After I got to Boston, I was sitting outside the hotel wondering how to get to the ball park. Kiki Cuyler came along. He said, 'You going to the ball park kid,?' I said I was. He said, 'Come on. I'll show you how to get there.' The two of us walked to the park and we talked back and forth. He seemed to take a real interest in me."

During the series with the Braves, Cavarretta got into his first major league game. He was sent up to pinch-hit, and was struck out by Boston pitcher, Fred Frankhouse.

"The first full game I played in was a few days later back at Wrigley Field against Cincinnati," Cavarretta remembers. "My first time up, I hit a home run. We won the game, 1-0, with Lon Warneke beating Whitey Wistert (Wistert's only major league decision). The funny thing was, exactly one year later, I hit a home run off of Paul Dean to beat the Cardinals, 1-0."

After hitting .381 in 21 at-bats as an 18-year-old, Phil took over the regular job at first base in 1935. He hit .275 and the Cubs won the National League pennant.

"The '35 team was the best of the three pennant winners I played on," says Cavarretta. "We had Billy Herman, Billy Jurges and Stan Hack in the infield, Gabby Harnett catching and guys like Chuck Klein, Augie Galan, Kiki Cuyler and Frank Demaree in the outfield. Lon Warneke, Charlie Root and Bill Lee were on the mound.

"We were young and we had a real good offense. It was a better all-around team than the others. At one point, we won 21 games in a row.

"I was in a trance," he adds. "Here I was, only 19 years old, and in the World Series. It was a big thrill, the biggest I ever had."

Another big thrill occurred a few years later. Cavarretta was present when playing-manager Hartnett hit his memorable home run into the falling darkness at Wrigley Field to help send the Cubs to the 1938 pennant.

The hit, coming in the bottom of the ninth inning, defeated the Pittsburgh Pirates, 6-5, and pushed the Cubs into first place ahead of the Bucs.

"I don't know how Gabby saw the ball, it was getting so dark," Cavarretta recalls. "They even had the lights on in the stands (there were, of course, no lights on the playing field). The funny thing was, Mace Brown, the Pirates' reliever, struck out the first two batters with fastballs. He got two strikes on Hartnett with fastballs, but then he threw him a slider, and that's what Gabby hit. I could never understand why he threw that pitch."

In 1938, as in the other years, the Cubs lost in the World Series. They bowed to Detroit, four games to two in '35, to New York, 4-0, in '38 and to the Tigers again in '45, 4-3. All the while, though, Cavarretta turned in one solid season after another.

Although plagued off and on by injuries and shifted back and forth between first base and the outfield at the end of the 1930s, Phil really began to hit his stride in the early 1940s. In 1943, he hit .291. The following year, he burst over .300 for the first time, compiling a .321 average to rank fifth in the league while tying Stan Musial for the league lead in hits with 197.

But that was just a warmup. In 1945, Cavarretta became only the second Cub player ever to win a battling championship when he stormed through the league to post a .355 average. Phil, who also had a career high 97 RBI that season, edged Boston's Tommy Holmes for the crown by three points.

"I went down to the last day with Holmes," he says. "We were one or two points apart. I got a hit in the last time up to clinch it.

"It was a big achievement for me. In order to win a batting title, everything has to go your way. You still have to have ability, but everything has to fall in place. And even though it was a war year, you still had to work hard to get your hits. There was nothing easy about it."

The Baseball Writers' Association voted Cavarretta the League's Most Valuable Player, giving him 279 points to the runner-up Holmes' 175. For Phil, it was a fitting climax to his greatest season in pro baseball.

The following season, although his average dropped to .294, Cavarretta proved he was the ultimate team player. Phil, the established veteran, shifted to right field to make room for flashy fielding rookie first baseman, Eddie Waitkus.

Cavarretta was back to .314 in 1947. But by the next season, his career was beginning to wind down. In 1951, the Cubs named their aging captain a playing-manager, replacing Frankie Frisch late in the season.

The Cubs finished in last place that season, but Phil got them up to fifth in 1952. When the Bruins fell to seventh in 1953, Cavarretta was let go.

"Looking back, I think I made a mistake," he says. "I think I accepted the job too quickly. I didn't have enough experience. I should have worked in the minors first.

"Being a playing-manager was rough," he adds. "There are so many things to think about. You really can't do both jobs well."

Phil Cavarretta (left) was one of the mainstays of the 1940s Chicago Cubs. Here he is in 1943 joined by Cubs' manager Jimmie Wilson.

After Cavarretta relinquished the Cubs' managerial reigns, he joined the White Sox as a part-time player. Phil spent two seasons with the Chisox before retiring as a player in 1955.

The next 10 years were spent managing in the minor leagues, working first for the Kansas City A's, then the Cleveland Indians and the Oakland A's. His 1957 Buffalo club went to the Little World Series.

Phil returned to the majors in the late 1960s as a coach with the Cubs. Later, he joined the New York Mets as a coach, eventually taking over as the Mets' hitting instructor under his pal, Yogi Berra.

Looking back, Cavarretta cites many highpoints of his career. He is credited with having gotten the only hit in a game three times—in 1937 against Lee Grissom, in 1949 against Rex Barney and in 1950 against Ewell Blackwell.

"Actually, I broke up no-hitters twice against Blackwell," Phil says. "Once it was with a line drive. But the second time, he jammed me. The bat broke into four pieces and it stung the hell out of my thumb. The ball blooped over third base. Blackie cussed me out; oh, did he cuss me out.

"He was the toughest pitcher I ever faced. He was mean. And even though he was righthanded, with that sidearm fastball of his, the ball moved all over. It never moved the same way twice in a row. He always threw it on the inside of the plate, too.

"Another tough pitcher was Harry Brecheen. He was cute. He had a real good screwball, two kinds of curves and he was sneaky fast. His control was super, too. He'd knock you back."

Cavarretta says his greatest moment as a hitter came after he had taken over as Cubs manager. "We were playing a doubleheader against the Phillies," he recalls. "Robin Roberts pitched the first game, and I hit a two-run triple and scored a run to beat him.

"Curt Simmons started the second game for the Phillies, but we knocked him out in the late innings. They brought in Robbie in relief with the bases loaded. I had benched myself for the second game, but when Robbie came in, I went up to pinch-hit. He threw me a slider, and I hit a grand slam homer to win the game.

"In two swings of the bat, I had a triple, a home run and six RBI—all off of Roberts. And he was a great pitcher, too."

Cavarretta, who says his idol as a boy was Lou Gehrig, didn't save many items from his playing days, but he has a few special treasures from the game. He has his 1945 Cubs uniform, a few old gloves and many pictures. His favorite picture is one taken of him and Babe Ruth. At the time, Phil was just an 18-year-old kid while Ruth, who signed the photo, was at the end of his career.

Once in a while, Cavarretta looks at that picture, and the memories of his fine career rush back.

"I beliveve the good Lord put me on this Earth and said, 'You're going to be a ballplayer,'" Cavarretta muses. "I'm glad He did that. There's nothing else I ever wanted to be."

Orlando Cepeda—
The Baby Bull with the Raging Bat

They called him "The Baby Bull." It was a nickname that fit him well. Big, strong, with rippling muscles and a body that exuded power, Orlando Cepeda was perfectly cast as the human symbol of the mighty bovine.

He had come out of Puerto Rico, the son of the island's greatest baseball star, and for 17 thunderous seasons, his raging bat snorted and charged around the game's pastures. No ball yard was ever big enough to contain him, and no pitcher was ever quite able to rope him in.

Cepeda entered the big leagues when the National League had one of the greatest collections of sluggers ever assembled at one time. Hank Aaron, Willie Mays, Ernie Banks, Eddie Mathews, Roberto Clemente and Frank Robinson—Hall of Famers all—gave the league a brilliant galaxy of batting stars. Cepeda was no less radiant.

In a career in which he played for six teams—the San Francisco Giants, St. Louis Cardinals, Atlanta Braves, Oakland A's, Boston Red Sox and Kansas City Royals—the 6' 2", 210-pound strongman had a lifetime batting average of .297 with 379 home runs among his 2,351 hits, 1,365 RBI and slugging average of .499. In nine of his 13 seasons as a regualar, Cepeda hit over .300. Fourteen times he homered in double figures, and five times he drove in more than 100 runs.

Cepeda was one of only 10 players in major league history to win a Rookie of the Year and later a Most Valuable Player award. He was a member of eight All-Star teams and three pennant-winners. And only two first basemen in the National League (Willie McCovey and Gil Hodges) have hit more home runs in their careers than he has.

At the peak of his career with the Giants, Cepeda teamed with Mays and McCovey to give San Francisco one of the most awesome home run trios in league history. Later, with the Cardinals, he joined Roger Maris, Lou Brock and company to drive St. Louis to two consecutive pennants and a World Series title.

Cepeda's career was one that was punctuated with knee problems and

Orlando Cepeda.

salary squabbles, both of which played a part in his somewhat frequent (for a player of his caliber) trades. But when it came to bashing a baseball, few hitters possessed the sheer strength and power of Cepeda, whose prodigious clouts left as many dents in pitchers' psyches as they did in distant spots in stadiums.

"I thought my career could have been better if it hadn't been for all those injuries," Cepeda says. "But I have no regrets. I played with the best players in one of baseball's greatest eras. I had a good career with some great years."

Cepeda had two particularly great years. In 1961, he won two legs of the Triple Crown, leading the league with 46 home runs and 142 RBI. He batted .311 that year, well behind Clemente's league-leading .351.

In 1967, when he was voted MVP, he hit a career high .325 while slamming 25 homers and leading the league with 111 RBI. That year, his Cardinals won the National League pennant; then defeated the Boston Red Sox in a memorable seven-game Series.

"I think that is the year I'll always remember best," says Cepeda. "I played with a great club, had some great teammates, and we won the championship. It was the most enjoyable year of my career."

There were other enjoyable years, though beginning with Orlando's rookie season in 1958 when he hit .312 with 25 homers and 96 RBI and led the circuit with 38 doubles. That year, he was voted Rookie of the Year by both the Baseball Writers' Association and *The Sporting News*.

Cepeda had burst on the scene after a short but sparkling minor league career during which he had won two batting championships and hit over .300 in each of his three seasons.

He had come out of a difficult environment to reach that point. His father, Peruchio, was considered the Babe Ruth of Puerto Rico and was the idol of legions of the island's baseball fans. Comparisons between father and son were inevitable, but, as is often the case, the youngster suffered the problems of playing in the huge shadow cast by his elder. It was not until Orlando reached the United States that he began to emerge as an excellent player in his own right.

"Having a father like that worked against me in some ways," Cepeda recalls. "In Puerto Rico, it was very hard to develop on my own. People were always making comparisons. My father's reputation wasn't much help to me."

But in 1954, Cepeda's fellow countryman, Roberto Clemente, still a minor leaguer himself at that point, brought Orlando to spring training in the United States. Clemente took Cepeda to the New York Giants' camp. The Giants, one of the earliest teams to sign black players, welcomed Cepeda with open arms.

A third baseman then, Orlando wound up hitting .393 at Kokomo, leading the Class D Mississippi-Ohio Valley League in hitting. The following year, he hit .355 at St. Cloud to top the Class C Northern League in batting and in homers with 26. Jumping all the way to Class AAA in 1957,

Cepeda hit .309 with 25 home runs for Minneapolis of the American Association.

That earned him a promotion to the Giants. By then, Cepeda had been switched to first base, and in 1958 he took over for aging veteran Whitey Lockman.

Cepeda joined the Giants in time for their first season in San Francisco. It was an exciting year for the whole ball club as the Giants surged to third place. For Cepeda, though, the excitement was somewhat tempered by the strangeness of a new land.

"Looking back, it was hard to adjust," he says. "Being black and not knowing the language made it difficult. But I learned to deal with the situation."

He dealt especially well with opposing pitchers. After winning Rookie of the Year honors, he ignored the sophomore jinx by posting even better numbers his second year with a .317 batting average, 27 homers and 105 RBI.

Cepeda slipped to .297 in 1960, but bounced back with four straight big seasons after that. From 1961–64, he went .311–46–142, .306–35–114, .316–34–97, and 304–31–97.

During his big year in 1961, Cepeda teamed with Mays (40 homers) to give the Giants a mighty one-two punch. That year, Orlando drove in eight runs in one game. He also hit the first of five Giant homers in one inning. Only three other teams in major league history have hit five homers in one inning.

Cepeda, who by then was also playing some outfield, helped the Giants to the National League pennant in 1962. He batted only .158 in the Series as the Giants lost in seven games to the New York Yankees, but his three hits in the sixth game combined with a three-hitter by Billy Pierce to lead San Francisco to a 5-2 victory.

In 1963, Cepeda combined with McCovey (44) and Mays (40) to give the Giants one of the top home-run-hitting trios in National League history.

Cepeda's batting spree continued until 1965 when a knee injury put him out of action for most of the season. During his absence, the Giants moved McCovey to first base from the outfield. Cepeda became expendable.

Early the following spring, Cepeda was traded to the Cardinals for pitcher Ray Sadecki. It was a good trade for the Cardinals; a bad one for the Giants.

"I was glad to move on," Cepeda recalls. "I had hardly played in '65 because of my knee. When they put McCovey on first full-time, somebody had to go. I kind of figured it would be me."

Cepeda started crushing the ball again, and in 1967 he came through with his MVP season. "I was the first MVP from the islands, so it really meant a lot to me," he says.

He hit only .103 in the Series that year. Given another chance in 1968, he upped his Series average to .250, but this time the Cards bowed to the Detroit Tigers in seven games.

Cepeda had slipped from his MVP season to a mere 16-homer, .248 average in 1968, so the next spring St. Louis shipped him to Atlanta in a swap for catcher-first baseman Joe Torre.

The Baby Bull, who during his career hit two or more home runs in one game 23 times and who had five five-hit games, helped the Braves to the Western Division title in 1969. But despite his .455 average in the playoffs, Atlanta was swept by the New York Mets.

From a .257 average in 1969, Cepeda bounced back with a .305 mark with 34 home runs and 111 RBI in 1970. But it turned out to be his last big season in the majors.

Cepeda spent one more year with the Braves, then was traded to the Oakland A's for pitcher Dennis McLain and cash. He spent most of the season on the disabled list, and got into only three games with the A's.

That winter, the A's released him, and he was signed by the Red Sox. A year as a designated hitter produced a .289 average with 20 homers and 86 RBI. After that season, though, he was sold to the Royals.

Cepeda played in 33 games for the Royals in 1974, but by late spring, with pain pounding unmercifully in his knees, he decided to call it a career.

A year later, however, he was back in the news. He was arrested by Federal agents in the San Juan airport with 160 pounds of marijuana in the trunk of his car. Charged with drug-smuggling, Cepeda wound up in jail, serving 10 months of a five-year sentence.

He avoids talking about the incident now. "It was stupid. I did something wrong, and now it's behind me," he says. "I don't like to talk about it."

Nevertheless, Cepeda clearly feels that his mistake has kept him out of the Hall of Fame. Credentials like his would normally usher a player quickly into the baseball shrine, but so far, Cepeda is still on the outside looking in. It hurts him deeply.

"I think I should be there," he says. "I have the credentials. I think it's very unfair. I paid my dues. What happened is all history."

Cepeda has tried diligently to get back into the good graces of organized baseball. He put in brief stints as a minor league hitting instructor with both the Philadelphia Phillies and the Chicago White Sox. He is a willing participant in old-timers' games. And, after running a baseball school for several years in Puerto Rico, he is doing what he can to share his considerable knowledge of the art of hitting with youngsters in this country.

He runs a baseball camp in California, near where he lives in Burbank. Boys enroll for a solid week of live-in baseball instruction.

"I'm available any time anybody wants me," he says. "I enjoy teaching youngsters. I think I know enough about hitting that I can be helpful to them.

'I faced some of the toughest pitchers in baseball history," he adds. "Nobody was tougher than Juan Marichal, Bob Gibson, Sandy Koufax, Don Drysdale and Jim Bunning. You've got to know I learned something from batting against those guys."

You also have to know that Orlando Cepeda hit those guys and most others pretty well.

Spud Chandler—
Tough Competitor on the Mound

In the long and storied history of the New York Yankees, the team's rich tradition of great hitters has often overshadowed the fact that many heroic pitchers also toiled in the Bronx.

From Pennock to Pipgras, from Gomez to Guidry, the Yankees have been favorably endowed with some of the finest arms ever to grace an American League mound. They are seldom mentioned in the same breath as Ruth, Gehrig or DiMaggio, but in their own ways, they are as much a part of the Yankee legend as their more widely heralded batting brethren.

One of the pitchers who fits snugly into this category was a cagey right-hander who went by the name of Spud Chandler.

Spud (an abbreviation of his real first name of Spurgeon) Chandler was a 6' 0", 180-pound bulldog who came out of the University of Georgia, labored five and one-half years in the minors, then at the not-so-tender age of 29 launched a big league career that took him on a colorful, 11-season journey with the Yankees.

By the time his career ended at age 40, Chandler had rung up a 109-43 record with a 2.84 earned run average in 211 games, and had played on seven pennant winning teams. His .717 career percentage ranks as the highest in major league history for a pitcher with 100 or more decisions.

Chandler, who gave up 1,327 hits, struck out 614 and walked 463 in 1,485 innings, was the American League's Most Valuable Player in 1943. A four-time member of his league's All-Star team, he was a two-time 20-game winner and twice led the league in ERA. His 1.64 ERA in 1943 was the lowest ever recorded by a Yankee hurler, and his 20-4 record that year stands as the 10th best won-lost record in American League history.

Known during his playing days as a pitcher with exceptional tenacity and determination who would begin to study the opposing lineup two days before he was scheduled to pitch, Chandler was a fierce competitor who refused to yield even the slightest margin to the other side.

"I was damned hard to beat," he says when asked to describe himself. "I wasn't about to give in to anybody. And I had a good assortment of pitches and good control.

"I had five pitches altogether," he adds. "I kept developing pitches as I went along. I had a good slider, a good curve, a decent screwball, which I used for a change-up, a forkball and a 90-mile-an-hour fastball. I was able to get all five of those pitches over the plate. That made pitching a lot easier."

Chandler lives in St. Petersburg, Florida. Until retiring in 1984, he was a scout for the Minnesota Twins. A few years back, he had the Twins talked into drafting a young pitcher from nearby Tampa by the name of Dwight Gooden. The Twins elected to take outfielder Kirby Puckett on the first round, and were going to draft Gooden on the second round. The New York Mets, of course, never gave them that chance.

Chandler never gave American League hitters much of a chance, either. During his big league career, he never lost more than eight games in one season. In the 184 games he started, he completed 109 of them, 26 of which were shutouts.

Chandler is ranked sixth on the Yankees' all-time list for career shutouts and ERA. He has the best winning percentage of all the Yankees who ever pitched.

The path that led Chandler to the Yankees was a lengthy one. A three-sport star at the University of Georgia, Spud was a second-team All-American halfback and an excellent punter who was drafted by the New York Giants of the National Football League.

"I was a little bitty skunk, weighing only 160 pounds then," Chandler recalls. "It wasn't a difficult decision to make to choose between football and baseball. Baseball was the game I loved."

Before he graduated with a degree in agriculture, Chandler had been approached by both the Chicago Cubs and St. Louis Cardinals about playing baseball for them.

"I didn't want to sign with them, so I stayed in school," he says. "Eventually, Johnny Nee signed me for the Yankees."

In his first minor league season, Chandler posted a 12-1 record while playing for Springfield and Binghampton. The only game he lost was in 13 innings.

"After that, I went everywhere," he says. "Newark, Syracuse, Minneapolis, Oakland, Portland. Things were going along real well for a while until they started to shift me from one team to another. I never did have another good year in the minors after that first one. But I lived through it."

Chandler spent five full seasons in the minors. After a 14-13 record at Newark in 1936, he was brought up to the Yankees the following year, making the squad as a 29-year-old rookie.

The 1937 Yankees featured five future Hall of Famers, including pitchers Lefty Gomez and Red Ruffing as well as Bill Dickey, Lou Gehrig and Joe DiMaggio. They won the pennant that year by 13 games.

"The first game I pitched, I had a four-hitter, but lost to Thorton Lee and the Chicago White Sox, 1-0." Chandler recalls. "Zeke Bonura hit a

Spud Chandler.

home run in the seventh inning to beat me. After that, I went out and won three straight games.''

Chandler won seven out of 11 decisions, but developed a sore arm and late in the season was sent back to Newark. There, he joined what is generally regarded as the finest minor league team in baseball history. The Bears, with Charley Keller and Joe Gordon leading the way, won the International League pennant by 25 1/2 games, then defeated Kansas City, another Yankee farm club, to win the Junior World Series.

After a 1-2 record at Newark in 1937, Chandler rejoined the Yankees in 1938. He posted a 14-5 record as the Yankees won their third of four straight pennants and World Series'.

It looked like Spud was on his way to becoming one of the better American League pitchers, but a broken ankle, suffered while he was working out during the off-season in 1939, sidetracked his career. Chandler appeared in only 11 games that season, posting a 3-0 record.

The next year, Chandler recorded an 8-7 mark, then followed that with 10-4 and 16-5 logs. The latter, coming in 1942, propelled Chandler into the upper echelon of American League pitchers.

That year, Chandler was the starting and winning pitcher in the American League's 3-1 victory in the All-Star game.

In 1943, Chandler improved on his credentials when he had one of the finest seasons of any pitcher in American League history. Spud won 19 of his first 21 decisions and finished the season with a 20-4 mark. He lost two of his last three decisions, all extra-inning games.

He led the league in wins, ERA (1.64), winning percentage (.833), complete games (20) and shutouts (five). At the end of the season, he not only became only the second pitcher awarded the American League MVP by the Baseball Writers' Association (Lefty Grove was the first), he was named *The Sporting News* Player of the Year. He also won two World Series games, beating the Cardinals, 4-2, with a seven-hitter in the opener and blanking St. Louis, 2-0, on 10 hits in the final game (Chandler had lost a 3-2 decision to the Brooklyn Dodgers in the 1941 Series and a 2-0 verdict to the Cardinals in 1942).

The MVP award turned out to be a bittersweet triumph, Chandler says.

> Naturally, I was very happy to win the award. It was a great honor. Not every player gets that award, so I appreciated it. But the one thing I have always regretted was that I got nothing for winning the MVP—no trophy, no plaque, no nothing. I don't have a single thing to show for it, and I've always wondered why. I know it was during the war, and they were cutting back on a lot of things, but you'd think the league would've done something at some point to recognize the MVP.

Uncle Sam, however, did what the league didn't. He recognized Chandler by sending him a draft notice—even though Spud was 36 years old.

Thus, at the peak of his career, Chandler marched off to join the Army. He missed most of the 1944 and 1945 seasons. But in 1946, he picked up where he left off in 1943 by posting a 20-8 record with a 2.10 ERA.

That year, Chandler almost had a no-hitter for the second time in his career. In 1943, he had pitched a one-hitter against the Washington Senators, giving up just a leadoff double to Ellis Clary. In 1946, Spud had a no-hitter against the Boston Red Sox broken up with one out in the ninth inning when Bobby Doerr slammed a single.

These were two of Chandler's finest games with the arm. He also had a couple of pretty good games with the bat. One in particular occurred in 1940 when he drilled two home runs, including a grand slam, and collected six RBI in a 10-2 victory over the Chicago White Sox.

Chandler was not one of those people to end his baseball career quietly. In his last season in 1947, at the age of 40, he led the league in ERA with a 2.46 while fashioning a 9-5 record. By the end of the season, though, his arm was giving him so much trouble that he decided to retire from the game. His memories, however, have lingered through the years.

"The Yankees were just a great ball club to be on," he recalls. "They always had the right amount of determination, the right spirit and the right desire. Of course, they had ability, too.

"Probably the best team of all the ones I played on," he continues, "was the 1937 team. We had Gehrig, DiMaggio, Rolfe, Crosetti, Lazzeri, Dickey and Henrich. Some of the other clubs were terrific, but this was an awful good club, and we ran away with the pennant (while winning 102 games).

"Gehrig was a great athlete and a great person," Chandler adds. "And Dickey was a terrific player and a good leader. He was always down to earth, never high hat.

"Joe McCarthy was a terrific man and a terrific manager. He demanded respect. If he wanted to call you on the carpet, he'd call you into his office and talk to you privately.

"He never tolerated dissension. The club was like a family, and everything ran smoothly."

As for the opposition, Chandler says he had trouble pitching to "a whole bunch of guys," including Hank Greenberg, Rudy York, Joe Cronin and Rip Radcliff. One he didn't have too much trouble with was Ted Williams.

"I never threw him his pitch," Spud says. "I always threw him change-ups. I struck him out twice on 3-2 pitches with the bases loaded. He was a great hitter, but I had pretty good luck with him."

Chandler also pitched against Joe DiMaggio when both played in the Pacific Coast League in 1935. Spud fared a little differently against his future teammate and one of his later roommates.

"I was at Portland and he was at San Francisco," Chandler remembers. "I never will forget one game I faced him. He hit a home run and a couple of doubles off me. The fourth time he came up, I decided I would deal him a sidearm delivery. He drilled it right through my legs.

"The next day, I said to him, 'Look, you're going up to the Yankees, and I'm a member of the Yankees. I just hope you remember me when I get up there and you get me some runs.' "

Chandler's arrival was a year after DiMaggio's, but by that time, Spud was a grizzled veteran of the pro baseball wars.

"Sometimes I wonder if I had signed as an 18 or 19 year old what would've happened," he muses. "I could have started a lot younger than I did, and that certainly would've changed my record around a bit."

One thing that probably wouldn't have changed was Chandler's record of longevity. Starting with his first year in organized baseball in 1932, he spent more than 50 years in the game as a player, coach, manager and scout.

Chandler managed in the minors for the Cleveland Indians and won three pennants during his tenure as a pilot. He also spent five years as a pitching coach with the Kansas City A's. He served as a full-time scout for the Yankees, Indians and Twins.

While with the Yankees, he wanted to sign Frank Lary and Herb Score, but the front office turned him down. In 1962 with Cleveland, Chandler signed former Yankees' manager Lou Piniella to his first pro contract.

Dick Groat—
A Rare and Gifted Athlete

Thumb through the pages of his career, and it becomes obvious all over again that Dick Groat was a rare and gifted athlete.

Time may have slightly eroded that impression, but a trip back through the record books serves as a perfect reminder. National League batting champion and Most Valuable Player; member of two World Series winners; five-time All-Star shortstop; pro basktetball player; two-time all-American and national scoring champion in college basketball, Groat was an outstanding all-around athlete.

His most noteworthy feats, of course, came in the employ of the Pittsburgh Pirates, a team he served for nine of his 14 big league baseball seasons. Groat was the Bucs' sparkplug and captain; their clutch hitter, a dependable fielder, a smart, unselfish, team player who was the head and heart of some of Pittsburgh's finest teams.

No less an authority than the venerable southpaw, Warren Spahn, once observed that Groat was "the player the Pirates could least afford to lose." Fellow shortstop Alvin Dark claimed that for years, Dick was the "most underrated player in the National League."

In a big league career that also included three seasons with the St. Louis Cardinals, a little more than one year with the Philadelphia Phillies and a few games at the end with the San Francisco Giants, Groat had a lifetime average of .286. He had 2,138 hits, and four times during his career hit .300 or better for the season.

Groat retired in 1967, a year after he and former Pirate teammate Jerry Lynch had designed and built a golf course in Ligonier, Pennsylvania. Since then, the two have continued to run the course, which is rated as one of the five best in western Pennsylvania.

Dick says he works 14 hours a day during the golf season. In the winter, he also works as a manufacturer's rep—he has been in sales for 22 years—and he broadcasts University of Pittsburgh basketball games.

Trim, dapper and as engaging and articulate as he always has been, Groat says he keeps in close touch with ex-Buc teammates such as Bob Friend,

Bill Mazeroski and Elroy Face who, like him, live in the Pittsburgh area. "I don't go to the ballpark very often," he says, "because I'm usually so busy during the summer. But I go to a few old-timers' games."

The father of three grown daughters, one of whom attended James Madison University in Virginia on a golf scholarship, Groat saw an article several years ago that really caught his attention.

"I read an article in the *Wall Street Journal* that said that those plastic statues (Hartlands) that they used to make of players are now worth over $300. Well, I'll tell you something funny. In 1960, they made one of me, and it cost $1.95. One of my aunts went out and bought 20 of them for various members of the family. Would you believe that today there's not a single one left in the family? I don't know where they are, but I can't find a one."

Something else Dick can't find are his two World Series rings. But he knows what happened to them. They were stolen. "Some of the guys at the golf course kept wanting to see them. So, one day, I brought them in, and passed them around while I was tending bar. Somebody left with them."

Groat had won the rings for being in the 1960 Series with the Pirates and the 1964 Series with the Cardinals. In both cases, his team beat the New York Yankees, four games to three.

"They were very similar teams," he recalls. "Both were closely-knit teams. Both lacked power; they never beat themselves; both scrambled a lot, and both had veteran pitchers."

The Pirates-Yankees clash was one of the great World Series' of all-time. Decided in the bottom of the ninth inning of the seventh game when Mazeroski slammed a Ralph Terry pitch for a home run to give the Bucs a 10-9 victory, the Series was the highpoint of Groat's career.

"Watching from the dugout, seeing Maz' ball go over the fence was the greatest thrill I've ever experienced," Groat says. "It was especially thrilling for me, growing up in the Pittsburgh area, playing for the Pirates and then seeing us win our first pennant in 33 years."

Although Mazeroski's home run, as well as Hal Smith's seventh inning three-run homer which had given the Pirates a brief lead, are the blows usually remembered, largely overlooked was Groat's seventh inning, RBI single. The hit, which followed Bill Virdon's famed hopper into Yank shortstop Tony Kubek's throat, was really what lit the fuse for the Bucs' improbable comeback.

It was this kind of key hit, though, that had been the trademark of the whole 1960 season for Groat. Lashing one clutch hit after another, Dick was the force behind the Bucs' pennant-winning drive, the steady man in a lineup that was peppered with good hitters such as Roberto Clemente, Virdon, Dick Stuart, Bob Skinner and Don Hoak.

Groat finished the season winning not only the National League batting championship with a .325 average—the first Pirate to win the title since Deb Garms did it in 1940—but also the league's Most Valuable Player award.

Although he would hit .319 for the 1963 Cardinals while leading the

Dick Groat.

league in doubles, and a year later would collect the highest number of All-Star votes in the league—when he anchored an all-Cardinals starting National League infield—1960 was by far the pinnacle of Groat's career.

Dick had come out of Swissvale in western Pennsylvania in the late 1940s, and blazed a trail through two sports that no individual has ever quite duplicated. At Duke University, he starred in baseball and basketball, earning All-American honors in the latter in his junior and senior years.

He led the nation in scoring as a junior with a then-NCAA one-season record of 831 points (25.2 average). The next year, Groat led the nation in assists, although he was edged for the scoring title by Kansas' Clyde Lovellette.

"When I was eight or nine years old," he recalls, "I wrote down some goals. I wanted to be an All-American basketball player. I wanted to play professional baseball and basketball. And I didn't want to play in the minor leagues.

"Basketball was the sport I played the best and loved the most," he adds. "But my father had a dream that he wanted a son to play major league baseball."

And so in 1952, Groat, who gives much of the credit for his success in basketball to Red Auerbach, who served briefly in the late 1940s as an assistant coach at Duke, signed a $25,000 bonus contract with Branch Rickey and the Pirates. Later in the year, he added his signature to a contract with the Fort Wayne Zollner Pistons.

Groat joined the Pirates in mid-season and immediately became the team's regular shortstop. Although the Bucs lost 112 games that year, Dick hit .284.

That winter, the Pistons flew him back and forth to games from the Duke campus where he had returned to finish his studies. He averaged nearly 12 points per game.

Groat spent the following two years in the Army. When he was discharged in 1954, he decided to stick exclusively with baseball. It was surely the correct decision for Groat.

Over the years, Dick was neither flamboyant nor terribly colorful. He was just amazingly effective. He was especially adept at moving a runner up. And, while not gifted with great speed, he was a sure-fingered shortstop who possessed a trememdous instinct for being where the ball was.

With Mazeroski, Groat formed the third-best (in 1962) and fifth-best (in 1961) single-season, double-play combinations in major league history, the pair participating in 264 and 261 twin-killings during those two years.

Groat also shares the National League record for most years (five) leading the league in double-play participation. On the other side of the ledger, he holds the major league record among shortstops for the most times (six) leading the league in errors.

Dick ranks Bob Gibson, Jim Maloney and Don Drysdale as the toughest pitchers for him to hit. But he always had a respectable batting average. He hit .315 in 1957 and .300 in 1958, and in 1960 had six hits (including three doubles) in one game.

Groat, who says he was "heartbroken" when the Pirates traded him to St. Louis in 1963, hit well right up to the end of his career. In his final regular season, he hit .260 for the 1966 Phillies.

"That was sad, playing on that team," Groat says. "Gene Mauch finally had the club he always wanted. It was filled with top players that the Phillies had picked up—Bill White, Harvey Kuenn, Bob Buhl, Larry Jackson—but they were all over the hill. They all really knew how to play, but they just couldn't do it anymore."

The following year, Dick decided he couldn't do it, either, and he retired, with regret, from baseball. "Till the day I die, I will always respect the game of baseball and what it did for me," he says.

Groat says he sometimes finds it hard to understand the behavior of some of today's players, including those who won't sign autographs or talk with the press. "The game has been too good to too many of us to be abused that way," he says.

"I have nothing but admiration for baseball, and for the way it treated me."

Jackie Jensen—
Football Star Turned Clutch Hitter

Throughout the 1950s, there was no righthanded hitter in the American League who pitchers faced with more trepidation than Jackie Jensen. Powerful yet swift afoot, Jensen could strafe enemy pitchers in a number of different ways, and he did so with remarkable consistency.

He was especially fearsome with men on base, a point that was reflected in the fact that between 1952 and 1959 he averaged more than 100 runs-batted-in per season. In that period, he won the American League RBI title three times (1955, 1958, 1959), the middle year of the three also being a season in which the Boston Red Sox's right fielder was named the Most Valuable Player.

The muscular blond, who broke into the major leagues in 1950 with the New York Yankees, was also an outstanding football player. In 1948 he was an All-American halfback at the University of California and one of the nation's leading rushers.

There were some other features of Jensen's career that were unusual, too. For instance, he was the winning pitcher in the final round of the first College World Series in 1947 beating Yale which, for students of political science, had a first baseman named George Bush.

Jensen was also the only player in the major leagues who played in the outfield with both Joe DiMaggio and Ted Williams. "To me," Jackie recalled, "that was one of the most memorable experiences in my baseball career. It was a wonderful opportunity, playing in the same outfield with those two, especially because they were my boyhood idols."

Jensen, who was interviewed three weeks before his death, had a history of heart trouble. He died suddenly in 1982 at the age of 55 from a massive coronary.

Although his boyhood was spent in San Francisco, Jensen made his home in recent years before his death in Scottsville, Virginia, a small community in the central part of the state. Jensen lived on a 75-acre farm where he and his wife Katherine grew Christmas trees. Jackie also coached baseball and worked as an admissions officer at nearby Fork Union Military Academy. In the summer, he operated a baseball camp there, too.

Jackie Jensen.

The curly-haired Jensen, although not specifically a collector, had some interesting memorabilia.

He had a letter from Ty Cobb in which the Hall of Famer tried to talk Jensen out of his premature retirement in 1960. He also had letters from Frank Lloyd Wright, Frank Sinatra and Dwight Eisenhower, a Joe DiMaggio bat, plus some of his own bats and his Red Sox uniform. Of course, Jensen had his MVP and All-American plaques, a pile of scrapbooks, which he claimed not to have looked at in years, and most of the baseball cards that were issued of him.

One item that Jensen didn't have but wished he did was the original piece of art of a locker room scene done by Norman Rockwell for a *Saturday Evening Post* cover. Jackie, along with Boston teammates Sammy White and Frank Sullivan, went to Rockwell's studio to pose for the illustration (which also included unposed images of Williams and Billy Goodman). The illustration's whereabouts are unknown, according to a Rockwell authority.

Jackie never had much time to search for the piece, anyway. With his various activities, which included keeping himself in extremely good shape, the former slugger maintained a steady pace.

The Jensens, who met in Nevada, moved to Virginia, near Katherine's home, in 1977. "Things are going pretty doggone well here," Jackie said. "We started from scratch when we moved to Virginia, but we've got it pretty well together now."

An extremely articulate and gracious man, Jensen had his share of adversity over the years. Personal problems helped to cut short his baseball career; then at the age of 41, he suffered a heart attack at a time when he was holding five jobs at once.

Jensen, the father of three grown children, had a variety of jobs after leaving the big leagues. For four years, he was the head baseball coach at the University of California. Later, he moved to Nevada where, at one time or another, he owned a golf course, operated a dude ranch, worked at an auto dealership, had a television sports show, was a network color commentator teaming with Keith Jackson to do college football games, worked for the state's economic opportunity office and for four years coached baseball at the University of Nevada-Reno.

Jackie's own baseball playing days in college were spent entirely as a pitcher. "I was a pitcher all through high school and college," he said. "I didn't become an outfielder until I signed a pro contract."

Jensen was a sophomore when he pitched California to the championship of the College World Series. Jackie was named a baseball All-American that season. Six months later, he was named All-American in football while leading California into the 1949 Rose Bowl—a game in which he made a 70-yard touchdown run.

That season, his junior year, Jensen set numerous rushing records for the Golden Bears. Many of them were not broken until Chuck Muncie came along some 25 years later.

Because he had his mind set on a pro baseball career, Jensen decided not to risk injury and to bypass his senior year of football. The decision was not widely applauded by pro football scouts, but it was an easy one for Jensen to make.

"I had no aspirations to play pro football," Jackie remembered. "Baseball was the number one sport in the country, and football hadn't really come around yet. I was only interested in playing professional baseball."

Although the Golden Bears failed to reach the College World Series again while he was in college, Jensen, a speech and rhetoric major as an undergraduate, signed a pro baseball contract with a fraternity brother's father who owned the Oakland Oaks of the Pacific Coast League. It was the first step toward Jackie's becoming one of a small number of college football All-Americans who went on to successful professional baseball careers, joining such players as his Berkeley predecessor Sam Chapman, UCLA's Jackie Robinson and Indiana's Ted Kluszewski.

Jensen hit .261 in his only minor league season. Afterward, the contracts of Jackie and teammate Billy Martin were bought by the New York Yankees.

Jensen joined the Yankees in 1950. He played sparingly over the next two seasons. Then, early in 1952, the Yankees sent him and three other players, including pitcher Frank (Spec) Shea, to the Washington Senators for Irv Noren and Tommy Upton. Casey Stengel would later call it the worst trade the Yankees ever made.

In 1954, Jensen was again swapped, this time to the Red Sox. Over the next six seasons he was one of the steadiest players in a Boston lineup that was bursting with solid performers. In addition to his RBI crowns, Jensen hit .315 in 1956, and he led the league in stolen bases once and in triples once. His finest all-around season came in 1958 when he hit .286, drove in 122 runs, stroked 35 home runs and was named the American League's MVP.

It was during his years with Boston that Jensen became a close friend of Williams. "He and Joe DiMaggio were completely different," Jackie recalled. "Ted was the best hitter, by far. Joe was the best all-around player. They were also very different temperamentally. Joe rarely showed any emotion. Ted let it all hang out, so to speak."

Jensen recalled the time he and Williams played in a golf foursome with Tony Lema, then one of the top pro golfers. "Ted couldn't understand why he couldn't hit the ball as well as Lema. It really bothered him."

Jensen, whose distaste for flying was notorious, retired from baseball following the 1959 season. But after a year's absence, he returned to Boston and played one more season before leaving the big leagues permanently.

Jackie ended his career with a lifetime batting average of .279. In 11 seasons, he hit 199 home runs and collected 929 RBI. He played on three All-Star teams. That number would have been higher, he confided, had he not written to Stengel requesting omission from other All-Star teams because of his desire not to fly.

His premature retirement was one of several regrets Jensen had about his athletic career. "I should have played four or five more years," he lamented. "I should have played football my senior year in college, too. One of my great regrets is not being in the college Hall of Fame. If I'd have played my senior year, I would have been in it.

"Actually," Jensen added, "there are a lot of things I'd like to do over again. For instance, I think the Fenway Park left field wall prevented me from being a better hitter. I was always told to pull the ball to left, and my hitting suffered because of that. I would have been much better off hitting to all fields.

"You can't second guess yourself, though. I gave it the best shot I could.

"I played at a good time," Jensen said. "It was kind of the last of an era. There were great stars then. It's different today. Things have changed— there are different motivations, different economics."

And there are far fewer players, it could be added, who hit with the consistent authority of one Jackie Jensen.

Hal Newhouser—
One of Baseball's Elite Lefties

Among the men who hurl baseballs for a living, no one in the last 40 years has accomplished as much as Hal Newhouser did during a stretch in the mid-1940s.

As stylish as he was talented, the hard-throwing, high-kicking lefthander was the ace of the Detroit Tigers' pitching staff, and one of the premier moundsmen in the American League. During a big league career that covered 15 full seasons and parts of two others, Newhouser had a 207–150 record and an outstanding 3.05 earned run average.

It was during a three-year period between 1944 and 1946, though, that Prince Hal, as he was called, really placed his name among baseball's pitching elite. Over that stretch, Newhouser won 80 games while losing only 27. Name any pitcher in modern times—Feller, Spahn, Roberts, Koufax, Gibson, Carlton—and there isn't one who put together three straight seasons that successfully.

During that period, the 6' 2 ", 180-pounder—whose records were 29–9, 25–9, and 26–9—led the league all three times in wins, and led twice in strikeouts and ERA (1.81 and 1.94). *The Sporting News* chose him major league Player of the Year in 1945 and pitcher on the major league all-star team in all three seasons. And in both 1944 and 1945, he was named the American League's Most Valuable Player, making him the only pitcher in big league history to win consecutive MVP awards (he also ended second in the voting in 1946), and only the second pitcher in major league annals (the other was Walter Johnson) to win the honor twice in a career.

Although he was a 20-game winner only once more after the streak (in 1948 when was 21–12), Newhouser continued to register impressive statistics, winding up the six-year period from 1944 to 1949 with a 136–67 record.

It is a record of which Newhouser is justifiably proud. And the still trim, erudite resident of Bloomfield Hills, Michigan, has some definite feelings about his career, one of which is that if he were pitching today, he would've had an even better record.

"I think I would have won 30 games three years in a row," he says.

"I say this in all modesty, but with the extended seasons and the designated hitter, which allows a pitcher to stay in the game longer, I think I would have done pretty well today."

Since his playing days ended in early 1955, Hal has done pretty well outside of baseball. For more than 20 years, he has worked for a bank in Pontiac, Michigan, where he is vice president in charge of marketing.

"After I retired from baseball, I scouted for the Baltimore Orioles for a while (six years)," he says. "We're the ones who put that club together. Then I scouted for the Cleveland Indians for three years. Eventually, I got tired of all the travel. I joined the bank. I didn't know a thing about banking except how to put it in and how to take it out. But it was the best thing I ever did. I really enjoy being in the business."

Newhouser says that his arm still hurts. "It doesn't bother me when I bowl or play tennis or golf," he asserts. "But I can't throw anything. As soon as I do, it hurts."

Although he has not thrown a baseball in years, Hal has not been forgotten by his legions of fans. He reports that he gets 150 to 200 letters per month. "I have no idea why I get such trememdous amounts of mail," he says. "But some of it is really interesting. A kid will write and ask me how to throw a fastball or curve. I get some cute ones sometimes, too, like the letter that started, 'My great, great grandfather said you were a great pitcher.'

"I'm not that old," Newhouser chuckles.

The smooth southpaw, who has saved a few of his own treasures from the game, including balls, pictures and a 16mm film of the 1945 World Series when the Tigers beat the Chicago Cubs in seven games, says he has been to several baseball card shows in recent years, and has formed some strong opinions about them.

"For one thing," he says, "they should charge the adults and let the kids in free. Also, I don't like the practice of charging for autographs. That's bad. I won't go to any show that does that."

Newhouser will go, he hopes, to the Hall of Fame. But he's no longer holding his breath. In fact, his rejection so far by baseball's shrine is a source of increasing irritation to Hal. And so it should be.

"I never said this before, but I think it's a complete farce," he says of his not having been elected to the Hall. "There's not another pitcher in baseball who won the MVP two years in a row. I won 200 games by the time I was 31. There are fellows in the Hall of Fame who can't compare to what I've done. Yet, I come up blank every year.

"I can't blame anybody," he adds. "But I can't understand it, either. It amazes me. I'm beginning to feel that if I don't get it soon, I'm going to tell the commissioner that I'm just not interested. Give my votes to somebody else. I think the whole thing is asinine, and I'm really losing patience."

The loss is justifiable. Newhouser did just about everything a pitcher

Hal Newhouser.

could do. At one time or another, he led the league in practically every favorable pitching category. Probably his greatest overall season came in 1945 when Hal won the triple crown of pitching, leading the league in wins, strikeouts (212) and ERA. He was also first in shutouts (eight), innings pitched (313), complete games (29) and winning percentage (.735).

Newhouser played in five All-Star games. And, in addition to his many awards, he won two World Series games, including the clinching victory in 1945.

That was one of Hal's most memorable moments in baseball, ranking with winning back-to-back MVP awards and his first 20-win season. Newhouser recalls:

> Getting the last out in a World Series is a thrill that almost can't be explained. You work all spring, then all summer; you battle back and forth and win the pennant on the last day of the season. Then you stand there on the mound and see a ground ball—a big, beautiful high bouncer—hit to our shortstop Skeeter Webb, and he throws to Eddie Mayo to get the force at second and end the game. It accomplishes everything you worked for. When it's over, you're drained. But what a feeling.

The 1945 Tigers, Newhouser claims, weren't graceful, but they had something that today's teams lack.

> We had hitters like Hank Greenberg and Rudy York and pitchers like Virgil Trucks and Dizzy Trout, all on one club. You don't have players like them on one club today. The good players are more scattered now. I'm not knocking the younger players, a lot of them are absolutely as good. But expansion has produced a lot of players who should be in Triple-A. And it has spread out the good players among 26 teams, rather than among just 16 as it was in my time.
>
> When I played, management told us what to do and we couldn't do a thing about it. Today, the players have a union, and things have gone to the other extreme. Somewhere along the line, they've got to settle this thing, and go back to playing baseball.

As a youth, Hal never worried about such things. In fact, growing up in Detroit, he was an avid ice hockey and football player. The son of a gymnastics instructor from Germany, Newhouser also spent long hours as a boy training with his father, one of the reasons, he feels, that he was later so graceful as a pitcher.

Newhouser was a lefthanded shortstop in baseball, and did not start to pitch until he was 15 years old. A self-described "hot-headed kid," he signed a contract with the Tigers at the age of 17, and spent a mere two and one-half months in the minor leagues before joining the parent club at the end of the 1939 campaign.

In his first full season with Detroit, Newhouser posted a 9-9 record, and the Tigers won the American League pennant. During the next three seasons, though, Hal struggled, never winning more than nine games and each year losing more than he won.

Then, from an 8–17 record in 1943, Newhouser suddenly rocketed to a 29–9 mark the following year, becoming, at age 23, the second-youngest pitcher in major league history to win that many games.

"What turned me around," Hal recalls, "is that I got a little older, and I began to do some thinking about my temper. Then Steve O'Neill came in to manage, and he was just like a father. And he brought in Paul Richards to catch, and he helped settle me down.

"I don't like to look back," Hal says, "but maybe if I had not gotten so angry in my early years, I would've done better."

From 1944 to 1950, Newhouser did superbly. But then one day in 1951 he was driving home from a game, his left arm resting on a window ledge of the car. When he want to get out of the vehicle, for some unexplainable reason, Hal could hardly move his arm. And it hurt terribly.

Whatever had occurred, it was, for all practical purposes, the end of Newhouser's pitching career. After two and one-half difficult seasons, the great lefty was released by the Tigers. The next year, despite continuing arm problems, he hooked on with the Indians, rejoining his former teammate, Greenberg, who had become Cleveland's general manager.

"Cleveland needed lefthanded pitching desperately," Newhouser recalls. "So I made an agreement with Greenberg to stay around until Herb Score was ready to be brought up from the minors."

Pitching mostly in relief, Newhouser posted a 7–2 record for a team that set an American League record that still stands of 111 wins (in 154 games) while racing away with the American League pennant.

"That team," Newhouser says, "had the greatest pitching staff ever assembled. I don't know why the media never mentions it. We had Bob Feller, Bob Lemon, Early Wynn and Mike Garcia as starters. Three of them are in the Hall of Fame. We had Don Mossi and Ray Narleski in the bullpen. And we had Art Houtteman and myself. It was a terrific stafff."

Just as terrific, you could say, as the streak one of its members put together almost a decade earlier.

Bobby Shantz—Elfin Southpaw
Was Spectacular in 1952

In 1952, a diminutive lefthanded pitcher with a dazzling curve ball was the toast of the baseball world. He stood no higher than 5'7"—some said it was 5'6"—and no amount of calories could push his weight above 150 pounds.

Viewed from the stands, Bobby Shantz never looked much bigger than the fielder's mitt on his hand. But the elfin southpaw was no pygmy when it came to projecting a baseball. In an era awash with good pitchers, there were times when he could throw as well as anybody.

Shantz spent 16 years in the major leagues. It was during the 1952 season, though, that he reached his crowning achievement in baseball.

Pitching for the Philadelphia Athletics, Shantz posted a 24–7 record, winning virtually one-third of his team's total number of victories (74). Never before—and never since—had a hurler of such short stature had such a magnificent season in the big leagues.

And Shantz didn't even pitch the full season. With three weeks remaining, his left wrist was broken by a Walt Masterson fastball. No matter. Bobby was voted the American League's Most Valuable Player, an honor that going back to its origin in 1911 had previously been claimed in the American League by only four other pitchers—Hal Newhouser (twice), Spud Chandler, Lefty Grove and Walter Johnson (twice).

That wasn't all there was to 1952 for Shantz, either. In the All-Star game that year, played at Philadelphia's Shibe Park, Shantz relieved Bob Lemon in the fourth inning and struck out the side, fanning Whitey Lockman, Jackie Robinson and Stan Musial. Subsequently, the game was rained out in the next inning before Shantz could take the mound again, enabling the home team National League to steal off with a 3–2 victory.

The rain that day may have denied Shantz a special place in baseball history, but overall, the 1952 season was one that neither Shantz nor A's fans of that era ever have difficulty recalling.

"It was just one of those years when everything went right," Shantz recalls. "The A's had the best doubleplay combination in the league in Eddie

Bobby Shantz.

Joost and Pete Suder. It seemed like every time the ball was hit, it went right to one of them.''

Bobby has vivid memories of the All-Star game. Although he had been a member of the American League team the previous year, the 1952 game represented his first All-Star appearance. "I was nervous as hell," he says. "I was just trying to throw strikes. Fortunately, I was able to do that.''

Shantz did a lot more that season—leading the league in wins and in won-lost percentage (.774) while working 280 innings in 33 games and logging a 2.48 ERA. It was a season that few would have predicted a couple of years earlier.

Shantz had a fairly undistinguished record in his first two big league seasons of 1949 and 1950. Then in 1951 he came forward with an 18–10 mark, laying the groundwork for what would take place the following year.

"In 1951, I could feel it coming," Shantz says. "Maybe I was learning how to pitch; learning to change speeds, to throw to spots and to keep the hitters off balance. Whatever it was, it seemed to carry over into 1952.''

Unfortunately, Bobby never had another season like the 1952 one. The broken wrist, he feels, seemed to affect his ability to throw the sharp curves that were his bread-and-butter pitches, and, perhaps because he tried to compensate, he developed arm trouble and worked in only 18 games over the next two years.

By the time the arm recovered, the A's had given up in Philadelphia and moved to Kansas City. After two seasons there, Shantz was traded to the New York Yankees as part of a nine-player deal.

Shantz got a reprieve on his career in New York. In 1957—his first season as a Yankee—Bobby posted an 11–5 record, led the league in ERA (2.45), was named to his third All-Star team, and played in his first (of two) World Series.

Thereafter, Shantz toiled mostly out of the bullpen, pitching through the 1960 season with the Yankees, then moving on to a series of stops in the National League at Pittsburgh, Houston, St. Louis, Chicago, and Philadelphia.

His last season was 1964, part of which was spent with the Phillies as they frittered away the National League pennant. By then, Bobby recalls, his arm was so sore that he needed daily injections. Although he was offered a contract for the next season, he turned it down.

"I hated to quit," he says. "But I just couldn't throw anymore. I was in real pain. In fact, my arm still hurts.''

For his career, Shantz wound up with a 119–99 record, pitching in 537 games (171 as a starter) and posting a 3.38 ERA. In 1,935 innings, he gave up 1,795 hits, struck out 1,072 and walked 643. As a starter, Bobby hurled 15 shutouts, and as a reliever he registered 48 saves.

Shantz, whose brother Wilmer played briefly in the big leagues as a catcher, also won eight Gold Glove awards.

It was a pretty nice career for a guy who was not only dwarfed by most big league pitchers, but who hadn't even been a pitcher until he was well out of high school.

Shantz, who grew up in a little town just outside of Pottstown, Pennsylvania, was a 4' 11" outfielder in high school. He was still an outfielder when he played in a semipro league in Philadelphia where his family had moved.

"I used to pitch batting practice," Shantz remembers. "The manager saw the way I was throwing, and got me started as a pitcher. Then the A's signed me when I was 21 years old."

At the time, Bobby was working in a saw mill, earning 73 cents an hour. "It was a terrible job," he says. "But I didn't think I could play in the big leagues. My dad had to talk me into going."

In 1948, his first and only season in the minors, Shantz stood the Western League on its ear, fashioning an 18-7 record and leading the circuit in wins and strikeouts. That was enough for the A's. Connie Mack, despite his penchant for pitchers who were big, strong and could throw hard, brought Bobby to the big team the following season.

"It was a shot in the dark for me," Shantz says. "I never had any idea I would be able to stick with the A's. They had a great pitching staff—Dick Fowler, Alex Kellner, Lou Brissie, Joe Coleman, Phil Marchildon, Carl Scheib. I was very skeptical about making the team.

"When I got to spring training, I saw all those big guys. They were all way over six-feet tall. I wondered what I was doing there. But then I saw them pitch, and they couldn't throw any better than me."

Shantz pitched one of his most memorable games in his first season with the A's. In a game against the Detroit Tigers, Bobby came in from the bullpen in relief of Scheib in the third inning, and pitched no-hit ball for the next nine innings. Although he gave up two hits in the bottom of the 13th, a home run by Wally Moses in the top of the inning gave Shantz a 5-4 win. Bobby recalls:

> The best game I ever pitched, though, was in 1951 in Yankee Stadium. We won, 2-1, in 14 innings. Micky Mantle hit a home run in the seventh to tie the score. In the bottom of the 14th, after we had taken the lead, I got the first two batters out. Then Mantle hit a line drive that hit the top of one of those field-level scoreboards. One umpire signaled home run, but he was overruled and Mantle was given a double. Then I got Yogi Berra for the last out.

As tough as Mantle was to pitch to, Shantz says the hitter he feared the most was Ted Williams. "I had pretty good success against him, but I had fear in me every time he walked to the plate," Bobby says. "Hank Aaron and Willie Mays were that way in the National League, which I always thought had tougher hitters than the American League."

During his career, Shantz played for three of the game's top managers— Mack, Casey Stengel and Gene Mauch. He gives the nod for best manager of the three to Mauch.

"Mr. Mack was a real nice man," Shantz states. "He never said much. Stengel was a good manager, but he had real good coaches and real good players. But I always felt that Mauch was the best baseball man. He had a little trouble with some guys, but nobody in baseball was, or is, as smart as that guy. And he'd do anything to win, too."

Playing for Mauch was an enjoyable experience for the personable Shantz. But then, so was mostly everything else during his big league days. "I enjoyed every minute of my career," Bobby says. "In fact, I'd like to go back and do it all over again—all 16 years of it, and even for the same money."

Shantz mentions that his top salary as a player was $25,000. In his big year in 1952, he earned $12,000, which was $5,000 more than he had been paid the previous season.

"I never made a lot of money," he says. "But I feel like I was the luckiest guy in the world. Playing big league baseball was the best thing that ever happened to me."

Today, Bobby looks trim enough to be ready to step out on the mound tomorrow. He hasn't seen a major league game in six or seven years, but he occasionally attends old-timers' games. And once in a while, he makes a guest appearance at a card show.

"I love those shows," he says. "I've been to a few of them, but I wish I could get asked to do one every week. I'd be glad to do it."

Shantz lost much of his personal collection of baseball memorabilia in a house fire a number of years ago. What remains is displayed at the Bull Pen, a dairy bar and restaurant that he's owned for the last 20 years in Chalfont, Pennsylvania.

Bobby, the father of four children, also used to own a bowling alley with former A's catcher Joe Astroth. After buying out his partner some years back, Shantz sold the establishment several years ago.

Bobby keeps a busy schedule. He plays golf nearly every day, all year long. He's a high 70s, low 80s shooter. In the mornings and evenings, he is usually at the Bull Pen, working hard, enjoying life, just as he always has done.

Bucky Walters—
Switch to the Mound Paid Off

The pathways of baseball are littered with stories of players who switched from one position to another. Some did it successfully, while others simply demonstrated the art of futility.

A classic example of the former was Bucky Walters. Originally an infielder, Walters was converted into a pitcher after reaching the major leagues. Ultimately, he became one of the top hurlers in the National League in the late 1930s and early 1940s.

Walters was a three-time 20-game winner for the Cincinnati Reds, and the National League's Most Valuable Player in 1939. Altogether, he won 198 games and played in 19 seasons, far more than he would have had he continued to pursue his livelihood as a third baseman.

Bucky was an outstanding sandlot infielder in his native Philadelphia when he signed a minor league contract in 1929. At the time, he was also a prominent semipro basketball player, earning as much as $150 a week playing in a league operated by Eddie Gottlieb, who would become the owner of the Philadelphia Warriors and one of the founders of the National Basketball Association.

The 6' 1" Walters, who still lives in the Philadelphia area, spent five seasons in the minors, playing mostly at third base. He was an outstanding defensive player, a skill that would later earn him the reputation as the Reds' "fifth infielder."

He was a good hitter, too. In 1931, he hit .326 while playing for Williamsport, a team managed by Glenn Killinger, later the legendary football coach at West Chester (Pennsylvania) State College. Two seasons after that, he hit .376 for San Francisco in the Pacific Coast League.

Because he had a strong arm, Walters pitched in 16 games in 1929 at High Point, North Carolina. "But I only did it to help out," he recalls. "I didn't give any serious thought to pitching."

Walters didn't pitch again in the minors. Nor did he pitch in partial seasons in the early 1930s with the Boston Braves and Boston Red Sox.

In 1934, the Red Sox sold Walters to the Philadelphia Phillies. That year, he was the club's regular third baseman, and hit .260. Toward the end of the season, manager Jimmie Wilson had Bucky pitch in two games.

That was enough to convince Wilson that his third baseman might really be a pitcher. The manager, also one of the team's catchers and an astute handler of pitchers, pursuaded Walters to give it a try. "Before I'm through with you, you'll be one of the best in the game," Wilson told his new moundsman.

"It looked like I wasn't going to make it as a third baseman," Walters recalls. "I wasn't hitting that well. Wilson asked me to try pitching because he thought I could do better there. It was either that or head back to the minors.

"I had a pretty good arm. I wasn't as fast as Grove or Feller, but I could throw a pretty good sinker. So I took the gamble.

"As it turned out, the switch wasn't that hard. I knew where I had to throw the ball. I used to pay attention at the team meetings, and I knew what the hitters liked and didn't like."

The conversion began in earnest in spring training of 1935. At first, Bucky had trouble with his control. In one of his early outings, he was so wild that he was lifted because Wilson feared an opposing hitter might get hurt.

The manager, though, stuck with his new pitcher, even offering a case of champagne to Bucky if he made the transition successfully. That summer, Walters worked into the regular rotation, and posted a 9-9 record in 24 games.

The following season, Walters led the league in losses while posting an 11-21 record for the last place Phillies. He was 14-15 in 1937, and was chosen for the National League All-Star team, his first of five such selections.

All the while, Bucky was filling in occasionally as an outfielder or infielder. He pitched, for example, in 37 games in 1937, but also played in eight games at third base, subbing for Pinky Whitney after he was injured.

In those days, the Phillies were regular occupants of the National League's lowest levels, and they played in a decrepit old bandbox known as Baker Bowl. There were three constants: losses, pop flies over or against a right field wall that stood just 280 feet from home plate, and the eventual departure of good players through trades.

Walters was liberated in 1938 in a swap that sent him to the Reds. "I didn't really want to go," he says. "But it turned out pretty well for me."

A year after his arrival in Cincinnati, Bucky—teaming with Paul Derringer to win 52 games—filed a 27-11 record while leading the league in victories, earned run average, strikeouts, games started, complete games and innings pitched. He won the MVP award, the second of three Reds (Ernie Lombardi and Frank McCormick were the others) to win the honor in consecutive years.

The following season, Walters had a 22-10 mark, and led the league in wins, ERA, complete games and innings. The Reds won their second

Bucky Walters.

straight pennant, and Bucky's two victories—including the opening game victory—helped them beat the Detroit Tigers in the World Series.

At the end of the season, Walters was third in the sportswriters' balloting for the nation's Top Athlete of the Year, placing behind Tommy Harmon and Hank Greenberg and ahead of Ben Hogan, Cornelius Warmerdam, Bryon Nelson and Sammy Baugh.

Walters was 19–15 in 1941 as the Reds slipped to third place. He won 15 in each of the next two years, then, at the age of 35, came back with a 23–8 mark in 1944. That year, an eighth-inning single by Connie Ryan robbed Bucky of his closest bid for a no-hitter.

Bucky worked three more full seasons. During the 1948 campaign, he was named manager of the Reds, and retired as a pitcher, although he returned to work in one game in 1950 for the Braves.

He finished with a 198–160 career record with a 3.30 ERA in 428 games. In 3,104.2 innings, Walters struck out 1,107 and walked 1,121 while allowing 2,990 hits.

"Half those walks were intentional," he says. "If a guy bothered me too much, I'd just walk him."

Always a good-hitting pitcher, Walters had a lifetime batting average of .243, which included a .325 mark in 1939. He hit 23 home runs.

"I would rather have played every day," he suggests. "That's why I always played the infield during batting practice. The management didn't like it too much, but I wanted to keep busy, and it also kept me sharp as a fielder."

An engaging conversationalist, Walters tells some fascinating stories about his days as a player. He recalls how in 1930 he reported to spring training with the Providence, Rhode Island team in none other than Providence, Rhode Island. "The depression was on," he says. "Clubs, even whole leagues, were disbanding all over the country. You were lucky just to hang on."

Walters doesn't remember autographs being a popular commodity during his playing days. "Very few people asked for them," he says. "About the only place where they ever went after autographs was in Brooklyn. When you'd get off the subway, kids would follow you to the ballpark and ask for autographs. Usually, you were all dressed up, and invariably somebody would hand you a leaky pen, and the ink would get on your suit."

The ex-pitcher says he has saved hardly anything from his playing days. He has a warmup jacket from 1940 hanging in the closet. "I used to have part of a uniform and another jacket, but some guy came to the house a few years ago, and I gave them to him. They were moth-eaten and just hanging there. I didn't pay much attention to them."

The uniform, though, did suggest to Bucky just how far players' livery has come. "I compared my old uniform to the new ones. My God, the old one was like a horse blanket. I couldn't believe there was so much difference."

Walters also cites the difference between the old and new stadiums. "The new ones all look like Disneyland," he says. "I don't even go to games anymore because you wind up having to park your car three miles from the gate."

A member of the Ohio Hall of Fame, Walters sold industrial supplies after leaving baseball. He also became a prominent golfer in Philadelphia amateur circles. Bucky retired from his sales job 15 years ago.

While he was still in baseball, Walters managed the Reds until late in the 1949 season. When he was replaced, his team was in seventh place, the same spot in which it had finished the year before.

"I didn't like managing," he says. "At first, I thought I would. But it was too much. I was glad to get out."

Walters spent the 1950 and 1951 seasons as the pitching coach of the Boston Braves. "Of course, how the hell are you going to coach Spahn and Sain?" he muses.

He returned to managing in 1952, leading the Milwaukee Brewers— with Wally Post, Bill Bruton, George Crowe and Gene Mauch—to the American Association pennant. Then he stayed in Milwaukee to become the newly arrived Braves' pitching coach again for the next three seasons. He was the pitching coach of the New York Giants in 1956-57, then, deciding not to go west to San Francisco, joined the Phillies as a minor league pitching instructor. Bucky left baseball after the 1958 season.

Walters' career spanned nearly 30 years in the professional ranks. His best moments, of course, came when he was playing.

Three events in particular stand out: the sixth game of the 1940 World

Bucky Walters (second from right) was the pitching ace of the 1940 Cincinnati Reds. Other key Reds were (from left) Jim Turner, Bill Werber, Jimmy Ripple, Gene Thompson, Ival Goodman and Frank McCormick.

Series when his home run and shutout pitching beat Detroit, 4–0; a game with the San Francisco Missions in 1933 in which he had five straight doubles and seven hits in seven at-bats during a doubleheader watched by Eddie Collins, who afterward signed him to a Red Sox contract; and a shutout victory in 1935 over the Gashouse Gang, the defending World Champion St. Louis Cardinals.

Bucky rates Phil Cavarretta, Rip Collins and especially Joe Medwick as the toughest hitters he faced. "Medwick was a great hitter," he says. "He hit them off his shoe tops, off his kneecaps and over his head."

"Actually," Walters qualifies, "everybody always thinks it was the big hitters who gave us pitchers the most trouble. It wasn't them as much as it was those damned 'taperitas' hitters like Stan Hack. They're the ones who'd really get you in trouble."

Men of Special Distinction

Larry Doby—
American League's First Black Player

  "I feel that those of us who are in a position to do something for other people, ought to."

The person who made that assessment is a reserved, soft-spoken man who has contributed much of himself to the betterment of the human race.

Larry Doby was an outstanding baseball player in his day—a two-time American League home run champion, owner of a .283 lifetime batting average, and a superb center fielder.

But his special place in history was assured with neither bat nor glove. By merely entering the lineup for the Cleveland Indians in the second game of a doubleheader with the Chicago White Sox in August, 1947, Doby became the first black man to play in the American League.

That was the start of Doby's contributions to mankind, and his efforts have continued to this day with Larry now working to improve the lives of inner-city youth through basketball.

Basketball? Doby is Director of Community Affairs for the New Jersey Nets of the National Basketball Association, the only team in the league with such a position. One of Larry's jobs is to assemble basketball programs and leagues for junior high school boys in the inner-city areas of the north Jersey cities of Newark, Jersey City and Paterson. More than 1,000 boys participate in the program.

In a conversation, the sensitivity and quiet dignity of the man is particularly evident as he describes his interest in helping others.

"I never thought I'd be in a position like this where I could help so many kids," he says, "particularly the way the world is today. It's a great feeling. I wouldn't trade it for anything."

Doby, who joined the Nets in 1982, says that his program stresses the importance of academics and discipline. "We have summer camps, we give lectures, particularly on why not to get involved with drugs and alcohol. I'm given a great deal of responsibility. It's a good program, and I have seen some very positive changes in some of the kids."

Doby, of course, knows first-hand about positive change. As a skinny,

22-year-old, he pioneered his race's entry into the American League after signing a contract with Indians' owner, Bill Veeck.

As considerable a feat as that was, it is often overlooked in the rush to celebrate the major league's first black player, Jackie Robinson. Yet, although it was seldom mentioned then and is rarely discussed today, Doby had all of the same problems and encountered all of the same abuses as Robinson.

"The only difference is that Jackie Robinson got all of the publicity," Doby says. "You didn't hear much about what I was going through because the media didn't want to repeat the same story. My experiences weren't newsworthy anymore because they'd already been reported with Jackie."

Doby's experiences, however, often were unpleasant. He was, as was Veeck, assailed by opposing players, owners and fans. It was a situation that the frightened and lonely youngster found extremely confusing.

"I grew up in a neighborhood of mixed groups. There were Italians, Jews, Blacks all living together," says Doby, who was born in Camden, South Carolina, but grew up in Paterson, New Jersey. "As a kid, you never thought about what you were. If I had been younger when I came up, I wouldn't have been mature enough to deal with some of the things I faced. Fortunately, I was just old enough to have the ability to be able to adjust and deal with the situations.

"Of course, I couldn't react to those situations from a physical standpoint," Doby adds. "My reaction was to hit the ball as far as I could."

After a shaky start, Doby did that with increasing frequency. In his first season, Larry, who had no minor league experience although he had played in the Negro National League, got into 29 games, hitting .156.

Originally, Doby was an infielder, playing first base, second base and shortstop during the 1947 season. At the start of his second season, he was converted to an outfielder. Although his defense needed several years of polishing before Doby became one of the top fielding center fielders in the league, his hitting perked up as soon as he became a regular.

In 1948, playing on a star-studded Cleveland team, the lefthanded power hitter compiled a .301 average, helping the Indians to the American League pennant. That fall, Larry hit .318 as the Indians downed the Boston Braves in the World Series, four games to two.

Doby's 410-foot home run off of Johnny Sain in the fourth game gave Steve Gromek and the Indians a 2–1 win, and a 3–1 lead in the Series. The blast provided Larry with one of the top thrills of his career.

"The thing that was especially satisfying to me." Larry says, "was the picture that ran the next day in newspapers all over the country. It showed Gromek and me in a tremendous embrace. A white guy and a black guy. It was just like when we were high school kids and would hug each other after we won. I got a big kick out of that picture.

"I often think about the '48 World Series," Doby adds. "It was such a thrill for me to play in it. I look at so many guys who never had that opportunity, and I think how fortunate I was."

Larry Doby.

Doby was fortunate enough to have played in the 1954 Series, too. He and catcher Jim Hegan were the only Indian starters remaining from the 1948 team. In 1954, however, Cleveland went down in four games to the New York Giants in a Series that was noteworthy mainly because of the pinch-hitting exploits of Dusty Rhodes and Willie Mays' spectacular catch of Vic Wertz's 460-foot drive to deep center field.

Probably the finest overall season for Doby occurred in 1950 when he hit .326 with 25 home runs, 102 RBI and 110 runs scored. At a time when great center fielders were in abundance, he was named that year the major league All-Star center fielder by *The Sporting News.*

Larry also put together outstanding seasons in 1952 and 1954, leading the league in home runs in both years with 32 each time. He led the league in runs (104) and slugging percentage (.541) in 1952, and RBI (126) in 1954. Five times during his career he drove in more than 100 runs.

In the late-40s, Doby anchored a stellar outfield which had Dale Mitchell in left and usually Bob Kennedy in right. In the mid-50s, his outfield running mates were Minnie Minoso and Rocky Colavito.

Doby was swapped to the Chicago White Sox in 1956 for Chico Carrasquel and Jim Busby. Two years later, he was shipped to the Baltimore Orioles during the winter and then back to the Indians before the season began. In 1959, the Tribe traded Doby to the Detroit Tigers, who that same season sold him to the White Sox.

Doby finished his major league career in 1959, although he played several more years in Japan. In his 13-year career, Larry had 1,515 hits, including 253 home runs. He drove in 969 runs and scored 960 times. He also wound up with a highly commendable lifetime fielding average of .984.

Doby, a member of six American League All-Star teams, regrets that he has few treasures from his playing days. His most cherished items are his 1948 uniform and a picture of that Lou Boudreau-managed team.

"I never thought during my playing days that such items would get to be that important," he says. "So, I didn't save anything."

After his career ended, Doby owned a tavern and restaurant for five years. Then he took a job as director of traffic safety in a north Jersey city. In 1968, he returned to baseball with the Montreal Expos.

Over the next five seasons he held positions as scout, minor league instructor and coach with the Expos. Later, he served as coach with the Indians, Expos again and White Sox.

In mid-season in 1978, Doby was named manager of the White Sox. Relieved of his duties at the end of that season, he decided it was time to leave baseball for good.

"I thought it was best to get away from the game because I was becoming a little bitter," he says. "That wasn't good; once you become bitter, you can't function.

"Now, I find it much more comfortable," he adds, "to look at the situation (baseball) from the outside."

Larry looks back on his playing career, and particularly his crusading efforts as a black player, with a great deal of pride.

"It gives me a real sense of satisfaction, a real feeling of pride to know what I accomplished," he says. "As a player, I had good years and bad years. But overall, I enjoyed my career very much.

"Baseball has been good to me. Without baseball I wouldn't have gone to a lot of places that I went. It gave my family and me an experience we never would've had any other way."

Doby, who attended Long Island University before becoming a professional baseball player, says that the game gave him the opportunity to far surpass his goals as a youth.

"My ambition when I got out of high school was to be a high school coach." he says. "Baseball broadened my scope. I learned about different places. And I learned about different people. Playing was one of the great things that happened to me."

Don Larsen—
Perfect Game Pitcher

There are many significant dates in sports history. But October 8, 1956 stands in a class by itself.

It is a date when everyone who was a sports fan then remembers where he was that day. It is a date when the sports world, indeed most of the nation, came to a stop to follow the event that was unfolding.

On that date, an angular, fun-loving, 27-year-old righthander named Don Larsen pitched the greatest game in baseball history.

With a nationwide audience riveted to radios and television sets, and with 64,619 fans watching hysterically at Yankee Stadium in New York, Larsen pitched a perfect game in the fifth game of the World Series, hurling the Yankees to a 2-0 victory over the Brooklyn Dodgers.

It was the only perfect game ever pitched in a World Series, and the first perfect game in the major leagues in 34 years.

Larsen used 97 pitches, striking out seven, including pinch-hitter Dale Mitchell on a called third strike to end the game.

The feat, probably the greatest single achievement in all of sports history, was especially astounding not only because it came amid the normally heavy pressure of a World Series when the spotlight glares the brightest, but also because it came against a team that had one of the heaviest-hitting lineups ever to take a baseball field.

It was a lineup that included four future Hall of Famers (Jackie Robinson, Pee Wee Reese, Duke Snider and Roy Campanella), plus three other outstanding hitters (Gil Hodges, Carl Furillo and Jim Gilliam). What's more, the opposing pitcher was the venerable Sal Maglie, who that day pitched a distinguished game himself with a five-hitter.

Larsen had also been the starting pitcher in the second game of the Series, but had been knocked out in the second inning, in the process losing a 6–0 Yankee lead by dishing out one hit, four walks and four runs.

It had been such an ineffective performance that Larsen wasn't sure he'd even pitch in the Series again.

"I didn't know I was going to start the fifth game until I got to the

Don Larsen.

ballpark that day," Larsen remembers. "Casey (Stengel) told me, and I went
out and warmed up. I knew I had good stuff.

"During the game, I was making a lot of good pitches. But the main
difference between the second and the fifth games was my control. I never
had such good control in my life. In fact, I can't recall ever pitching another
game without walking a batter."

Larsen still thinks often about the game that made him an instant hero
with guaranteed recognition for the rest of his life.

He lives in San Jose, California now, a salesman for a multi-product
company, and often appears at old-timers' games around the country.

Larsen has lived in the San Jose area for the last 19 years, prior to which
he lived in San Diego. A native of Michigan City, Indiana, he had moved
as a child to San Diego, and grew up there.

Although people don't make quite as big a fuss over him as they once
did, Larsen is still a fellow who enjoys life and the status that his famous
game has brought him. And his mind is never far from that game.

"Sometimes, I can be driving along, and I'll start thinking about the
game," he says. "I still go over the game in my mind quite often. I'll think
of certain hitters I faced, and the way I pitched to them. Of course, I'll never
forget the end when Yogi (Berra) came running out and jumped into my
arms. By then, the whole place was sheer bedlam.

"When Yogi jumped on me," he adds, "my mind just went blank.
Earlier in the game, though, I had been very conscious of what was happening. But I never realized I was pitching a perfect game. I knew it was a no-
hitter, but I didn't know it was a perfect game.

"On the bench, nobody would talk to me. That made me really nervous. The only time I felt comfortable was out on the mound.

"Finally, in the seventh inning, I looked up at the scoreboard, and I
said to Mantle, 'Hey, Mick, only two more innings to go.' I thought when
I said that he was going to pass out. He looked like he'd just seen a ghost."

Larsen says that he threw mostly fastballs and hard sliders during the
game. He recalls going to three balls on only one batter—Reese, the Dodger
shortstop.

"I threw a few slow curves to Robinson," he says. "But most of the
time, I threw hard stuff. I shook Yogi off once or twice on signs, but that
was only to throw the hitters off. I came back each time with the same pitch."

The Dodgers may have been needling Larsen during the game—they
were a team that was good at such tactics—but if they were, Larsen was
oblivious to it.

"If they were on me, I didn't know about it," Don says. "The only
thing I was paying attention to was their hitters. They had some great hitters on that team, and I was just trying to get them out."

Larsen was helped in that respect by some sparkling plays in the field
by his teammates.

"The best one was on the ball Robinson hit to Andy Carey at third,"

Larsen says. "It was a hard shot, and it hit off of Carey's glove and over to Gil McDougald at short. Gil threw to first to get the out.

"The long flyball that Hodges hit probably would've been a home run in any other park," he adds. "But Mantle chased it down, and made a great catch. (Sandy) Amoros also hit a ball that I thought might get out of the park, but it went foul by a foot and a half."

As the game wore on, the crowd became more and more tense. So did Larsen's teammates. But Don swears he was able to remain calm.

"I wasn't really nervous," he says. "By the time Mitchell came up, though, I was pretty pumped up. He was a helluva hitter. I said to myself, 'You've come this far, so you better get this last one.'

"The first pitch was a ball. Then I threw him a strike. He fouled off the next pitch. I was throwing him nothing but fastballs. Finally—and the crowd was going crazy by now—he took a little half-swing for the third strike, and all hell broke loose."

Fans and players alike tumbled out onto the field in a frenzied dash to Larsen. What followed was one of the wildest celebrations ever to take place on an athletic field.

"And we hadn't even won the World Series, yet," Larsen muses. "It took us two more games to do that."

The story of Don Larsen's career did not, of course, start and end with that one brilliant game in 1956. There was much more to his 14-year stay in the big leagues.

It was a stay that began with the St. Louis Browns in 1953 and ended with the Chicago Cubs in 1967. In between, Larsen pitched for the Baltimore Orioles, Yankees, Kansas City A's, Chicago White Sox, San Francisco Giants and Houston Astros.

Don had a career record of 81–91 with a respectable 3.78 earned run average. He worked 1,548 innings in 412 games, giving up 1,442 hits, striking out 849 and walking 725.

Along the way, the 6' 4", 215-pound righthander was a colorful performer who enjoyed having fun and who pitched in some other pretty big games.

In 1955, he beat the Boston Red Sox in Fenway Park on the next to last day of the season to give the Yankees the American League pennant. Coming down the stretch in September, 1956, he hurled four consecutive four-hitters to lead the Yanks to another flag.

Larsen also won three other World Series games. In 1957, he pitched seven and one-third innings of relief to get the win in a 12–3 decision over the Milwaukee Braves. The following year, he tossed seven shutout innings to beat the Braves, 4–0. And in 1962, while working for the Giants, he earned a decision in relief in a 7–3 triumph over the Yankees.

Originally, Larsen had signed in 1947 with the Browns as a 17-year-old, who in high school had been more noted for his basketball exploits than for his baseball talent.

"I didn't really pitch that much in high school," he says. "I was a better basketball player. But I started to pitch a lot in a semipro league, and that's when the Browns saw me. I signed with them because I figured if I was going to do anything I could do it with the Browns."

After spending time in both the minors and the military service, Larsen finally arrived in St. Louis in 1953. It was the Browns' last year in baseball.

"I loved that year," says Larsen. "Satchell Paige was with us. What a character he was. And he knew so much about pitching. We also had Bob Elliott, Virgil Trucks, Vic Wertz and Dick Kokos—we even had Tom Lasorda for a while.

"We had a fair club, but we didn't draw anybody. We were just trying to survive. St. Louis just wasn't an American League town. Bill Veeck, our owner, tried everything he could think of. He was a great man. I think he did as much for baseball as anybody.

"But it was sad. Sometimes we had as few as 300 or 400 people in the stands. The only option was to move the team to Baltimore. I was disappointed when the club was sold, but it was exciting, going to a new place."

In 1954, the St. Louis Browns became the Baltimore Orioles, and Larsen, with Bob Turley and Joe Coleman, was ticketed as one of the club's top pitchers. That year, however, as the Orioles lost 100 games, Larsen finished the season with an unflattering 3–21 record, leading the league in losses.

Before the next season, Larsen, Turley and others were sent to the Yankees in an 18-player trade that brought, among others, Gene Woodling, Gus Triandos, and Willie Miranda to the Orioles. It was the biggest trade in baseball history.

"I don't even remember all the players who were involved," Larsen says. "I do remember that I had an awful year, and if I hadn't had that record, I probably wouldn't have been traded. But I think Jim Turner (Yankees' pitching coach) spotted something about me that he liked, and he got the Yankees interested in me.

"When I joined the Yankees," Larsen continues, "I didn't know how to take it. Here were guys like Mickey and Yogi who had been my idols. Now, I was on the same team with them."

By his own admission, Larsen reported to spring training in 1955 in less than peak condition. As a result, the Yankees soon sent him to Denver of the American Association where he not only posted a 9–1 record, but hit .360 with 10 home runs. The Yanks recalled him at mid-season, and Don went on to post a 9–2 mark the rest of the way.

Larsen did not appear in the 1955 World Series as the Yankees lost to the Dodgers, four games to three. Little could anybody predict at the time what lay ahead for the big hurler.

The eventful season of 1956 got off to a turbulent start in spring training when Larsen crashed his car into a telephone pole at 4 a.m. When asked what his pitcher was doing out at that time of the morning, Yankee manager Casey Stengel playfully told reporters that Don was merely "mailing a letter."

"I was just very tired, and fell asleep at the wheel," Larsen explains. "I hadn't been partying, like they said at the time. The thing that really made me mad was that I cracked up my beautiful new Olds convertible."

Larsen survived the crash and spring training to take his place as one of the top hurlers on the Yankees' staff. His performance was aided by another strange quirk—Don's mid-season decision to eliminate a full wind-up, and convert to what was basically a no-windup delivery.

"I wasn't doing that well. I had something like a 7–4 record at the time," Larsen remembers. "So I asked Turner if I could try something new. He said, 'As long as you win, I don't care what you do.' "

Larsen caught everybody by surprise in the first game that he trotted out his new delivery.

"Nobody knew that I was going to pitch that way," he says. "Not even Turner or Yogi knew. When I made my first pitch, the outfielders weren't even set. But I figured if I could deliver the ball a little quicker, the opposing team couldn't pick out my flaws and get the message to the hitters in time. It worked, and I had everybody screwed up.

"I think it kept the hitters a little off balance," he adds. "You need every advantage you can get when you're pitching, and this was mine. The interesting thing is, that what I did was considered revolutionary at the time.

The scoreboard showed all zeros for the Brooklyn Dodgers as Don Larsen threw the final pitch of his perfect game in the 1955 World Series.

But now, a lot of the pitchers use some variations of the same no-windup delivery."

Larsen stayed with his no-windup delivery, or at least some variation of it, for the rest of his career.

It was a career that continued to flourish, even after the perfect game. In his five years with the Yankees, Don posted a 45–24 record (including 11–5 in 1956 and 10–4 in 1957). He also blossomed into an outstanding hitter, winding up with a lifetime batting average of .242, a career slugging average of .371, which is the 10th highest among 20th Century pitchers, 72 RBI and 14 home runs, including a grand slam in 1956 off of Frank Sullivan of the Red Sox.

In the winter of 1959, Larsen was again part of another trade that had a major impact on the history of baseball. He was sent with Hank Bauer, Norm Siebern and Marv Throneberry to the Kansas City A's for three players, one of whom was Roger Maris.

Larsen played only briefly with the A's, then began a sojourn that took him on a lengthy path through the major leagues. In the final years of his career, he was used mostly in relief, never winning more than eight games in a season after leaving the Yankees.

Although he had a memorable career, it is his perfect game for which Larsen is mostly remembered.

He says he has "made a few extra dollars" because of that game, but it did not produce instant wealth for him, nor did it drastically alter the course of his life.

Don still has the hat, glove, shoes and the final ball from that game. Eventually, he says, he will give them either to his son or to the Hall of Champions in San Diego.

Larsen is somewhat annoyed that the Yankees never gave him a memento for his perfect game, although he did get a cash bonus. He had a plaque made up himself that he later distributed to his friends.

It was, indeed, a moment to remember—the greatest game ever pitched in baseball history.

"I like to think it was," Larsen says. "I guess every pitcher is entitled to a good game. I don't know why this particular one happened to me. I guess the man upstairs was with me."

So, too, that day, were millions of others who were scattered from one end of the country to the other.

Danny Litwhiler—
First Errorless Outfielder

The mere fact that he has a three-page resume tells you something about Danny Litwhiler.

He is not your basic ex-ballplayer.

Author, inventor, college professor, coach, international participant, Litwhiler has gone considerably further than being simply a fellow who put in 11 good seasons in the major leagues.

In 1988, baseball will be a regular part of the Olympic Games. Credit Danny Litwhiler for that.

Litwhiler has been the driving force to get baseball included as an Olympic sport while serving as a member of the U.S. Olympic Baseball Committee from 1969–1983. He was a technical advisor to the Olympic Games in 1984 when baseball was played as an exhibition sport.

The former outfielder has long been involved in baseball on a worldwide level. He was international president of the United States Baseball Federation from 1978–1983, a member of the U.S. State Department's international athletics panel of experts, and has conducted clinics in countries throughout the world.

Litwhiler's activities hardly stop there. He has written five books, four on baseball fundamentals and one a glossary of baseball terms translated from English into seven other languages. He has developed six different baseball products, including the Jugs Speed Gun, a widely used device that times the speed of a thrown baseball.

Litwhiler is a member of six halls of fame, including the Helms Foundation. For 20 years, he was the head baseball coach and professor of physical education at Michigan State University where he recruited and coached such future major league stars as Steve Garvey, Kirk Gibson and Mike Marshall (the pitcher). And for nine years before that, he had the same titles at Florida State University. Altogether, he has sent more than 100 players into professional baseball, also including major leaguers Dick Howser, Rick Miller, Woody Woodward and Ken Suarez.

A graduate of Bloomsburg (Pennsylvania) State College, where he majored in science and social science, Litwhiler, the father of 10 children, is still going strong. After retiring from Michigan State in 1983, he went to work for the Cincinnati Reds for whom he has been the club's minor league batting instructor.

Litwhiler always did know how to hit. While playing for the Philadelphia Phillies, St. Louis Cardinals, Boston Braves and Reds, he had a career major league average of .281 with 982 hits in 1,057 games.

It was as a fielder, though, that Litwhiler gained his highest level of distinction in the majors. A two-time Gold Glove winner, in 1942, while playing left field for the Phillies, he became the first outfielder in major league history to play a full season of 150 or more games without making an error. He went 151 games that year, accepting 317 chances without a bobble. The streak extended to 187 straight games before Litwhiler finally booted one.

"You have to be very lucky to do that," he says. "You can make a perfect throw, but it could hit something and take off or it could hit the guy sliding in and you would get an error.

"You have to have good hands, too," he adds. "And you have to learn to block a ball. I could have been given some errors, but by moving in close and blocking the ball I didn't get charged with errors because I was able to prevent the runner from moving up a base.

"Stan Hack used to hit down the left field line," Litwhiler recalls. "One time he hit one down the line, and I went over to block the ball, but it hit something and started to get by me. I stuck my foot out and blocked it, then picked up the ball and threw Hank out at second. I almost had an error that time."

Litwhiler recalls another time in late September when he was actually charged with an error, but the decision was later reversed.

We were playing in the Polo Grounds against the New York Giants. It had been raining, and there was a big puddle in left field. Johnny Mize hit a line drive, and I ran over and made a shoestring catch. Willard Marshall had been on second, and he was running for home. I figured I had him doubled at second. I caught the ball, and just as I went to plant my feet to throw, I hit the water. My feet went out from under me, and I slid about 20 feet. Water was flying everywhere, and I dropped the ball.

I looked up and saw a big E on the scoreboard. After the game, I was getting on the train to go back to Philadelphia, and I got a newspaper. But there was no error in the box score. The next morning, I got up at 6 a.m. to get another paper, and still there was no error listed. So I went through the whole season without an error.

About 10 years later, I'm at a banquet in New York and Mel Allen says to me, "Remember the season you fielded 1.000? Do you know how you did it?" I told him I had a lot of luck.

He reminded me of the incident at the Polo Grounds. When the game was over, he told me, Mize rushed right up to the press box in his uniform to see the official scorer. "How can you give that kid an error on a play like that?" he roared. "Here I am trying to hit .300. Hitting is my bread and butter, and I'm hitting .299, and you take a hit away from me."

Danny Litwhiler.

The scorer told Mize that he thought it was a legitimate error. Then he
turned to Allen, and said, "What do you think?" Mel said he thought it was
a hit, so the official scorer changed it from an error to a hit. So that's why
the error never appeared in the papers. In all those years, I had never known
what happened.

Litwhiler also credits the groundskeeper at Shibe Park with an assist
in helping him maintain the streak. "I used to ask him to let the grass grow
a little longer in left field, and he did," Danny recalls. "One time, Joe
Medwick said to me, 'How in the world do you keep from tripping out there;
the grass is so long?' "

The streak finally ended early in the 1943 season in Philadelphia. "A
ball was hit to left-center," Litwhiler remembers. "I went over to cut it off,
and it hit something and bounced back behind me. I ran right by it. They
gave me an error. It was the only one I made all that season."

During his 187 consecutive errorless games—at the time a major league
record—Litwhiler played every inning. "The glove I used during the streak
is in the Hall of Fame," he says. "I am very proud of that record."

In those days, the Phillies were a downtrodden bunch that not only
finished last each season, but were the worst teams in the club's history.
Litwhiler had joined the club during the 1940 season.

Originally, Litwhiler had been signed for $200 by the Detroit Tigers
while he was still a four-sport star at Bloomsburg. He spent three seasons
in the minors, but after advancing to Toledo, tore up his knee on opening
day in 1939 and was eventually released by the Tigers.

The Phillies signed him, and after playing most of the 1940 season in
the minors, Litwhiler was brought up by the parent club late in the season.
Danny proceeded to hit in 21-straight games and finished the year with a
.345 average. He got a $500 bonus for the streak.

Litwhiler hit .305 in 1941, his first full season in the majors. That year,
he also hit a home run in every National League park.

"That meant a lot to me because it indicated that you could hit a ball
as hard as anybody," Litwhiler says. "One ball I hit that year cleared the
roof at the Polo Grounds. I got knocked down three straight pitches by a
guy named Ace Adams. I figured he couldn't knock me down again; he had
to come in with it. He did, and I knocked it over the left field roof."

While Litwhiler played with the Phillies, he came into contact with
several future Hall of Famers.

"Chuck Klein," he says, "was a very likeable person. He was a good
man, and he was good for me because he would talk to me and help me
a lot. He helped to build up my confidence. He had a good, relaxed style
of hitting, and I tried to emulate it.

"Lloyd Waner was another person who helped me," Litwhiler continues.
"The year I fielded 1.000, he was the center fielder. With him next to me,
I could always concentrate on catching the ball because he would be there
to tell me where to throw it. He always let me know what to do with the ball."

Litwhiler hit .271 in 1942, and was named to the National League All-Star team. Then on June 1, 1943, he was traded to the Cardinals. "I was heart-broken," says the upstate Pennsylvania native of Ringtown. "I loved it in Philadelphia. I actually cried when they told me I had been traded.

"I think the reason the Cardinals wanted me stemmed from a game in 1942. I always had the attitude that we could win, no matter what. One day, I slid hard into Walker Cooper at home in a game against the Cardinals, and we both got knocked out. But I think the Cards liked that. Billy Southworth, their manager, said 'Anybody who can hustle for a last place club like that should help a first place club like us.' "

Litwhiler not only went from last place to first, he joined what he feels was one of the best teams in baseball history.

"You'd have to rate the Cardinals of that era one of the top teams of all time," he says. "We had guys like Stan Musial, the Cooper brothers, Mort and Walker, Whitey Kurowski, Marty Marion. They were all guys who could win.

"Playing with the Cardinals was so different from playing with any other team I played on," he adds. "They went out there every day thinking they were going to win. They never expected to lose. And if they did, their attitude was, 'We'll win tomorrow.' "

Litwhiler's 1943 Cardinals lost in five games in the World Series to the New York Yankees, but they came back to win in six in 1944 against the St. Louis Browns. Litwhiler's solo home run in the fifth game helped the Cardinals snap a 2-2 deadlock in the Series and gain a 2-0 win.

Danny remembers:

> I guess you'd have to say that was my biggest thrill in a baseball game. It came in the eighth inning off of Denny Galehouse. He threw a slider, outside and high, and I hit it to right. I'd never hit a home run to right before. I just started running with my head down, and all of the sudden, the crowd started to cheer. I thought the guy in right had made a sensational catch. When I looked up and saw it was a home run, I was so elated. I don't remember touching a base all the way around.

After hitting .272 in 1943 and .264 in 1944 as the Cards' regular left fielder, Litwhiler missed the 1945 season because of military service. He missed the World Series in 1946 because after getting discharged from the Army and rejoining the Cards, he was sold to Boston in June.

Danny wound up the 1946 season with a .286 average. He spent 1947 with the Braves, hitting .261; then the following season was traded to the Reds, thus missing out on another World Series as Boston won the National League pennant.

Litwhiler stayed with the Reds through the 1951 season, his best year having been 1949 when he hit .291. He was a player-coach for the Reds in '51, but the following year went back as a full-time player with Oakland in the Pacific Coast League.

A serious leg injury ended Litwhiler's playing career in 1952. He wound up the season managing in the Reds' chain in Fargo, North Dakota.

Danny managed two more seasons in the minors. As he had done as a player, he continued to teach high school social studies during the off-season.

"In 1955, I was offered the job at Florida State," he says. "I wanted something more settled, and so I took it."

Litwhiler produced some outstanding teams at both Florida State and Michigan State. He is a firm believer in the place of the college sport in the overall baseball picture.

"College baseball is never going to replace the minor leagues, but it is very much needed by professional baseball," he says. "Professional baseball needs a training ground, and they don't get it in the minors. The colleges are serving that function, just as they do for professional football and basketball.

"At this point," he adds, "75 to 80 percent of the professional baseball players attended some college. So the game at the college level has a very definite place in the baseball structure."

Much of the reason for that is attributable to Litwhiler, a man who enjoyed a successful career as a big league player and who for nearly 30 years was one of the most prominent people in baseball at the college level.

Roger Maris—Nobody Hit More Homers in One Season

During the course of baseball history, there have been only a few years that can be clearly identified with special individual achievements.

Mention the year 1927 and the mind readily connects it with Babe Ruth's 60 home runs. 1920—Wambaganss' triple play. 1938—VanderMeer's two no-hitters; 1941—DiMaggio's 56-game streak; 1947—Robinson's emancipation.

To that august group, it is easy to add the year 1961.

That was the year that Roger Maris broke Ruth's all-time single-season home run record. He did it on the last day of the season with a blast at Yankee Stadium against Tracy Stallard of the Boston Red Sox.

Maris' 61 home runs in 1961 has become one of the most notable one-season accomplishments in baseball history, and it climaxed a marvelous summer of baseball that was watched breathlessly throughout the world.

The lefthanded-hitting New York Yankees' right fielder had waged a torrid home run battle with teammate Mickey Mantle through most of the season. Maris finally pulled away from his friend, but Mantle's 54 home runs, coupled with Bill Skowron's 28, gave the Yankees the most productive home run trio the game has ever seen with 143 four-baggers. (Maris and Mantle combined for 115 for the best twosome in baseball history.)

During the season, Maris enjoyed one banner game after another. On May 30, he, Mantle and Skowron each hit two home runs and Yogi Berra added one as the Yankees beat the Red Sox, 12–3. On July 25, Roger hit four homers in a doubleheader. From August 11 to 16, he hit a home run in six straight games.

Maris was the first player in baseball history to hit his 50th homer in August. He hit his 60th on September 26 at Yankee Stadium against Jack Fisher of the Baltimore Orioles.

When the season finally ended, Maris not only led the league in home runs, he topped the American League with 142 RBI and 132 runs while batting .269.

Despite Maris' season-long home run barrage, it was a year that raged with controversy. Roger suffered the abuse of fans and press for daring to challenge a legend. He was often cast as an upstart, one-shot wonder who had neither the right nor the talent to tamper with a record as sacred as Ruth's. And as a final insult, then-baseball commissioner Ford Frick ordered an asterisk placed next to Maris' record because he hit the 61 home runs in 162 games, while Ruth had hit his 60 in 154.

Such abuse never sat well with Maris, and until his death in 1986, he bristled at the mention of the trouble he had dealing with the pressure surrounding his pursuit of the Babe.

"I really didn't have that much pressure on myself," he said. "The big problem was the media. They created the pressure.

"It didn't matter that it was New York," he added. "The pressure wouldn't have been different anywhere else. It was just a lot of guys (writers) trying to make names for themselves, and you have them anywhere."

Maris, who died at the age of 52, always wore the crew cut that was popular in his playing days.

For the previous 19 years, Roger had owned and operated a beer distributorship in Gainesville, Florida.

Father of six children and the grandfather of two, Maris lived long enough to see the Yankees finally get around to retiring his No. 9 at a 1985 ceremony at Yankee Stadium in which the late Elston Howard's number was also retired. That year, a Roger Maris Museum was opened in Fargo, North Dakota, the town where the ex-player grew up and got his start playing in youth baseball leagues. Located in a mall in Fargo, the museum contains trophies, photographs, a taped narration of Maris' drive for 61 homers performed by long-time Yankee broadcaster, Mel Allen, and various other souvenirs of Roger's career.

"Basically, everything I had I gave to the museum," Maris said, noting that some 1,800 people turned out for the grand opening. "That kind of response was really gratifying. I was surprised that so many people are interested in my career."

And a fine career it was. As the years went by, Maris' pride in his 1961 record seemed to heighten.

"That year was a fine year, and it made my career," he said. "It got much more difficult in later years with all the people on my back all the time."

Maris, perhaps justifiably, allowed some bitterness to creep into his conversation, especially while discussing the press, the asterisk and the frequent characterization of him as a one-season ballplayer.

He was hardly that. In 1960, Roger hit 39 home runs and led the American League in RBI with 112 and in slugging average with .581. As he would the following year, too, he was named the league's Most Valuable Player.

Although he never approached 61 homers again, Maris hit home runs in double figures nine times in his 12-year career, averaging 36.4 homers a season during one five-year period.

Roger Maris.

The 6' 0", 197-pounder finished his career with 275 homers, a batting average of .260, 851 RBI and 826 runs.

A member of four American League All-Star teams and five Yankee pennant winners, Maris ranks sixth on the Yankees' all-time slugging list and seventh in home runs.

But Roger was not just an offensive standout. He was an excellent base-runner with fine speed, and he was an outstanding defensive player with an especially strong arm. In fact, Maris' 1964 fielding average of .996 is the highest ever recorded by a Yankee right fielder.

Maris broke into professional baseball in 1953. After playing at Fargo, Keokuk, Tulsa, Reading and Indianapolis, he made the big leagues in 1957 with the Cleveland Indians.

"My first major league game was probably the biggest event of my career," he said. "I went three-for-five. That and my first All-Star game (1959) and my first World Series (1960) were the most memorable games I played in."

After hitting .235 with Cleveland, Maris was swapped to the Kansas City A's in 1958. He played one and one-half years for the A's before KC sent him to New York along with first baseman Kent Hadley and shortstop Joe Demaestri for pitcher Don Larsen, first baseman Marv Throneberry and outfielders Hank Bauer and Norm Siebern.

"When I got traded to the Yankees, it really didn't mean anything to me," Maris recalled. "I'd have sooner stayed in Kansas City because I really liked it there. But I had no choice in the matter.

"It turned out to be the best move of my life. But those are the kinds of things you never know about. You can never count on the unknown."

In 1960, Maris hit 11 more home runs than his previous high, and led the league with a ratio of one home run every 7.8 times at bat. But there was little indication of what would come the following year.

Maris chased Ruth's record relentlessly. In June he set a major league record with 15 home runs during the month. He had eight two-home run games, and, ironically, did not receive an intentional walk the entire season. He struck out only 67 times.

At the conclusion of the season, Maris was again voted MVP. He also won the Hickok Belt as the top professional athlete, and was named Player of the Year by The Sporting News, Man of the Year by Sport magazine and Sportsman of the Year by Sports Illustrated.

The following year, Maris' home run total dropped to 33, but he had 100 RBI. Over the next two years, his home run totals were 23 and 26 as injuries began taking their toll.

Maris played most of the 1965 season with a broken hand. He planned to retire after the 1966 season, but the Yankees traded him to the St. Louis Cardinals where Roger played two more years.

The Cardinals' regular right fielder for those two years, Maris got into two more World Series, bringing his total to seven. He retired after the 1968 season.

"Looking back," Maris said, "I was not real satisfied with my career. It should have been a lot better. Under the circumstances, with all the adverse conditions, though, I couldn't really get the maximum out of myself."

He did, though, for one great year in 1961. It's a year that baseball will never forget.

Bill Mazeroski—Great Gloveman
Whose Home Run Won a World Series

It is the fantasy of nearly everyone who ever played baseball to come to bat in the bottom of the ninth inning of the final game of the World Series and hit a home run that wins the championship.

Every kid has that dream. But only one has had it come true.

Bill Mazeroski of the Pittsburgh Pirates.

Remember that day? Seventh game of the 1960 World Series. Bottom of the ninth. Score tied, 9-9. Ralph Terry on the mound for the New York Yankees.

Mazeroski steps to the plate. After taking a ball on the first pitch, he slams a drive over the left-center field wall for a home run., Pandemonium breaks loose. The crowd of 36,683, filling every speck of space in Forbes Field, goes beserk while Mazeroski, hat in hand, dances ecstatically around the bases, finally crossing the plate as a mob of happy fans races behind him and his teammates wait to engulf him.

The Pirates have won their first World Series in 35 years.

In a sport that thrives on memorable events, it may have been the most dramatic home run in the history of baseball.

It certainly was one that has followed Mazeroski wherever he has gone.

"I'm still asked about it all the time," says the soft-spoken former second baseman as he reflects on that memorable occasion. "Year after year, people still want to know about it."

Each time he is asked, Mazeroski patiently relives the moment. "I didn't think the ball was going to go out," he says. "I thought it would be off the wall. But it ended up going over the wall.

"I hit a high fastball," he adds. "Terry said it was a high slider. If it was, it didn't slide.

"I was digging all the way. I didn't see the ball go out. It sure was a good feeling when I learned that it did.

"I was really happy. I was just so glad we beat the Yankees. I had thought we were going to lose when they tied it up in the top of the ninth."

For the Pirates, Mazeroski's hit ended what had been a cinderella year.

200

Bill Mazeroski.

In fourth place the season before, the Bucs, under popular manager Danny Murtaugh, rode to the National League pennant with a hefty seven-game lead over the second place Milwaukee Braves. Pitted in the Series against a powerful Yankees club that had stormed to the American League title with an eight-game cushion over Baltimore, the Pirates were a decided underdog as the October gala opened in Pittsburgh.

But the experts had not figured on Mazeroski's bat. It is often obscured by his seventh game homer, but Bill actually won two other games for the Pirates. His two-run homer off of Jim Coates gave the Bucs a 6–4 triumph in the first game. And his two-run double put the Pirates ahead to stay in a 5–2 victory in the fourth game. Maz wound up the Series with a .320 average, second only to Smoky Burgess among Pittsburgh regulars.

"Nobody thought we could beat the Yankees because they had Mantle and Maris and Berra and all those other big sluggers," Mazeroski recalls. "But we had a pretty good team, too. We didn't have a lot of power. But we had good starting pitching and good relieving. And we did little things that worked well. Whatever it took to win, we did it."

Nobody did it better than Mazeroski.

During a 17-year career—all with the Pirates—it is somewhat ironic that Mazeroski should be best remembered for one swing of the bat. A solid but not overwhelming hitter, Bill registered a lifetime average of .260 with 2,016 hits, including 138 home runs. He had 853 RBI.

Except for that one indelible moment in 1960, it was as a fielder that Mazeroski really carved his nitch in the baseball arena. To many appraisers of the game, he was simply one of the best, if not *the* best, defensive second baseman there ever was.

He was especially adept at making the doubleplay, getting rid of the ball with such cat-like quickness that he was given the nickname "No Touch." Sometimes, it looked like he barely touched the ball.

Mazeroski was such a skillful gloveman that opposing players often stopped what they were doing to watch Bill take infield practice. Even the American League players did that before All-Star games.

Mazeroski rolled up some generous statistics in the field, including still-standing major league records for second basemen for most years leading the league in assists (nine) and doubleplays (eight), most doubleplays in one season (161) and most doubleplays in a career (1,706). He also holds a National League second base record for most years leading the league in chances (eight) and is tied for most years with 500 or more assists (five).

In 1966, Mazeroski and Pirates' shortstop Gene Alley participated collectively in 289 doubleplays, most ever recorded in the major leagues. Mazeroski is listed in the top five in that category three times (twice with Dick Groat).

His record for most doubleplays in one season by a second baseman, also set in 1966, is just one of five times Mazeroski's name appears in the top nine places on that all-time list.

Strangely enough, despite performing in the big leagues from 1956 to 1972 as one of the game's premier defensive second basemen, the 5' 11", 183-pound native of Wheeling, West Virginia, didn't even play that position originally.

"I always played shortstop as a kid," Maz says. "I was a Cleveland Indians' fan, although I didn't get to see many of their games because they were too far away. My idols were Dale Mitchell, Ken Keltner and especially Lou Boudreau."

Even after he was signed by the Pirates, Mazeroski spent his first year in pro ball (1954) as a shortstop at Williamsport (Pennsylvania) of the Eastern League. The following year, though, Bill made the switch to second base.

"Branch Rickey put me at second," Mazeroski recalls. "We had about 15 other shortstops in the Pirates' organization. There was just no more room there. So he put me at second, and told me I was staying there.

"It turned out pretty well," Mazeroski adds. "Nobody really showed me how to play the position. It just came naturally. I didn't study the great second basemen. Everything I did was through trial and error."

Mazeroski arrived in Pittsburgh from Hollywood of the Pacific Coast League in mid-season of 1956, and immediately took over as the Pirates' second sacker. With Roberto Clemente, then in his second year in Pittsburgh, Dick Groat finally getting established at shortstop and Bill Virdon just joining the club from St. Louis, Mazeroski's arrival supplied one more ingredient to the mixture that would lead the Bucs to the World Championship in 1960.

Bill clearly remembers his arrival in the big leagues.

"My first major league game was in the Polo Grounds against the New York Giants," he says. "I got a hit off of Johnny Antonelli. I also got my first doubleplay in that series. The ball was hit by Willie Mays."

It didn't take Mazeroski long to establish himself as one of the league's premier second basemen. In 1957, he hit .283—the highest batting average of his career. In 1958, he hit a career-high 19 home runs while batting .275.

Mazeroski made his first All-Star team in 1958. He was selected for the team in six additional years, although he was replaced in 1963 because of an injury.

Bill was named Major League Player of the Year in 1960, a year in which he was also selected as the second baseman on the major league All-Star team, picked by *The Sporting News*.

He won a Gold Glove eight times, and by the time he retired, he had played more games at second base than any player in Pirates' history. Although he is well behind Joe Morgan and Rogers Hornsby, his home run total ranks as the third-highest of all National League second basemen.

On the Pirates' list of all-time career leaders, Mazeroski ranks fifth in games, sixth in at-bats, home runs and RBI, seventh in singles, and eighth in hits, doubles, total bases and extra base hits. Considering the rich history of the Pirates and the many outstanding players who have performed in

Pittsburgh, Mazeroski's multiple appearances on the Bucs' all-time lists are excellent testimony to his fine, all-around play.

Maz, who hit home runs in double figures six different times, was always a good RBI man, despite usually batting in the lower part of the Pirates' lineup. He had 82 RBI in 1966 and 81 in 1962 for career highs.

Bill was also noted as a fellow who rarely complained about umpires' calls, and is highly regarded by many veteran arbitrators for that practice.

Toward the latter part of his career, Mazeroski played a handful of games at third base. It was an uncomfortable situation for him.

"I tried to play there, but it was terrible," he remembers. "I had no idea what I was doing."

Since his retirement as a player, Mazeroski has been in and out of the big leagues. He spent a year as a coach with the Pirates in 1973. Later, he worked in 1979–80 as a coach with the Seattle Mariners. In 1984, he performed as an instructor with the Montreal Expos, working with the club's infielders.

Mazeroski, who owns a golf course and who has dabbled in local politics, still lives in a suburb of Pittsburgh. He has the bat with which he hit his famous home run in 1960, and a few other items from his career.

He still sees a number of his former teammates, particularly at golf tournaments and other events around the Pittsburgh area. In 1985, he saw many of them at a 25-year reunion of the Pirates' World Championship team of 1960.

For Mazeroski, of course, that Series provided him with the high point of his career. But it was a career that had many other successes.

"I never believed," Bill says, "that I would last 17 years in the big leagues. As a kid, all I dreamed about was just making the big leagues and being a decent ballplayer."

Bill Mazeroski was that and then some.

Bobby Thomson—
Baseball's Most Memorable Homer

There have been well over 100,000 home runs hit in major league history. They have come in all forms in all situations by all kinds of hitters. But there is one home run that stands out above all others.

It is the home run by Bobby Thomson, the "shot heard 'round the world" that clinched the Miracle of Coogan's Bluff.

The date was October 3, 1951. The location was the Polo Grounds in New York. The event was the third game of a best-of-three National League playoff between Thomson's New York Giants and the Brooklyn Dodgers.

There have been other noteworthy home runs in baseball, but because of the conditions surrounding this particular one, no homer was ever more dramatic or had a greater impact. It was, without question, the most famous four-bagger ever hit.

The saga had begun in mid-August when the Giants, trailing the league-leading Dodgers by 13½ games, opened a miraculous stretch drive. Winning 37 of their final 44 games, the Giants vaulted into a tie for first place as the regular season ended, necessitating a special playoff to decide the league's representative in the World Series.

The teams split the first two games, and Thomson was a factor in each one. His two-run homer off of Ralph Branca won the first game, 3–1, and his two errors and a base-running blunder contributed to a 10–0 Dodgers' win in the second.

In the final game the Giants, trailing 4–1, faced almost certain elimination after Dodgers' starter, Don Newcombe struck out the side in the bottom of the eighth inning. But a spark of hope flickered an inning later when Alvin Dark led off the bottom of the ninth with a single and Don Mueller followed with another single. Monte Irvin fouled out, but Whitey Lockman sliced a double to left that scored Dark. Misfortune struck the Giants on the play, however, as Mueller, sliding into third, suffered a broken ankle.

During the commotion that followed, Branca was brought in to replace Newcombe on the mound, and Clint Hartung was sent in to pinch-run for the injured Mueller, who was carried off the field on a stretcher.

Thomson, the next batter, took Branca's first pitch for a strike, but swung at the next offering, also a fastball, and laced a line shot to deep left field that carried over the head of Brooklyn's Andy Pafko and into the stands for a game-winning, three-run homer.

The dramatic blast not only jetisoned the Giants into the World Series (which they eventually lost to the New York Yankees, four games to two), but also sent the stunned Dodgers down in one of the greatest collapses in baseball history.

The fact that the home run produced the Giants' first pennant since 1937 gave the blast special meaning. Coming in New York between two bitter rivals, and as one of the early nationally televised broadcasts just added to the melodrama. It was, with all due respect to some other highly dramatic home runs, unrivaled as the most memorable round-tripper ever poled.

Thomson remembers the hit as clearly as if it just happened. He says there was no great pressure when he came to bat in the bottom of the ninth.

> You have to back up before that and realize the circumstances. It was a very unusual situation. We were down, 4–1, going into the bottom of the ninth. I remember running into the dugout after the top of the inning, and being totally disgusted. I threw my glove down. I just felt terrible that we weren't going to beat the Dodgers.
>
> I was the fifth batter up in the inning, so I was totally wrapped up in the game. I wasn't thinking about myself, just how we could avoid defeat. Then Mueller got hurt. I was the next batter, and I ran down to third where he was lying, and I still had the bat in my hand. He was my friend. When I saw him lying there in pain, it got my mind totally off the game. I was more concerned about him.
>
> In fact, I didn't even know the Dodgers had made a pitching change until I got back to the plate. But I'd never been in a spot like that, so I was cursing, talking to myself, telling myself to wait and watch. I wasn't nervous. In a situation like that, you just follow your instincts.
>
> I was determined to give myself a chance to hit the ball. I just wanted to do a good job in that situation and I was concentrating totally.
>
> Branca threw me a fastball inside. He said that he made a good pitch. I just happened to move my hands quickly and get the bat around.
>
> At first, I thought the ball was going over the wall. Then it started to sink. I thought, "Oh, Geez, it's not going to make it." Then when it did, I just jumped up. I was never a hot dog, but looking at it later, I realized I was hopping up and down. Then I started running around the bases, and things were happening so fast; it was hard to realize what was going on. I was hyperventilating. I'd never done that before. I was aware of what I was doing, but it was crazy. The whole situation was so different from anything I had ever experienced before. I had no thoughts. Everything was just a blur.

When Thomson reached home, chased there by wildly jumping manager Leo Durocher, he was immediately engulfed by his ecstatic teammates. Then, half-carried, half-washed along in the tide of jumping, shouting players, Thomson was swept to the center field clubhouse. By then, bedlam reigned on Coogan's Bluff.

Bobby Thomson.

Except for his white hair and glasses, Thomson looks very much the same today as he did that fall afternoon many years ago.

Since his retirement from baseball in 1960, Bobby has worked for a New York City paper company. He is a national sales rep for the firm. He also works as a volunteer in an alcohol and drug program for children in his home town in northern New Jersey.

"Branca and I agree that we both would have been forgotten long ago if it hadn't been for that home run," Thomson says. "The fact that I hit it has kept my name in the news and gotten me invited out a lot more than I would have been otherwise.

"It's nice to be remembered. But having had to go out and work and become an ordinary citizen tends to put things in perspective. So the home run hasn't been a focal point of my whole life. I don't really think about it much anymore unless somebody comes along who wants to talk or write about it."

Thomson, who says the main items he saved from the game were some pictures, says he and Branca have become good friends over the years and see each other at occasional gatherings. "But he's really had enough of it," Bobby says. "It was kind of tough on him."

Although the home run was certainly the highlight of his career, Thomson was hardly a one-event ballplayer. Bobby had a fine 15-year career that included many other memorable occasions.

He had a career batting average of .270 with 1,705 hits, including 264 home runs. He had 1,206 RBI. He was a member of the National League All-Star team three times.

Bobby reached double figures in home runs in 12 different seasons, hitting a high of 32 in 1951, a year in which he batted .293 and drove in 101 runs.

Probably his finest all-around season was 1949 when he hit .309, had career highs in hits (198) and RBI (109) and socked 27 home runs.

A native of Glasgow, Scotland, Thomson moved with his parents to the United States at the age of two and one-half. Settling in Staten Island, Thomson eventually became an outstanding baseball player. While still in high school, he was playing shortstop in a fast semipro league when he first attracted the attention of the scouts.

"The Dodgers had been paying some attention to me, and they said, 'Don't sign with anybody else until you talk to us,'" Thomson relates. "But I had gone to a tryout with the Giants. I was a Giants fan—my heroes were Mel Ott and Billy Jurges—so I signed with them for $100 a month."

Shifted to third base, Thomson broke into the professional ranks in 1942. Then, after three years in the military service, he spent the 1946 season at Jersey City in the International League before being called up to New York at the end of the campaign.

"My first big league game was in Philadelphia, and I think I got a hit in that game," remembers Thomson.

In 1947, Thomson was shifted to the outfield, and he became the regular center fielder on a Giants team that set a National League record with 221 home runs. Bobby had 29 homers, while Johnny Mize led the league with 51, Willard Marshall had 36 and Walker Cooper 35.

"I was just a young kid, but it was a pretty big thrill to play with those guys. The team was managed by Ott, so that was a thrill, too, playing for my old idol. He helped me a lot. When you're young like I was then, you always single out guys like that. I listened to Ott and Hank Greenberg."

After hitting .283 his rookie year, Thomson slumped ot .248 in 1948. He blames it on his youth.

"When you're a young kid, you have a mind of your own," he says. "I guess I was a pain in the neck. I got a little headstrong, and didn't listen to anybody."

Thomson, however, bounced back in 1949, and from there put together five straight solid years, including four with more than 100 RBI. In 1952 he led the league with 14 triples.

Along the way, he had some other memorable hits.

In 1949 in a doubleheader against the Phillies, Bobby hit a two-run homer that gave the Giants a 4–2 victory in the 15th inning in the opener. In the nightcap, he came back with two singles and a home run and scored all the runs in a 3–0 New York triumph.

That year, Thomson also played in an all .300 hitting outfield. His .309 was joined by Marshall's .307 and Lockman's .301.

Thomson hit a single right at the end of the 1951 season to beat the Phillies in a game that kept the Giants in the pennant race. The following season, he hit a memorable, two-out, bottom of the ninth inning grand slam homer to give the Giants a come-from-behind 5–4 win over the St. Louis Cardinals.

Durocher had been managing the Giants since mid-1948, and Thomson enjoyed playing for the fiery ex-Dodger pilot.

"He could run a team pretty well," Thomson says. "He had good leaders on the field in Dark and (Eddie) Stanky. If you hustled and did the job, there was no problem. He was all for you. And you could argue with him, and the next day, it was all forgotten. He was not one of those petty guys. What he said made a lot of sense."

Durocher, however, had brought Thomson in from the outfield to third base to make room for Willie Mays when the latter came up in 1951. Willie went into the Army in 1952, and when he came back in 1954, Durocher considered Thomson to be expendable.

As a result, Thomson and catcher Sam Calderone were traded to the Milwaukee Braves for pitcher Johnny Antonelli and three others plus cash.

"I wasn't really surprised about the trade," Thomson recalls. "I had had a disappointing year in 1953 (he hit .288 with 26 home runs and 106 RBI), and I kind of expected it. Besides, Willie was coming back from the Army, and the Giants needed pitchers."

Thomson spent a little less than two and one-half season with the Braves. He missed half of the 1954 season after breaking an ankle in an exhibition game in March, and never did get untracked in Milwaukee. In mid-1957,

It was a joyous scene for Bobby Thomson (right) and manager Leo Durocher after the New York Giants' outfielder hit his pennant-clinching home run.

the Braves, badly in need of a second baseman, shipped Bobby and two others back to the Giants in exchange for Red Schoendienst.

Thomson was traded to the Chicago Cubs the following spring, and in 1958 enjoyed a strong comeback, hitting .283 with 21 homers and 82 RBI. But after the 1959 season, Bobby was swapped to the Boston Red Sox. He played most of the 1960 season with the Bosox, but wound up the campaign with the Baltimore Orioles. At that point, he retired from the game.

Thus ended an excellent career that was made even finer by Thomson's dramatic home run in 1951. It was a career that Thomson feels fortunate to have had.

"With the natural ability I had, I think I should have done more than I did," he says. "I'm not completely satisfied with my performance. But it's too late to worry about, and I'm not going to go through life feeling bad about it.

"I consider myself fortunate to have played ball, especially in New York, and in a great era in baseball history. I had one day in the sun, so to speak. You have to be a little lucky for things like that to happen.

"You can't ever sit down and explain why that happened to me. Things like that just happen and that's it. You just have to be thankful for small blessings."

Johnny Vander Meer—
Two No-Hitters in a Row

In the 11½ decades that baseball has been played professionally, no achievement by a pitcher was ever more spectacular than Johnny Vander Meer's two consecutive no-hitters in 1938.

It was a feat unmatched in baseball history, and when it occurred it catapulted the Cincinnati Reds' hurler into the national spotlight. Johnny's remarkable performance generated the kind of coast-to-coast excitement that surfaces on rare occasions in sports.

Vander Meer, a hard-throwing but sometimes wild lefthander, was in his first full major league season when he recorded his back-to-back no-hitters. The first one came on June 11 against the Boston Bees. In his next starting assignment on June 15, Vander Meer blanked the Brooklyn Dodgers.

As astonishing as the twin no-hitters were, it is seldom remembered that Vander Meer pitched three-hitters on either side of his no-hit spree. In the game prior to his first no-hitter, the 6'1", 190-pound southpaw gave up two hits in the first inning to the New York Giants, and a pinch-hit, broken bat single by Hank Lieber in the ninth. Following his second no-hitter, Johnny yielded just three hits to Boston.

During that period, Vander Meer pitched 21⅔ innings without allowing a hit, a major league record that will probably stand until they stop playing baseball.

Vander Meer, now retired after 20 years as a district sales manager for a major brewery, lives in Tampa, Florida, where he keeps busy playing golf, fishing and tending his large yard. Although his no-hitters occurred nearly 50 years ago, Johnny recalls every detail of his famous feat.

"I didn't go for a no-hitter in either game until the ninth inning," the affable ex-hurler remembers. "Before then, I was just going for the shutout.

"In the first game, I threw a lot of fastballs. I had good control that day, and Boston hit a lot of ground balls.

"In the second game, I was real quick, real fast, but my curveball was hanging. I only threw three curves in the first seven innings. By the eighth, I was starting to lose my fastball, but the curve came back to me.

"In both games," Johnny adds, "I figured if they're gonna beat me, they're gonna beat my good stuff.

"One of the things I remember most about the games was that in the second game, which was at night, it was probably the only time in the history of Ebbets Field that the fans weren't pulling for the Dodgers. Brooklyn fans were probably the most loyal fans in baseball, but when they saw what was

Johnny Vander Meer

going on, they pulled for me. When Buddy Hassett hit a liner to the box to end the game, they let out a big cheer. That really gave me a thrill.''

Happily, Vander Meer still has that ball as well as the one that ended the Boston game. They're locked in a safe deposit box, and John wouldn't part with them if he was down to his last penny, which, incidentally, is hardly the case.

The Prospect Park, New Jersey native also has a fine assortment of other items from his playing days; in fact, Johnny has retained more memorabilia than most players. He has the uniforms he wore in the 1939 and 1940 World Series. He also has heaps of scrapbooks filled with clippings from his playing days.

His prized possessions, though, are the baseballs he's kept from all of his complete games. ''I'm probably the only ex-player in the country with 70 to 75 baseballs,'' Vander Meer says. Written on each ball is the date, the line score and the batteries. Johnny says he has 35 to 40 of the balls on display in his house.

The balls represent an awful lot of good pitching. During a career that covered all or parts of 14 seasons, excluding two years in the Navy in World War II, Vander Meer had a lifetime record of 119–121 with a 3.44 earned run average. He led the National League in strikeouts in 1941, 1942 and 1943, in walks in 1943 and 1948, and in complete games in 1943.

Vander Meer joined the Reds in 1937, after playing half the season at Syracuse. He posted a 3–5 record his first year. In his legendary 1938 season, Johnny had a 15–10 record with a 3.12 ERA. During the season, he won nine straight games, and he also pitched three five-hitters.

He was the starting and winning pitcher for the National League in the 1938 All-Star game, allowing one hit in three innings of a 4–1 triumph. At the end of that season, Vander Meer was named the major league's Player of the Year by *The Sporting News*.

''Double No-Hit,'' as he came to be called, was at the time part of an outstanding Cincinnati pitching staff that included Paul Derringer and Bucky Walters. But in 1939, Johnny hurt his arm, and not only dropped out of the starting rotation, but was eventually sent back to the Reds' Indianapolis farm team, a stunning development for a guy who just a year earlier had been at the pinnacle of his profession.

The Reds reactivated Vander Meer in time for the 1939 World Series, which they lost to the New York Yankees, four games to zero. Although Johnny didn't pitch in the Series, his arm was sound again.

Proof of that had come during a game late in the 1939 season. It was a game in which Johnny beat the Phillies and Hugh Mulcahy, 3–2 in 13 innings to clinch the National League pennant for the Reds.

''The no-hitters are probably what I'm most known for,'' Vander Meer says, ''but to me, that game was the biggest thrill of my career. I was still going strong in the 13th inning. I knew my arm was back. To me, that was my greatest game.''

In the ensuing years, John had a number of fine seasons. He posted records of 16–13 in 1941, 18–12 in 1942, 15–16 in 1943 and 17–14 in 1948. Vander Meer worked three innings in relief in the 1940 World Series in which the Reds beat the Detroit Tigers, four games to three. He hurled in two more All-Star games, his most notable performance coming in the 1943 contest at Shibe Park in Philadelphia. Johnny struck out six American Leaguers in 2⅔ innings of pitching.

Throughout the 1940s, Vander Meer worked consistently while other Cinci hurlers came and went. "I pitched every three days, sometimes every two," he says. "And I always pitched batting practice to five hitters in between starts. I don't think pitchers today throw enough. They never throw between starts like we used to."

Johnny used a special technique while he was on the mound. "I finished about 52 percent of the games I started, which was pretty good for somebody as wild as me," he says. "What helped me was that I used to count myself down from the seventh inning on. When I hit the seventh inning, I would start to count the number of pitches. By the ninth inning, I figured I usually had 20 good pitches left, and I had to make them count."

The Dutch Master, as he was sometimes referred to, played his last season in Cincinnati in 1949. He spent the 1950 campaign with the Chicago Cubs, working mostly in relief, then finished his career in the livery of the Cleveland Indians in 1951.

Vander Meer looks back at his career with a healthy dose of satisfaction. "I had a very exciting and successful career," he says. "No job in the world would have been more enjoyable. I accomplished something that was of great satisfaction to me. A fellow who can play in the big leagues for 10 years or more has the best job ever made.

"I remember," Johnny says, "hunting one time with Babe Ruth. We were sitting in a duck blind, talking about getting booed. I recall saying, 'When they don't boo you anymore, you know that things are tough.'"

After leaving the playing field, Vander Meer managed for five years in the Reds' farm system. Johnny manged Pete Rose in his second year in baseball at Tampa of the Florida State League.

"He was probably the most dedicated player I ever managed or played with," Vander Meer says. "When he would ground to first, he'd run just as fast as if he'd hit a single. If he hit a single, he barreled into second. I always thought he would be a good hitter because he always made contact. He was never that good with the glove at second base because he couldn't go to his right. I wanted to put him at third base or left field.

"One day I said to him, 'Do you always run to first base like that?' Rose said, 'I'm just looking for a job.' At practice, he was the first man on the field and the last man off of it. After an inning, he made a point of getting to the dugout before anybody else. When you're a manager, you notice things like that.

"Dedication is extremely important," Johnny adds. "It's important in every walk of life. You can't be without it if you're going to be successful. Rose certainly had it."

A guy named Vander Meer must have had it, too, because without it, he never would have achieved the astonishing feat of back-to-back no-hitters.

Home Run Kings, Batting Champs and RBI Leaders

Del Ennis—
Big RBI Man for the Phillies

Ask any real fan of the Philadelphia Phillies to name the top sluggers in club history and, without hesitation, the name Del Ennis is always one of the first ones mentioned.

Names such as Mike Schmidt and Chuck Klein readily come to the tip of the tongue, too. And that should tell you all you need to know about the kind of company that Ennis is keeping.

More than 30 years after he hung up his Phillies uniform for the last time, Ennis still ranks second on the club's all-time list in home runs, third in RBI and total bases, fourth in hits, and extra base hits, and fifth in doubles, at-bats, and games played.

One of the premier power-hitters of his era, Ennis, a three-time member of the National League All-Star team, was *The Sporting News'* Rookie of the Year in 1946, the league leader in RBI in 1950, and was annually among the league's top home run and RBI men.

During a career that spanned 14 big league seasons—11 with the Phillies, two with the St. Louis Cardinals and one divided between the Cincinnati Reds and Chicago White Sox—Ennis drilled 2,063 hits and 288 home runs, collected 1,284 RBI and wound up with a lifetime batting average of .286.

He drove in more than 100 runs seven times, and seven times he cracked 25 or more home runs in his career that ended in 1959.

Between 1946 and 1959, only Stan Musial with 1,678 drove in more runs than Ennis.

Ennis recalls:

> With men on base, I made a habit of studying pitchers. I would concentrate when a pitcher got in a jam, see what his best pitch was. Was he a fast ball pitcher or a curve ball pitcher? What was his best pitch? When a pitcher is in trouble, he is not going to try to get you out on his worst pitch. He'll try to get you out on his best pitch. If you know the pitchers and look for their best pitches when they are in jams, nine times out of 10, you'll get that pitch eventually.

The best season for the big outfielder was in 1950 when he helped the Phillies win their first pennant in 35 years. Del hit .311 with 31 home runs,

34 doubles and 126 RBI. That year, Ennis was fourth in the MVP voting, which was won by teammate Jim Konstanty.

During the season, Ennis had tied the National League record for most RBI in two consecutive innings when he drove in seven runs against the Chicago Cubs. He doubled with the bases loaded in the seventh inning, then hit a grand slam home run in the eighth. With 41 RBI in the month of July, Ennis went on to win the league's RBI title.

"I always had it in the back of my mind that I would like to win some kind of title," Ennis says. "I was shooting for the RBI title that year, although the main thought on my mind was to win the pennant."

The Phillies won the pennant on the last day of the season when Dick Sisler hit a three-run homer in the top of the 10th inning to defeat the second place Brooklyn Dodgers, 4–1. The Phillies then bowed to the New York Yankees in four straight games in the World Series.

"After we won the pennant, the World Series was an aftermath," Ennis says. "It was a big thrill for us to win the pennant on the last day of the season, going down to the wire. If we had won earlier, we might have given the Yankees a much better battle. We had real good pitching.

"It was wonderful," he continues, "to play with a bunch of guys who worked together so well. We had 25 guys on that club and every one stuck up for one another. To win, you have to work together. It was a team effort."

Even though the Phils lost the Series, it was still the most memorable experience in Ennis' career.

"That's what all players point for—playing in the World Series," he says. "It's an experience that's not like anything else in the game."

Today, Ennis is a partner with Johnny Wise, a former Phillies traveling secretary, in a 36-lane bowling alley in suburban Philadelphia. The two opened the place called Del Ennis Lanes one year before Del concluded his major league career.

"Sometimes, I miss playing baseball," says Ennis. "But being in the bowling business is a little like being in baseball because there's a lot of contact with people. I enjoy that."

Del, who played only one minor league season after graduating from a high school in Philadelphia that later produced two other big leaguers—infielder Lee Elia and outfielder Al Spangler—divides his time between homes in Jenkintown, Pennsylvania, and Ocean City, New Jersey. The father of six children, Del is an avid fisherman and golfer. He used to bowl every day, he says, but quit because there were too many interruptions while he was bowling.

Ennis was signed by the Phillies right out of high school in 1942.

"I was in my senior year at Olney High when Jocko Collins came out to one of our games," Ennis recalls. "I think I drove in about 12 runs with three homers and a double. Jocko was there to watch one of our pitchers, but after the game, he came over and talked to me. I had no thoughts at the time of playing professional baseball. I was going to go into the Navy after graduation."

Del Ennis.

Instead, he signed with the Phillies and played the 1943 season at Trenton in the Inter-State League.

Ennis hit .346 at Trenton. He led the league in total bases with 320, cracking out 37 doubles, 18 homers, and a league-leading 16 triples. Ennis drove in 93 runs while scoring 104.

The Phillies knew that they had a player with a future. But they had to wait because Del missed the next two seasons while serving in the Navy. He was out in time to join the 1946 Phillies.

"I didn't really expect to stay with the Phillies, but they had to keep me because I was on the national defense list and they had to give me a 30-day trial," Ennis says. "I never had spring training. I pinch-hit in Pittsburgh in my first game, then I got into the starting lineup. A few days later against the Cubs in Chicago, I hit two homers in one game."

Del hit .313 in his rookie year with 17 home runs, which at the time was a club rookie record. *The Sporting News,* voting for the first time for a Rookie of the Year, gave the award to Ennis. Del was also named to the National League All-Star team.

The Phillies' fifth place finish that year was their highest since 1932. "Ben Chapman, our manager, did a good job with that club," says Ennis. "Personally, Schoolboy Rowe helped me the most. He told me that I should know the pitchers. He used to sit on the bench when he wasn't pitching and help me with the pitchers. He could pick up the pitches real good. From the pitchers' motions he could tell whether they were going to throw a fast ball or a curveball. Rowe would whistle when the pitcher was going to throw a curve. Of course, Schoolboy was a good hitting pitcher himself."

The following season, Del's average dropped to .275 and he hit only 12 homers. But he drove in 81 runs and he had a 19-game hitting streak, the longest in his career.

Ennis came back strongly in 1948, hitting .290, driving in 95 runs and smashing 30 homers. He also established the club record at the time for most homers hit in a season on the road with 22.

The following year, the Phillies finally escaped the second division by moving up to third place. It was the highest the club had finished since the 1917 season when it came in second. The Phillies had finished in the first division only one other time between 1918 and 1948 (1932 when they came in fourth). In 1949, the Whiz Kids were starting to come together.

"In the last six weeks of the 1949 season, we were all starting to mature as ballplayers," Ennis says. "We were all starting to concentrate and learn how to play, and we were fortunate that Eddie Sawyer could field eight of us without injuries for the most part. In fact, you used to play whether you were injured or not. If you came out, you might not get back in. There were about 60 outfielders in the farm system waiting to take your job."

Del helped the Phillies with a strong finish as he hit .302 with 25 home runs and 110 RBI, fifth best in the league. His 39 doubles were second best in the league, two behind the leader, Musial.

Ennis was also a part of history that year when the Phillies tied a National League record for most homers in an inning with five against Cincinnati at Shibe Park. When the Phillies came to bat in the bottom of the eighth, they were trailing the Reds, 3-2. Del led off the inning with a homer. The Phillies went on to score 10 runs in the inning. Andy Seminick hit two homers while Rowe and Willie Jones each hit one.

Ennis, who had played left field in 1946, 1947 and 1949 and right field in 1948, was switched back to right in 1950 as Sisler went from first to left.

"The biggest adjustment going back to right field was that most of the sun fields then were in right," Ennis says. "In the later part of the game, the sun would come over the stands. It was a tough field to play. The only reason I moved back to right was I had a little stronger arm than Dick. I didn't mind playing there."

After the Phillies' exciting season in 1950, the team never came close to winning another pennant. Ennis was the National League's starting right fielder in the 1951 All-Star game, but he ended the season with a .267 average, just 15 home runs and 73 RBI. By then, the fans had started to boo him, a practice that was to continue throughout the rest of his years in Philadelphia.

Ennis was probably booed more than any player in Phillies' history. It was largely because he was a hometown product, and the fans apparently expected too much of him.

"The booing didn't bother me much," Ennis says. "At first when it started, I thought about it. But I made up my mind I was going to play ball or go home. I kept it out of my mind, even though I used to get a standing ovation of boos. It seems that after I left, they picked a guy to concentrate their booing on each year."

Despite the boos, Ennis had a strong season in 1952, hitting .289 with 20 home runs and ranking third in the league with 107 RBI. That year, he had one of his most memorable hits, a 17th inning home run that defeated the Boston Braves, 7-6, in a game in which Robin Roberts went the distance to get his 23d win of the season.

"I broke my wrist during that game and didn't know it," Ennis remembers. "I did it in about the third inning. They kept icing it during the game. I had no feeling in it when I hit the homer. But I missed only two games. They put my wrist in some kind of pressure cast. I didn't want to come out of there."

Del had another fine season in 1953, hitting .285 with 29 homers and 125 RBI, fourth best in the league. His average dipped to .261 in 1954, but he was fifth in the league with 119 runs batted in and he hit 25 homers. After playing left in 1952 and 1953, he played both left and right in 1954. He also played his first and only game at first base that year.

"I remember that one game I played there," he recalls. "Willie Jones threw a ball to me that hit me on the knee cap. It was a sinker. They got me out of there in a hurry."

The 1955 season began with Ennis hurt. He and Ashburn collided chasing a line drive by Mickey Mantle in a game against the Yankees in Wilmington, Delaware right before the home opener. Ennis missed the first three games. He went on to hit .296 with 29 homers. His 120 RBI were third in the National League.

Not only was Ennis voted to the All-Star team as the starting left fielder, that year, he had one of his biggest days as a hitter. He hit three home runs and drove in seven runs against the Cardinals as the Phillies beat St. Louis, 7–2. On August 9, Del got his 1,000th career run batted in when he hit a sacrifice fly to drive in Herman Wehmeier against the Pirates in a 9–1 Phillies win.

Del's average slipped to .260 in 1956. He hit 26 home runs, but his

Del Ennis (right) was a member of a fine Philadelphia Phillies outfield in 1950 along with Dick Sisler (left) and Richie Ashburn.

RBI dropped to 95. That November he was traded to the Cardinals for Rip Repulski and Bobby Morgan. It wasn't a good trade for the Phillies.

Ennis recalls:

> The thing that shocked me about the trade was that I had dinner with Wister Randolph, one of the team's vice presidents, and I didn't leave him until midnight. When I got up in the morning, a writer called me and told me that I was traded to the Cardinals. At the time, Bob Carpenter was away, so I called Randolph and told him I had been traded. He said, "You have got to be kidding." I said, "No, I was traded to the Cardinals." He called Bob and Bob knew nothing about it either. I think Roy Hamey, our general manager took it on his own to trade me.
>
> We almost won the pennant in St. Louis in 1957. We lost in the last week to the Braves. I drove in 105 runs batting in front of Musial, who was also my roommate. We used to talk about pitchers more than hitting.

The 1957 season was Del's last big year. After spending 1958 with St. Louis he played briefly with Cincinnati and the Chicago White Sox in 1959 before calling it a career in June.

"The toughest pitcher I ever faced was Ewell Blackwell," remembers Ennis. "I didn't like to hit against him, dreaded the thought of hitting against him. As it turned out, I had real good luck against Blackwell. My shots were mostly to right field, and fortunately for me, found some holes out there."

Over his distinguished career, Ennis hit a lot of other shots that also found holes. Despite an abundance of excellent hurlers in his era, Ennis usually knew what to do with the pitches that came his way. His record clearly indicates that.

Carl Furillo—
The Man with the Golden Arm

In the era that extended from 1946 to 1957, the Brooklyn Dodgers were one of the most successful baseball teams ever to take the field.

During that period, the Dodgers won six National League pennants. Two other times they finished in ties for first before losing in special playoffs. The club placed second four times and third twice, its lowest finish in those 12 years.

Through most of those years, the Dodgers fielded a starting eight that was as potent as any that ever stepped onto a diamond. Eventually, four of them became members of the Hall of Fame.

Perhaps the most under-rated player of this star-studded group was the right fielder. His name was Carl Furillo, and he was as vital to the club as any of his more publicized teammates.

For one thing, he had the best throwing arm of any outfielder of his and probably any other era. He was also an outstanding hitter.

Furillo won the 1953 National League batting championship with a .344 average. Four other times he hit over .300 during a 15-year career in which he posted a lifetime .299 average.

A dangerous clutch hitter, Furillo drove in more than 80 runs nine times in his career. he wound up with 1,058 RBI while scoring 895 runs and whacking 192 homers.

When he batted eighth in the order—which he did for part of his career—he was often described as the best number eight hitter in baseball history.

But it was his throwing arm that really attracted attention. Furillo, who played the tricky right field wall at Ebbets Field like a violin, had an arm that uncorked throws like a howitzer fires shells. So powerful were his pegs that most enemy runners refused to test them. If they did, they were usually gunned down like clay pigeons at a shooting range.

Furillo, nicknamed The Reading Rifle, led National League outfielders in assists only twice (1950 and 1951). Because his arm was so feared, opposing base-runners simply didn't dare run on him.

Carl Furillo.

Today, Carl lives in Stoney Creek Mills, Pennsylvania, a suburb of
Reading, in a house that sits just a few blocks from where he grew up.

Refreshingly candid, Furillo has had some ups and downs since his glory
days in Brooklyn, including leukemia. Medication, he says, has pushed the
disease into remission. Carl's healthy looks are reassuring.

Furillo has been involved in a variety of endeavors since leaving baseball
in 1960. Currently, he works at a Reading industrial company as a security
guard, a position he has held the last nine years.

When he first retired from the game, he returned to Reading to become
part owner of a kitchen cabinet business. Later, he shifted to New York where
he was a partner in a delicatessen in Queens. That was followed by a short
stint as an assistant manager of a grocery store in the Bronx and seven years
as an ironworker, installing elevator doors in New York City. Carl helped
to put up the doors on the World Trade Center.

Although he has owned the house in which he lives for 36 years, Furillo
returned to it permanently 13 years ago. Just a few blocks away is the place
where he learned to play the game of baseball.

Furillo recalls:

My mother and father were immigrants, and they didn't want me to play
ball. But we had two or three acres behind the house that my father had built,
and there was a ballfield back there. At first, I played mostly softball. I was
also the mascot for one of the sandlot baseball teams. When I was 15, the
manager told me to go out and shag some flies. "It's time you went out and
played some baseball with the big boys," he said.

Furillo played with local teams until he was 18. In 1940, he was given
a tryout by Pocomoke City, a team in the Eastern Shore League and a farm
club of the Reading International League team. Carl made the team, and
his professional career was launched.

He progressed from Pocomoke to Reading—a team which while he was
there was bought by the Dodgers for $5,000—to Montreal to the Army before
getting his first action with Brooklyn in 1946.

"I was home from the Army for just 24 days when the Dodgers told
me to report to an advance spring training camp in Sanford, Florida," he
recalls. "I hadn't played ball in three years. Most of the time, I was stationed
on the Phillipines, and there was no service ball there."

Although he was ticketed for Montreal, Furillo made the Dodgers,
anyway, and in his rookie season hit .284. He followed that with a .295 and
a .297 before exploding to a .322 in 1949. That year and the following one,
Carl drove in 106 runs each season—his career high.

Furillo's best year was 1953 when he won the batting crown. Amazingly,
he had just come off an eye operation in which he had had grit removed
from one eye and a growth removed from the other.

"I was a very determined person," he recalls, "and I wasn't going to
let anything stop me. I was determined not to kill the ball, just meet it, and

I practiced hitting to right and up the middle all the time. Everything I did was right."

Furillo followed his batting title with seasons of .294, .314, .294, .306 and .290. He hit a career-high 26 home runs in 1955.

All the while, though, people wanted to talk more about his arm.

"I got more of a thrill out of throwing out a runner than I did getting a base hit," Carl confides. "I used to love it. I really gloated on it. But once in a while I'd get annoyed because nobody ever talked about my hitting.

"I always had a good arm," he adds. "I was one of those kids who threw stones a lot. And I worked in an apple orchard as a kid, and threw a lot of apples. One time, I even hit a rabbit in the head.

"Later, I worked for a construction company and we hauled rocks all day. When you do that, your arm is bound to get strong.

"But it was basically more God-given talent than anything," he says. "That and a lot of practice. I still practiced all the time, even when I was in the big leagues. A lot of times, the other team would stop to watch me throw.

"Campy (Roy Campanella) and I used to have contests every day. We'd stand back of home and have somebody put a glove up at second. Then we'd throw for accuracy. We'd keep score. We were always about even."

Furillo talks animatedly about the technique of throwing. To him, it is a science, and he knows it perfectly. One wonders why some ball club hasn't utilized his expertise on the subject.

"I was always taught to use the arm, wrist, shoulder and body," he says. "If you're throwing from center field, you aim for the top of the pitcher's mound so that the ball will hit half way between the mound and the plate. From right field, you try to hit the cutoff man in the chest. You've got to get the ball out of your hand quickly. You have to charge the ball, come up with it and throw all in one motion.

"Most players don't do that today. There are a lot of scatter arms around. All they want to do is show off."

Furillo had some memorable throws in his career, once even throwing out Mel Queen at first base on what would have been a clean single to right.

"I threw out Marty Marion at the plate in St. Louis," Carl recalls. "And he could run. After the game he said to me, 'Either I'm getting slower or you're getting stronger.'

"The throw I remember best, though, was in Boston in 1952. We won the pennant that day. Sam Jethroe was on first. The batter hit a low, line shot toward right-center. Jethroe tried to go to third, but I fired the ball in and it hit 20 feet in front of Billy Cox at third. The ball just scooted right into Billy's glove. Jethroe was out by 1½ steps. It was pouring rain. We got the next out, the game ended and we won the pennant."

Furillo's Dodgers were frequent visitors to the World Series, although the only time they won in Brooklyn was in 1955. But they were great teams, nonetheless.

"We had a few prima donnas," Furillo says, "but when you got on the field, it didn't matter who you were or what color you were. We all stuck together."

Furillo, who first roomed with Gil Hodges and later Sandy Koufax, played in Brooklyn at the time when the club was twice involved in history-making events; first when it made Jackie Robinbson the first black major leaguer and later when it shifted the franchise to Los Angeles.

At the time, stories associated Carl with a clubhouse conspiracy that opposed Robinson's joining the club. But he says he was falsely connected.

"Dixie Walker, Dixie Howell, Hugh Casey, Kirbe Higbe and Pete Reiser, all of whom were southern boys and they used to condemn the hell out of blacks," he says. "They wanted to get up a petition against Jackie. I knew him from when he played in Montreal and we trained in Havana.

"When Branch Rickey heard about the petition, the southern boys tried to blame me, but I had nothing to do with it."

Something else Carl wanted nothing to do with was the Dodgers' move to Los Angeles in 1958. "The majority of players didn't want to leave Brooklyn," he says. "Only the California guys like (Duke) Snider and (Ron) Fairly did.

"Brooklyn was very special to us. And the people there were special. You could feel them. They'd be on top of you at Ebbets Field, and you could hear them and they were almost part of the game. And they'd always want to treat you. They were great. It was like one, big family.

"When we moved from Brooklyn, it was very traumatic. Los Angeles just didn't feel right. All everybody did was talk about Hollywood. Everybody wanted to meet movie stars or see who was in the stands. Nobody had his mind on the game. We didn't have a bunch of players who were hungry."

Furillo didn't stay long on the West Coast. In fact, about the only positive memories he has from his days in LA were two pinch-hit singles in 1959, one that won the pennant against the Milwaukee Braves and another that won the third game of the World Series against the Chicago White Sox.

Early in 1960, Carl was abruptly handed his release in an episode that ignited an unpleasant end to his career with the Dodgers. Furillo, who sued the club for his salary for the full year—and won—left baseball with a bitter taste that took a number of years to overcome.

Presently, Furillo ranks high in many categories on the Dodgers' all-time career hitting lists; fourth in RBI; fifth in triples; sixth in home runs, hits, and extra base hits; seventh in total bases and eighth in runs and games played.

His accomplishments came in an era when good pitchers were in abundance in the National League.

"Sal Maglie was about the toughest. He never gave you a ball down the middle." Furillo says. "Robin Roberts was also tough. He was a spot pitcher, but he could throw hard and he moved the ball around. Ewell Blackwell—we called him the Octopus—had a motion that you didn't know where the ball was coming out of. Warren Spahn had a real good screwball, and Lew Burdette and Bob Rush were tough.''

Furillo says he didn't like hitting against that group any more than he liked dealing with Leo Durocher, his Dodger manager briefly in the late 1940s and the hated pilot of the New York Giants' later. The two had a celebrated fight in 1953.

"He always tried to scare the hell out of you with that big mouth of his," Carl says. "I never trusted him. We didn't get along. He was always against me. Why, I don't know."

Furillo has had little contact with baseball in recent years, although he participated in the Dodgers' dream week one year at Vero Beach. "I'll watch a couple of innings of a game on television and then I pack it in," he says.

Carl has, however, retained some personal items, such as his silver bat for the batting title, two bronzed gloves, his World Series rings and some uniforms. He also has a sizable scrapbook from his playing days.

In it are clippings that reaffirm the point that Carl Furillo was truly one of the outstanding members of an outstanding team.

Billy Goodman—
The Ultimate Utilityman

Billy Goodman was the ultimate utilityman, a high-average hitter and a versatile fielder who could, and did, play every position except pitcher and catcher.

He also represented the ultimate dilemma for several of his managers, particularly while he played for the Boston Red Sox. Despite his status as a utilityman, Goodman was too good to keep out of the regular lineup, even though it was never easy finding a spot for him on the talent-laden Bosox of the late 1940s and 1950s.

Consequently, during his nearly 10 seasons in Boston, as well as in subsequent years with the Baltimore Orioles, Chicago White Sox and Houston Colts, Billy had few seasons in which he held a regular position. Every year, though, he wound up with close to or more than 500 at bats.

As an illustration of his versatility, Goodman, during his 16-year big-league career, played 624 games at second base, 406 at first base, 330 at third base, 111 in the outfield and seven at shortstop. He played each position skillfully, but seldom for too long.

Goodman won the American League batting championship in 1950, running away with the title with a .354 average. Billy, however, had no regular position, dividing most of his time between the outfield and first and third bases.

The Red Sox' starting lineup that year had Walt Dropo at first, Bobby Doerr at second, Vern Stephens at short, Johnny Pesky at third, Ted Williams in left, Dom DiMaggio in center, Al Zarilla in right and Birdie Tebbetts catching. With a lineup like that (the lowest average was Doerr's .294), it was no easy job getting enough at-bats to qualify for the batting crown. But, due in part to Ted Williams' breaking an elbow in the All-Star game, Billy squeezed into 110 games, and the slender North Carolina native went to the plate often enough to beat George Kell for the title by 14 points.

"With all the guys on that squad, I couldn't be too choosy about where I was playing," Goodman recalled. "The only thing that mattered was that I played somewhere."

Billy Goodman.

When he won the batting title, Goodman was only in his third full season in the major leagues. He was just 24 years old at the time, one of the youngest batting champs in big league history.

"I was so young, I didn't realize what I'd done," Billy said. "It was exciting, but the year was a little disappointing because we didn't win the pennant."

The Red Sox finished in third place, which was a typical finish for Boston teams in those days. Despite having the most talented starting eight in baseball, the Sox except in 1946, lost the pennant chase every year either to the New York Yankees or the Cleveland Indians.

Goodman, who lived in Sarasota, Florida, died in 1986 at the age of 59.

Billy often wished he still had his old baseball cards. "When I was playing I always gave the cards away," he said. "I just handed them out to kids. If I'd kept all those cards, I'd really have something now."

Billy kept one of his first baseman mitts. He also had some of his caps. And he was particularly fond of a bronze plaque which he received at a benefit for Joe McCarthy. "Of course, I've got a lot of clippings," he added. "But they're hardly worth a cup of coffee."

Billy said that Hoyt Wilhelm was one of the toughest pitchers he faced. "As I look back, he was the hardest guy to make contact against," he said.

"Bob Feller was the fastest. The first time I saw him was when Joe Cronin sent me up to pinch-hit. I watched three fast ones go by. That made a lifelong impression on me."

Goodman made some sizable impressions, himself. Essentially a singles and doubles hitter—he had 19 career home runs—Billy finished his career with a .300 batting average, which included 1,691 hits.

A lefthanded batter, Goodman broke into organized baseball in 1944. In his three years in the minors (he was also in the military one year), Billy hit .336, .389 and .340.

He joined the Red Sox at the end of the 1947 season. In his rookie year in 1948, Goodman hit .310. That year and the next, he played mostly at first base. Billy led American League first sackers in fielding in 1949.

In 1950, Boston brought up Dropo, a hard-hitting first baseman who tied with Stephens for the league lead (144) that year in RBI. Knocked off of first base, Goodman won the batting crown while playing 45 games in the outfield, 27 at third base and 21 at first. Although he had no regular position, Goodman came to the plate 424 times.

In his nine full seasons with the Red Sox, Billy never hit lower than .293. He hit .306 in 1952 and .313 and .303 in the next two years. His 1953 mark tied with Minnie Minoso for third place in the batting race behind Mickey Vernon and Al Rosen.

Because of his irregular status, Billy never had a 200-hit season. By far, the most games he ever played at one position in one season was in 1955 when he manned second base in 143 games.

A two-time member of the American League All-Star team (1949, 1953), Goodman was traded to the Orioles in 1957 for pitcher Mike Fornieles. At the end of the season, he and Larry Doby were the key figures in a seven-player deal with the White Sox.

Billy spent four years in Chicago, playing mostly at third base. He was the Chisox' starting third baseman when they won the American League pennant in 1959.

Chicago gave him his release in the spring of 1962. One month later, Goodman hooked up with the expansion Houston Colts. That was his last major league season.

Goodman joined the Milwaukee Braves system, and for the next two years managed a minor league team at Durham in the Carolina League. At Durham, Billy was a playing-manager, hitting .354 and .325 in part-time roles. The club finished second and fifth.

In 1965, Goodman signed as a scout with the Houston Astros. But in May, he was sent to manage the team's Cocoa farm club in the Florida State League. The following year, Billy joined the Red Sox as a scout. He was a hitting instructor in the Kansas City farm system the year after that. In 1968, he rejoined the Braves as a coach with the parent team. He stayed there until the end of the 1970 season.

Since then, Goodman did spot work as a minor league hitting instructor for the Braves and coached with the club's Richmond farm team.

After leaving baseball, he worked at a ranch near his home in Florida and looked after his commercial properties. He also spent time working at his wife's antique store.

Sometimes, visitors would enter the store and recognize the slender man waiting on them. Billy Goodman, a one-time batting champion and certainly the finest utility man of his and perhaps any other day, was anything but forgettable.

Ted Kluszewski—
Hard-Slugging Muscleman

Mention the name Ted Kluszewski and the first picture that leaps into the mind is that of a big guy wearing a uniform with cut-off sleeves. He was probably the first baseball player ever to cut off the sleeves of his shirt at the shoulders.

It caused a bit of a stir when he did it. But Kluszewski altered the satorial effects of his Cincinnati Reds' shirt for a good reason. And it had nothing to do with what was occasionally suggested as a desire to exhibit his rippling muscles.

"I just did it to be more comfortable," reveals the former slugging first baseman. "We had those old flannel uniforms that didn't have any give. I couldn't move my arms at all. I tried to get them to tailor the sleeves for me, but they wouldn't do it. So, one day, I just got some scissors and cut them off."

Kluszewski, of course, had arms that would've made a blacksmith proud. Put him underneath a spreading chestnut tree, and Big Klu, with his bulging biceps hung on a 6'2", 225-pound frame, would've looked like the perfect village smithy.

The large frame was something that gave Klu an advantage in the sports world long before he discovered the pleasures of socking baseballs into distant lands. As a youngster, Ted was notorious throughout his native Indiana for his exploits on the football field.

He attracted All-American attention at the University of Indiana as a rugged end on a team that featured future Philadelphia Eagles Hall of Famer, Pete Pihos, at fullback.

When he finally got around to taking baseball seriously, Kluszewski became one of the great hitters of his era. For 15 seasons, starting at the end of the 1947 campaign, Ted was one of the most intimidating sights in baseball, a giant in baseball clothing who could crush an enemy pitcher's delivery with the certainty of a man squashing a bug.

By the time he retired after the 1961 season, Big Klu had a .298 lifetime batting average. One third of his 1,766 hits were for extra bases, including 279 home runs, and he collected 1,028 RBI to go along with 848 runs scored.

From 1949 to 1956, he had few peers in the National League when it came to hitting a baseball. In seven of those eight years, he hit over .300, going .309, .307, .259, .320, .316, .326, .314, and .302. In one stretch between 1953 and 1956, his home run totals read 40, 49, 47 and 35.

Ted Kluszewski.

Kluszewski had his biggest year in 1954 when he won two legs of the triple crown with 49 home runs and 141 RBI for the fifth place Reds. Only seven other National League players have hit more home runs in one season. His .326 batting average was fifth in the league.

"It was a great year," recalls the ex-slugger, "although I didn't feel that I did anything different from previous years. It was just one of those things. I hit the ball well, and I had a lot of men on base when I did."

Klu had almost as fine a season the following year when he led the league in hits (192) while clubbing 47 homers, second in the circuit, driving in 113 runs and batting .314.

That year, Klu's homers combined with teammate Wally Post's 40 four-baggers to gain a third place tie (with the 1947 New York Giants' Johnny Mize and Willard Marshall) on the National League's list of all-time top home run-hitting duos. The following season, Klu's 35 homers, Post's 36, 38 by rookie Frank Robinson, 29 by Gus Bell and 28 by Ed Bailey gave the Reds the highest five-man one-season total in National League history.

Kluszewski was the starting first baseman on the National League All-Star team for three straight years from 1953 to 1955. In four All-Star game appearances, he hit .500, three times getting two hits in the game.

Despite his size, Ted was an excellent fielder, too. In 1955 he set a record which still stands by leading the league in fielding for the fifth consecutive season. And in 1956 he tied Frank McCormick for the major league mark of most consecutive years leading the league in double plays with four.

Strangely enough, first base was not Kluszewski's original position. When he broke into organized baseball in 1946, Ted was an outfielder.

"But they decided that first base should be my position," recalls Kluszewski. "I was starting to run over people in the outfield, and I guess they were afraid I'd hurt somebody. So I was switched to first base at spring training in 1947.

"I struggled for about two years at first base; I made errors you wouldn't believe. One guy said I couldn't catch a ball in a telephone booth. I had a real tough time getting used to the mitt. They even brought in Bill Terry to work with me one spring training."

Klu could be excused for his unfamiliarity with the glove, or for that matter with baseball in general.

"Before I signed a pro contract, I had played no more than 50 games of baseball in my life," Ted says. "I was a Cubs' fan , but I really didn't follow baseball. I played one season of baseball in high school. Mostly I played slow-pitch softball around my hometown. But I was basically a football player."

Ted went to Indiana University on a football scholarship and became the Hoosiers' starting fullback. When Pihos returned from military service, Klu was switched to end to make room for the returning star. Ironically, Pihos made his mark in the pros as an end.

Kluszewski began playing baseball in college almost as an afterthought.

"The main reason I did it," he says, "was because if you played baseball you didn't have to go out for spring football.

"I found I could hit pretty well," Kluszewski adds. "Then in my second year, the Reds held spring training at the college. They saw me play and we won the Big 10 that year. They offered me the opportunity to play baseball. I felt I could play, and anyway, football wasn't that lucrative as a pro sport. So, I signed with the Reds after my sophomore year."

In his first year in the minors, Klu played at Columbia (South Carolina) and led the Sally League in hitting with a .352 average. The following season at Memphis, he hit .377 to lead the Southern Association in hitting.

"I probably had a natural talent for hitting," Kluszewski recalls. "When I first played, I was a line drive hitter. But the Reds taught me to pull the ball."

After reporting to Cinci at the end of the 1947 season, Kluszewski made the club permanently in 1948, a season in which he took over from Babe Young and hit .274 with 12 home runs.

From there, Ted went on to become one of the Reds' all-time leading hitters. Five times he led the team in home runs, RBI and average in the same season. Klu was elected to the Reds' Hall of Fame in 1962.

Klu had some memorable moments with the Reds. "I especially remember two home runs I hit," he says. "One was against the Giants. Eddie Stanky was playing second base for them, and I hit a line drive that was low enough that he jumped for the ball. It kept going and went over the right-center field fence.

"Another home run I remember was one I hit off of Preacher Roe. With two outs in the ninth and a curfew approaching, I hit one that won the game. Hit it so hard that Roe didn't even turn around to watch. He just put his glove in his pocket and headed for the clubhouse."

Klu also remembers a spectacular doubleheader in Memphis. He hit for the cycle in the first game. In the second game, the absence of a triple kept him from hitting for the cycle again.

One game that Klu would like to forget was a late 1950 outing in which he hit a screaming liner into the face of Phillies' pitcher Bubba Church. In the midst of a fine rookie season at the time, Church was never the same pitcher after the accident.

"When it hit him, I didn't know what to do," remembers Kluszewski. "I didn't know whether I should go to him or to first. The hit wasn't important at that point.

"It was scarry," Klu adds, recalling how Church staggered in pain around the mound before finally crumbling into a bloody heap. "He was a friend. I was really worried for him."

Most other times, Klu didn't have such compassion for enemy pitchers. He attacked their offerings vehemently.

Klu faced numerous good pitchers in his day, but the one he claims gave him the most trouble was Howie Pollet, a stylish lefthander who hurled for the St. Louis Cardinals and later in the National League the Pittsburgh Pirates and the Chicago Cubs.

"He used to give me fits," relates Kluszewski. "I never hit him well at all."

Through all his years with the Reds, Klu never came close to playing with a pennant-winner except in 1956 when the Reds finished third, two games behind the league-leading Brooklyn Dodgers.

It took until 1959, by which time he had been traded to the Pirates and then to the Chicago White Sox, for Ted to get into a World Series.

But what a World Series he had!

Although the White Sox lost in six games to the Dodgers, Klu hit .391 in the Series with three home runs. His 10 RBI and five runs scored accounted for all but eight of the Sox' runs in the Series.

In the opening game of the Series, Klu hit two home runs and collected five RBI to power Chicago to an 11–0 victory. He also hit a two-run homer in a losing cause in the final game.

"It really meant a lot to me to play in that Series," says Klu, "even though we lost. I had been around (pro baseball) for 14 years, and I hadn't played in one. I was really happy to get the opportunity when it finally came."

Two seasons after that Series, Klu wound up his career with the Los Angeles Angels. Although he turned 37 that season, Ted still managed to hit 15 home runs, one of the big league's highest career-ending totals.

"I could still hit, but I had a bad back. It was really bothering me," says Klu. "It had gotten to the point that it wasn't much fun playing anymore."

Once he retired, Kluszewski found opportunities in new ventures. He opened a restaurant in Cincinnati and ran it for 12 years. Meanwhile, he also did television sportscasting for five years.

Along the way, the Reds called Ted back as a coach. He joined the club in 1970 and stayed with them through 1983. He was named the club's hitting coach in 1979.

In recent years, the Reds have used Klu's expertise with the bat as a minor league hitting instructor. He travels through the farm system, spending time with each of the team's minor league clubs.

"I enjoy working with kids," Ted reflects. "You get plenty of time to teach. I like that."

Ted spends the off-season back home in suburban Cincinnati where his trophy room is filled with memories of an outstanding career.

"I have a lot of bats, plaques, trophies, newspaper clippings and a couple of uniforms," he says. "I have the last bat I used as a player, plus some bats from the World Series and the rest of my career."

Kluszewski says he gets 100 to 200 fan letters each month, considerably more than he did when he was playing.

"I guess a lot of people remember me," he says.

Indeed, they do.

Bill Nicholson—
The Fans Called Him Swish

He would stand up there at the plate, a big guy with a massive chest, arms like a blacksmith's and shoulders that seemed as wide as a highway, and as he would take his practice swings, a roar would come down from the stands.

"Swish," the crowd would chant. Each time he swung the bat, "Swish, Swish, Swish."

In the annals of sports, few athletes have provoked such a massive vocal outpouring from the fans as Bill Nicholson, the powerful lefthanded batter who in the early to mid-1940s was one of the most feared hitters in baseball.

Wherever he went, the cry always rang out. "Swish, Swish, Swish."

It was the fans' way of having a little fun while recognizing not only one of the lustiest swings in the game but one of the more popular players of the era.

And the chant wasn't limited to Wrigley Field where Nicholson toiled for the Chicago Cubs and won two home run crowns. It followed him all the way around the league.

"It really started in Brooklyn," recalls Nicholson who, although he was known as Swish to the fans, was called Nick by friends and teammates. "Pretty soon, it caught on in other cities. In fact, the fans probably did it more in some of the other cities than they did in Chicago."

Why did they do it?

"Well, every time I came to the plate, I would take a few practice swings to sort of measure the pitcher," Nicholson says. "After a while, the fans just started yelling 'swish' with each swing."

Once he stepped to the plate, the chants ceased and the sound became that of ball against bat as Nicholson lit into enemy pitching. That was something he did with considerable frequency.

In a 16-year big league career, the 6' 0", 205-pounder clubbed 1,484 hits, including 235 home runs and 272 doubles. He finished with a career batting average of .268 with 948 RBI in 1,677 games.

Nine times in his career, Nicholson homered for the season in double figures. During one five-year stretch, he averaged 27 dingers per season. He reached double figures in doubles 10 straight times.

Nicholson won back-to-back home run and RBI titles in 1943 and 1944. In the former, his best season in the majors, Bill smashed 29 homers, drove in 128 runs and had a .309 batting average. In 1944, he led in home runs with 33, and RBI with 122 while also leading the league in runs scored with 116. That year he hit .287.

Nicholson had a number of other fine seasons, hitting .295, .297 and .294, and in 1945 helping the Cubs win the National League pennant.

Now much trimmer than he was in his playing days, Nicholson lives on his 128-acre farm about 10 miles outside of his native Chestertown, Maryland. He keeps busy by tending to the many chores on his property and hunting in the game-rich, nearby meadows with his battery of retrievers.

After his playing days ended following the 1953 season, which culminated with a five-year hitch with the Philadelphia Phillies, Nicholson tried his hand at a variety of occupations, including the operation of a bowling alley, selling real estate, working as an inspector at a race track and farming.

There are few clues that the handsome home in which he lives houses a former ballplayer. A painting of Nick in a Phillies uniform, given to him when the team celebrated the 25-year anniversary of the 1950 Whiz Kids, provides a rare hint. Nicholson has not retained most of the mementoes of his career, having given most of them away.

"I did have an old Cubs uniform," he relates, "but I had it out in the shed and the termites ate it up. I gave a Phillies uniform I had to a museum over in the next town."

Nicholson is somewhat of a local hero in this quiet area of the Eastern Shore. Not only did he grow up there, he went to college there and has always lived there except during baseball seasons.

Bill attended Washington College in Chestertown where he was a math major, a National Merit Scholar and an all-around athlete.

"I began as an engineering student, but I never followed it up," he says. "I always wanted to be a ballplayer, even though I didn't actually expect to make it because I didn't think I was good enough."

When Nicholson began at Washington College, there was no baseball team. Instead, he ran track while playing baseball with a town team. He also played basketball, was an all-state selection in football and maintained a B average.

Washington finally added baseball in time for Nicholson's last two years. By the time Bill got his degree, he was not only the talk of the Eastern Shore, he was being scouted by the major leagues.

Ironically, Nicholson was playing near the birthplace of Jimmie Foxx. who was born in Sudlersville, about 20 miles from Chestertown. The two, however, never met until many years later.

Bill Nicholson.

"He was my idol as a kid," Nicholson recalls, "but he was already a big star in the major leagues when I came along. I didn't meet him until I was in the minors. Later on, we were teammates in Chicago (1943-44). He was an awfully nice fellow. I liked him very much."

Following his graduation from college with a bachelor of science degree, Nicholson was signed to a contract with the Philadelphia A's by veteran scout and former catcher, Ira Thomas.

Nick was sent briefly to Oklahoma City, then reported to the A's late in the season and got into 11 games, mostly as a pinch-hitter. After that, the A's sent him back to the minors where he played over the next three years for Williamsport, Portsmouth and Chattanooga, hitting over .300 and more than 20 homers each year.

"I hit well in the minors," remembers Nicholson, "but apparently the old man (Connie Mack) didn't like me."

Eventuallly, the Cubs bought Nicholson from Chattanooga for $35,000. Bill launched his career in the Windy City in mid-1939. He was immediately installed in right field, and hit .295 the rest of the season for the fourth place Cubs.

After a .295, 25-home run, 98-RBI season in 1940, Nicholson was a fixture in Wrigley Field and was on his way to becoming one of the most popular players in Chicago.

He made the National League All-Star team in 1940, 1941, 1943 and 1944, ultimately carving a place for himself in Cubs' history with his big seasons in 1943 and 1944.

"My first five years in Chicago, I thought I did really well," he says modestly. "I always had power, even as a kid, and I was a pretty consistent home run hitter. When I won the home run titles in '43 and '44, it really gave me a good feeling."

It was at about that time that Nicholson almost met with an early demise.

"My top salary in baseball was $18,000," he explains. "So one year after winning the home run title, I wanted a raise, Instead, they offered me a cut of $3,000. I held out all spring.

"Finally, I decided to fly to Catalina Island, where the Cubs trained, and meet with them. I went to get on a plane, but they wouldn't let me on because it was full. So I had to get the next plane.

"When I got to camp, the players gave me a big welcome. It seems the plane I was originally supposed to get had crashed and everybody was killed. They thought I was on that plane, too. They were really suprised when I showed up."

Along the way, Nicholson also had some memorable games. In one doubleheader at the Polo Grounds in New York in 1944, he hit four consecutive home runs (three in one game). He is only the seventh National League hitter to accomplish that feat.

"I hit two in a row off of Bill Voiselle," Nick recalls. "I always could hit him. Actually, I had five home runs, plus a single, in seven at-bats in that doubleheader. None of the homers was cheap, either. They were all line drives to right-center. I was hot. When you're hot, you can hit anything. Of course, I had some terrible slumps in Chicago, too."

Several pitchers, Nicholson says, contributed heavily to those slumps.

"I always had trouble with Max Lanier and Alpha Brazle when they were with the Cardinals," he says. "We used to go into St. Louis, and they would throw four straight lefthanders against us. One was Howie Pollet. I liked to hit against him. And once in a while, I'd get one against Harry Brecheen. But I could never hit Lanier or Brazle.

"One time I talked to Lanier about that. I asked him how come he always got me out? He said, 'It just seemed like I always pitched you good.'

"Bob Feller was awful quick," Nicholson adds. "But Ewell Blackwell in that one, great year he had (1947) was about as fast as anybody."

He wasn't so fast, though, that Nicholson didn't stop Blackwell's 16-game winning streak that year. It came in a memorable 11-inning battle that the Cubs won, 2-1.

Nicholson hit a sinking line drive that Reds' center fielder Bert Haas misplayed for a two-base error and scored on Lenny Merullo's swinging bunt for the Cubs' first run. Then Nick blasted a home run in the 11th to win it.

"I had a single, home run and should have had a double, but they gave him an error," Nicholson recalls. "We also had a triple play in that game when Merullo caught a liner by Babe Young."

Bill also has vivid recollections of a home run he hit off of Carl Hubbell. "It was the longest ball I ever hit," he says. "It was a low line drive that just kept going. It finally went 440 feet over the bullpen."

Nicholson, who was such a fearsome hitter that the Dodgers once walked him with the bases loaded (electing to give up one run in a 9–6 game rather than risk giving up more), slipped to a .243, 13-homer season in 1945 when the Cubs won the pennant. As it turned out, there was a good reason for Bill's slump.

"I was feeling awfully tired and rundown that season," Nicholson says. "I didn't know it at the time, but it turned out I was probably getting some early signs of diabetes, which I later came down with. But it was a great thrill to win the pennant. A lot of great players have played their whole careers and not been in a World Series. I felt very fortunate.

"Of course, it was the last year of the war. A lot of teams were not up to par. Some players wouldn't have played in normal times.

"The whole season was very exciting, though. We came from pretty far back and beat the Cardinals, who had a real good team."

The Cubs lost to the Detroit Tigers in the Series, four games to three.

Nicholson, who was not drafted in World War II because he was color blind, spent three more years in Chicago. Demonstrating that he was also a fine defensive player, Bill led National League outfielders in fielding percentage in 1947, posting a .990 mark while committing only three errors.

He hit 26 home runs in 1947 and 19 in 1948. But after that season, the Cubs traded him to the Phillies for 1947 batting champion, Harry Walker. In a way, Nicholson was happy to leave Chicago.

"The fans were absolutely the greatest in the world," he says, "but I didn't enjoy playing in Wrigley Field because it was so hard to see the ball and it was sometimes so cold and windy. I'd rather play in any other park than Wrigley Field.

"I hit many, many balls that would've been home runs that were stopped by the wind and became just big outs," he adds. "But the worst thing was all the white shirts in the center field bleachers. Someltimes, you just couldn't see. It was really dangerous.

"The players used to complain to management all the time about hitting against that white background. But nothing was ever done about it until the year after I left. Then they roped off a section and painted it green.

"On bright, sunny days, it was especially brutal. Some guys got hit in the head and got their skulls fractured because they never saw the ball. We used to love cloudy days because then we could see."

Nicholson started out in 1949 as the Phillies' regular right fielder. But midway through the season, he tore a muscle in his rib cage while making a play in the outfield on a ball hit by Bobby Thomson. He saw only spot duty the rest of the season.

Bill was the Phillies' chief lefthanded pinch-hitter when the club captured the National League pennant in 1950. On successive weekends, he hit pinch-hit home runs that season to beat the Dodgers, breaking up a 4-4 tie with a three-run homer in the eighth inning off of Ralph Branca and a 1-1 deadlock with a three-run homer in the ninth off of Don Newcombe.

Unfortunately, Nicholson missed not only the Phillies' stretch drive in September, but also the World Series. The diabetes which his body had been quietly harboring, suddenly erupted and put Bill in the hospital where he stayed the entire month.

Nicholson lost 30 pounds during the siege. Although he eventually recovered, he has had to give himself daily shots of insulin since then.

The big lefthander stayed with the Phillies through the 1953 season, serving as a utility outfielder, pinch-hitter and elder statesman on the young club. At the close of that season, he retired, ending what had been a long and productive big league career.

It was a career in which he did some outstanding hitting, played some fine defense and contributed to two pennant-winners. What's more, he had his own cheering section in nearly every city.

Tony Oliva—
Member of a Select Group of Hitters

In the modern era of baseball, just 14 men have won a batting championship three times or more.

The list includes names such as Cobb, Wagner, Lajoie, Hornsby, Williams, Musial, Carew and Rose—some of the greatest players ever to tote a bat to home plate.

Being a great hitter, though, does not assure one a place on the list. It contains no Speaker, no Sisler, no Terry. Nor is there a DiMaggio, a Mantle or a Mays, a Ruth, a Gehrig or a Foxx to be found.

Nestled comfortably among the 14, though, is Tony Oliva.

Tony Oliva of the Minnesota Twins not only won batting titles in 1964, 1965 and 1971, he is the only player in baseball history to have captured a batting title in his rookie season.

A slender, 6' 1", 175-pound lefthanded hitter, Oliva was an artful batsman whose deft control of the ash enabled him to drill hits to all fields, usually on the line and often with considerable power.

In 15 seasons as a big league swatter, from 1962 to 1976, all with the Twins, Oliva rang up a .304 career batting average. He had 1,917 hits, 220 home runs and 947 RBI.

In 11 seasons as a regular—either as a right fielder or for three years as a designated hitter—Oliva went over the .300 mark six times. The rest of the time, his average never went below .285.

Oliva led the American League in hitting with .323, .321 and .337 averages. He also led the circuit in hits five times, in doubles four times, in slugging average once and in runs once.

He hit 22 or more home runs five times and drove in 92 or more runs five times.

Tony was a member of eight American League All-Star teams, hitting .263 in 19 at-bats.

Naturally, Oliva ranks as one of the great Twins' hitters of all time. He is the club's all-time leader in doubles, ranks second (to Harmon Killebrew) in both home runs and RBI, and is second in hitting (among players with 2,000 or more at-bats) to Rod Carew.

Tony, who played with the Twins longer than any player in club history, had two 17-game hitting streaks. Eighteen times he hit two home runs in a game. And 28 times he had four-hit games.

A native of Pinar del Río, Cuba, Oliva first set his sights on the big leagues as a small boy.

"I played all the time, every chance I could," he recalls. "All the time, I was thinking, I want to get to the big leagues someday.

"We used anything we could find for a ball. Sometimes it was a rubber ball, sometimes it was a bottle cap, sometimes it was just rolled up pieces of paper. We didn't always have 18 guys to make up two teams. Often we'd have as few as six guys. We'd play with one, big, long base.

"As a kid," Oliva adds, "I followed the Cuban Professional League. I'd listen to the games, although I never had a chance to see them. Minnie Minoso and Camilo Pascual were my heroes."

When he was old enough to sign a professional contract, Oliva joined the Washington Senators, one of the first teams to recognize the abundance of talent in the Latin American countries. Tony hit .410 in 249 at-bats in 1961 in his first year in pro ball. He followed that with .350 and .304 years.

Before he got to the big leagues, though, the Senators had moved to Minnesota to become the Twins. Oliva played with the Twins briefly in their first and second years there, then joined the team on a permanent basis in 1964.

That year, he led the American League in hitting (.323), hits (217), doubles (43) and runs (109). Adding in 32 home runs, he easily won the Rookie of the Year award. His hits total was the most ever recorded by a rookie.

"It was an unbelievable year," Oliva says, shaking his head. "Here I was, just 22 years old, and just being in the big leagues was the most exciting thing that ever happened to me. America was such a big country, but to come from a small island, compete and then win a batting title, it was unbelievable.

"All my playing career was a big thrill to me," he adds. "But winning that title was the biggest.

"It was the most satisfying of the three, too," he adds. "All three titles were thrilling to me, but the first one meant a little bit more because it said I could play in the big leagues with the best of them."

Oliva didn't rest on his laurels. The very next year, he won the batting title again, this time hitting .321. The Twins, meanwhile, having finished seventh the previous year, romped to the American League pennant, winning 102 games. They lost to the Los Angeles Dodgers, four games to three in the World Series with Oliva hitting just .192. But Tony's RBI-double helped the Twins to a 5–1 win in the second game as Jim Kaat beat Sandy Koufax. He also homered off of Don Drysdale in a 7–2 Twins loss in the fourth game.

In the ensuing seasons, Oliva continued to hit well. In 1970, he again led the league in hits with 204, while his .325 average was just four points less than Alex Johnson's winning mark.

Tony Oliva.

That year, the Twins won their second straight West Division title, but for the second year in a row lost in three straight games to the Baltimore Orioles in the League Championship Series. Oliva, who had hit .385 in the '69 playoffs, hit .500 in the '70 series.

Oliva finally notched his third batting title the following year when he ripped up American League pitching with a .337 average. He also led the league in slugging percentage (.546) that year.

The following year, a knee injury limited Oliva's playing time to 10 games. When he came back in 1972, he was moved into the designated hitter's spot. He had three more good years with the bat, then after his weak knee worsened in 1976, he retired from the game.

It was a game, though, in which Oliva had played well and in which there were many memorable moments.

"My whole career has been a thrill to me," he says. "There were so many good games, it would be hard to pick out the most memorable one. I remember one in Kansas City where I hit the ball out of the park. They said it went 517 feet. I couldn't believe it was me who hit it.

"Another game I remember well," he adds, "was the All-Star game in 1968. I had to face Tom Seaver, and I was lucky enough to hit a ball to left-center that hit the top of the fence. If it had gone out, we would have won. Instead, we lost, 1–0."

Another big game for Tony came in 1964 when he, Bob Allison, Jimmie Hall and Killebrew hit consecutive home runs. Two years later, on June 9, 1966, Oliva began another home run barrage, in which he, Don Mincher and Killebrew hit consecutive homers.

That trio of homers was part of the greatest four-base outburst in American League history. Earlier in the same inning (seventh), Rich Rollins and Zoilo Versalles had also hit home runs, giving the Twins the league record with five homers in an inning.

During his career, Oliva often had trouble holding onto the bat. Frequently, he would swing, and the bat would go flying out of his hands.

"When I batted, I held the bat very loose," Oliva explains. "Sometimes a pitcher would make a good pitch and fool me, but by holding the bat loose, I had a better chance to follow through. When you're tense, you tie up your hands too much.

"I always took my time," Oliva adds. "I would step out of the batter's box a lot. I was a smart hitter. When I'd go up to home plate, I'd take a look around—see how the outfielders were playing, see how the infielders were playing, see how the wind was blowing. I was able to see all of those things, and that would help me be a better hitter. No one would ever call me a stupid hitter.

"I'd also practice a lot," Oliva says. "Anybody should be able to do that if they want to take the time and pay the price."

Oliva says two of the toughest pitchers he faced were Sam McDowell of the Cleveland Indians and Nolan Ryan when he was with the California Angels.

"They both threw 100 miles an hour and they were wild," Oliva says. "You really had to be ready to get out of the way when they were pitching.

"As tough as they were, though," Oliva continues, "the toughest of all was Hoyt Wilhelm. You knew what he was going to throw, but you still couldn't hit it."

Most of the time, Oliva not only knew what was coming, he also hit it. But he says he was not a one-dimensional ballplayer, who could hit and do nothing else. Because he could hit and was also a good all-around player, Oliva feels that he deserves more consideration for the Hall of Fame.

"People only talk about my hitting," he says. "They don't talk about how I could field, how I could throw and how I could run.

"I was a good all-around ballplayer. I won a Gold Glove. I could steal bases. And I hit with power as well as for average. Before I hurt my knee, I averaged 23 home runs a season."

Today, it is still Oliva's hitting that has perpetuated his career in baseball. Tony is putting his considerable expertise on the science of hitting to use as the Twins' hitting instructor.

Oliva had been the Twins' hitting instructor and first base coach for the first two years after he retired as a player. Then in 1979, the Twins decided to put him to work in the minors with the young hitters.

For five years, Tony helped to develop future Twins stars such as Kent Hrbeck and Kirby Puckett. Then he rejoined the big team in 1985.

"I love working with hitters," he says. "I always had it in my mind that I was a good coach. Even before I stopped playing, I often helped the young guys on the ball club with their hitting.

"I managed winter ball for five years," Oliva adds. "I was preparing myself because I wanted to get to the big leagues again. It was a sacrifice for myself and for my family, which I had to leave behind in Minneapolis. But I made the sacrifice because I wanted to prepare myself to be able to do anything in the big leagues.

"Every coach has his own approach," Oliva adds. "I tell my hitters to hit the ball in the hole and hit it on the ink. I believe you should not try to change a guy's stance. I think you should bring a guy to the park, and have him practice hitting and work on his concentration. That's what it takes, practice and concentration. I also like to give a hitter confidence. Work with him a lot on that level. But I don't want to force anything. It should all come naturally."

That's certainly the way it worked when Tony Oliva was hitting. He was a hitter who ranks in a special group of baseball's most select hitters.

Mickey Vernon—Bat Champ
Who Fielded with a Velvet Touch

Of all the things that can be remembered about Mickey Vernon, the image that has lingered longest is of the way he handled himself at first base. The man could play the position!

He was so smooth. So graceful. So stylish. Vernon played first base the way that Perry Como sang. With the Washington Senators' "W" flapping on his chest for most of his career, Mickey made playing the bag look as easy as bicycling to the corner candy store.

As a hitter, Vernon had a textbook swing, which guided him to two American League batting championships. Mickey was one of the better hitters of his day, and his impeccable batting stroke was memorable in its own right. But he was a classic first baseman. Tall, angular and lefthanded, he played with a velvet touch, gliding around the bag as though engaged in a form of outdoor ballet.

Because of Vernon, coming to the ballpark early to watch fielding practice was obligatory for admirers of his elegant style. And among his peers, he was in a class by himself. Only Earl Torgeson, George McQuinn and perhaps Eddie Waitkus seemed remotely comparable in smoothness. Certainly, Vernon gets no competition from today's band of cloven-hoofed pretenders who are sent to stumble around the initial sack because it is thought of as the post of least liability.

James Barton Vernon, though, was not merely an artist. He was also a master fielder whose handling of the leather easily matched the grace of his style. And with his 20-year career in the big leagues, longevity joined with talent to give him some of the game's most durable records.

Vernon holds the major league records for first basemen for most assists in a season (155) and a career (1,444), and the American League marks for most lifetime putouts (19,754) and chances (21,198). Annually the leader or near the top in fielding percentage in the league, he also holds records for having two unassisted doubleplays in one game and for participating in a doubleheader that went 23 innings.

During his big league career—which went from 1939 to 1960 when he

retired as one of only a handful of players who performed in four decades—
Mickey saw action at first base in more games than any first sacker in the
history of the American League. While playing 13½ years with the Senators
plus 4½ more with the Cleveland Indians and Boston Red Sox, he was
stationed at the bag in 2,237 games.

Except for his first year of baseball as a boy ("I was too small to play
first base"), his two years during World War II on a Navy team (Johnny
Mize played first and Mickey, because of his speed, was sent to the outfield),
and a couple of games in the outfield at the close of his career, Vernon was
always a first baseman.

"It was the only position I ever wanted to play," he says. "Of course,
being lefthanded, I was limited to first base, pitcher and outfield. But I really
loved playing first."

His style around the bag, he adds, "wasn't developed." It just came
naturally. "Some guys are helter-skelter; for others, it's just something you're
born with."

Mickey Vernon.

Vernon was born in Marcus Hook, Pennsylvania, a town of oil refineries along the Delaware River. At about age 12, he got to know a kid named Danny Murtaugh from nearby Chester. The two became lifelong friends.

As a boy, Vernon hitchhiked to Philadelphia to watch the A's play at Shibe Park. His heroes were the A's Jimmie Foxx, Lefty Grove and Mickey Cochrane and the Tigers' Charley Gehringer, and he would go to see them every chance he got. "I was crazy about baseball," he recalls. "In fact, I've been crazy about baseball as long as I can remember."

Mickey attended Villanova University for one year, then in 1937, he and Murtaugh joined a class D team in Easton, Maryland, the same team that spawned Foxx. Although the club was affiliated with the St. Louis Browns, Vernon was signed by the Senators after hitting .287 his first season.

The Senators called Mickey to Washington in 1939. By 1941, he had become a regular, hitting .299 that year. Vernon went on to a long and distinguished career in the nation's capital, playing there through 1948, then being traded to Cleveland. He returned in 1950 to D.C., where he played through 1955, when another swap moved him to the Red Sox. Ultimately, Vernon spent two years in Boston, another year back in Cleveland, a year with the Milwaukee Braves and 1960 with the Pittsburgh Pirates where, after 22-years apart, he rejoined his buddy Murtaugh as batting coach and was activated late in the season during the Bucs' pennant-winning stretch drive.

During all of those years, Vernon was compiling some noteworthy statistics. Altogether, he appeared in 2,409 games, playing in more than 100 games for 16 consecutive seasons. He collected 2,495 hits in his career, while driving in 1,311 runs and scoring 1,196. A lefthanded swinger who hit to all fields, Mickey was never noted as a power hitter. His highest one-season production was 20 homers. He finished his career with 172.

Vernon, who played in seven All-Star games and was named the Senators' all-time first baseman, ended with a lifetime batting average of .286. He won American League batting titles in 1946 with a .353 average and in 1953 with a .337 mark. Ironically, in his 20 seasons, Mickey hit over .300 only two other times, although he finished in the .290s on five other occasions, including 1958 when he hit .293 at the age of 40.

Mention the batting titles, and they generate some fond memories for Vernon. "In 1946," he recalls, "Ted Williams was right behind me. When a fellow who's as great a hitter as he was breathes down your neck all season, it really puts some pressure on you." Vernon, who had been in the service the entire previous year, wound up beating the Red Sox slugger by 11 points.

In 1953, Vernon again edged Williams as well as the Indians' Al Rosen, who led in the race most of the season, but missed out on the triple crown by losing the batting title. Early the following season, Vernon was presented his title-winning silver bat by President Dwight Eisenhower at a special ceremony at Griffith Stadium.

Ike was often quoted as saying that Vernon was his favorite player. Mickey was also said to have been the favorite player of Jacqueline Kennedy

Onassis when she was stationed in Washington. Meeting Presidents and other Washington dignitaries was one of the few benefits of playing for the Senators, perennial occupants of the American League's second division.

"I remember one time I hit a home run off of Allie Reynolds to beat the Yankees in extra innings," Vernon says. "Right after I'd crossed the plate, some big guy—a Secret Service man, it turned out—comes up, grabs me by the arm and takes me over to the President's box. Eisenhower was at the game, and he wanted to congratulate me for the home run. That was one of the top thrills of my career.

"Just playing was a thrill, though," Vernon adds. "I'm very glad I played when I did and with the kinds of players I played with and against. I think I could have done a little better as a hitter, but overall, I feel very good to have been able to do something that I wanted to do—namely, be a big league ballplayer. That's the dream of a lot of kids. It certainly was mine."

Vernon, who always enjoyed a reputation as an unassuming, clean-living, classy gentleman, lives today in comfortable surroundings in Wallingford, Pennsylvania, in the same county in which he was raised. He is one of the favorite sons of Delaware County, a densely populated area in the southeastern corner of Pennsylvania which takes enormous pride in its native athletes. Heisman winner John Cappelletti, bonus pitcher Lew Krausse, lonesome end Bill Carpenter of Army, NBA star Jeff Petrie, Jets' ace Joe Klecko and Dodgers' catcher Mike Scioscia are just a few of them.

The den in Vernon's home is lined with photographs, autographed balls, baseball books, hats, trophies, and various other bits of baseball memorabilia. Among his prized possessions is a framed montage made by a friend, consisting of all of the Vernon baseball cards that have been issued.

Mickey doesn't get much time to savor his mementoes these days. Actually, he never has. Still active, Vernon has spent more than 50 years in organized baseball.

Vernon has never held a full-time job outside of baseball. Since his playing days ended, he has been either a coach, manager or employed in some other capacity by nine different major league teams.

Vernon was the first manager of the expansion Washington Senators, piloting the Nats from 1961 to early 1963. He has also been a batting coach for the Pirates, Cardinals, Dodgers and Expos, a minor league batting instructor for the Royals and manager of minor league teams in Vancouver, British Columbia (A's), Richmond, Virginia (Braves), and Manchester, New Hampshire (Yankees).

After spending three years as batting instructor for the Yankees' six farm teams, Vernon joined the parent club as the hitting coach and performed in that capacity for several seasons. Later he was the Yanks' Triple A batting coach. In recent years, he has been a major league scout for New York.

"Working with a minor league team is a lot different from working with a major league team," he says. "In the majors, most of the hitters have been around for a while, and they know what's going on. You don't really try to change major league hitters. You do more observing, trying to analyze what fellows are doing wrong and working with them to straighten out their problems."

Vernon says the art of hitting instruction has changed considerably since his days as a player. The instruction is more scientific and employs devices and techniques that were unheard of 30 or 40 years ago. "There's also more individual instruction now," Mickey says. "And more personal involvement than when I broke in."

Lifelong pals Mickey Vernon (left) and Danny Murtaugh got together as rival managers during an exhibition game in Cleveland.

The pitching, he thinks, is also tougher today. "Overall, from the first to the 10th man, the pitching is better," Vernon says. "The four or five starters are no better today than when I played. But the relief pitching is much better."

Vernon says that the hardest pitchers for him to hit were Bob Feller, Hal Newhouser, Whitey Ford, Allie Reynolds (who once said that he pitched more carefully to Mickey than to any other hitter) Tex Hughson and Thornton Lee. "Actually," he says, "they were all tough, as you can tell by some of those years I had."

They were years, it should be noted, that most players wish they could have had.

Pitchers of Excellence

Steve Barber—
Orioles' First Mound Ace

In the years that they have resided in the city that gave us Babe Ruth, Edgar Allen Poe and the *Star Spangled Banner*, the Baltimore Orioles have always had generous assortments of good pitching.

Almost from the time that they relinquished the unwanted appellation, St. Louis Browns, the team has been noted for the quality of its moundsmen. Names such as Pappas, O'Dell, Wilhelm, Estrada, Roberts, Bunker, McNally, Cueller, Dobson, Palmer, Flanagan, Stone, McGregor and Boddicker have made pitching the crown jewel of the Orioles' franchise, supplying an unbroken line of strong arms that have positioned the club in the first division in 22 of the 25 years leading up to 1987.

Of all the great names in the Orioles' galaxy of stars, the one who made the first real glitter was a handsome lefthander whose blazing fastball left a trail of victims throughout the American League in the 1960s.

His name was Steve Barber. He was the first Orioles' pitcher to win 20 games.

The 6-foot,195-pounder came out of the suburbs of Washington, D.C. (Takoma Park, Maryland), to give the Orioles seven and one-half seasons in a 15-year career that extended from 1960 to 1974. His sizzling fastball was one of the fastest ever recorded in the major leagues, at 95.5 mph, and it was wild enough that for a time no sight was more terrifying to a batter than that of Barber about to deliver another high hard one.

Hampered by arm trouble during parts of his career, Barber had a 121–106 record in 466 games. He had a career earned run average of 3.36. In his 1,999.2 innings pitched, he struck out 1,309, walked 950 and gave up 1,818 hits.

It was a career dotted with many memorable games, not the least of which was the one in 1967 when Barber joined with Stu Miller to hurl one of only four combined no-hitters in big league history.

Barber pitched eight and two-thirds innings, only to lose the game in the ninth inning, 2–1, when the Detroit Tigers pushed over one run on his wild pitch and scored another with Miller pitching on an error by a young

Mark Belanger. Although he gave up no hits, Barber walked 10, hit two and threw two wild pitches.

"Anybody who pitched like that deserved to lose," he reminisces. "I was lucky I didn't get beat, 10–1."

Barber can recall the ninth inning like it just happened. "Baltimore scored in the eighth inning to get a 1–0 lead," he says. "In the ninth, we put in Belanger at second base for defensive purposes. I gave up two walks and a sacrifice bunt. Willie Horton fouled out. Then I threw a wild pitch to let in a run. I wound up walking Mickey Stanley. Miller came in. He got the batter to hit a grounder to (Luis) Aparicio at shortstop. He threw to Belanger covering second; Mark dropped the ball, and the winning run scored."

Two starts before that game, Barber recalls, he had gone into the ninth inning with a no-hitter against the California Angels. Jim Fregosi broke up that bid with a double.

There were other memorable games, though. In 1967, Barber combined with Wally Bunker, Eddie Watt, Ed Fisher and Miller to strike out 21 Washington Senators in a 19 inning game. Five years earlier, Steve had been on the losing end of a 2–0 no-hitter by the Angels' Bo Belinsky.

Fame always seemed to follow Barber, sometimes catching him, sometimes not. He looks back on his career with somewhat mixed emotions.

"I did some things, had some experiences that I never would have had," he says. "When I look at it that way, I have few regrets. I had a lot of fun.

"But I don't feel that I ever fully reached my potential. I was never able to put two good years back-to-back. I always had minor arm problems. Had we known then what we know today about sports medicine, I would never have had the trouble I had.

"From that standpoint," he adds, "I'd like to do it all over again. I'd like a full career with a healthy arm."

Barber resides in Las Vegas, Nevada, where he works as a salesman for an auto dealer. He has been in the auto business for a number of years. He worked in Phoenix, Arizona, for about 10 years before moving slightly north.

"In 1969, I was drafted by Seattle, and we trained in Tempe (Arizona)," he says. "That was my first exposure to the Southwest. I liked it and decided to stay."

He has little contact with baseball other than to see a few Triple-A games each year and to participate in a couple of old-timers games.

"To be honest," he says, "I'm not a fan in any way, shape or form. Even as a kid, I wasn't a fan. I was interested in playing, but didn't like to watch.

"I saw my first game when I was about six years old," he continues. "It was the Senators. But after that, I didn't see more than five or six games until I reached the major leagues."

Reaching the major leagues was not much of a problem for the flame-

Steve Barber.

throwing southpaw. A high school sensation, he was the object of a major recruiting battle in his senior year.

"I had 12 clubs after me," he says. "I put them all down. I said I was not interested in playing professionally. I was going to college."

Barber enrolled as a student in electrical engineering at the Unversity of Maryland, but decided he didn't like it and dropped out after two months. Shortly afterward, the Orioles signed him for a bonus.

Barber was sent to the low minors, and wound up spending three years there, twice leading leagues in walks. "In my rookie year, I led the league in walks, wild pitches, hit batters, everything," he says. "But my coaches helped me with the mechanics, and eventually I overcame those problems.

"Cal Ripken, Sr., helped me a lot in the minors," Barber says. "He was my catcher in Pensacola and Amarillo. I had quite a temper as a kid, and he and later Paul Richards and Harry Brecheen helped me tone it down."

Eventually, although he had won only 22 games in three minor league seasons, and advanced no higher than Class B ball, Barber arrived in Baltimore in 1960 as a raw 21-year-old.

"The first game I started in the big leagues," he recalls, "was against Washington. I didn't win, and I didn't lose. Then I beat the Red Sox, 2-1, in Boston."

Barber's fastball was attracting attention all around the American League. "It was something I guess I had God-given talent for," he says. "I can't say I did anything consciously to acquire it. It was just there."

American League batters found Barber's fastball to be anything but friendly. As a result, Steve won 10 games in his rookie season and nearly doubled the total the following year. That year, while posting an 18-12 mark, Barber tied with Camilo Pascual for the league lead in shutouts with eight.

Two years later, Barber had his finest season, registering a 20-13 record with a 2.75 ERA. Then, continuing his on-again, off-again pattern (he was 9-6 in 1962, 9-13 in 1964), he checked in with a 15-10 log in 1965. Included were three three-hitters and nine wins in his last 11 starts.

Barber led the Orioles in wins and innings pitched in 1961, 1963, and 1965, and also led the club in strikeouts in the latter two years. In 1966, the second year in which he was chosen for the American League All-Star team (he was also picked in 1963, but was replaced due to an injury), arm trouble limited his record to 10-5. Baltimore won the pennant and swept the Los Angeles Dodgers in the World Series, but Steve's physical problems kept him out of the action.

Barber continued to struggle the following year, and in July the Orioles traded him to the New York Yankees for cash, a minor league player (Ray Barker) and two players to be named later.

Barber finished the season with a combined 10-18 record. What followed was an odyssey that took him over the next seven years from New York to the Seattle Pilots, Chicago Cubs, Atlanta Braves, California Angels and San Francisco Giants.

After leaving Baltimore, Barber never won more than six games in any one season (twice with the Yankees), and worked almost entirely in relief over the final five seasons of his career. Although he ended his career in 1974 in San Francisco, his heart belonged in Baltimore.

"The atmosphere on the Orioles was just great," he says. "There was so much camaraderie; there were never any cliques. Everybody could do anything with anybody. We had great team spirit. I never had that feeling of unity on any other team.

"I think it was set up by the organization. They had a program set up by Paul Richards. Everything we did was as a unit. It was as good a place to play as a ballplayer could have."

And for seven years in the '60s, nobody generated any more electricity while playing there than southpaw Steve Barber.

Ewell Blackwell—
"The Whip" Terrified Hitters

They called him "The Whip."

He was 6' 6", but a mere 195 pounds; a beanpole of a man with uncommonly long arms and long legs. He pitched with a sidearm motion, whipping blazing fastballs that looked like they were coming from third base and would surely hit you if you batted from the right side. They were paralyzing pitches, and they sent many terrified hitters trembling back to the dugout.

Ewell Blackwell was one of a kind. Pitching mostly for the Cincinnati Reds, he did not have a lengthy career. But it was a memorable one, not only because of his unusual style and physique, but because it included one of the greatest seasons any pitcher had in the history of major league baseball.

In 1947, his second full season in the major leagues, Blackwell buggy-whipped his way to a record that in modern times has not been equaled. Over a two and one-half month stretch, he won 16 straight games, a National League record for righthanded starting pitchers.

During the streak, Blackie was virtually untouchable, his sidearm deliveries boring in on righthanded batters and away from lefties. On June 18, the streak reached its apex when Ewell hurled a 6–0 no-hitter against the Boston Braves, a strong-hitting outfit that was one year away from winning the National League pennant.

Blackwell finished the season with a 22–8 record, leading the league in wins, complete games (23) and strikeouts (193) while posting a 2.47 earned run average in 273 innings of work. He was named a pitcher on *The Sporting News* major league All-Star team.

The feat was especially remarkable because the Reds of 1947 were a weak-hitting clan (Augie Galan, Bert Haas and Frankie Baumholtz carried the biggest bats) which finished a distant fifth in the National League standings. Other than Blackwell, the team had little pitching, reliever Harry Gumbert having the next-highest number of wins with 10.

The season, though, is still fresh in the mind of Blackwell, now a resident of Brevard, North Carolina, a small town in the western part of the state.

Still exceptionally thin and not given to too many words, Blackwell

Ewell Blackwell.

recalls that he "had real good stuff that year," the best he had in his 10-year major league career. "I won my first two games of the season, then lost the next two," he says. "Then I won the 16 in a row. Finished every one of the 16, too."

The Whip, a nickname that was the winning entry in a contest held that year by a Cincinnati theater, remembers the way the streak came to an end as though it just happened. "I lost to the Giants in 10 innings," he says. "Tried to brush back Willard Marshall, but I threw it down the middle, and he hit a home run."

Blackwell's power of recall is such that he has precise recollections of most of the events and numbers of his career. But he has had little contact with baseball in recent years. He attends a game now and then, but rarely sees any of his former teammates.

Except for one old-timers' game in 1983, Blackie has not played in an old-timers' game in years. "Every time I think about playing in a game, my arm hurts," he muses.

Blackwell spent his post-baseball working days in retail sales for a large distillery in the south. When he retired in 1973, he had become the company's sales manager for the state of South Carolina.

Today, Blackwell says he does a little fishing and plays a little golf. He has two grown children, but he and his wife stick close to home most of the time.

Ewell looks back on his career with a feeling of pride, although it takes some probing to find that out. "I was very happy being a baseball player," he says. "As a kid, that's what I wanted to be. I wish I had played longer, but I think I had a real good career."

Blackwell wound up with an 82–78 lifetime record. He had a 3.29 ERA. Ewell pitched in one World Series (1952) and in five All-Star games, including the 1950 game in which he was the winning pitcher.

The Fresno, California native originally signed with the Reds in 1942 after attending LaVerne College for part of one year. "The Dodgers, Phillies and Yankees all wanted to sign me," he explains, "but the Reds were the only team that would take me to spring training, so I signed with them."

Blackwell spent most of the 1942 season with the Triple-A Syracuse team (posting a 15–10 record), then joined the Reds at the end of the summer. He spent the next three years in the military, rejoining Cincinnati for the 1946 campaign.

In his rookie year, Blackwell led the league in shutouts (six), was fourth in the league in ERA (2.46) and posted a 9–13 record for the sixth place Reds. That year he was named to the All-Star team for the first time.

Blackwell's wicked sidearm offerings struck fear in the hearts of batters throughout the league. Especially terrifying was a pitch that was known as a crossfire. It was a pitch on which Blackwell would step with his left leg across his body toward the third base line, then whip the ball homeward, giving the distinct impression that it was coming from somewhere near third base.

Ewell says that he was the first pitcher to throw the crossfire. "It just came naturally to me," he says. "I threw it about 90 percent of the time. The hitters didn't like it. In fact, whenever I pitched against the Dodgers, Campanella, Furillo and Hodges (all righhanded batters) wouldn't play. The pitch was hard for lefthanders to hit, too."

Blackwell, who proudly points out that neither Stan Musial, Johnny Mize nor Willie Mays ever hit a home run off him, maintains that sidearm is a more natural way to throw than overhand, and thus is less taxing on the arm. Nevertheless, arm trouble plagued Ewell off and on during his career.

Following his sensational season in 1947, during which there was even a book published called *Secrets of Pitching,* by Ewell Blackwell, the slim hurler developed arm trouble in spring training in 1948. The problem, he says, resulted from his throwing on a cold, windy day.

Over the next two years, with the arm trouble taking its toll, Blackwell managed only 7–9 and 5–5 records. In 1950, however, Ewell's arm was fully recovered, and he came back to fashion a 17–15 record and register the third best ERA (2.97) in the league. Despite the Reds' continued weak-hitting attack, Blackwell posted a 16–15 log in 1951. But then he slipped to 3–12 the next season, and was traded to the New York Yankees in late August. He won one game for the Yanks that fall, then two more the following season.

"By the time, I went to the Yankees, I had arm trouble again," Blackwell recalls. "I was done. I just wanted to get it over with and get out."

At the age of 31, Blackwell went on the voluntary retired list. After sitting out the 1954 season, he tried to make a comeback with the Kansas City A's in 1955, but his return was brief. This time, his retirement was permanent.

It was the end not only of a career that had had some glittering moments, but of a particular way of pitching. There have been a few imitators since, but none who threw quite like The Whip.

Jim Bouton—
Maverick Pitcher, Author

"The key to success in baseball is having fun. Having fun will beat winning every time."

The originator of those words could not be cast as your basic ex-jock, a plodding, monosyllabic introvert whose focus rarely moves past scores and games of long ago.

No, indeed. This was Jim Bouton speaking. Jim Bouton—ex-pitcher, best-selling author, successful businessman. Jim Bouton—a man of intellect, imagination and wit; a skillful communicator and concerned citizen, and, most important, a free spirit and enjoyer of life and the challenges that it presents.

If there is anything that sets Bouton apart from the average former player, it is his ability to extract pleasure from life. It was an ability that he took with him on the baseball field, and it is an ability that he now uses in business.

"Oh, I wanted to win as much as anybody else," he says of his playing days. "But I absolutely enjoyed playing baseball. It was fun. Even if I had never made it to the big leagues, it still would have been worthwhile because I would have simply enjoyed the experience of playing baseball."

Today, Bouton lives in Teaneck, New Jersey, where he presides over his own product development company. He has developed several products, most notably Big League Chew, the shredded bubble gum that is meant to resemble chewing tobacco, and Big League Cards, a personalized, baseball-style card that he makes available to the public.

Bouton also serves as a popular speaker for business and college groups across the country (his special topic is motivation) and he still writes an occasional magazine or newspaper article.

If there was ever a player whose professional baseball career was merely one stop along life's winding trail, Bouton is he. For him, baseball was an interim step on the way to bigger and better pursuits in life.

Bouton does not cling desperately to the memories of his exploits on the baseball diamond, as do so many ex-players. Nor does he have any contact today with the major leagues or his former teammates.

270

Jim Bouton.

"I am not part of the baseball world, and don't want to be," he says. "That part of my life is behind me.

"There are benefits to my having played in the big leagues," he adds. "Because I was a big league player, it is easier to get to see people if I'm trying to arrange a business meeting. On the other hand, I've had to overcome the dumb jock image. I've had to deal with a stereotype of a baseball player, and that's not always been easy."

When he wrote his controversial, best-selling book, *Ball Four,* there were some mistaken perceptions of Bouton as a player who was anti-baseball. That, however, was hardly the case. While Bouton does not agree with some of the mores of the game and enjoys poking fun at them, he has a zest for the performing aspect of baseball that is rarely found among ex-players.

That is one reason he made a comeback nine years after he'd originally retired, and that is one reason he plays in the fast semipro league today.

With little prodding, Bouton talks about his career with a considerable amount of enthusiasm.

"Getting to the big leagues was beyond my wildest dreams," he says. "Here I was, a guy who sat on the bench his entire career in high school. I was known as Warmup Bouton because that's all the coach would let me do. But I kept going out for teams. By the time I was a freshman in college (Western Michigan University), I had developed into a pretty good pitcher."

Bouton finally got his chance when he was spotted pitching for a semipro team in a tournament in Chicago. Signed by his coach, a New York Yankees scout named Art Stewart, who is now the minor league director for the Kansas City Royals (Bouton was Stewart's first signee), Bouton trucked off to the minors where he spent three years developing his craft.

Jim arrived in the big leagues in 1962. He quickly won the hearts of the wizened New York fans with his blazing fastball, dazzling overhand curve and penchant for losing his cap while making his delivery.

After pitching two innings of relief against the Cleveland Indians in his first big league appearance, Bouton made his starting debut against the Washington Senators. He won, 8–0.

"It was the worst shutout in the history of baseball," he jokes. "I walked seven, gave up seven hits. The Senators stranded 14 runners. Hector Lopez bailed me out with three great catches in left-center.

"After the game, I was on a cloud. I came into the locker room, and Mickey Mantle had layed a path of towels to my locker. He was a great guy; a funny guy. All the players loved him."

Bouton went on to post a 7–7 record in his rookie year. Then, in 1963, he enjoyed what would be his finest season.

With a 21–7 record, a 2.53 ERA, six shutouts, an All-Star game appearance and a glittering performance in the World Series, Bouton put together the kind of season that had not only him but everyone else in New York celebrating the arrival of what surely seemed to be another in the long line of great Yankee pitchers.

"I felt so good that year, "Bouton recalls. "When you have a year like that, you think you are going to go on forever. I thought I could pitch like that for 10 more years, then go right into the Hall of Fame."

Bouton pitched two of his most memorable games that year. He beat Camilo Pascual of the Minnesota Twins, 2-0, to win not only his 20th game of the year, but also to clinch the pennant for the Yankees.

"It may have been the strongest game I ever pitched," Jim recalls. "They hardly hit a ball out of the infield, which was a good thing because my outfield was Johnny Blanchard, Phil Linz and Jack Reed. Ralph Houk (the Yankees' manager) didn't want me to win 20, so he put those three out there."

A few weeks later, Bouton hurled a masterful four-hitter only to lose, 1-0, to Don Drysdale and the Los Angeles Dodgers in the third game of the World Series. The only run came in the first inning on a walk, a wild pitch and a hard grounder by Tommy Davis that bounced off of the mound, hit Bobby Richardson in the shins, and rolled into short right field.

The following season, Bouton got off to a slow start, owning only a 5-8 record by the All-Star break. But he came back with a 13-5 mark in the second half to end up 18-13 (3.02 ERA) while leading the league in games started with 37.

Again, the Yankees went to the World Series (their fifth straight time), and again Bouton hurled brilliantly, although not quite as well, he says, as he did in his 1963 Series outing.

Jim gave up six hits and beat the St. Louis Cardinals, 2-1, in the third game of the Series. Then he won an 8-3 decision in the sixth game, yielding nine hits in 8⅓ innings.

"I had my best stuff in the '63 Series," Bouton says. "But I was a better pitcher in the '64 Series because I had a year more experience."

After winning 39 games in two years and moving into a position in which he joined Whitey Ford as the bellweathers of the New York pitching staff, Bouton came down with arm trouble in 1965. It would plague him the rest of his career.

Bouton won only four out of 19 decisions in 1965. Over the next three years, he won only five games in the majors, and spent parts of two seasons back in the minors.

In the fall of 1968, the Yankees gave up on Bouton, selling him to the expansion Seattle Pilots. It may not have been much of a break from a playing standpoint, but it turned out to be the most fortuitous move of Bouton's life.

While he languished in the bullpens of Vancouver of the Pacific Coast League, Seattle and eventually the Houston Astros, to whom he was traded in late August, appearing in 73 big league games and winning two of five decisions, Bouton spent much of his time away from the field telling his observations and experiences to a tape recorder.

By then, of course, Bouton's reputation as a free spirit and nonconformist preceeded him, and Jim had already begun to commit some of his views to published articles. The taped diary served as the basis for a book, which came to be known as *Ball Four*. In a word, it set the baseball world on its proverbial ear with its candid descriptions and no-holds-barred exposés that revealed the behind-the-scenes lives of baseball players.

The controversial *Ball Four* wound up selling 300,000 copies in hardback and four million copies in paperback. It was the toast of the literary world in 1970, and the bain of the baseball establishment.

Why did Bouton write it?

"I was dying to tell something," he says. "I had something to say, and I wanted to let it out."

And the less-than-ecstatic baseball patriarchs let Bouton out.

Jim spent one more season with the Astros, posting a 4–6 record in 29 games, and was then advised that his services were no longer required.

At the age of 31, Bouton had become an ex-ballplayer and a famous author, all in one virtual sweep of the hand.

"The book changed my life completely," Bouton says. "Before it came out, I was just a marginal relief pitcher trying to hang on in the big leagues. *Ball Four* put me in a different category. It lifted me above the level of baseball player and into a kind of level of social commentator."

The demand for Bouton's services skyrocketed. Jim was the darling of the talk shows, and his prose began appearing in print with regularity. He was hired as a television sportscaster and in 1971, he came out with his second book, one called *I'm Glad You Didn't Take It Personally*. A look at the backlash from *Ball Four*, the new book sold 50,000 copies.

Bouton spent six years doing TV sports in New York, but in 1978 gave that up.

"I really never saw myself as a career sportscaster," he says. "My idea was that people should enjoy participating in sports themselves, not just watch them on TV. So I would do a lot of offbeat things. The network really didn't appreciate that."

About that time, Bouton says he realized that "something was missing in my life. I needed a challenge. Something in the back of my head said I should go back and play baseball."

At age 39, Bouton began his comeback. Having developed a knuckleball, he found work in the deepest of the minor league bushes.

"I was 0–5 at Knoxville and I got released," he says. "I was 1–5 at Durango in the Mexican League and I got released. I did much better at Portland. I was 3–5.

"Then I ran into Ted Turner at a sports dinner in New York. I told him I thought I could make it back to the big leagues. He said I should come down to spring training with the Atlanta Braves."

Bouton went to spring training, and was assigned to the Braves' Triple

A farm club at Richmond. He was told to pitch batting practice, and if one of the club's young pitchers got hurt or transferred, he would pitch.

"Finally, after six weeks of pitching batting practice, they told me I could pitch against the Atlanta Braves in an exhibition game," Bouton recalls. "Everybody thought that was a great idea but me. The Braves had four guys hitting over .300, and I had done nothing but pitch batting practice for six weeks. I wasn't too sharp. Our players got up a pool to see what inning I would get knocked out. I chose the fourth."

Instead, Bouton pitched what he says was one of the best games of his career. He beat Atlanta, 3–1, scattering seven hits. The Braves rewarded him with a contract, and sent him to their Double A club in Savannah.

Bouton won 13 games there, and was called up to the parent club late in the season. He worked in five games for the Braves, winning one and losing three.

His comeback, though, was complete. At the end of the season, he retired again.

"To me, the appeal was going back to the minor leagues and seeing if I could make it back to the big leagues," Bouton says. "I wanted the experience of going back, not the experience of staying."

His major league career thus completed, Bouton finished with a lifetime record of 62–63 with a 3.57 ERA. He pitched in 304 games, worked 1,238.2 innings, gave up 1,131 hits, struck out 720 and walked 435.

As was the case during the 1969 season, Bouton again fell upon a stroke of good luck during the 1978 season.

Bouton was discussing chewing tobacco one day in the Portland bullpen with another pitcher, Rob Nelson. Nelson wondered why there couldn't be a product that looked like tobacco but tasted like bubble gum.

With the idea planted firmly in his fertile mind, Bouton eventually formed a partnership with Nelson, and Big League Chew was born.

After approaching the major baseball card gum companies with the idea of shredded gum in a tobacco-like pouch and getting turned down, Bouton finally found a willing sponsor in a gum company in Illinois. The product hit the market in 1980. In its first year, it had wholesale sales of $18 million.

Since then, it has had annual sales of $14 million with Bouton and Nelson getting royalties.

Four years ago, Bouton's entreprenuerial skills were at work again. This time, Jim came out with Big League Cards. Originally, the idea was to provide an inexpensive way for people to fantasize by having baseball cards produced with their pictures and personal information. Now, only about 25 percent of the market buys the cards for that reason; the other 75 percent uses the cards for business or promotional purposes.

"We call them hand-carried billboards," Bouton says. "They fill a need for people to transmit information about themselves or to carry a message."

Bouton has his own card, which along with the cards from his playing days, he signs readily for all comers.

"I always thought it was fun to sign autographs," he says. "I enjoyed giving interviews, too, and getting my picture in the paper. A lot of players don't understand how much fun that can be. A lot of them just don't enjoy playing the game of baseball."

Bouton did, and still does. He plays in a fast semipro league in northern New Jersey, pitching once a week. During the 1986 season, he had an 8–3 record with a 2.40 ERA, third best in the league.

"I throw a lot of knuckleballs," he says. "Couldn't get by otherwise. But I love it. It's a lot of fun."

Does he view playing at that level differently from playing at the professional level?

"Not at all," says Bouton. "It's just the same. I'm out there on the mound, I've got the ball in my hand, and I'm trying to figure out how I can keep the hitter from hitting it. When I strike out a guy in this league, it's the same thrill as if I'd struck out Harmon Killebrew."

Once nicknamed "Bulldog" because of his tenacity as a pitcher, Bouton preaches perserverance to the groups he addresses. But he is a somewhat different person now, he says, than when he was playing.

"I think I'm much more mellow now," he says, "and much less intense. I've learned more about people and about dealing with them."

Bouton is interested in social causes. His primary concern is nuclear weapons, and the threat they pose to the planet.

When he addresses that concern, he could easily pass as someone involved in the political arena. While he admits to thinking once in a while about running for office, he says he does not dwell on the idea.

He is content right now to remain an entrepreneur-social critic-philosopher-enjoyer of life. Those are roles he played as a baseball player, too. Then, as now, he plays them well.

Jim Lonborg—
His 1967 Season Was Memorable

The new group of names that in 1985 went before the Hall of Fame selection committee to be considered for induction into the baseball shrine included former pitcher Jim Lonborg.

It is doubtful that the 6' 5" hurler who was known as "Gentleman Jim" will ever enter the hallowed halls of Cooperstown. But he would have been a shoo-in had he had some other years like the one he had in 1967.

That year, Jim Lonborg was the toast of baseball, a Cy Young Award winner who took the Boston Red Sox from last place the previous season to the American League pennant, and then almost singlehandedly won the World Series.

Lonborg had entered the major leagues in 1965 after just one season in the minors following his graduation fron Stanford University. After two mediocre seasons in which he posted records of 9-17 and 10-10, Jim suddenly exploded into the upper echelons of the major league pitching fraternity.

He rang up a 22-9 record during the season with a 3.16 earned run average while tying for the league lead in wins and leading the circuit in strikeouts with 246 and games started with 39. He was second in the league in innings pitched (273) and winning percentage (.710).

Entering the final weekend of the '67 season, four teams were still in the race for the American League pennant. The Chicago White Sox dropped out on Saturday, leaving the Red Sox, Detroit Tigers and Minnesota Twins.

On the last day, Lonborg beat the Twins, 5-3, while the Tigers split a doubleheader with the California Angels,giving the Red Sox the pennant by a one-game margin over the other two contenders.

Too tired to pitch the World Series opener against the St.Louis Cardinals, Lonborg was saved until the second game. He responded with a scintillating one-hitter, only the fourth in Series history. Only a two-out, eighth inning double by Julian Javier kept Lonnie from a no-hitter as the Cards fell, 5-0.

Jim returned to the mound for the fifth game, and with the Red Sox needing a win to stay alive in the Series, he came through with a three-hitter, beating St. Louis and a young lefthander named Steve Carlton, 3-1. The only run for the Cards came on a homer by Roger Maris.

Boston won again the following day to send the Series to a seventh game. Again Lonborg was summoned to save the Sox. But pitching with only two days rest, Jim bowed, 7-2, yielding 10 hits in six innings. Bob Gibson went on to get the win, his third of the Series.

Despite the final game, Lonborg had put together one of the finer seasons by a pitcher in recent times. His Cy Young Award and selection by *The Sporting News* as the American League Pitcher of the Year added confirmation to that fact.

"It was," Lonborg acknowledges, "without a doubt the most pleasurable season, the best one I've ever been involved with. The Cy Young Award was very special. And so was pitching in the World Series.

"I was amazed at myself, being able physically to go out and pitch two complete games in a row. I couldn't have asked for any more, especially in terms of my control. (He walked one in 18 innings while striking out eight.)

"In the third game, I was a little tired, I was hoping that we could score some runs early, but we didn't. We tried our best, but he (Gibson) was destined to win."

What followed that winter may have been destiny, too, but for Lonborg, it was more like a tragedy. While on a vacation, Jim was seriously injured in a skiing accident. The result was a badly torn knee that nearly ruined his career.

"It took me a good two years to come back," he recalls. "For two years, I didn't pitch well. I lost my fastball, and then I had to start thinking of other ways to pitch. That's when I learned how to pitch, rather than just throw."

The accident seemed to have a settling effect on the free-spirited California native, but he also got tired of hearing about it. "For two years, that's all I heard," he says. "I became a little defensive."

In a way, so did the Red Sox. After winning only 27 games over the next four years, Lonnie was shipped to the Milwaukee Brewers where he posted a 14-12 record in 1972. That fall, the Brewers sent Lonborg and pitchers Ken Brett, Earl Stevenson and Ken Sanders to the Philadelphia Phillies for infielders Don Money and John Vukovich and pitcher Bill Champion.

"When the trade was made, I kind of laughed," Lonburg recalls. "It was almost exactly one year to the day earlier that the Red Sox had traded me to the Brewers.

"By that time, baseball in general had started to become kind of comical. I was going from the last place Brewers in the American League to the last place Phillies in the National League.

"But I looked at it as a new adventure, a new challenge. Going to a new league was certainly different."

For the better part of the previous decade, the Phillies had been a downtrodden assortment of castoffs and unfulfilled youngsters. But the

Jim Lonborg.

Phillies of the early 1970s were a club on their way toward shinnying up the National League pole, and Lonborg would play an important role in that ascent. Lonborg recalls:

> At that point, you could see where the Phillies were headed. You could see the talent there. Steve Carlton had been awesome the previous year (when he won the Cy Young with a 27–10 record for the last place Phils). And they had young talent developing in Mike Schmidt, Greg Luzinski, Bob Boone and some others. The pieces were starting to come together. You could tell that there wasn't going to be anything to hold them back.

The year after Lonborg's arrival, the club vaulted from sixth to third place, with Jim posting a 17–13 record. Then it jumped to second the following year and hasn't been too far from the pennant race most seasons since.

In four of his six seasons with the Phillies, Lonborg won in double figures. He had his finest season in 1976 when he rang up an 18–10 record with a 3.08 ERA. That year, the Phillies won 101 games, going over the 100 mark for the first time in club history and establishing a record equaled by the 1977 team.

Unquestionably, Lonborg's biggest game as a Phillie came in 1976 when he pitched a four-hitter to beat the Montreal Expos, 4–1, giving the Phils the National League's Eastern Division title. It was the first time the Phillies had won any kind of championship since the Whiz Kids captured the National League pennant in 1950.

"I just happened to be the winning pitcher that day, but it was a happy occasion for all of us," Lonborg says. "At the start of 1976, we felt we might have a pretty good ball club. It was pretty obvious to a lot of us that we were going to win. We just knew it was going to happen.

"When we finally clinched the division championship, it just confirmed what we had felt all along. It was a great moment."

In the League Championship Series that year against the Cincinnati Reds, Lonborg worked the second game. After hurling a no-hitter for the first five innings, he wound up losing, 6–2.

Following an 11–4 season in 1977—during which a shoulder injury kept him idle for nearly the first two months of the season—Lonborg also got the call in the second game of the Phillies' second straight appearance in the LCS. This time, he bowed 7–1 to the Los Angeles Dodgers after serving a grand slam homer to Dusty Baker.

The next year, Lonborg slid to an 8–10 record. Then, early in 1979, with younger arms crowding the premises, the Philies handed Jim his unconditional release.

At the end of his 15-year baseball career, Lonborg showed a record of 157-137 with a lifetime ERA of 3.86. He worked in 425 games, pitching 2,464.2 innings allowing 2,400 hits, striking out 1,475 and walking 823.

In a career plagued with injuries, both with the Red Sox and the Phillies, Lonborg won in double figures eight times. He was a member of the 1967 American League All-Star team, although he did not play.

Retirement from baseball at the relatively young age of 36 would have been a problem for some players. But Lonborg had little trouble finding a new direction.

"I had had an interest in health care for a long time," he says. "I was a pre-med student at Stanford. But it was a casual comment by my wife that really served as a catalyst. I was thinking one day after I had retired about what I was going to do, and she said, 'Why don't you become a dentist?'

"I pursued the idea, and the more I discussed it, the better I liked it."

A short time later, Lonborg enrolled in the dental school at Tufts University in Boston, near where he has made his home since his playing days with the Red Sox. Six semesters later, after being the oldest student in his classes, draining his finances, seeing little of his wife and six children and working himself to the point that he sometimes fell asleep in classes, Lonborg got his degree as a dentist.

After serving an apprenticeship, he entered a private practice in Marshfield, Massachusetts doing family dentistry. He also works several days a week at a clinic in Boston.

The transition from the roar of the crowds to the whine of the drill was, Jim says, not terribly difficult, once he battled his way through dental school.

"I was very strongly motivated," says the son of a college professor and a television hostess. "I had some absolutely great moments in baseball but baseball is not my whole life. It's behind me, and I have a new adventure ahead of me.

"Leaving baseball," he adds, "was not that big a deal. I didn't really enjoy the last two years I was playing. I was separated from my family. So, I don't miss the game."

Lonborg does concede, though, that there are similarities between pitching and being a dentist. "With dentistry, you have to make sure you do the best possible thing for every patient," says the ex-pitcher. "That's similar to baseball because in baseball you go out each game and try to do the best you possibly can."

Lonborg certainly did that enough times during his playing career, although he never got too excited about baseball as a youngster, he says.

"I didn't have any idols and never collected anything," he says. "I was into academics very seriously. I always pitched, though, even in little league. But I wasn't really that interested in baseball until one year I was pitching in the Basin League in Washington. That was in 1963. All of a sudden, my skills just came together."

If it hadn't been for various injuries, Lonborg easily would have won in excess of 200 games. But that doesn't bother him. "I played 15 years in the big leagues, and I had some good years and some bad years," he says. "I worked very hard to try to make a contribution to the game.

"I had the good fortune of being with some great organizations—the Phillies and the Red Sox—and you can't say that about every organization.

"But now, I don't think that much about the past. My commitment is to excellence tomorrow and in the future."

With such a commitment, a lot of cavities in the Boston area are now in big trouble.

Eddie Lopat—
Master Craftsman

It is an extinct description in today's baseball parlance, but the word craftsman was once a term of considerable honor and dignity when used to define certain pitchers and the way they plied their trade.

The word was employed with a careful degree of selectivity. Few hurlers qualified for the distinction of being called a craftsman. And in a world dominated by flame-throwers and junk-ballers, even fewer were ultimately chosen to wear such a mantle.

Eddie Lopat was one of them. A smooth-throwing, stylish lefthander, Lopat was a certified master craftsman who survived 12 seasons in the big leagues because he knew how to pitch and made full use of his talent.

It was not Lopat's style to try to blow hitters away with overpowering fastballs because he didn't have one. Eddie was a clever control artist who nibbled at the corners of the plate while using an assortment of off-speed pitches to keep hitters off balance. He was a master of the diminishing art of setting up the hitter.

In a career in which he spent four seasons with the Chicago White Sox, seven and one-half years with the New York Yankees and one-half of a season with the Baltimore Orioles, the 5' 10", 185-pound lefty won in double figures 11 straight seasons while posting a 166–112 record with a 3.21 earned run average. Lopat pitched in 340 games, working 2,439.1 innings, allowing 2,464 hits, walking just 650 and striking out 859. He completed 164 of the 318 games he started.

Steady Eddie, as announcer Mel Allen named him, enjoyed his finest years while wearing Yankee pinstripes. From 1948 until mid-1955, Lopat toiled in his native New York, for much of that time, teaming with Vic Raschi and Allie Reynolds to give the Yanks one of the greatest pitching threesomes in baseball annals.

But while the other two relied on their abilities to throw hard, Lopat made a science out of pitching. No hurler ever used his head and his physical tools any more effectively.

"I had limited ability," Lopat says. "I didn't have the great stuff that

283

some other pitchers had. So, I had to supplement what I did have with a variety of pitches, and by changing speeds and keeping my control sharp.

"Everything revolved around my screwball," he says, adding that he threw the pitch one way to righthanded batters and another way to lefties. "With righthanders, I dropped down to sidearm-three-quarters," he reveals.

"The screwball was a pitch I had learned in the minors," Lopat says. "I started throwing it in 1939. My manager showed me how to throw it, and I got to fooling around with it. I worked on it for a year and a half before I used it in a game."

During that time, Lopat was working on various other aspects of his trade, too, because he was relatively new to the pitching profession.

"I was originally a first baseman," Ed recalls. "The Brooklyn Dodgers signed me to my first contract, and my first year in professional baseball (1937) I played first base."

He hit .229. And the Dodgers didn't renew his contract, but Lopat hooked into the White Sox system. By this time, he had started to do some pitching. In his second year as a pro, Lopat became a full-time hurler.

He spent seven years in the minors, bouncing from one town to another. All the while, Lopat was learning the fine art of pitching.

His record showed it. In 1939, he had a 16–9 season at Longview in the East Texas League. He was 11–15 at Salina in 1941. Finally, after a 19–10 mark at Little Rock and leading the Southern Association in earned run average and innings pitched, Lopat made the White Sox in 1944.

"The White Sox had told me I had a good chance to pitch for them, and it turned out they were right," Lopat recalls.

Ed made his major league debut against the pennant-bound St. Louis Browns. "I had butterflies in my stomach," he remembers. "I was jittery and nervous. I lost to the Browns, 5–4, in Chicago. I didn't feel too good about that, but then in my second game, I beat Cleveland, 2–1. That made me feel much better."

Lopat finished his rookie season with an 11–10 record and was regarded as one of the up-and-coming moundsmen in the league. He went on to win in double figures in each of his four seasons with Chicago, although the White Sox were mired in the second division the entire time.

After playing for Jimmy Dykes in his early years in Chicago, Lopat got a big boost in his career when ex-pitcher Ted Lyons, a future Hall of Famer, was named to manage the club in 1946.

"Ted Lyons really put the finishing touches on my pitching," Ed says. "He polished me off and helped me become a real pro. He taught me all the knick-knacks of pitching."

But Lopat still had one other hurdle. "I managed to pitch .500 ball, which with a seventh place ball club was as good as you were going to get," he says. "But deep down, I wasn't convinced that I was a major league pitcher. I didn't really master the screwball until 1946. I figure if I had a good year in 1946, when all the fellows had come back from the war, I would know that I was a major league pitcher."

Eddie Lopat.

Ed had a 13–13 record in 1946 as the big leagues blossomed with the return of the World War II veterans. The following season, his record went to 16–13. There was no doubt about his status as a big league pitcher. The fact that the Yankees sought his services confirmed that.

After posting a 50–49 record in four seasons with the lowly White Sox, Lopat was swapped to the Yankees in the winter of 1948 for catcher Aaron Robinson and pitchers Bill Wight and Fred Bradley.

"It was a great thrill getting traded to the Yankees," Ed recalls. "I was born and raised in New York City, and as a kid the Yankees were my favorite team. Lou Gehrig and Babe Ruth were my favorite players. Getting traded to the Yankees was like a dream fulfilled."

Eddie didn't squander his opportunity. Teaming with Raschi and Reynolds, the trio pitched the Yankees to American League pennants and World Series championships in five years. From 1948 to 1953, the three captured 307 victories with only 143 losses.

"We were as good a threesome as ever pitched," Lopat says. "We usually didn't win 20 in a season because we pitched only every fifth day. But we pitched often enough. The Yankees were concerned about us staying strong. Our records confirmed the theory that pitching every fourth day is a tough assignment."

Lopat's record was brilliant. Except for 1952 when he had arm trouble, and won only 10 games, the crafty southpaw never won less than 15 games a season for the Bronx Bombers. He won 17 in 1948, and in 1950 he posted an 18–8 mark. The following season, he was 21–9 and made his only appearance on the American League All-Star team.

Despite a case of tendinitis, Lopat may have had his best year in 1953 when he rang up a 16–4 record while leading the league in earned run average (2.42) and won-lost percentage (.800).

"I set a couple of goals for myself," Lopat remembers. "I wanted to win 20 games, which I did, and I wanted to have the best ERA, which I did. I only pitched once a week in 1953."

While he was standing American League hitters on their ears, Lopat was also working his spell on National League sluggers as the Yankees ventured each fall into the World Series.

Lopat won four out of five decisions while hurling in five straight World Series'. In seven Series games over that period, Ed had a 2.60 ERA.

Particularly noteworthy was his performance in the 1951 Series against the Dodgers. Enroute to two victories and two complete games, Lopat gave up only one earned run and 10 hits in 18 innings. He beat Brooklyn, 3–1, in the second game, and 13–1 in the fifth.

Ed was also the winning pitcher in the fourth game of the 1949 Series when he defeated the Dodgers, 6–4, and in the second game of the 1953 fall classic when he also topped Brooklyn, 4–2. He went eight innings but didn't get the decision in a 3–2 Yanks' win over the Phillies in the 1950 Series.

In those days, the Yankees under Casey Stengel were an overpowering club with no perceptible weakness. "People said we had all that power in our lineup," Lopat notes, "but the thing that was most overlooked was that we had a fantastic defensive club and outstanding pitching.

"And Casey was easy to play for," he adds. "He was a good psychologist. If you put out, he wouldn't bother you. He was also a good strategist, and he had a fantastic memory."

Stengel's club failed to capture the pennant in 1954, although it won 103 games. That year, despite an arm that "popped out," Lopat had a 12–4 record. He was, however, approaching the end of his days as a Yankee.

By 1954, Raschi had been sent to the St. Louis Cardinals. And Lopat's roommate, Reynolds, retired after the '54 campaign.

After working half of a season with the Yanks in 1955, Lopat was sold on waivers to the Orioles. He played in Baltimore for the remainder of the season; then he, too, retired at the conclusion of the year.

Lopat went out as one of the top hurlers in Yankee history. He ranks high in a number of categories on the club's all-time list, including: seventh in percentage (.657); 11th in shutouts (20); 12th in wins (113); 14th in innings pitched (1497); 16th in career ERA (3.25) and 17th in complete games pitched (91). Considering the wealth of pitching talent the Yankees have had, ranking in the top 20 in any of the club's all-time pitching categories is a distinguished feat.

"Just being with the Yankees and winning that first pennant in 1949 were my greatest thrills," Lopat says. "Looking back, I couldn't have asked for a better career. I fulfilled everything I wanted to do as a player."

After his retirement as a player, Lopat remained in baseball. He managed at Richmond in the International League for three seasons. He was the Yankees' pitching coach in 1960, then joined the Kansas City A's. Ed managed the A's in 1963 and part of 1964, but that part of baseball wasn't terribly agreeable. "You had to scream and connive all the time," he says.

Following his resignation as manager, Lopat became the A's general manager, a post he held for six years. In 1968, he joined the Montreal Expos as a scout.

Lopat rejoined the Yankees as a major league scout in 1986. Today, a resident of Hillsdale, New Jersey, he covers all the American and National League clubs in the East and also cross-checks high school and college players for the free agent draft.

Lopat sees numerous pitchers in his travels. But few are the master craftsmen that he was.

Sal Maglie—
"The Barber" Was Mean

His nickname was "The Barber."

If you needed a shave, Sal Maglie was happy to oblige—only not with a razor but with a fastball around the whiskers. And then when he had knocked you off the plate, he would throw that big, nasty curve that would break across the outside corner.

Hitters did not like to go up against "The Barber."

He looked mean, and he was mean. Always looking like he hadn't shaved in a couple of days, and with a constant scowl and beady eyes, he resembled one of those gunslingers that the good guys were always chasing in the cowboy movies.

If Maglie ever smiled, nobody ever saw him—at least, not on a baseball field. When he was with the New York Giants, pitching against the Brooklyn Dodgers, he gave new meaning to the word, "hate." The Giants and the Dodgers had enough of a rivalry, but when Maglie pitched, he turned it into a war.

Maglie spent only 10 seasons in the big leagues, but what seasons they were. During his tenure, he was a central figure in what many consider to be the finest era in baseball—the 1950s.

Sal posted a career record of 119–62, which gave him a lofty .657 percentage. In 303 games, he had a 3.15 earned run average and gave up 1,591 hits in 1,723 innings.

Although not a strikeout pitcher, he fanned 862 while walking 562.

Maglie pitched a no-hitter, he won a crucial World Series game, and he was a winning pitcher in an All-Star game. At one point, he won 11 straight games. And during a three-year stretch from 1950 to 1952, he was as good a pitcher as there was in baseball, winning 59 games while losing the incredibly low total of 18.

The 6′ 2″, 180-pound righthander had a reputation as a pitcher who could put any pitch anywhere he wanted. He had pinpoint control, and he worked hitters with a delicate touch, moving the ball up, down, in, out, but never giving them a juicy pitch to hit.

Sal Maglie.

"I never threw a ball down the middle of the plate," Maglie recalls. "I always shaved the corners. I tried to keep the hitters off balance.

"The batters back then really knew the strike zone. Fellows like Pee Wee Reese, Richie Ashburn. They made it tough on a pitcher. You had to keep hitting the corners on them."

More than 30 years later, Ashburn still has vivid memories of the battles he had with Maglie. "He had great control," says the former Phillies' center fielder. "He'd put it under your chin, moving you back from the plate; then he'd get you with a pitch on the outside. He had a good fastball, a great curve and whole assortment of other pitches. He was really nasty."

Maglie says he never threw at a batter with the intention of hitting him. "But I would throw at his nose to move him back," he says.

"When I first joined the Giants," he adds, "the manager was Mel Ott. He had a talk with me and told me he wanted me to pitch high inside and low and away. 'And if you want to make money,' Ott added, 'you've got to beat the Dodgers.' "

In those days, the Giants and Dodgers had as fierce a rivalry as ever existed in professional sports. And some of Maglie's most memorable games were the shutouts he pitched against Brooklyn.

His most memorable game, though, was the no-hitter he pitched for the Dodgers in 1956 against the Phillies. It came on September 25, and he beat Jack Meyer, 5-0, striking out three and walking two. He also hit Ashburn on the foot with two outs in the ninth inning.

"I had real good control that day," says Maglie. "I remember Reese making a great play at shortstop. I also remember one of the Phillies, I think it might have been Del Ennis, hitting a shot to left that just curved foul before it went over the wall."

Maglie was also on the scene for some other memorable events. He was with the Giants when Bobby Thomson hit the home run in 1951 that won the pennant for New York. He was the starting pitcher in the World Series game in 1954 in which Willie Mays made his sensational catch in deep center field on Vic Wertz' drive for the Cleveland Indians. And he was on the losing end of Don Larsen's perfect game in the 1956 World Series.

"I didn't see Mays' catch," Maglie says, "because I was already in the clubhouse. But I did see Thomson's home run. When he hit it, I knew the score would at least be tied because I thought it would hit the wall and drive in the tying run. What a thrill that was."

By the time Thomson hit the home run that beat the hated Dodgers in the National League playoff, Maglie was firmly ensconced as one of the premier pitchers in the major leagues. It was, however, a designation that nearly escaped him.

After breaking into organized ball in 1938, he did little to attract much attention until 1941 when he rang up a 20-15 record for Elmira in the Eastern League, leading the circuit in games (43) and innings pitched (270). The following year, he was elevated to Jersey City and the International League, but posted only a 9-6 mark while pitching mostly in relief.

Disgusted, Sal quit organized ball and joined a company league in Canada. For two years, he worked for a firm during the day and played for its baseball team at night.

In 1945, Sal returned to Jersey City and by the end of the season was called up to the parent Giants for whom he was 5–4 in 13 games.

"That winter, I played in Cuba. I was getting $400 a month, which was good money at the time," he recalls. "I got to know Dolf Luque, the old Cuban pitcher who played in the National League for many years. He was the manager of our team, and he introduced me to some people who were involved with the Mexican League.

"That spring, I went to training camp with the Giants. But I didn't get to pitch much at all. I was pretty disgusted."

His disappointment, coupled with the urgings of former Giant, Danny Gardella and the lure of big money, convinced Maglie to jump to the outlawed Mexican League, which, at the time, was attempting to attract major league players to its teams.

"It seemed like a good opportunity, and so I went," says Maglie. "Mainly, though, I went because I wanted to pitch."

Maglie won 40 games in two years in the Mexican League. But he, along with Gardella, Max Lanier and a few others who had travelled south of the border, were banned from organized baseball.

It was not until November, 1949, that Commissioner Happy Chandler lifted the ban, and the players were allowed to return to their big league teams. Maglie rejoined the Giants in 1950, and after a few relief assignments, became the top hurler on a staff that already included Larry Jansen, Dave Koslo, Jim Hearn, and Sheldon (Available) Jones.

That season, Maglie fashioned an 18–4 record, leading the league in won-lost percentage with a glittering .818. Along the way, he won 11 straight games, at one point teaming with Hearn to pitch a doubleheader shutout in early September against the Phillies that nearly sidetracked the Whiz Kids from the pennant drive.

What was the difference between the Sal Maglie who had been a mediocre pitcher before he jumped to the Mexican League and the Sal Maglie who returned to the majors as such a brilliant moundsman?

"Looking back, the way things turned out, I learned a lot about pitching down in Mexico," Maglie answers. "The altitude down there was very high, about 7,000 feet, and my curve ball didn't break so well in that thin air. I had a sort of flat curve. So I had to learn to throw my curve differently. It broke more; it was sharper.

"What that meant was that I came back to the big leagues a much better pitcher."

Sal was so much better that he followed up his 1950 season with a 23–6 mark in 1951, tying Jansen for the league lead in total victories and placing second in winning percentage (.793), earned run average (2.93) and complete games (22) and ranking third in innings (298) and strikeouts (146).

That year, Maglie joined the distinguished gathering of Robin Roberts, Don Newcombe and Ewell Blackwell as National League pitchers in the All-Star game. Sal was the winning pitcher as the Nationals beat the Americans, 8–3, at Briggs Stadium.

In the fall, Maglie got one start in the World Series, but was saddled with a 6–2 loss to the New York Yankees.

But he was back to his old tricks in 1952, winning 18 and losing eight. By this time, Maglie's reputation as a pitcher so mean that he would surely brush back Santa Claus was at its peak.

Maglie chuckles when he talks about that. ''The press really made that up,'' he says. ''I just played along with it. But I wasn't so mean. I didn't hate every hitter. Sure, I did come high and inside on them. I'd knock them back. But that was part of the game. If a guy got a hit off me, I'd give him credit.''

A mild-mannered fellow off the field, the soft-spoken Maglie had such superb control, though, that he could toy with hitters, sending them into fits of despair. ''I remember one game late in my career,'' he says, '' when I beat Milwaukee, 3–0. I threw 111 pitches. Eighty-nine of them were curve balls, and 85 of those curve balls were strikes.''

Sal, who says he got his nickname, ''The Barber,'' from Jim McCullough, a baseball writer with the *New York Daily News* who first called him that in an article following a 1950 game in St. Louis, had an off-year in 1953 (8–9), then moved back up to 14–6 in 1954. That year, he was the Giants' starting pitcher in the World Series opener against the Cleveland Indians, but did not get a decision in New York's 5–2 win, which was pre-served by Mays' memorable catch.

In July the following season, after he had compiled a 9–5 record, the Giants sold Maglie to the team he had just pitched against in the World Series. Sal spent the rest of that season and part of the next pitching in only 12 games and failing to win any for the Indians. In May, 1956, Cleveland sold Maglie to his old rivals, the Dodgers.

Going to a team that was once such a bitter adversary may be traumatic for some players, but it didn't bother Maglie.

''I was happy to go there,'' he says. ''I wasn't getting any action in Cleveland. All I wanted to do was pitch. It didn't matter to me where I did that. I was in Brooklyn to pitch, that's all.''

The first player Sal met when he joined the Dodgers was his old nemesis and former enemy Carl Furillo. ''We were only enemies before because we both wanted to win so badly,'' Maglie says. ''Once I joined the Dodgers, we turned out to be real good pals. We roomed together, hung around together.''

Maglie had a 13–5 record that season for Brooklyn, including his no-hitter against the Phillies. In the World Series that fall, he started the first game for the Dodgers and beat the Yankees, 6–3. Then, despite a five-hitter, he was the losing pitcher (2–0) on the day that the Yankees' Don Larsen pitched the only perfect game in World Series history.

Once again the next season, Maglie was sold to a team he had just faced in the previous World Series. Sal joined the Yankees and worked for them until mid-1958 when he was sent to the St. Louis Cardinals. He retired as a player at the end of the season.

Maglie stayed with the Cardinals the following season as a scout, then joined the Boston Red Sox in 1960 as a pitching coach. He spent three seasons with the Bosox before going to Buffalo where he coached for three more seasons. Sal rejoined the Red Sox for the 1966-67 campaigns, then moved to the Seattle Pilots, first as a minor league pitching coach, then as a coach with the parent club.

In recent years, Maglie worked in sales for a distillery and for a convention center in his native Niagara Falls, New York. Seriously ill several years ago, Sal recovered after undergoing major surgery.

Maglie is now retired, but still active. He follows baseball closely, is a guest at an occasional baseball card show, and once in a while sees a former teammate or opponent.

The opponents don't get mad at him anymore. But there was a time when they couldn't stand the very sight of the bearded, scowling, sneering "Barber," standing on the mound, ready to give another batter another close shave.

Vinegar Bend Mizell—
From Baseball to Government Service

Presidential elections should be of interest to all Americans, but for an ex-major league pitcher with an outrageously colorful nickname, they are particularly important occasions.

Each time there's a presidential election, his job is on the line.

Wilmer (Vinegar Bend) Mizell, who once toiled in the vineyards of the St. Louis Cardinals, Pittsburgh Pirates and New York Mets, now plays for a team located in Washington, D.C. And, depending on the outcome of that club's contest every four years in November, the former hurler either remains in the big time or returns to the farm in North Carolina.

Mizell, a former U.S. Congressman, is currently Assistant Secretary for Governmental and Public Affairs in the Department of Agriculture. A presidential appointee, he has held the job since Ronald Reagan ascended to the Presidency in 1980. In the position, Mizell says he deals in congressional and international governmental relations and public information.

Fancy titles like his are abundant in the nation's capitol, but Mizell does not fit the mold of your basic bureaucrat. He is, after all, a relative newcomer to this game, and he approaches it in the same, serious manner that he used to approach a pitching assignment.

It is, furthermore, not such a regular occurrence to have dark, good-looking, 6'4" ex-ballplayers ambling around the halls of the federal government. In recent years, several ex-athletes, notably baseball's Jim Bunning, basketball's Bill Bradley and football's Jack Kemp turned their attention to Washington. But the jock-turned-politician phenomenon does not happen often.

"Sports can open the door for you," says Mizell. "But in politics, once the door is open, you have to win people's confidence on your own. There's no guarantee that you'll be successful."

In Mizell's case, though, success is a condition with which he had been rubbing elbows long before he came to Washington. As a lefthanded pitcher, Vinegar Bend had a nine-year major league career, six of them ones in which he won in double figures.

Vinegar Bend Mizell.

Until injuries forced a premature end to his career, Mizell posted a 90–88 record and a 3.85 earned run average. He appeared in 268 games, working 1,528.2 innings, allowing 1,434 hits, striking out 918 and walking 680. He had 61 complete games and 15 shutouts.

When he was on the mound, Mizell was a sight to behold. He would launch his pitches with a big exaggerated windup, punctuated by a high kick. What usually followed was either a blazing fastball or a big sweeping curve.

The motion combined with an easy-going Southern manner, his country humor and his absorbing nickname to make Mizell one of the game's more colorful personalities.

The nickname, a moniker that both Presidents Ford and Reagan address him by, was pinned on him by a sportswriter during his first year in the minor leagues. Vinegar Bend was the town in Alabama where the young pitcher lived.

It was a town, though, that was so small it nearly kept Mizell from the majors.

"We had no baseball team in high school," Mizell explains. "In fact, we had no teams of any kind, the town was so small. Until I signed a pro contract, I never played on a regular team. All the games we played as kids were pick-up games. We just played out in the country, using whatever equipment we could find."

Mizell often pitched to his brother Curtis when there was a break in their plowing chores on the family farm. And in 1948, inspired by his apparent prowess as a barnyard pitcher, the young Wilmer traveled several hundred miles to Biloxi, Mississippi, for a Cardinals' tryout camp.

The last player to pitch before a heavy rain storm washed out the remainder of the two-day camp, Mizell struck out the side. That winter, St. Louis scout Buddy Lewis signed the 18-year-old youngster to a $175-per-month contract.

Leaving his job in a sawmill, Mizell reported to Albany of the Georgia-Florida League where the manager was a man named Chief Bender (not the A's Hall of Famer). "For the first six weeks, he wouldn't let me pitch," recalls Mizell. "I begged him to put me in, but he wouldn't. Finally, one game we were getting beat, 15–0, and he let me go in.

"Needless to say, I was nervous. Hal Smith (who would later team with Mizell on both the Cardinals and Pirates) was the catcher. I threw the first pitch 20 feet high. Eventually, I walked six batters. But I also struck out seven of the nine outs I got."

Mizell went on from there to win eight games in a row and finish the season with a 12–3 record. "But I was so green," he says. "I had no training. All I knew to do was look toward home plate and just throw the ball.

"Bender was very patient. He really helped me. So did the pitching coach, a man named Bob Klein. Later, I also got a lot of help from another minor league pitching coach named Al Hollingsworth. He was a lefthander and had pitched in the majors. He really helped me develop a better curve and better control."

After his initial season in Albany, Mizell spent a year with Winston-Salem (17–7) in the Carolina League and a year with Houston (16–14), then in the Texas League. He led both leagues in strikeouts—in the latter fanning 18 in one game to break a league record held by Dizzy Dean.

Having registered 484 strikeouts in 445 innings over the previous two seasons, Mizell was summoned by the Cardinals for the 1952 season. He had a 10–8 record in his rookie year while leading the National League in walks (103) and ranking fourth in strikeouts with 146.

The following season, Mizell had a 13–11 mark with 173 strikeouts, third best in the league. He spent the 1954–55 seasons in the Army, and when he came back in 1956 he was the Cards' top winner with a 14–14 record while placing fifth in the league in strikeouts (153). But his Army service was not without penalty. A suitcase had fallen off a rack in a train and landed on Mizell's left shoulder. The injury that resulted probably kept him from being a 20-game winner in '56.

In 1958, the Cardinals got big years on the mound from Larry Jackson and Lindy McDaniel and made a run at the pennant before finishing second to the Milwaukee Braves. Mizell's record slipped to 8–10 after he hurt his ribs while slipping on wet grass around the mound.

Over the next two years, Mizell went 10–14 and 13–10. Then, early in the 1960 season, he was traded with infielder Dick Gray to the Pittsburgh Pirates for second baseman Julian Javier.

Mizell provided the Pirates with the additional lefthanded pitcher they needed to win the pennant. Teaming with Bob Friend, Vern Law and Harvey Haddix, Mizell gave Pittsburgh a fourth solid starter as he posted a 13–5 record (14–8 overall).

"That September, I pitched in what I consider to be my most memorable game," says Vinegar Bend. "We were playing a doubleheader with the Reds. At the time, we had only a two or three game lead over the Dodgers. Law won the first game, 5–4, and I won the second, 1–0, with a three-hitter. That just about clinched the pennant for us."

Although the Pirates defeated the New York Yankees four games to three in a memorable World Series, Mizell didn't fare so well. He failed to last through the first inning in a 10–0 loss to the Yanks in the third game. Later, he relieved in the sixth game.

"Despite what happened to me," he says, "playing in the World Series was the climax of my baseball career."

It was a career that was over two years later. Mizell developed arm trouble in 1961 and slipped to a 7–10 mark with the Pirates. The following season, the Bucs sold him to the fledgling New York Mets. During the season, the Mets released Mizell. The big southpaw went back to the Pirates' Triple-A farm team at Columbus with the promise of a new chance the following season with Pittsburgh if he performed well. But arm trouble continued to plague him, and at the end of the season, Mizell hung up his glove and spikes at the age of 32.

"It was a good career, and I enjoyed it," he says. "I thought I played at a great time in baseball. It was very satisfying to me.

"My only regret is that a couple of injuries kept me from winning a lot more ball games than I did. It was frustrating."

Soon after he retired, Mizell got into a new kind of game. First, though, he took a job as a sales supervisor for a soft drink company in Winston-Salem, North Carolina, the city in which he had made his home since he played there in the minors.

"But some friends thought I should get into politics," he recalls. "I had never considered running for office before, although some of my family had been in politics when I was small. But I had always been interested in government. As a baseball player, traveling back and forth across the country, I had become more and more interested in our government.

"I had thought a lot about our country and the ways the government operates. In fact, I had switched parties from Democrat to Republican because I felt that in the South we had had a one-party system too long."

When Mizell finally decided to get into politics, he ran for County Commissioner. Then in 1968, he ran for Congress. Defeating the grandson of a local tobacco tycoon, Mizell rode the Nixon landslide to victory.

His seat in the House of Representatives lasted three terms, and during that time Mizell served on the powerful Public Works and Agriculture Committees.

"I really enjoyed my terms in Congress," Mizell says. "Campaigning, representing the views of the voters, it was all very enjoyable. I always worked to inform the people as much as possible because I figured that if you presented both sides, people would make good judgements."

When the backlash of Watergate influenced much of the 1974 elections, Mizell tumbled to defeat in his bid for a fourth term in Congress. He returned home to Winston-Salem to ponder life without politics.

He didn't ponder long. Soon, President Ford appointed Mizell Assistant Secretary of Commerce for Economic Development. In that post, the ex-pitcher was responsible for directing funds to small communities in need of money for building themselves up.

When Ford was defeated by Jimmy Carter, Mizell went home once again, this time to become an executive with a furniture parts company. That job lasted until Reagan called four years later.

Since then, Mizell has been heavily involved in government service. He still has his home in Winston-Salem , but lives in an apartment in a Virginia suburb of the District of Columbia. Except for an occasional appearance in an old timers' game, his days and many of his nights are taken up with the Washington whirl of political and social activities.

Most people, though, still remember his days on the ballfield.

"Actually," he says, "there are many similarities between baseball and politics. For one thing, you're constantly meeting and dealing with people in both of them. In fact, baseball really helped me in this regard. It provided one of the best opportunities to meet people.

"In Congress," he continues, "you're representing not only your country, but also your constituents. That's very much like when you play ball; you're representing your team.

"The relationship you have with your colleagues is also very similar. The cloak room, which is just off the House floor, is very similar to the clubhouse. In both cases, that's where you meet and talk with your fellow members."

Does he miss that life? "Yes," says Mizell. Will he run for office again? "I haven't said I wouldn't," he says, smiling.

"When you think of it," the amiable ex-hurler drawls, "I have had a really great life. It has been a great honor to have played major league baseball and to have been on a World Championship team, and then to have served my country in government. It's an experience I wouldn't want to replace with anything else."

Milt Pappas—
A Winner in Two Leagues

Put a microscope to the career of Milt Pappas, and it is not hard to be struck by the realization that here is a player who seemingly accomplished a little bit of everything.

Boy wonder at the age of 18, no-hit pitcher at the age of 33. Consistent winner year after year. Home run hitter. Controversial player representative. Pappas had a career that was not only successful, but was anything but placid.

The name Milt Pappas is not one that should disappear quietly into the ranks of oblivion. While he may not have reached the same plateau as some of his Hall of Fame peers, he did earn a place as one of the top hurlers of his era.

In 16 full seasons as a starting pitcher, the 6'3", 190-pounder won 209 games (losing 164) while playing for clubs that were usually also-rans. When he retired following the 1973 season, Pappas was just one victory short of the rare achievement of having won 100 games in both the National and American Leagues.

As any big league manager will quickly attest, there is no greater luxury than having a pitcher who is dependable, durable and consistent. Pappas was all of those and more.

Between 1958 and 1972, he won in double figures 11 straight times and 14 times in 15 seasons. He never won 20 games, but he won 17 twice, 16 three times and 15 twice.

Pappas pitched in 520 games during his career, allowing 3,046 hits in 3,185 innings while striking out 1,728 and walking 858. His career earned run average was 3.40, and he hurled 43 shutouts, which rank among the top 35 in baseball history.

In addition to his no-hitter, which was one out away from being a perfect game, Pappas hurled one one-hitter and six two-hitters. And twice he was a member of the American League All-Star team.

A hard-throwing righthander who specialized in fastballs and sliders, Pappas was mostly noted for his pitching with the Baltimore Orioles. But he also toiled for the Cincinnati Reds, Atlanta Braves and Chicago Cubs in a career that began in 1957 when Pappas was just 18 years old.

Milt Pappas.

"The fact that I lasted all those years was an achievement in itself," says Pappas, now a salesman with a building products company near Chicago. "I really have Paul Richards (Orioles' manager) to thank for that. He was quite a guy, and he helped me enormously to become what I did. He was a great handler of pitchers.

"When I first came up," Pappas continues, "he would only let me stay in for 90 pitches. Then he would take me out. That helped to strengthen my arm, and I thank God that Richards did it that way. He prolonged my career and I never had arm trouble."

Pappas had been a high school phenom in Detroit, hotly pursued by an army of major league scouts, when he signed with the Orioles in 1957.

"A scout for the Orioles had first seen me when I was 12 years old, playing in the sandlots of Detroit," Pappas recalls. "He followed me all through high school. In my senior year, I had offers from 12 of the 16 clubs. I looked at all the pitching staffs, and tried to figure out with which team I could make it to the big leagues fastest. Baltimore was at a point where it was having a changing of the guard. The team was on the verge of going with young players, so I decided to sign with the Orioles."

Pappas pitched in only three minor league games (at Knoxville in the South Atlantic League) before getting the call to report to the Orioles. Soon afterward, just a few months out of high school, he made his big league debut. What a debut it was.

"We were playing the New York Yankees," he says. "At the time, they had a dynasty. They were the most powerful team in baseball.

"I didn't think Richards would pitch me against them, but during one game, he told me to warm up. While I was doing that, Mickey Mantle hit a ball off the scoreboard. I had never seen a ball hit that far.

"Harry Brecheen was our pitching coach. A little while later, he said, 'You're in.' I said, 'You're crazy.' I came in from the bullpen and when I went to walk into the dugout, I was so nervous I fell down the steps. Then I went out to the mound, and the first pitch I threw was over the catcher's head."

The first four batters Pappas faced were Enos Slaughter, Mantle, Yogi Berra and Bill Skowron, three of them future Hall of Famers. Somehow he survived.

"I don't remember how," Milt says. "All I can remember is how scared I was."

From that rugged beginning, Pappas went on to become one of the mainstays of a kiddie corps Orioles pitching staff that eventually included such other youngsters as Steve Barber, Chuck Estrada and Jerry Walker. By 1960, not only had Pappas become a consistent winner, but the Orioles had grown from the woeful, transplanted St. Louis Browns of the mid-1950s to an exciting pennant contender, even though Baltimore fans hadn't exactly taken the team to their bosoms.

"At the time," Pappas recalls, "the Colts were the dominant team in

Baltimore. We were just step-children. The Colts had all those great players. When anybody would mention the Orioles, people would say, 'Oh, that's the baseball team.' It took us a long time to turn it around in Baltimore. It was very difficult winning over the fans.''

But win they finally did. Meanwhile, Milt was posting records of 15-9, 15-11, 13-9, 12-10, 16-9, 16-7 and 13-9 with the upwardly mobile Orioles.

Pappas' finest season with the Birds came in 1964 when he registered the 16-7 mark with a 2.97 ERA. That year, he tossed seven shutouts, including three in a row, and blanked the Minnesota Twins with a one-hitter.

By then, Milt was also making a name for himself in two other areas. He had become one of the better hitting pitchers of his day; in fact, his 20 career home runs rank 12th on the all-lime list for pitchers. And he was a leader in the players' union.

''I had been the assistant player rep in Baltimore,'' Pappas remembers. ''Mike McCormick was the player rep, but when he got traded, I inherited the job. It was a tough time for the player reps. I wound up doing it for 10 years in both the American and National Leagues. We had out first strike while I was player rep in 1972 in Chicago.''

Although he ranks among the team's all-time leaders in a number of pitching categories (including fourth in shutouts, fifth in strikeouts, sixth in wins, seventh in innings pitched and ninth in won-lost percentage), Pappas' career with the Orioles came to an abrupt end after the 1965 season when he was traded along with pitcher Jack Baldschun and outfielder Dick Simpson to the Cincinnati Reds for outfielder Frank Robinson. The trade led to the 1966 pennant and World Series victory for the Orioles, but was nothing but pure disappointment for Pappas.

''I didn't want to be traded,'' he says. ''I was very disappointed when it happened. It was totally unexpected. I had thought that the club might trade Barber because he had had a big argument with one of the club's officials and wanted to be traded. But I enjoyed Baltimore, had made my home there, and it was quite a shock when I was traded.''

Milt pitched two and one-half seasons in Cincinnati, winning 30 games, including 16 in 1967. In June 1968, the Reds swapped him to the Braves in a six-player deal. Pappas pitched for two more years with Atlanta. While there, he saw the only post-season action of his career when he worked two and two-thirds innings in relief in the 1969 League Championship Series in which the New York Mets swept the Braves in three games enroute to a World Series victory over Milt's old team, the Orioles.

Pappas discovered some big differences between pitching in the American and National Leagues.

''The National League had better hitters,'' he says. ''When I pitched in the American League, it hadn't signed many black superstars. But the National League had two or three real good black players on every team.

''The strike zone was also different. American League umpires had trouble seeing low strikes because they still wore those big chest protectors. The American League strike zone was higher.''

In June, 1970, the Braves sold Pappas to the Cubs in what would be Milt's last stop on the baseball trail. His career, though, was still flying high.

Pappas was 17–14 and 17–7 in his first two full seasons with the Cubs, and wound up winning 51 games in Chicago.

And in 1972, in his next to last season in the majors, Pappas pitched a no-hitter at Wrigley Field against the San Diego Padres. Milt struck out six while winning, 8–0, and had a perfect game with two outs in the ninth inning.

"I had retired 26 men in a row, and on what should have been the last batter, Bruce Froemming missed three pitches and I wound up walking Larry Stahl," he remembers. "Later, I ran into Stahl, and he said he hadn't intended to swing anyway. I said, 'Why didn't you let me know that? You could've winked or something.'

"But I still wound up with a no-hitter, which was some consolation. I was so elated. I had never pitched a no-hitter in my whole career. I wasn't thinking too much about it during the game because I was so engrossed in the game itself. But I got a lot of phone calls that night, and then it really started to sink in. It was by far the biggest moment of my career."

Pappas retired from baseball after the 1973 season, having won 110 games in the American League and 99 in the National. He stayed in Chicago to enter the business world, and has been there ever since.

Looking back, he says, "I think I had a helluva career. When I broke in, nobody thought I was going to be around too long. But I was extremely fortunate, especially to last as long as I did, to win that many games and to get a no-hitter."

Mel Parnell—The Epitome of the Stylish Lefthander

Remember the phrase, "stylish lefthander?"
You don't hear it much anymore. But there was a time when the words were fairly common around major league baseball parks.

And the word, "stylish" was the exclusive property of lefthanders. You never heard anyone referred to as a "stylish righthander."

Actually, there weren't really that many stylish lefthanders. The phrase was reserved for a pretty elite group. To qualify, one had to be about six-feet tall, rather slender, and most important, throw with a smooth, easy motion.

You couldn't have your arms and legs flapping all different ways. You couldn't have what they used to call a herky-jerky delivery. And you couldn't be one of the guys who just rared back and threw with everything he had.

Stylish lefthanders were fluid. They had nice, big windups with high kicks, textbook deliveries and perfectly balanced follow-throughs. They always pitched like pitchers should pitch.

No pitcher ever earned the label of stylish lefthander with any more certainty than Mel Parnell. He had a few challengers, to be sure; guys like Howie Pollet and Hal Newhouser and Warren Spahn. But Mel Parnell was the king of the post-World War II stylish lefthanders.

But not only was the 6-foot, 180-pound southpaw stylish, he could pitch with the best of them, too.

His big league career wasn't that long—10 years, all with the Boston Red Sox. But he had six straight seasons of winning in double figures, including two campaigns with more than 20 wins.

Parnell had a lifetime record of 123–75 with a 3.50 earned run average. He worked in 289 games and 1,752.2 innings, allowing 1,715 hits. One of his games was a no-hitter.

Parnell pitched for the Red Sox during some of the team's most powerful years. Breaking into the majors in 1947, he was the bellwether of the late-40s, early-50s staff. From 1947 through 1951, the Red Sox never finished lower than third place, and through 1956 they finished out of the first division only once.

Although the Red Sox have never made a habit of overloading with left-handed pitchers because of the closeness of the left field wall at Fenway Park, Parnell is generally regarded as one of the top lefthanders in the team's history. When Mel was working for Boston, he was hailed as the finest southpaw on the club since Lefty Grove.

While he doesn't inhabit big league pitching mounds anymore, Parnell is still stylish. Now, though, he is stylish as a person instead of as a pitcher.

A slightly balding gentleman, Parnell still lives in his native New Orleans, where for the last 15 years he has operated a pest-control business.

This venture followed a period in which Mel attempted to hang on in baseball after his playing days ended. He managed in the Boston system for three years—at Alpine, Texas, York, Pennsylvania and Seattle—but "threw in the towel because there were too many headaches." He also spent seven years in the broadcasting business, covering Red Sox games for six years and the Chicago White Sox for one.

Parnell had a stroke six years ago. "I was completely paralyzed on my left side for four days," he says. "I was laid up for four months altogether."

Fortunately, he was in good shape, and made almost a full recovery, except for a slight paralysis in his left arm.

"When something like a stroke happens," Parnell says, "it gives you a lot to think about."

One of the things he thought about was slowing down his business activity, and following more leisurely pursuits, such as gardening, following sports in Louisiana and playing golf three times a week, maintaining a nine handicap.

"I've somewhat divorced myself from baseball, however," notes the soft-spoken ex-pitcher. "Oh, once in a while I go to an old-timers' game. I think the fans like to see how much hair's left on your head and how fat you've gotten.

"I cross paths with some of my ex-teammates," he adds. "Jack Kramer and I often have lunch together. I used to see Zeke Bonura (prior to his death in 1987). And I keep in contact with Milt Bolling because he's a Red Sox scout in Louisiana."

Parnell, whose Boston roommates were Maurice McDermott, Billy Goodman, Bob Porterfield, Bill Wight and Jackie Jensen, is a member of the Louisiana Sports Hall of Fame.

Mel marvels at the way the game of baseball has changed since he played it.

"Our time was taken up entirely with the game. Even when we were traveling, we talked baseball," he says. "Today's fellows are more businesslike. They carry briefcases and divide their time between sports and business. It's a little different kind of ballplayer today.

"We were much closer than the players are today," he adds. "We rode mostly on trains, and that kept us together. We didn't fly much, although I remember one particular time we did. The plane fell 1,500 feet. One of

Mel Parnell.

the coaches got two broken ribs. Several of the fellows were about to go beserk. Ted Williams was very upset.''

Mention the name Ted Williams, and all kinds of memories come back to Parnell.

"As a person, he was tremendous," says Parnell. "Of course, he was a great player. He was just a great fellow to have on the club. He was a guy you had to admire, a great professional, a perfectionist and a great student of the game. He never got any special treatment. But everybody looked up to him because he was the big name on the ballclub.

"One of my greatest thrills was just being on the ballclub with him, and seeing some of the things he did," Parnell continues. "They were just unbelievable. If there was a better hitter in the game, I never saw him.''

There were a couple of hitters, though, he would've liked to have seen less of. "I guess the toughest batter I faced was Joe DiMaggio," Parnell recalls. "Harvey Kuenn and Lou Boudreau were tough, too. They weren't really power hitters. They made contact with the ball.''

Parnell had no notion of how tough the hitters would be when he began playing baseball. "I was always a first baseman as a kid," he explains. "Mel Ott was one of my idols. I used to throw batting practice in high school, and my ball moved pretty well. So they made me a pitcher. One game, I struck out 17 batters.

"I grew up with baseball on my mind," he says. "People used to tell my dad, 'That kid's going to be a ballplayer.' ''

By the time Parnell's high school career was approaching an end, he had attracted a parade of big league scouts. The top candidates for his services were the Red Sox, New York Yankees, Detroit Tigers and St. Louis Cardinals.

"Branch Rickey sat at my home," Parnell says. "But in the end, I signed with the Red Sox. Being Irish and Boston being a great Irish town swayed my decision.''

Parnell broke in with Centerville of the Eastern Shore League in 1941, then two years later went into the Air Force for three and one-half years. He got out in time to play for Scranton in 1946. He divided the 1947 season between Boston and Louisville, then moved in permanently with the Red Sox the following year.

Mel posted a 15-8 record as a 26-year old rookie, teaming with Jack Kramer, Ellis Kinder and Joe Dobson to hurl the Red Sox to a first place tie and a special post-season playoff with the Cleveland Indians, which Boston lost.

In those days, the Bosox were in the fight for first place every season, but except for 1946, never quite made it to the top. The lineup was filled with top sluggers—Williams, Bobby Doerr, Vern Stephens, Dom DiMaggio, Johnny Pesky, Al Zarilla and others.

"But the team lacked speed," Parnell says. "Other than that, we had it all—hitting, pitching, defense. Unfortunately, we were always a step slower than some of the other clubs.''

Playing in Fenway Park was a problem, too, especially for lefthanders like Parnell. Working there caused the southpaw to change his whole method of pitching.

"When I was coming up through the minors, I was a fastball pitcher," Mel relates. "But I had to change my style to pitch in Fenway Park.

"You know, there was a mark on the left field wall at Fenway that said it was 315 (feet) down the left field line. One time, we took a measurement, and it was 297.

"But it was still a great ballpark. It had a tremendous atmosphere.

"The best pitch I threw there was a slider. As a lefthander, you have to keep it inside to righthanded hitters. I always wanted to keep the ball inside to the hitters, anyway. The left field fence was not my main concern. I always thought I could protect myself against that. My main concern was the lack of foul territory. You got outs in other parks that were just foul balls in the stands at Fenway."

Nevertheless, Parnell went from a fine rookie season to a sensation sophomore one. The '49 campaign turned out to be the best of his career as he registered a 25–7 record, leading the American League in wins, earned run average (2.77), innings pitched (295.1) and complete games (27). He also was the starting AL pitcher in the All-Star game.

Parnell's 25th win came in a 4–1 victory over the New York Yankees with one week left in the season. The win moved the Red Sox temporarily into a first place tie with New York, climaxing a surge in which Boston had stormed back after being 12 1/2 games out of first in July. The Bosox wound up losing the pennant by one game.

Parnell also had another memorable game that season. He and Virgil Trucks of the Detroit Tigers hooked up in a torrid pitching duel that went 12 innings before Mel's single drove in the winning run in a 3–2 Boston victory.

His performance in 1949 made Mel the premier pitcher in the American League and, teaming with Kinder, who won 23 games that year, gave the Red Sox the circuit's top one-two punch. It was a year in which one-two punches flourished, with the likes of Feller and Lemon, Raschi and Reynolds, Newhouser and Trucks and Kellner and Brissie.

Mel, who was being compared to another top lefty who played for a while with Boston, Herb Pennock, combined with Kinder for a 48–13 record in 1949. Then, over the next two seasons, Parnell won 18 each time and in 1951 worked in his second All-Star game.

He slipped to 12–12 in 1952 as the Red Sox tumbled all the way to sixth place. But Parnell, whose nickname was Dusty because he liked to throw the ball in the dirt, reblossomed the next year. He fashioned a 21–8 record, again taking his place as one of the league's top hurlers.

By this time, Parnell had led the Red Sox five straight years each in wins, ERA, innings pitched and complete games (although not simultaneously in all four categories). But in 1954, he began developing arm trouble. Over the next three years, he won only 12 games.

But there was one more big game in 1956. On July 14, Mel pitched
a no-hitter against the Chicago White Sox. He struck out four and walked
two while winning, 4–0.

"You have to have something working for you on days when you pitch
a no-hitter," says Parnell. "That was one of those days I had a good screwball.
I was setting up the hitters with my slider, then throwing the screwball.

"A no-hitter is something every pitcher dreams about," he adds. "You
feel like you're on Cloud Nine. I wasn't thinking no-hitter. I just wanted

*Mel Parnell (left) was the pitching ace and Lou Boudreau was the manager of some fine
Boston Red Sox teams in the early 1950s.*

to win. Of course, I knew I had a no-hitter going. I can't agree with those fellows who say they didn't know what was going on when they were pitching no-hitters.''

The no-hitter was Parnell's last major achievement in baseball. At the end of the season, after posting a 7-6 record, he retired as a player.

"I had a whole lot of arm trouble the last couple of years from throwing the screwball so much," he recalls. "It was time to bow out."

When he retired, Parnell left a record that to this day places him among Boston's all-time pitching leaders. He ranks second in career wins (behind Cy Young), third in innings pitched and games started, fifth in shutouts, and sixth in games and complete games. He is also first in walks.

"It was a very satisfying career," Parnell says. "I was very happy with the organization I played for. The Red Sox had a reputation for being a country club ballclub, but that really wasn't the case.

"Contrary to what was written and said, we had great harmony on that club," he adds. "Anybody who couldn't play for Tom Yawkey couldn't play for anybody."

Parnell not only played for him, he played exceptionally well...and with exceptional style.

Camilo Pascual—
Master Curveballer

In the days before all kinds of fancy names were used to label breaking pitches, back when a curve ball was a curve ball, nothing more, nothing less, there were few pitchers who could make a ball bend any better than Camilo Pascual.

Pascual was a dark-eyed righthander who had pitched his way out of Cuba and into the American League, working the better part of his career with the Washington Senators and Minnesota Twins. He played 18 years in the big leagues, a feat largely attributable to his masterful curveball.

What a curveball it was! Pascual would start it out with a big, easy motion, punctuated with a high kick, and then with a sweep of the arm would come straight overhand toward the plate. The ball would spin madly toward the batter, and then, at the last second, would break away with a huge, roundhouse arc.

The curveball, of course, wasn't Pascual's only pitch. But it was the most essential weapon in his arsenal and the pitch that provided him with two 20-win seasons, the league lead in strikeouts three consecutive years and three All-Star Game performances.

And it was the pitch that carried him to a 174–170 career record, a 3.63 earned run average and 2,167 strikeouts in 529 games and 2,930 innings.

In 1986, Pascual ranked 32d among the major league's all-time strikeout leaders. Thirty-nine times during his career, he struck out 10 or more batters in one game. He averaged 6.6 strikeouts per nine inning game during his 18 seasons in the majors.

Pascual had several memorable strikeout games. Twice he fanned 15 batters in one game, once in 1960 while pitching for the Senators against the Baltimore Orioles, and once in 1961 when he was on the mound for the Twins, facing the Los Angeles Angels. In 1964, he also whiffed 14 batters in a 12-inning clash with the Kansas City A's.

During the early part of his big league career, which began in 1954, Pascual pitched for teams buried deep in the American League's second division. In four of his first six seasons, his Washington Senators finished dead last.

312

Camilo Pascual.

Pascual never pitched for good teams until the Senators moved in 1961 to Minnesota. By the time the Twins won a pennant in 1965, Camilo's talents had started to fade, even though he hung on with an assortment of teams until the the end of the 1971 season.

At the peak of his career, though, Pascual was one of the premier pitchers in the Anerican League. His best season statistically was 1963 with the Twins when he posted a 21-9 record while leading the league for the second straight year in complete games and the third year in a row in strikeouts.

Pascual was a hard-thrower, but it was his curveball that American League batters had the most trouble with. It was a pitch that Camilo had started to develop as a youth back in his hometown of Havana, Cuba.

"I started throwing a curveball when I was 10 years old," says Pascual, now a resident of Miami, Florida. "It just seemed to come naturally to me. From then on, I just practiced and practiced throwing it all the time. It never bothered my arm; in fact, I never got a sore arm from throwing a curveball."

It didn't take long for the young Pascual to begin attracting attention with his curveball. As a teenager, he had scouts watching him, as well as his older brother, Carlos, who eventually had a brief fling with the Senators in 1950 and went 1–1 in two games.

In those days, the Washington Senators were far ahead of all the other big league teams in scouting and signing players from Latin America. The Senators were especially interested in Cuban players.

"Baseball was the main sport in Cuba," Pascual recalls. "It was the only sport I remember playing as a youngster.

"When I was 17 years old," he adds, "my brother recommended me to Joe Cambria, a Senators' scout. They signed me, and sent me to the minor leagues. It was hard getting used to playing in the States, but I survived. By that time there were about 30 Cuban players in professional baseball in the States."

Pascual played for three different Class D teams his first year, then performed for Havana in the Florida League for the next two years. After posting a 10–6 record in his second season with Havana, Pascual was called up to the Senators for the 1954 season. He had just turned 20.

"My first year in Washington, I was used mostly in relief," he remembers. "I didn't pitch very much."

Pascual worked in 48 games, only four as a starter. He had a 4–7 record.

The following year, Pascual moved closer to the starting rotation, starting 16 of his 43 games, but winning only two of 14 decisions. That year, the Senators lost 101 games while finishing 43 games out of first.

Beginning in 1956, Pascual became almost a full-time starter, but Washington continued to flounder and Camilo won just 22 games (losing 47) over the next three years.

In 1959, though, with the Senators finishing in last place for the third straight year, Pascual made his move into the upper levels of big league hurlers. The 5' 11", 165-pounder fashioned a 17–10 record while leading the league with 17 complete games and six shutouts.

"I really think that was my best year in baseball," Pascual says. "As a team, we didn't win that many games (63) that year, so my total was a big percentage of the club's victories."

The following season, Pascual slipped to a 12–8 mark as the Senators rose all the way to fifth place. By then, though, the Nats had other things on their minds.

After being one of the original American League teams in 1901, the Senators were moving to Minnesota. It was a traumatic experience for the players.

"It had always been a big thrill to play in the nation's capital," says Pascual. "The President always threw out the first ball, and there was a lot of tradition there. After I came to Washington, I liked it so much I never went back to Cuba.

"It was sad to move from Washington. In the beginning, I felt real bad about it. I had played so many games in Washington and gotten used to the people there.

"The first year in Minnesota, I was kind of homesick. Of course, I later found out that Minnesota was a beautiful place. But I was really happy in Washington, and if I was starting over again today, I'd want to play there again."

Nevertheless, Pascual had his greatest success in Minnesota. Camilo had four straight years with wins in double figures, surrounding 20 and 21-win seasons with two 15-win campaigns.

In 1961, Pascual led the league in strikeouts (221) and shutouts (eight) while posting a 15–16 record. The following year he went 20–11 while leading the league again in strikeouts (206), and shutouts (five) and complete games (18).

"I'll never forget the first year that I won 20 games," he recalls. "It had always been my dream to win 20. I beat the Baltimore Orioles, 1–0, in the last game of the season. Harmon Killebrew got a hit that won the game."

Camilo came back the next year with a 21–9 record and led the league for the third time in strikeouts (202) and in complete games (18). That year, he had the best earned run average (2.46) of his career. He was also the losing pitcher in the first All-Star Game that year, pitching the middle three innings and giving up two runs in a 3–1 American League loss in Washington.

It was one of three All-Star Games in which Pascual pitched. He also hurled in the second game in 1961 and the game in 1964. He had been named to four other All-Star teams, but did not play in them.

In 1964, the Twins finished seventh, but Pascual registered a 15–12 record. He struck out 213, which missed by five his winning a fourth straight strikeout title. It was, however, the last big year for Camilo.

In 1965, while the Twins soared all the way up to first place, Pascual slipped to a 9–3 mark, taking a back seat to new Minnesota mound stalwarts, Mudcat Grant, Jim Kaat and Jim Perry. Camilo, however, did get the starting assignment in the third game of the World Series against the Los Angeles Dodgers. He bowed to the Dodgers and Claude Osteen, 4-0.

The 1965 season was significant for another reason for Pascual. That year, against the Cleveland Indians, he had become one of the few pitchers in baseball to have hit two grand slam home runs when he poked a bases-loaded shot out of the park against Stan Williams. Pascual had hit a grand slam against the New York Yankees and Bob Turley in 1960.

The 1966 season turned out to be Pascual's last in Minnesota. He spent one month of the season on the disabled list with arm trouble, and finished with an 8-6 record. After the season, he was traded to the expansion Washington Senators.

Pascual spent two and one-half years in Washington, winning 12 one season and 13 the next. In mid-1969, the Senators sold him to the Cincinnati Reds. The Reds released him at the end of the season, and he was signed by the Dodgers for the 1970 campaign. After spending that year in LA, he moved on to Cleveland for the 1971 season.

Pascual captured just four of 11 decisions over his last three seasons in baseball, working mostly in relief for the final two years. He retired after the 1971 season.

Eventually, Pascual returned to Minnesota as a coach in the Twins' system. He spent three years there. In recent years, he has been the East Coast scout for the Oakland A's.

Gaylord Perry—
Few Pitchers Were More Durable

It is the rare athlete who can perform for 20 or more years in the major leagues as a pitcher.

Long before that time, one of two possibilities usually occurs. Either he succumbs to the ravages of age, and his curve ball ceases to curve and his fastball is no longer fast, or his arm, once as sturdy as an oak limb, beats with such pain that he is no longer able to throw without the feeling that he has been stabbed by some treacherous demon.

Throughout baseball history, only a handful of pitchers have been active for more than 20 years. Most of them have their names emblazoned on plaques in the Hall of Fame.

One who does not have his name there yet, but surely will, is Gaylord Perry, a colorful throwback to an earlier era who pitched in the major leagues for 21 seasons.

There have been pitchers who have been faster, pitchers who have been slicker and pitchers who have been more dominant. But few ever put together all the ingredients of good pitching over as long a time as Gaylord Perry.

Perry worked the big league arenas from 1962 to 1983, along the way passing one milestone after another. When he retired near the end of the 1983 season, he had climbed into 10th place on the list of baseball's winningest pitchers (he has since been passed by Steve Carlton and Phil Niekro). Gaylord's 314 wins (265 losses) made him one of only 16 moundsmen who won 300 or more games in their careers.

Perry won more than 20 games four times (1966, 1970, 1972, and 1978). He won in double figures 17 times.

He pitched for eight teams—San Francisco, Cleveland, Texas, San Diego, New York (A), Atlanta, Seattle and Kansas City. He won Cy Young Awards in each league, played in five All-Star games and pitched a no-hitter in 1968.

During his career, Gaylord went to the hill 777 times in the majors. He pitched 5,353 innings (fourth highest in baseball history), struck out 3,534 (third on the all-time list) and had a 3.10 career ERA.

For Perry, whose career in organized baseball began in 1958, those figures should easily earn him a trip to the Hall of Fame. It is a thought that Perry savors, and then savors some more. He is eager to be initiated into the baseball shrine on the first ballot.

"It would mean something extra to go in on the first ballot," he says. "But just being elected would be very flattering because it would mean I would have the honor of really being one of the best in my business.

"That," he adds, "would make all the hard times worthwhile. The days and nights of being away from my family and loved ones, staring at four walls, watching the same TV programs that you've seen a dozen times already—going into the Hall of Fame would make all those times worth it."

Sometimes, when he is out riding around deep in the hills of North Carolina, Perry thinks of those times and smiles. It is not easy to break a relationship after 26 years. The residue can be barren, lonely, painful. The separation affects some players more dramatically than others, but all must in some form or another come to grips with life when the roar of the crowd stops.

"I'm fortunate because I keep very active," says Perry. "I stay so busy that it's pretty hard to be bored or to think too much about baseball.

"I don't really miss the game. I do miss the fellowship, but there were some parts of the game that were becoming hard work."

So now, Perry pumps his energy into other forms of hard work. He had a farm in Williamston, North Carolina, the same town in which he was born, where the soft-spoken ex-pitcher tended 500 acres of corn and soybeans and 120 acres of peanuts.

But the farm went bankrupt and Perry has had to find other ways to make a living. He is the head baseball coach at a small, local college. He is also involved in selling mementoes from his playing career. He runs advertisements in collectors' publications, and frequently ventures out to appear at baseball card shows to sign autographs and to operate a table where he sells caps, uniforms, autographed pictures, peanut bags, balls and assorted other paraphernalia.

Gaylord has been criticized for what some people classify as huckstering. A big league player becoming a dealer and selling his own items is certainly unusual. But Perry has his reasons for doing it.

"I have collected so much stuff over the years that it's just piled up in the attic," he says. "I have too much of it. So I figure, I might as well sell some of it to people who'll enjoy it. Also, there are so many people out there getting forged stuff. If you get it from me, you know it's the real thing."

And there's still plenty left over for Gaylord. "I've saved a lot of stuff," he says. "I have a household full of stuff—all my major awards, the Cy Youngs—*The Sporting News* Pitcher of the Year awards and a couple hundred baseballs, including the one from my no-hitter and my 300th win."

When he was growing up, Perry never had even one bubblegum card. "We didn't have any money to buy cards," he recalls. "Things were tight on the farm."

Gaylord Perry.

Between chores, Gaylord and his older brother Jim still found plenty of time to play baseball, though. On their high school team, Jim, two years older, was the pitcher. Gaylord was the third baseman.

"I always played third in high school because Jim pitched twice a week and that was all the pitching we needed," Gaylord says. "But one year we went to the playoffs, and we were playing three-four games a week and needed another pitcher. That's how I got started."

The 6'4" Gaylord, who professes to have had no baeball idols as a boy, was signed out of Campbell College by the Giants in the summer of 1958 for a reported $90,000. Four years later, he got his first big league exposure.

By that time, brother Jim was an established big league hurler. Jim went on to a 17-year career in the majors, working mostly for Cleveland and Minnesota. Jim's 215 wins combine with Gaylord's 314 to make them the winningest brother combination in big league history, although the record should be passed by the Niekro brothers.

Longevity—and some say the spitter—provided the key to Gaylord's lofty win total.

"When I started out, I never thought I'd get to 300 wins," says Perry. "But they just kept piling up. The 300th was kind of icing on the cake.

"The thing that helped me get there," he continues, "was staying healthy. That gave me the opportunity to keep pitching, whereas pitchers such as Sandy Koufax, Juan Marichal and Bob Gibson never got to 300 wins because they had injuries. I never had a serious injury in my career.

"My arm was always strong, and I guess it was because I always did a lot of physical work on the farm. That, plus the fact that I always kept in shape. Every year, I started a workout program on January 1, and I would be ready to go by spring training."

As he has always done, Perry adroitly avoids a direct answer about charges that he threw a spitball.

Did he throw the wet one? "I don't have a set answer to that," he says. "I always liked the hitter to believe that I was throwing one. I couldn't say I never threw one because then the hitters might believe me."

Whatever the case, Perry had some memorable years and tossed some memorable games.

His Cy Young years—when he was 24–16 with a fifth place Cleveland team in 1972 and 21–6 with a fourth place San Diego team in 1978—his 1–0 no-hit victory over the St. Louis Cardinals in 1968, and his 300th, coming at the age of 43 while pitching for the Seattle Mariners in 1982, highlight a career that puts him among the all-time kings of pitching.

Perry, who rarely played for a contender and never in a World Series, rates his no-hitter and the 300th win as his most thrilling experiences in baseball.

"The 300th win was especially memorable because before I got it, it was like a big burden on top of my shoulders. It took a long to get, but I finally put it together. I was really relieved."

Another milestone should eventually be reached when Perry's exemplary career is officially recognized by his selection to the Hall of Fame.

As he joins the other immortals of baseball, how would Perry like to be remembered?

"I'd like people to remember me," he says, "as a guy who when his turn came did a consistent job, day in and day out."

Ken Raffensberger— Crafty Control Artist

Ask a National League hitter who played in the 1940s or 1950s to name the most difficult pitchers to bat against, and invariably the name Ken Raffensberger enters the conversation.

Raffensberger wasn't overpowering; he didn't have a crackling fastball that blew like a thunderbolt past opposing hitters. He wasn't menacing; he didn't try to intimidate hitters by throwing at them.

Raffensberger was a guy who pitched with his head and his heart. He was a guy who had fantastic control. And he had an assortment of tantalizing pitches that would drive batters nearly crazy as he toyed with them, setting them up, nibbling at the corners, getting them to chase pitches that they didn't really want to go after.

He was a craftsman. He had style. Class. And most of all, a left arm that in its day gave its possessor a rating as one of the premier hurlers in the National League.

The pity of it all was the 6' 2", 185-pound southpaw never got to play with a winner. In a big league career that went from 1939 to 1954, and included stops with the St. Louis Cardinals, Chicago Cubs, Philadelphia Phillies and most prominently the Cincinnati Reds, Raffensberger never even played for a team that finished in the first division.

Yet, six times he posted wins in double figures. Twice he led the National League in shutouts. He pitched four one-hitters, two in one season. He is the only Phillies pitcher ever to get the win in an All-Star game. And he ranks as one of baseball's all-time control leaders, yielding just 1.13 walks per game during a career in which he pitched 2,151.2 innings.

Raffensberger walked 449 and struck out 806 during his career. He had a lifetime earned run average of 3.60 with 31 shutouts. Of the 396 games in which he appeared, he completed nearly half (133) of those he started (282).

With decent teams, Raffensberger's lifetime record would surely have been better than the 119–154 it is. But then, luck was never one of Ken's biggest allies.

Ten times he pitched complete games and lost,1–0. The reputation as a hard-luck pitcher was one that followed him throughout his career.

322

Ken Raffensberger.

It was, nonetheless, a career that earned the respect of those who had to go up against him.

"I'll never forget the time I was watching the Ed Sullivan Show," Raffensberger recalls. "Sullivan had Stan Musial on the show, and he asked him to name the toughest pitcher he ever faced. Musial named me. I thought that was a pretty good honor, coming from a fellow like him.

"I never had that much trouble with Musial," he adds. "I had a lot more trouble with Enos Slaughter. Carl Furillo and Roy Campanella were also rough on me. Bob Elliott was tough, too."

None was so tough that he ever gave Raffensberger any anxiety attacks. When he pitched, Ken was as relaxed as he was fearless. And he had a knack for getting stronger as a game wore on.

"They always said, 'Get him early,' when I was pitching," Raffensberger says. "If I went over the second, third or fourth inning, usually I was going to get a complete game."

Today, Raffensberger recalls many of those games with fond memories. Born and raised in York, Pennsylvania, he still lives there.

He worked as a bartender after his playing days were over. "I still work every other Saturday night," he says.

"I took a lot of kidding, but it never bothered me," he adds. "It (his career) was always good conversation, and it always kept them around for a few extra drinks.

"I'm just sorry I'm not playing now. With the salaries so much bigger, my earnings certainly would have been different today."

Although Raffensberger's best years were with Cincinnati, he had attracted attention long before he shifted to the Rhineland. One of the attention-getters was his masterful control.

"My dad always preached control when I was learning to pitch," he says. "Even when I was little, he had me working on it. He would hold up his glove, and I would hit it.

"I always had good control. I never believed in knocking anybody down. I wouldn't want it on my mind that I ever hit a guy in the head and killed him; I never believed in that kind of pitching. If I couldn't get them out without throwing at somebody's head or knocking them down, then I shouldn't be a pitcher.

"Warren Spahn, Robin Roberts and myself were usually one-two-three in fewest walks allowed," he continues. "But we were usually one-two-three in home runs allowed, too. A home run was only one run, but if you walk somebody and then if someone busts one, that's two runs. I always thought, make them hit the ball."

Raffensberger not only learned control from his father, he also received inspiration.

"My dad was the instigator in my career," Ken says. "He was determined that I was going to be a ballplayer. My mother wanted me to be a piano player."

His father having won that debate, Raffensberger embarked on a baseball career that led him through high school, American Legion and semipro ball. Eventually, he was offered a tryout by the Washington Senators and, in 1937, went to spring training with the Nats' farm club.

"I stayed until two days before they broke camp," Raffensberger says. "They wouldn't give me a contract, so I went home to York. Then the Cardinals signed me, and I went with Cambridge of the Eastern Shore League."

Raffensberger had an 18-6 record there, then moved up the following year to Triple-A Rochester of the International League where he had a 15-10 mark. He began the 1939 season with St. Louis, appearing in one game before getting sent back to Rochester where he posted a 15-15 record the rest of the season.

That winter, the Cardinals traded him to the Cubs. In his first game in 1940, he relieved against his own team.

"It was so cold," he remembers. "The first three pitches I threw, I damned near put them in the stands. Then I threw two strikes, and finally got the batter to pop up. I got the next batter out and that saved the game for the Cubs."

Raffensberger didn't spend long with the Cubs—just a little more than one season—but he was in Chicago long enough to learn a valuable lesson from his manager in 1940, Gabby Hartnett.

"He told me, 'You will never be a winning pitcher until you learn to change speeds on your curveball,' " Ken says. "I took his advice to heart, and it really helped my career."

The advice took a little while, though, to take effect. First, the Cubs sent Raffensberger back to Triple-A, and he spent three seasons there, one with St. Paul of the American Association and two with Los Angeles of the Pacific Coast League. He won 46 games during that period.

Late in the 1943 season, Raffensberger's contract was purchased by the Phillies. It didn't matter to Ken that his new club was the long-standing doormat of the National League.

"The main thing was, I was coming back to the big leagues," he says. "That's all that mattered.

"I joined the Phillies just in time to get a start at the end of the season. The Reds and Bucky Walters beat me, 3-0."

Ironically, Walters and Raffensberger were later teammates on the Reds when Bucky was nearing the end of his career and needed just two wins to reach 200 career victories.

"Bucky was managing the Reds. I told him, 'Why don't you start a couple of games, and I'll will come in and save them for you and you'll get the wins?' He never did that, and he ended up wih 198 wins," Raffensberger says.

In 1944, Raffensberger ended up with a 13-20 record, leading the league in defeats. But he picked up one of the most important victories of his career when he got the winning decision in the All-Star game at Pittsburgh's Forbes

Field. It was the only win ever recorded by a Phillies pitcher in an All-Star game.

"Walters had started the game, and I went in when we were behind, 1–0," Ken recalls. "I pitched the fourth and fifth innings. In the bottom of the fifth, we scored four runs. Bill Nicholson pinch-hit for me, and hit a double that drove in what turned out to be the winning run. We went on to win, 7–1."

Despite his record, Raffensberger didn't have a bad season in 1944. His ERA was a fine 3.06. And he led the league in fewest walks, passing just 45 batters in 258.2 innings. The Phillies won only 61 games the entire season, finishing 43 1/2 games out of first.

"I lost a lot of one-run games that year," Raffensberger remembers, "including one in 16 innings against the Cardinals. I pitched the full 16 innings. It was the longest I ever pitched. I had struck out Whitey Kurowski three or four times that day, but in the 16th, I didn't get the pitch where I wanted it. He hit it up on the roof at Shibe Park, and I lost the game."

It was a game in which the Phillies cracked out 19 hits and left 17 men on base. Raffensberger gave up 13 hits and walked just one.

In 1945, the Phillies did their spring training for the second straight season in Wilmington, Delaware.

"It was a little chilly," Raffensberger recalls. "We weren't allowed to go south because of the restrictions on travel during the war."

The war soon claimed Raffensberger. Ken spent most of the season in the Navy. He came back to baseball for the 1946 season, and spent the next year and one-half with the Phillies before being traded to the Reds. Philadelphia received reserve catcher Al Lakeman in what was one of the club's worst deals.

Raffensberger blossomed in Cincinnati. Although the Reds weren't much better than the Phillies, Ken became the club's most consistent pitcher over the next five years, averaging slightly more than 15 wins a season during that period.

In 1948, Raffensberger won 11, but two of those victories were one-hitters against the Cardinals.

"Marty Marion broke up the first no-hitter with a single in the fourth inning," Raffensberger recalls. "Nippy Jones got the only hit in the second game with a single in the eighth. I didn't want to walk anybody, so I just laid it in there for Jones, and he almost knocked me off the mound."

In 1949, Ken had his biggest season, posting an 18–17 record with a 3.39 ERA. He led the league in games started with 38 and in shutouts with five.

From there, Raffensberger recorded 14, 16 and 17 win seasons. Along the way, he lost two more no-hitters.

"We had lost 18 or 19 straight to Brooklyn," he says. "I was scheduled to pitch on Sunday, but I had gotten tangled up with too many beers on Saturday night. I figured, 'What the hell. We're just going to lose, anyway.'

"But I went out, and I beat Joe Hatten, 1–0. Gil Hodges got the only hit in the eighth inning.

"The other one-hitter," Raffensberger adds, "was against the Cubs. Eddie Miksis got a hit on a swinging bunt down the third base line. If Bobby Adams, our third baseman, had let the ball go, it would have rolled foul."

Raffensberger led the league in losses again in 1951 with 17 and in shutouts again in 1952 with six. For most of his years with the Reds, he was the bellweather of a Cinci staff that included hurlers such as Ewell Blackwell, Johnny Vander Meer and Herm Wehmeier.

Raffensberger pitched nearly seven seasons in Cincinnati. His final full season was in 1953 when he dipped to a 7–14 record. The following year, after pitching in six games, Ken was cut loose by the Reds and wound up playing in Havana, an International League club at the time.

His 10–9 record there attracted the attention of New York Yankees' scout Johnny Neun. For a while, it looked as though the Yanks were going to sign Raffensberger, just as they had so many other former National League pitchers. But the deal fell through.

Ken returned to Cuba in 1955, but with his wife at home, pregnant, he quit early in the season and returned to York. There he hooked up with the local Piedmont League club in the Baltimore Orioles' farm system.

As a graybeard pitching among fuzzy-cheeked hopefuls, Raffensberger carved out a 13–3 record at York. The call he hoped to get from the Orioles never came, and at the end of the season, the crafty southpaw decided to retire from the mound.

Raffensberger spent the next two years managing in the Cubs' farm system. Then, deciding that baby-sitting raw recruits was a lousy way to make a living, Ken took his leave of baseball for good

Raffensberger had spent more than 20 years in the game. It was an experience that was mutually beneficial.

Allie Reynolds—
Ace of the Yanks' Big Three

Among former baseball players, none is a more engaging individual nor had a more fascinating life than Allie Reynolds, the ex-New York Yankees' pitching great.

Reynolds came out of Oklahoma, a brilliant all-around athlete who rejected an offer from pro football's New York Giants, and became one of the top pitchers of his era. He was the American League's first player representative, a World Series hero and one of only five hurlers in major league history ever to throw two no-hitters in one season.

When his playing days ended, Reynolds returned to his native state to become one of the pillars of the community, a highly successful businessman who achieved substantial prosperity in Oklahoma's thriving oil industry.

A congenial fellow whose reputation as a deadly serious pitcher no longer precedes him, Reynolds is now an articulate spokesman for the game of baseball and the benefits that can acrue to its players.

"It is one fine privilege to play in the major leagues," he says, "and in my days, we were all proud that we could. We came out of the Depression, and playing professional baseball was very special."

As a pitcher, so was Allie Reynolds. In slightly more than 12 years in the majors, the 6' 0", 195–pound righthander compiled a 182–107 record with a 3.30 ERA. He struck out 1,423 and walked 1,261 in 2,492.1 innings. He led the American League in strikeouts in 1943 and 1952, a year in which he also topped the circuit with a 2.06 ERA while posting a 20–8 record.

Originally a member of the Cleveland Indians, Reynolds broke into the big leagues late in the 1942 season. Despite playing for mediocre teams, he had some good years with the Tribe, especially in 1945 when he went 18–12.

In the fall of 1946, Allie was traded to the Yankees for second baseman Joe Gordon and reserve infielder Eddie Bockman. It was a swap that benefitted both teams.

In New York, Reynolds was soon joined by Eddie Lopat and Vic Raschi, forming one of the ablest mound trios of the last 40 years. Reynolds, though, was the ace of the Big Three. Although each played eight seasons

Allie Reynolds.

in Yankee uniforms, Allie's 131 victories surpassed both Raschi (120) and Lopat (113).

Those were scintillating years, playing for the Yankees. The club won five straight World Championships and six Series titles in seven years. Reynolds was one of 12 players who performed for the five successive championship teams.

"Until I was traded, I didn't know how good it was to play with a team like the Yankees," Reynolds says. "It was just great to get on that club because everybody on it wanted to win. Going to the Yankees was like getting out of prison."

Reynolds, who is part Creek Indian, recalls those days with a twinkle in his eye and excitement in his voice. He is somewhat heavier now than he was in his playing days, but walking through a crowded hotel lobby, he is easily recognizable.

He is a wealthy man, today, having parlayed a keen business sense and good timing into a successful company of his own.

"We service oil field drilling sites," he says. "Our product is fluids. We've been doing it for 25 years. I was president of the company, but I sold it; now I'm retained on a consulting basis.

"Over the years, we've also drilled some oil wells and financed some others," he adds. "I'm also a stockholder in the Oklahoma City (89ers) baseball team."

That is Reynolds' main remaining contact with baseball, although he is an occasional participant in old-timers' games. He doesn't go to baseball card shows, but is a willing autographer, something he didn't used to be.

"It was hard for me to sign autographs as a player," he says. "It used to irritate the devil out of me. But now I get 12 to 24 requests a week in the mail. I'm amazed at some of the things I get. I sign every one of them. Even if they don't have a stamped return envelope. Sometimes, the kids forget to put them in. It doesn't matter, I give them pretty good treatment."

Despite his many triumphs, Allie has few mementoes of his career. His no-hit balls went to the Hall of Fame in Cooperstown. A uniform wound up in the Smithsonian Institution.

"The pitching rubber from Yankee Stadium was sent to me after one of my no-hitters," he remembers. "At first, I didn't know what it was. Then I gave that to the Hall of Fame, too."

Some people say Reynolds himself should be in the Hall of Fame. Although Allie doesn't speculate on that, it's hard to deny that he was certainly one of the finest hurlers in an era when fine hurlers were in abundance.

Ted Williams ranks Reynolds as one of the toughest pitchers he faced. Crafty old Casey Stengel once said that Reynolds "can take care of a hitter quicker than any pitcher I ever saw."

Reynolds was a fierce competitor who threw hard and who never gave in to an opponent. Allie was sometimes accused of throwing at hitters, but he now denies that charge.

"I don't like that reputation," he says. "I didn't throw at hitters. I would throw close to them, sure, because the toughest ball to hit is one that's up and in. But the hitters knew I didn't do that to be vicious. To me, that pitch was just one of the weapons a pitcher has."

Allie had many other weapons as a pitcher, not the least of which was a crackling fastball. Considering he came to baseball relatively late, his development as a pitcher of elevated stature was extremely impressive.

Reynolds didn't play baseball until he reached college. The son of a minister who forbade playing sports on Sundays, Allie was a track and football star as a youth.

After high school, he attended Oklahoma State University (now Oklahoma A & M) on a track scholarship. He was also a 210-pound, two-way back on the football team, and an outfielder on the baseball squad. "I relieved some, too," he adds. "But I was a little on the wild side."

When he graduated with a degree in psychology, Reynolds was drafted on the third round by the football Giants.

"There was no money in football then," he says. "By that time, I was married and had two children. I was offered a $1,000 bonus to play baseball, so I picked that."

Reynolds began in the minors in 1939. By the end of 1942, he was in the majors.

After winning 51 games (47 losses) in four full seasons with Cleveland, Reynolds moved to New York where his career blossomed.

Following a 19-8 record in his first year with the Yankees (1947), Reynolds strung together records of 16-7,17-6, 16-12, 17-8, 20-8, 13-7 and 13-4.

"I think I eventually became a good pitcher," Reynolds says of his transition from a mediocre hurler at Cleveland to a superb one at New York. "The first four years, I kind of fiddled around a lot. I didn't get my mind into the game the way I should have. Then, when I did, I began to make strides. Eventually, I got as much as my ability would allow.

"I think I was very fortunate to have had those abilities. When I look back, I see places I could've improved. But hindsight has little value.

"I am very pleased with my career. I won some fine awards. I wasn't a half-assed athlete. I could do it all, and I enjoyed my career."

The highlight of Reynolds' career came in 1951 when he hurled two no-hitters. Nolan Ryan (1973), Jim Maloney (1965), Johnny Vander Meer (1938) and Virgil Trucks (1952) are the only other pitchers to have tossed two no-hitters in the same season.

In his first one on July 12, Reynolds beat Cleveland and Bob Feller, 1-0. Feller had just thrown a no-hitter 11 days earlier. Reynolds struck out four and walked three.

The second no-hitter came on September 28 when Allie bested Mel Parnell and the Boston Red Sox, 8-0. This time, he fanned nine and walked four.

At the time, the no-hitters didn't really impress Allie. "It wasn't a big thrill," he recalls. "I didn't think it was until later.

"Actually, no-hitters are not very glamorous. A player doesn't look at them the same way as a fan. People ask, 'Did you know it was going on?' Of course, you do.

"I remember in the first one, I was sitting on the bench between innings with Eddie Lopat, who was my roommate. He was very superstitious. I said to him, 'Do you think I can pitch a no-hitter?' He got so bothered by that, he got up, went to the clubhouse, got dressed and left the ballpark. They fined him $50 for that. But I paid it.

"Bobby Avila was the last batter and I struck him out. He swung so hard on the last pitch, he fell down. He landed right on his fanny. I was standing on the mound laughing my head off.

"Gene Woodling hit a home run for the only run of the game.

"The Boston game was a lot different. We built up an early lead. A win meant we would tie for the pennant.

"Ted Williams was the last batter up. On the first pitch, I got him to pop up (foul). The ball got caught in the wind, and Yogi (Berra) missed it. I said, 'Well, we'll just have to go back and try him again.' I threw him the same pitch in the same place, and he popped it up again. This time, Yogi caught it. I told Ted, 'That was your last chance. I'm not going to stand out here all day.'

"Actually," Reynolds adds, "you're so uptight when you're pitching a no-hitter. In a way, I didn't feel much pressure, but I knew it was there. Pretty soon, you start telling jokes. You do anything to calm your nerves.

"You need a lot of luck, though. No matter what you're throwing, the other team's going to hit so many hard balls. They just have to be within somebody's reach. That's where the luck comes in.

"It was never easy being a pitcher," Allie adds. "When I pitched, every mound was a different size, and they used different kinds of dirt. Some of them were so high they were like Pike's Peak. The toughest time in a game for a pitcher is when he first goes to the mound, and has to adjust to it."

During his career, Reynolds achieved special distinction as a hurler who won the big games. Perhaps his most shining hours came in World Series games.

Reynolds had a particular knack of winning the big ones in the Series, as his 7-2 record in six fall classics attests. He is tied for second for the most wins in Series history. He also ranks among the Series leaders in numerous other pitching categories.

Allie hurled some noteworthy Series games. He beat the Brooklyn Dodgers, 1-0, with a two-hitter in the 1949 Series opener. In 1952, he lost a 4-2 opener to the Dodgers, then came back with a 10-strikeout, four-hit, 2-0 victory in the fourth game and a 4-2 win in relief in the seventh game. Reynolds also beat the Dodgers in relief in the final game of the 1953 Series, 4-3.

He won at least one game in each of the six Series' in which he played. He also had a .308 batting average in those games, his eight hits ranking second only to Christy Mathewson's Series record (for a pitcher) of nine safeties.

Reynolds, a member of five American League All-Star teams, was the winner of the famed Hickok Belt in 1951 as the nation's top professional athlete. The following year, he was runner-up to Bobby Shantz for the American League's Most Valuable Player Award.

As successful as he was on the field, Reynolds was equally successful off the field as the American League's first player representative. He and his counterpart in the National League, Ralph Kiner, laid much of the groundwork that led to today's multitude of player benefits.

"We were just trying to get something so we could break even," Reynolds remembers. "We certainly didn't envision what they've got today.

"Mainly, we were attempting to get a decent pension plan, using money from the All-Star game and from radio rights. Our approach was altogether different than today's. And certainly, we never even thought about a strike.

"But I don't mind seeing the boys today make the kind of money they do. The only thing I don't like are the long-term contracts. I think they're wrong. They take away from a player's desire to excel."

Reynolds never had that problem. Even toward the end of his career, when he split his time between starting and the bullpen, Allie always gave his best.

"Casey wanted to make me a reliever in the early 1950s. I went to the bullpen (where in 86 games for the Yankees, he won 15 and saved 41), but I think I would've lasted longer if I hadn't relieved.

"But I always had the desire to excel. And the fact that I had the ability to play in a game like this and was able to stay away from injuries and have a long career, has been very satisfying."

Allie's major league career might have lasted longer had it not been for a freak accident in Philadelphia. In 1953, the Yankees' team bus struck an overpass, and Reynolds suffered a back injury. The injury persisted throughout the 1954 season, and although he won 13 of 17 decisions that year, Reynolds was forced to retire at the end of the campaign.

He retired with a winning percentage (.686) and a strikeout total that are each fourth best in Yankee history.

Bob Veale—
An Imposing Sight

If a pitcher's looks could get batters out, Bob Veale would have been the modern baseball era's first 40-game winner.

It was enough that Veale was a 6'6" giant with huge hands and arms like tree limbs, who, when he stood on the mound, made the hitters seem like Lilliputians.

But his presence was made all the more menacing by a gruff, stoic demeanor that was usually complimented by a perpetual glower. Whether intended or not, it made Veale look like just about the nastiest guy ever to stomp around a pitcher's mound.

Just to add another touch to his imposing appearance, Veale wrapped his scowls with a pair of big, ugly, thick dark-rimmed glasses. The mere suggestion that his eyesight might be less than perfect gave hitters sufficient reason to tremble.

And if his looks didn't do it, surely his pitches would. The towering southpaw could get a ball up to the plate just about as rapidly as anybody of his era. What's more, he was a trifle wild.

With all this, and a considerable talent, too, it was no wonder that Veale was one of the better National League pitchers in the 1960s.

Bob's career spanned 13 big league seasons, beginning in 1962 with the Pittsburgh Pirates and ending in 1974 with the Boston Red Sox. In between, the Birmingham, Alabama native had seven stellar seasons in which he won in double figures.

Veale's years with the Pirates (1962–72) covered a time when the Bucs had slipped off the lofty pedestal that accompanied their magnificent 1960 World Series victory over the New York Yankees. At one point, the club fell as low as seventh in the then one-division league before starting a climb that would lead back to the World Series in 1971.

Through all those years, Veale (with the principle exception at one point of Woodie Fryman) was the lone southpaw on decidedly righthanded staffs that featured names such as Bob Friend, Vern Law, Don Cardwell, Steve Blass, Tommy Sisk, Bob Moose, Jim Bunning and Doc Ellis.

Bob Veale.

In a league in which good lefthanders have always thrived, Veale was a 19-game winner once, a 17-gamer another time and twice a 16-game victor.

"I never won 20," he laments, "but I could have very easily. A timely hit here, a timely hit there would have made the difference. But we never seemed to play up to our potential."

Nevertheless, Veale finished his career with a 120–95 record and a highly satisfactory 3.08 earned run average. In 397 games and 1,925 innings, the fireballing portsider struck out 1,703 while walking 858 and allowing 1,684 hits.

Veale was a member of two National League All-Star teams (1965–66), although he played in neither.

Bob was always known for his strikeouts. In fact, he ranks second (behind Friend) on the Pirates' all-time career strikeout list. And he is fifth in the major leagues (behind Nolan Ryan, Sandy Koufax, Sam McDowell and J.R. Richards) in strikeouts per nine inning game for a career with 7.96.

Two of Veale's most memorable games were high-strikeout performances. In 1965, he struck out 16 Philadelphia Phillies. A year earlier, he fanned 15 Milwaukee Braves.

One of the games Veale remembers best, though, was a contest in which he pitched only two-thirds of an inning. It was in the 1971 World Series. Bob, by then approaching the twilight of his career, relieved in the second game against the Baltimore Orioles during a six-run Bird uprising that led to an 11–3 victory.

It was the only World Series appearance of Veale's career.

"Just pitching in a World Series was a thrill," Veale says. "It was one of the most memorable experiences I've had."

There were, of course, others. Another was a rain-delayed win over the Phillies. "The game kept getting interrupted by rain," Veale remembers. "I pitched the whole game, but it didn't end until about two o'clock."

Veale's best season was in 1964 when he posted an 18–12 record with a 2.74 ERA. He led the league that year in strikeouts (250)—the last Pirate pitcher to do so—and walks (124), one of the four times he topped the senior circuit in bases on balls. He also set a Pirates' club record that year with 18 wild pitches.

The following year he was 17–12 with a 2.84 ERA and 276 strikeouts. He was 16–12 and 16–8 over the next two seasons, then 13–14 in both 1968 and 1969. All the while, Veale was pitching well in excess of 200 innings as the bellwether of the Pirates' staff.

Veale, who was signed out of St. Benedict's College in Atchison, Kansas, was noted for his crackling fastball.

"I always threw hard, even as a kid," he says. "What helped was that I always worked hard, always kept in good physical condition."

Veale says that he had no baseball idols as a youth, but that his father constantly talked about baseball to him.

"I started playing when I was about seven or eight years old," he says. "I pitched and played first base."

He began his professional career in 1958 with Las Vegas in the California League. After moving up the ranks with stops at Wilson (Carolina League) and Columbus (International League), he saw his first action with the Pirates in 1962, then made the club on a permanent basis in 1963.

Veale worked in the Yankees' farm system for several years, serving as a pitching coach, prior to which he spent six years as a pitching coach with the Atlanta Braves' minor league teams. One of the hurlers he helped to develop was Larry McWilliams, most recently with the Pirates.

"I enjoyed that kind of work very much," says Veale, who got into coaching two years after he retired as a player. "It kept me in touch with baseball, and it was really rewarding to see kids develop."

Back home in Birmingham, where he still lives, Veale still has some remembrances of his playing days.

"I have a uniform, a couple of gloves and a few balls," he says.

"I don't have a lot of things. I was just glad I got the opportunity to play. A lot of kids didn't get the chance to play like I did. I was one of the fortunate ones."

Solid Performers, One and All

Smoky Burgess—
His Bat Was Always on Call

It has often been said that if Smoky Burgess were hauled out of bed in the middle of the night and sent to the plate to hit, he'd belt a line drive to the outfield.

As a hitter, Burgess was always ready. And similar to what used to be claimed about postmen, neither wind nor rain nor hail nor sleet—and in Smoky's case, nor opposing pitchers—could stop him.

Burgess hit, no matter what the situation. During an 18-year major league career, his average nearly always hovered around the .300 level, even when he wasn't playing regularly.

Smoky's position was catcher. But a weak throwing arm, brought about by a jeep accident while he was in the Army, kept Burgess out of the starting lineup during part of a career that began in 1949 and extended through 1967.

His bat, though, was always on call. It was his ability as a hitter that made Burgess a valuable member of the teams for which he played.

Burgess' particular ability to hit coming off the bench made him one of the top pinch-hitters in baseball history. The lefthanded hitting North Carolina native holds the major league record for the most pinch-hit appearances (507) in a career, and he is second to Manny Mota in most career pinch hits (145). He hit 16 career pinch-hit home runs (two less than record-holder Jerry Lynch) and he had seasons in the American League of 20 and 21 pinch hits—the latter, three below Dave Philley's league record.

"I was fortunate," Smoky says as he looks back on his outstanding career. "I could always go up to the plate and swing hard right away. A lot of hitters can't do that. But I could swing hard on the first pitch.

"I didn't have to worry about the weather, either. Cold never bothered me. In fact, I can remember one time when I was with Cincinnati, and we were coming north from spring training. We were playing Washington, and Camilo Pascual was pitching. It was about 34 or 36 degrees. By the last inning, they had already packed the bats away so they could get out of the cold in a hurry. I was sent up to bat, and I just grabbed the first bat I could find. I hit a home run over the right field wall to win the game.

"Pressure. That's what I liked. It made you bear down that much more when you went up to the plate. But I guess my being able to hit was just a gift.

"I never thought anybody could throw the ball past me," he adds. "Of course, there were some pitchers who gave me trouble. Dave Koslo was a sidearm lefthander who was tough. Nelson Potter had a real tough screwball. And I always had trouble with Johnny Antonelli.

"I always went up to the plate looking for a fastball. If I got it, I was ready. As a pinch-hitter, you have to study the pitchers. You have to know what pitches the pitchers threw. Batters don't study pitchers any more. They just want to hit the home run."

Burgess figures he could still hit today. In fact, he often demonstrates his present hitting prowess with line drives in old-timers' games.

"I think if I were playing today, I'd be helped a whole lot by the Astroturf," he says. "As for the pitchers, I don't think they throw any harder now. They might be a little smarter because of better coaching. But I don't think they're quite as mean. You don't have anybody around now who was as mean as some of those guys I faced, such as Ewell Blackwell."

A roly-poly, 5'9", 185-pounder as a player, Smoky, who's considerably slimmer today, played for the Chicago Cubs, Philadelphia Phillies, Reds, Pittsburgh Pirates and Chicago White Sox. He ended his career with a .295 batting average, 1,318 hits and 126 home runs.

Burgess made the National League All-Star team in five different years. He was also the regular catcher for the Pirates' 1960 World Championship team.

"Playing in that World Series was my most memorable experience," Forrest Harrill Burgess says. "It also meant a lot to me to play in those All-Star games with guys like Musial, Mays, Aaron, Koufax and Roberts. It makes you feel good to be in there with that kind of company."

Smoky, who got his nickname because his father was called Smoky, saved his uniform from the 1960 World Series. That, a bronzed catcher's mitt, and the bat he used when he broke the existing major league pinch-hit record of 114, held at the time by Red Lucas, are the most treasured possessions from his playing days.

These days, Smoky is a scouting supervisor and minor league hitting instructor for the Atlanta Braves. He's been doing that for the last 11 years.

Although modesty prevents him from blowing his own horn, Burgess worked with many of the present Braves when they were in the minors, including Dale Murphy, Bruce Benedict, Glenn Hubbard and Rafael Ramirez.

Given his own background as a hitter, Burgess makes the ideal batting coach.

"I had my years in the big leagues, and now I enjoy helping somebody else get there," he says. "But I'm a different kind of hitting instructor than most people. My philosophy is to see the ball and hit it solid. You have to be an aggressive swinger. But the main thing is to hit the ball solid, and hit it where it's pitched."

Smoky Burgess.

As a player, Burgess certainly practiced what he now preaches. Smoky could smoke liners to all fields. And he hit lefthanders and righthanders equally hard; in fact, he calls managers penchants to platoon "hogwash."

Burgess began building his reputation as a hitter at an early age. As a boy, his favorite team was the New York Yankees—because he could get their games on radio in North Carolina—and his idol was Bill Dickey.

Smoky, who was originally an infielder, was playing American Legion ball when he signed with the St. Louis Cardinals in 1943. Trouble was, he was still in high school. Commissioner Landis vetoed the contract because Burgess was too young.

The following year he put his name on a pact with the Cubs. He spent that summer and the early part of the next season in the low minors, then joined the military for two years. The jeep accident occurred in Germany.

In 1947, Burgess, by then discharged, landed in Fayetteville (North Carolina) where he led the Tri-State League with a .387 average. A year later, his .386 average at Nashville led the Southern Association.

Burgess was up briefly with the Cubs in 1949, went back to the minors, then came up to stay in 1951 when he got into 94 games and hit .251 for Chicago.

At the end of the season, the Cubs traded Burgess to the Reds. Two months later, Cincinnati shipped Smoky to the Phillies in a seven-player swap that had Dick Sisler and Andy Seminick going to the Reds.

In Philadelphia, Burgess came into his own. Taking over as the Phillies' regular backstop, Burgess hit .296 and .292 in his first two seasons.

Then, in 1954, Smoky virtually went berserk as a hitter. He hit .368, far and away the best average of any regular in the National League. But Burgess was not awarded the batting title because he had only 345 plate appearances—55 at bats short of the mandatory 400. The crown went to Willie Mays with a .345 average.

Early the following season, in one of the many curious trades made by the Phillies in the 1950s, Burgess was sent back to Cincinnati as part of a six-player deal that also returned Seminick to Philadelphia.

Burgess hit .306 for the Reds in 1955 (.301 over the whole season, with career highs of 21 home runs and 78 RBI). But the next year he lost his starting job to Ed Bailey. Smoky had three more good years at the plate in Cincinnati, then was involved in 1959 in a seven-player trade in which he wound up in Pittsburgh.

Smoky resumed his regular catching duties when he joined the Pirates. In successive years, he hit .297, .294, .303 and .328. In 1961, he was named the catcher on *The Sporting News'* National League All-Star team.

Burgess' career seemingly began winding down in 1963. Late in the 1964 season, the Pirates sold him to the White Sox. But instead of slowing down more, Smoky got a second wind as a pinch-hitter.

Over the next three seasons, Burgess led the American League in pinch-hit at bats three times and in pinch hits twice. In 1965, he broke what at the time was the major league record for the most career pinch hits. The old mark of 114 had been set during the 1920s and 1930s by Lucas, who played for the Reds and Pirates.

"It made me feel real good to set that record," Burgess recalls. "It was a big thrill, although Lucas was a real good friend of mine."

Burgess finished his big league career in 1967. He returned to North Carolina, and opened an auto agency, which he ran until joining the Braves in 1976.

Smoky looks back at his long and successful career with a considerable amount of pride.

"Everything went well," he says. "I have no regrets. I don't know a thing I would have changed.

"If I hadn't played baseball, I would have probably had to work in the cotton mills. That's real hard work. I'm certainly glad I had baseball."

Johnny Callison—
Mainstay of the 1960s Phillies

In the decade of the 1960s, keeping track of the Philadelphia Phillies' roster was not only difficult, it was sometimes impossible. Players moved in and out of town with the regularity of a morning sunrise.

As the team's fortunes fell, rose, then fell again, only a handful of players remained with the Phillies for more than a couple of years. Even fewer lingered many seasons as starters. In fact, rare was the lineup that carried the same names as the one before it.

The team had only one player who was a member of the starting lineup throughout the decade. Johnny Callison held down a regular berth in the Phillies' outfield for 10 seasons starting in 1960.

If any one player was synonomous with the Phillies of the '60s, it was Callison. The lithe slugger not only survived the entire decade with the team, he was a solid contributor who provided the Phillies with a wealth of natural talent, both offensively and defensively.

During a 16-year career, which began with the Chicago White Sox and, after a layover with the Chicago Cubs, ended with the New York Yankees, Callison had a lifetime batting average of .264. He hit 226 home runs while collecting 1,757 hits and 840 RBI.

John, a three-time member of the National League All-Star team, led the senior circuit in doubles (40) in 1966 and in triples in 1962 and 1965. Always one of the league's better outfielders defensively, Callison led his peers in assists four times (1962 through 1965).

To baseball fans outside of Philadelphia, Johnny is probably best remembered for his game-winning three-run homer with two outs in the bottom of the ninth inning of the 1964 All-Star game at Shea Stadium. The blast gave the Nationals, who began the inning behind, 4–2, a 7–4 victory.

Callison breaks into a big smile when reminded of that game. "That was unquestionably the biggest thrill of my life," he says.

"I didn't really expect to play that much," he recalls. "I figured I'd pinch-hit. But Hank Aaron got sick, so I got in the game and got a couple of at-bats."

346

Johnny Callison.

The pitcher he hit the homer off of, John has no trouble recalling, was the Boston Red Sox' Dick Radatz. "I swung at the first pitch," he says. "It was up and tight. I got around on it. I was using Billy Williams' bat, which was lighter than mine. I was looking for a fastball because that's all he threw. If he'd have thrown me an off-speed pitch, I probably would've fallen on my face."

Although he is not a collector of items from his playing days, Callison has the ball from that home run. It was retrieved, he says, by Rocky Colavito and given to Jim Bunning to give to John.

At present, Callison works as a bartender in suburban Philadelphia. Prior to that, he sold cars for five years before which he sold electronics equipment.

A resident of a Philadelphia suburb, Johnny has little contact with baseball or with former teammates. He participates in occasional old-timers games, but is generally content to avoid the limelight. "I really don't want the pressure," he says. "It's nice to be out of the spotlight. I enjoy being able just to sit back and relax."

Does he miss baseball? "I miss the people in it, but I don't miss the game," he says. "It had become just a job to me."

Callison is still easily recognized by Phillies fans. He's a few pounds over his 175-pound playing weight, but the 5 ' 10 " ex-outfielder closely resembles the look of his playing days, despite recent open-heart surgery.

Although he became the most popular Phillies' player of the 1960s, Johnny was far from happy about joining the club. Originally signed in 1957 by the White Sox the day after he graduated from a Bakersfield, California high school, the Oklahoma native—his family had moved to California when John was five years old—had thought he had a solid future in Chicago.

In his first big league game, Callison, then 19, went three-for-three against Boston's Frank Sullivan. John, who admits he was "scared to death" at the time, spent parts of the 1958 and 1959 seasons with the White Sox. But in December 1959, he was traded to the Phillies for Gene Freese.

"I was playing winter ball in Venezuela," says John, whose boyhood heroes were Ted Williams and Mickey Mantle. "I saw my picture and Freese's in the paper. The writing was in Spanish, so I had to find somebody to translate it for me. That's when I learned I'd been traded.

"I was really disappointed. I was going from a first place club to a last place club. Philadelphia was the last place I wanted to come to. I could've signed with the Phillies in 1957. I didn't want to then, but here I was being traded to them, anyway."

To make matters worse, the young Callison had the additional pressure that accrued from his being labeled another Mantle. And he was joining a team managed by a young dynamo named Gene Mauch, who had taken over the team after Eddie Sawyer quit following the first game of the 1960 season.

"Mauch was pure hell those first two years," Johnny remembers. "He was a young guy then, and he thought he could outsmart everybody. He platooned all the time, and nobody ever got a chance to play regularly. Finally, he let me just go out there and play.

"I'll tell you one thing about Mauch," Callison adds. "Basically, he was the best manager I ever played for as far as baseball strategy goes."

In Callison's second year in Philadelphia, the Phillies lost 23 straight games, a modern major league record. "We were so lousy," Johnny recalls. "And we had no confidence. We'd be ahead, and we'd wait for something to happen. We knew we were going to lose. It was such a helpless feeling."

The following year, Callison, who had been switched from left field to right field, began to blossom. He hit .300, the highest average of his career, with 23 home runs.

Two years later, Callison, hitting .274 with 31 homers and 104 RBI, teamed with rookie Dick Allen to give the Phillies a powerful one-two punch that propelled them to the top of the National League standings. With 12 games left in the season, the Phillies had a 6 1/2-game lead, and the pennant virtually clinched.

But 10 straight losses, comprising one of the most notorious collapses in major league history, detached the Phillies from the pennant, and sent not only the team but the entire city into a state of shock that by any measure really lasted until 1980.

The memory of that season still haunts Johnny, as it does most of the other 1964 Phillies. "It was," says Callison, "the worst disappointment I ever had.

"It was such a great year, otherwise. Everything we did was right until the last 12 games. We didn't have the best team in the league, but I never saw any other team that was as together as much as that one. Everybody pulled for everybody else. At the end, we just hit a streak that we couldn't get out of. Balls took funny bounces, we lost in funny ways, we got beat by funny people."

Did Mauch, as Phillies fans will forever insist, make a mistake by using Bunning and Chris Short too much during the losing streak? "In a way he did," Callison says. "But they wanted the ball. They had to have it, and he gave it to them. Personally, I think the bigger mistake was using Jack Baldschun so often in the middle innings in relief. He was our late-inning stopper, and should have been saved for that, rather than thrown into games and used up in the earlier innings."

Callison notes that the Phillies fully expected to come back and win the pennant the following year. But they finished sixth, despite John's 32-home run, 101 RBI season.

The Phillies never came close to first place again during the '60s. As for Callison, several injuries took a toll on his performance as the decade wore on.

In 1968, though, John achieved the rare feat of going through the season without an error. His 1,000 fielding average was compiled in 109 games.

"Actually, I had better years fielding," Callison says. "When you have a year like that, you're not making many mistakes, of course, but you're also not doing a lot. You're more careful. Most of my errors came on throws, but I usually only had four or five a season, anyway. So, I never considered that record that outstanding. It was just a year when the ball didn't take any bad hops."

By the end of the decade, John says, he was ready to leave Philadelphia. "It was so hard to deal with Quinn (general manager John Quinn)," he says. "I never felt that I was paid what I should have been. After 1965, I was always getting hurt, and he always wanted to cut my salary. It was really disappointing. Finally, I just told him to get me out of here."

After the 1969 season, Quinn traded Callison to the Cubs for Dick Selma and Oscar Gamble. Johnny helped Chicago to a rare second place finish in the East Division in 1970. But, citing a knee injury and manager Leo Durocher's dislike for him, Callison slumped in 1971, and was sold that winter to the Yankees.

Teammates mobbed Johnny Callison after his three-run homer in the ninth inning gave the National League a 7–4 victory in the 1964 All-Star game.

He played two years in New York before retiring after the 1973 season at the relatively young age of 34.

"I would have liked to have played a couple more years," Callison says, "but my knees were bad and my arm was hurt. I couldn't go on."

John looks back at his career with few regrets. "I'd liked to have hit a little higher," he says. "But I made good money. And I got to play with some of the greatest players of all time, guys like Aaron, Mays, Seaver, Rose, Koufax. I don't think you have that many great players today."

Despite all the pitching greats he faced, Callison says the toughest hurler for him to hit was Hal Woodeschick, a mediocre lefthander who spent the National League part of his career as a reliever with Houston and St. Louis. "Everybody else on the team always pounded him, but I could never hit him," Johnny says. "He had a funny motion, and I just couldn't pick up the ball."

At least during his career with the Phillies, Callison didn't have that trouble with too many other pitchers. On the club's all-time list, he ranks among the leaders in nine of the 11 hitting categories. He also ranks as the club's most consistent player during the decade of the '60s.

George Case—
Speed Merchant Who Could Hit

Gather a list of the fastest men ever to blaze across the diamonds of professional baseball, and one of the names would surely be a comet who did most of his running in Washington.

Appropriately, his name was George Washington Case, and he was not only the premier stolen base artist of his day, he was one of the most successful pilferers of all time.

Possessed with the speed of a world-class sprinter, Case tore up American League basepaths for 10 seasons, leaving a trail of stolen base titles in his wake, including five straight crowns—at the time a league record. Altogether, Case roared to the league lead in steals six times and placed second twice.

A list of the great stolen base kings of baseball begins with Lou Brock and Ty Cobb, and then drifts down through the likes of Honus Wagner, Eddie Collins, Max Carey, Jackie Robinson, Maury Wills and Rickey Henderson. Case is right there with them.

Although George's career total of 349 steals ranks just 39th on the all-time major league list, his per-season average (35) is in the same company as Cobb (37), Carey (37), Wagner (34), Bert Campaneris (34) and Collins (30).

Had his career not been cut short at the age of 31 by a severe back problem, Case would no doubt have ranked among the all-time leaders in career totals, too.

Case was not just a speed merchant. He could hit and field. In a career that went from late 1937 to mid-1947 and included one season with the Cleveland Indians and all the others with the Washington Senators, the 6' 1", 183-pound righthander registered a lifetime batting average of .282. Twice, he finished fifth in the league in batting and once led in runs scored. He also led AL outfielders in assists once.

Because of his blinding speed, Case was one of the hardest players to double up. In 5,017 career at bats (1,226 hits), he hit into only 42 double-plays, which ranks among the all-time leaders in that category.

He is also one of only a handful of outfielders ever to have made an

George Case.

unassisted doubleplay, a feat he accomplished in 1944 against the Philadelphia A's.

A leadoff hitter throughout his career, Case, an outstanding bunter, was not a power hitter (he had only 21 lifetime home runs). But he was often among the league leaders in doubles, and four times in his career scored more than 100 runs in a season, despite the often lowly stations of the Senators.

"I think one of the things I'm most proud of," says Case, "is the fact that in four of the six years I led the league in stolen bases, I scored more than 100 runs four times. To me, that statistic is really meaningful."

A native of Trenton, New Jersey, Case lives now across the Delaware River in Morrisville, Pennsylvania, his home since 1941. He is still active in baseball as an advisor to the Seattle Mariners.

When he talks about his career, it is obvious to a listener that Case enjoyed himself. With good reason, too. He was well-liked by teammates as well as opponents, and he played in a glorious era with some of the great stars of the game.

Moreover, Case made his own mark in baseball history. He, as much as any other player, was the bridge between the stolen base era of Ty Cobb and the resurgence of the steal in the modern era. Until Case came along to revive it, the stolen base had mostly gone the way of the spitball and the bottle-handed bat—into the attic of baseball oblivion.

"Running came naturally to me," he says. "I could run the 100 in 9.9 in full uniform. It was said that if I had trained, I would've been a world-class sprinter.

"I was completely dedicated to baseball," he adds. "I knew what I had to do, and I could do the job."

Case says he holds the world record for circling the bases. He did it in 13.5 seconds before a game at Griffith Stadium.

"It was a big promotion," he recalls. "They billed it as an attempt to beat the record of Hans Lobert. It was played up in all the papers. We had AAU officials time it. The infield was manicured. I started with one foot on home plate. When they announced the new record, the crowd went nuts."

Case often loaned his speed to promotional efforts. In fact, after he joined the Cleveland Indians in 1946, he was involved in the first big league promotion ever staged by Bill Veeck. Then the new owner of the Indians, Veeck put Case in a race against Olympic sprinter, Jesse Owens.

"He beat me, but it was a good race. I didn't lose by much," Case recalls. "Of course, we were both past our primes then. But that was the only time I ever lost a race while I was wearing a baseball uniform.

"I used to race all the time," he adds. "I picked up a lot of extra money that way. They'd stage match races. They were 100 yards. I won as much as $1,000 in one race when I beat Gil Coan."

Ironically, Case had no background as a runner. George was strictly a baseball player in the spring at Peddie School, a private boarding school in New Jersey. His main position was pitcher.

As a schoolboy, Case attracted the attention of A's scout, Ira Thomas, who invited George to a tryout at Shibe Park. After pitching batting practice to the regulars, Case was approached by A's coach, Lena Blackburne.

"He said, 'I understand you can hit the ball pretty well, young man. Why don't you stick around for another day and hit?'

"After the second day," Case continues, "Connie Mack invited me up to his office, and asked me what I had in mind. I said, 'I'd like to get into professional baseball.' I had a lot of college offers, but I wasn't interested in them."

When Mack proposed signing Case and sending him to the Texas League, George declined, saying he wasn't interested in a job that far away. Mack then said he would recommend him to Joe Cambria, at the time a minor league club owner.

Eventually, Case signed with Cambria's York club in the New York-Penn League. Two weeks after he reported, the York franchise was moved to Case's hometown of Trenton.

Case spent two seasons at Trenton, and in the second one (1937) emerged in a three-way tie for the batting title with a .338 average while leading the league in stolen bases. At the end of the season, his contract was sold to Washington. He played in 22 games in September for the Senators.

"I remember my first big league game, I sure do," says Case. "I was scared to death. It was at Shibe Park, and a lot of people from Trenton had come down to see me. I was just 21 years old. Didn't hit a thing. In fact, I went 0-for-10 to start. I didn't hit a ball past the pitcher."

Among Washington's outfielders at the time were aging Hall of Famers Al Simmons and Goose Goslin.

"It was a tough outfield to break into," Case remembers. "They didn't even know I existed. Nobody ever talked to me. Cecil Travis and Buddy Lewis were the only ones who did and that was because they were my age. The next season, Al Simmons didn't even recognize me, although he wound up being one of the best friends I ever had. He really took me under his wing. He helped me tremendously."

Case began the 1938 season platooning in right field with Johnny Stone. But partway through the season, Stone developed tuberculosis, and was forced to retire from baseball. Case moved in as a full-time player, and proceeded to team with Simmons and Sammy West to give the Senators an all .300-hitting outfield. George led the way with a .305, while the others each had .302 averages.

Case came back the next year with a .302 mark, then followed that in succeeding years with .293, .271, .320 and .294. In each of the last two, he placed fifth in the league in batting, and in 1943 led the circuit in runs scored with 102. That year, he also was selected for the American League All-Star team, starting in right field in his side's 5-3 victory in Philadelphia.

By then, Case had long been regarded as the base-stealing king of the majors. At a time when 15 to 20 steals usually were enough to capture the league lead, George was dwarfing that number.

Starting in 1939, he led the league with 51, 35, 33, 41 and an unheard-of-for-the-time 61 in 1943. He was second to Snuffy Stirnweiss the next two years, then came back to win the title again in 1946.

"When I first came up, they brough Clyde Milan, the old base-stealer, out of retirement to coach me," Case says. "It was like having a private coach.

"Eventually, they let me run on my own, something they usually didn't do. Bucky Harris, our manager said, 'Get the jump whenever you can, but don't abuse it.'

"Bucky was really something," Case adds. "He was a great manager. I never saw him make a technical mistake in baseball. He was a ballplayer's manager. And he had the same disposition whether you won or lost."

Case says that the hardest catcher to steal a base on was the Detroit Tigers' Paul Richards. The easiest was the A's Frankie Hayes.

"Richards always seemed to outguess me," says Case. "He was the toughest to run on. Hayes only threw me out once."

Case studied the opposing catchers as well as the pitchers. He doesn't buy the modern theory that a base-runner steals mostly on the pitcher.

"That's a misnomer," he says. "It's only about 50 percent true. Every pitcher has some move that gives him away. You have to study them, guess with them. But about 60 percent of all stolen bases are gifts. It's amazing. Most of those are gifts either from the catcher or the fielder who's out of position or makes a poor tag. The one thing a good runner has to overcome is the pitchout. But there are always going to be catchers who give away the pitchout."

Case says that today's base-stealers are much better than the ones of past eras. "They're faster, and the black players, especially, are hungry," he says. "They know they can make big money, and they are completely dedicated. They work and work."

Despite all of his own work at stealing bases, Case rates his most memorable experience in baseball as having come with the bat. In 1940, he tied a major league record with nine hits in a doubleheader. He currently shares the mark with seven others.

"Any time you get nine hits in a doubleheader, it's got to be a big thrill," he says, remembering the afternoon clearly. "It was against the A's. I went four-for-five the first game. The fifth time up, I hit a rope that Sam Chapman made a shoestring catch on. I went five-for-five in the second game with two bunt singles."

Case also considers it a thrill to have played in the era in which he did. Even though part of that time was during World War II, George says that period took a back seat to none.

"To me, the war years were by far the most fascinating years in baseball history," he insists. "You can't believe some of the things that went on.

"For one thing, players were coming and going every day. You'd go into the clubhouse and see guys packing to go off to the service. Sometimes, we'd play with makeshift lineups. Some of the players weren't even close to being major leaguers, but you had to have bodies, so you had them in the lineup.

"Beside that, travel was unbelievable. In peace time, each club traveled by Pullman, often with your own dining car attached. But travel was restricted during the war. You didn't have your own car, and you had to take what they could give you. Twice, we went from Washington to Boston and had no seats. We had to sit in the aisles on our bags.

"And they wouldn't service you in the dining car. All the servicemen had to eat first. Sometimes, you wouldn't get into the dining car until 10 o'clock. By then, they'd be out of meat. The only thing they'd have was eggs.

"One time on the road, we went one week without meat. It was starting to get to us, our being athletes and not having any protein. Often, we couldn't get meat or coffee.

"Dutch Leonard, one of our pitchers, always seemed to get what he wanted, though. He gave away autographed baseballs like they were water and always got something for them.

"Of course, every off-day, we had to play at an Army or Navy base. And it was always hard getting to Washington from our homes at the beginning of the season because of gas rationing. One year, I had to go before the local board here in town to get extra gas stickers just so I could get to spring training."

Case, himself, had been rejected for military service and declared 4F because of a shoulder injury that had occurred early in his career. The shoulder repeatedly popped out, and, unable to raise his arm above his shoulder, George spent his summers playing baseball and his winters working in an airplane factory in Trenton. Eventually, material was removed from his leg and used to repair the shoulder.

"Spring training was different, too," Case continues. "Twice, we held it at the University of Maryland. We worked out outside, and one spring it was really cold. In real bad weather, though, we worked out in the artillery hall. They gave us a dormitory to stay in. We had a private dining room and our own cooks. Sometimes, we worked out in the snow.

"We played under great hardship in those years. But we kept going. During the war, there was talk about closing down baseball, but Clark Griffith went to President Roosevelt and asked him to keep the game going. He though it would help to keep the morale of the country up, and Roosevelt agreed. So we kept playing."

Playing in the nation's capital, not only during the war, but before and after it, was a special experience.

"It was altogether different from playing anywhere else," Case says. "We had politicians in the clubhouse all the time. When he was a senator, Happy Chandler was in the clubhouse every home stand. He was crazy about baseball. And during the war, you wouldn't believe the people we had. Generals Bradley, Wainwright, Secretary of State Stitineous. Eisenhower used to come in. It was really something.''

After the 1945 season, when he helped the Senators to their second second place finish in three years (the club was eighth in between), Case was traded to the Indians for outfielder Jeff Heath.

''It was the biggest disappointment of my life,'' he says. ''Washington was looking for a long ball hitter, and I was the only guy Cleveland would accept. I was really unhappy about going. But Lou Boudreau met me at the train station; he was so glad to have me.

''I had the worst year I ever had in baseball. I was hurting all the time.''

Case had back spasms so bad that at times he could hardly stand. He hit just .225, although he led the league in stolen bases with 28. After the season, Washington bought him back. The 1947 season wound up being his last as a player.

''It was a game in August,'' Case remembers. ''I went down for a grounder, and couldn't get up. They had to carry me off the field. I never played again. I couldn't even tie my shoes.''

Forced out at the young age of 31, Case entered the famed Johns Hopkins Hospital in Baltimore and learned that heavy amounts of scar tissue from all the years of sliding had accumulated in his lower back. George underwent surgery, then came home to Trenton to run the sporting goods store he had opened a year earlier.

He operated the store for a number of years, and along the way also took on an assignment as head baseball coach at Rutgers University. In his first year, Case piloted Rutgers to second place in the College World Series.

Case coached at Rutgers from 1950–60, turning out seven players who entered the professional ranks, including a catcher named Harding Peterson, who later became executive vice president and general manager of the Pittsburgh Pirates.

In 1961, Case joined his former Senators' teammate and long-time friend, Mickey Vernon, when the latter took over as Washington manager. Case was a coach and then, after Vernon's dismissal, a scout with the Nats until he was named manager of the club's Hawaii team in the Pacific Coast League in 1965.

Case spent two years in Hawaii, at one point becoming the first American to go to spring training in Japan. Hired as an instructor, he spent two weeks in Japan, working with the hitters and base-runners.

After another minor league managerial stint, Case joined the Minnesota Twins in 1968 as a coach. In 1969, he left to take over as manager of the New York Yankees' farm club in Oneonta, New York, where he won two pennants in four years.

Case spent five years as a minor league hitting and base-running instructor with the Texas Rangers, then five more years in the same capacities with Seattle. He then became an advisor to the Mariners providing instructional tapes and other materials to the team.

George is amazed by today's major league salaries.

"It's unbelievable," he says. "Mike Schmidt gets more for one base hit than I made in a whole year.

"When I played," he adds, "there were only 12 or 13 guys making over $10,000 in the entire American League."

Case is also somewhat amazed by the autograph requests that his mailman delivers.

"I get cards to sign every week," he marvels. "I've been out of baseball for 40 years, and yet I still get maybe 10 autograph requests every month. Sometimes, it's 10 a week. Some of the cards that come in are ones that I never saw before."

Not too long ago, Case was one of the featured subjects in a video about baseball's greatest base-stealers. Brock, Wills, Campaneris and Jackie Robinson were the others.

The tape put Case in some pretty fast company. But that's exactly where he belongs. He was, after all, one of the swiftest players ever to scorch the basepaths.

Whitey Kurowski—
Crack Third Baseman of the 1940s

At one point or another during conversations with former major leaguers, the subject always seems to get around to the high salaries of current players. It is a subject that most ex-players discuss freely and without rancor, despite the great disparity in wages between the generations.

George (Whitey) Kurowski doesn't have to look far to be reminded of this disparity. He keeps it right in his wallet.

Tucked between the cards and papers is the stub from Kurowski's first major league paycheck. It shows that in 1942, the St. Louis Cardinals paid their rookie third baseman $226.61 for two weeks' work.

If he was playing today, that figure wouldn't come close to paying Whitey for one time at bat. In fact, Kurowski would be worth a heaping sum now.

When Kurowski played, good third sackers such as Bob Elliott, Stan Hack and Sid Gordon were in abundance in the National League. Whitey ranked among the best of them.

He had a nine-year career in the majors during which he was the Cardinals' third baseman in four World Series. He was a member of the National League All-Star team three times (1944, 1946, 1947), and in 1945 was the third baseman on the major league all-star team of *The Sporting News*.

His lifetime batting average was .286, which included three seasons in which he hit above .300 and three seasons of 20 or more home runs. Whitey had 925 hits and 106 homers during his career.

Kurowski wasn't a one-dimensional player. In addition to being a good, solid hitter, he was also a top fielder. He led National League third basemen in fielding twice, in putouts three times, in assists once, and he holds a record at his position for most putouts (13) in a seven-game World Series.

Whitey doesn't regret not getting the big money he surely would have received today.

"I had my turn. I had my fun," he says. "It was more fun playing when I did. Today, they don't want to be tops in hits or tops in home runs. All they want to do is lead the league in money. But how much money do they really need?

Whitey Kurowski.

"In my day," he adds, "you were happy if you played anyplace in the big leagues. You wouldn't care where you played, as long as it was in the big leagues."

Kurowski now lives in an apartment in Shillington, Pennsylvania, a suburb of Reading, the city where he was born and raised. The father of four children and the grandfather of nine, Whitey is retired from his job as a sealer of weights and measures for Berks County.

Prior to that job, he managed in the minor leagues from the end of his playing days in 1949 until 1965. He ran teams for the Cardinals in Lynchburg (Virginia), Allentown, Peoria, Billings, Denver, Winnipeg and Tulsa, for the New York Mets in Buffalo and for the Cleveland Indians in Reading. Along the way, he won pennants at Tulsa in the Texas League and at Winnipeg in the Northern League.

Whitey spends his time now relaxing and playing golf two or three times a week. He keeps up with baseball through the newspapers and television while occasionally watching the present Reading (Phillies) farm club or a major league game.

He plays in old-timers games once in a while, but otherwise doesn't have much contact with his fellow players. He also appears as a guest at card shows in the Reading area. And he gets, he says, five to 10 autograph requests per week in the mail.

"I don't mind signing autographs at all," he says. "It's good that somebody remembers me."

Kurowski didn't mind signing autographs as a player, either, and he bristles at the thought of current players refusing to give out their signatures to fans.

"When I played," he says, "we loved to sign autographs. First of all, we didn't have anything else to do after games, anyway. So, we'd stand there and sign as long as anybody was around. And the kids appreciated it. It was just a thing we enjoyed doing.

"I'll tell you something else," he adds. "It ticks me off to see that some of these shows charge for a player's autograph. That's ridiculous. Those autographs should be for free."

Kurowski has a modest collection of plaques and trophies in his home, but the few items he saved from his playing days—a bronzed glove, a uniform, some bats—have been given to his children.

Of his four World Series rings, two were stolen a number of years ago. One was later recovered, but Whitey's 1942 ring, the one he cherished the most, is still missing.

One of his favorite possessions is a plaque that honors the members of the all-time Rochester Red Wings team. He is the third baseman in that select group.

Kurowski played for the Red Wings for three years from 1939-42. He broke into organized ball in 1937 in Class D with Caruthersville (Missouri). The following year, he played at Portsmouth and led the Middle Atlantic League in batting with a .386 average.

Kurowski almost didn't play pro baseball.

When he was eight years old, Whitey, who got his nickname because "my hair was snow white as a kid," fell off a fence and landed on broken glass. His right arm was badly slashed. Kurowski developed a serious case of blood poisoning, which turned into osteomyelitis, the same ailment that afflicted Mickey Mantle. An operation proved unsuccessful and, eventually, the ulna, one of the two arm bones, had to be removed.

As a result, Kurowski was obliged to go through life not only with a partial arm, but with one that was three to four inches shorter than his other arm. And it was his throwing arm that was injured, too.

"Actually, they wanted to take the whole arm off," he recalls. "But I found out later that my sister wouldn't let them do it."

Despite his handicap, Kurowski took to baseball like weeds take to a garden. He played constantly as a youth, and ultimately became one of the top players in the avid baseball area in which he lived.

"Because of the arm, though, professional teams were reluctant to sign me," he says. "But finally, a guy named Harrison (Muck) Wickel took a chance on me.

"He was the manager of the team in Caruthersville, and was from the Reading area. One winter he came home and asked one of the local sportswriters, a guy named Doc Silva, if he knew of any infielders. Wickel needed an infielder for the following season, and Silva suggested me. I signed a contract for $70 a month."

Kurowski entered organized ball as an 18-year-old. After five seasons in the minors, the Cardinals brought him to the majors at the end of the 1941 campaign. Another youngster they brought up at the same time was a lefthanded former pitcher named Stan Musial.

In 1942, the Cardinals came from 13 games back in early August to overtake the Brooklyn Dodgers and win the National League pennant with 106 wins (the Dodgers won 104). It was the first of three straight flags for St. Louis.

In the World Series in which the Cards upset the favored New York Yankees, four games to one, the rookie Kurowski won the second game with an RBI triple and the final game with a two-run, ninth inning homer.

The Series-clinching homer, which was hit against Red Ruffing, provided Kurowski with his greatest thrill as a player. "That was my most memorable hit because it helped, and I emphasize helped, win a World Series," he says. "It always takes nine to win a ball game, and I was just one of them. But it was a great feeling getting that home run because we were such underdogs in the Series."

In the ensuing years, Whitey had some other memorable experiences. He had a 22-game hitting streak in 1943. In 1944, he was the middle man between Walker Cooper and Danny Litwhiler when the trio hit consecutive home runs.

When the Dodgers and Cardinals finished in the first tie for first place in major league history in 1946, Kurowski was one of the heroes of St. Louis's two-game playoff sweep. He drove in the tying run and scored the winning run in the Cards' 4–2 victory in the first game. And he scored the sixth run and batted in the next ones with a two-run single in an 8–4 triumph in the second game.

"That was a great thrill," he says, "because it was always nice to beat Brooklyn."

In the ensuing World Series, Kurowski and teammates Enos Slaughter and Joe Garagiola and Boston's Wally Moses set a record with four hits each in the Cards' 12–3 fifth game romp.

Kurowski had his best season in 1945 when he hit .323 with 21 homers and 102 RBI and in 1947 when he batted .310 with 27 home runs and 104 RBI. His highest World Series mark was .296 in 1946.

"I was strictly a pull-hitter," he recalls. "I had a little power and I hit some home runs. I always figured that a bat was made to swing. The hell with taking pitches. If the ball was in there, you swing at it."

The toughest pitcher Whitey says he had to swing at was Cincinnati's Ewell Blackwell. He recalls one time when the Reds' side-armer fired a pitch that went between his head and his cap, which was in the process of flying off his head.

"He wasn't throwing at me," Kurowski says. "Blackie never threw at anybody. He even apologized to me as he came off the field.

"Actually," he adds, " most pitchers back then were pretty easy-going. One pitcher might hit you in the ribs. The other pitcher would retaliate. Then you'd go back to playing. Sometimes there'd be a little battle, but it would be over and forgotten in a hurry. Now, you knock a hitter down, and he wants to get up and kill somebody."

Whitey remembers that he also had trouble with Fritz Ostermueller, the old Pittsburgh Pirates' southpaw, although he loved to hit against him. Another rough hurler to face, he notes, was the Dodgers' hard-throwing but wild Rex Barney.

The rivalry between the Dodgers and the Cardinals in the 1940s was one of the most intense in baseball, but Whitey claims he always enjoyed playing against Brooklyn. "They were real competitive, and always gave us a good battle," he says. "Brooklyn was a good place to play, too, because the fans were very good. It was the best road stop."

Travel was one of the things that Whitey enjoyed most about his playing career. "Getting to travel around the country was very enjoyable," he says. "The second best part was meeting so many fine people all over the country."

Kurowski retired early in 1949. By then, he had had 13 operations on his arm and elbow, which contained pinched nerves caused by the condition of the arm. The arm was bothering him so much that he could no longer play, even though he was only 31 years old.

"I can't complain, though," he says. "I was fortunate enough just to have been able to play. It's the dream of every kid, and I was able to fill that dream. That was enough for me."

During his big league career, Kurowski had the distinction of having never played for a team that finished below second place. The Cards were second in 1941, 1945, 1947 and 1948 which, coupled with their four pennants (and three World Series victories) during a five-year period from 1942 to 1946 gave them one of the best records of the modern era.

"I would have to say that we compared favorably with the great teams in baseball," Kurowski states. "We were equal to the great Yankees and Dodgers teams.

"Although I think the 1946 Series (when the Cardinals beat the Red Sox, four games to three) was the most exciting one we played in, I think our best team was the 1942 club," Kurowski adds. "We had better overall talent with Musial, Slaughter, (Marty) Marion, (Johnny) Hopp, the Coopers (Milt and Walker), Johnny Beazley plus a fine team captain in Terry Moore.

"The thing about our ball club was that we all stuck together. We talked about a ball game after the game was over. If a guy made a mistake, others would try to help him correct it. They'd offer constructive criticism, not jump down his throat.

The 1946 St. Louis Cardinals fielded a team of heavy hitters that included (front from left) Stan Musial and Whitey Kurowski, and (top from left) Red Schoendienst, Enos Slaughter and Marty Marion.

"We always traveled in Pullmans. We'd sit in the club car and go over and over the ball game. It was more like a family affair then. Everybody tried to help everybody else.

"I think that's lacking today," he says. "Don't get me wrong. There are good ballplayers today. But if I'm making $500,000, who are you to tell me what to do? Also, with these four and five year contracts, there's no incentive.

"The talent's the same now as it was when I played. I can't say one era is better than another. In fact, years ago, maybe there was less talent. But the players pushed themselves more. A good case in point was Eddie Stanky. He didn't have all the talent in the world, but he was a helluva player. He fought for everything he got.

"That's the way it was with us. We had to fight to keep our jobs. Even if we were only getting $600 a month."

Minnie Minoso—
An Exciting Free Spirit

Throughout the 1950s no player in the American League generated more excitement than a flashy little former sugar cane field worker from Cuba.

His name was Saturino Orestes Arrieta Armas Minoso—everybody called him Minnie—and he played the game with verve and with flair.

Sometimes volatile, sometimes happy-go-lucky, Minnie Minoso was a free-spirited individual, and he loved baseball and life with equal intensity.

Bill Veeck once said of Minnie, "I've never seen anyone who wanted to play as much as Minoso."

And play he did. In 11 seasons as a regular with the Cleveland Indians and Chicago White Sox, Minoso hit over .300 eight times. The other three times, he hit .280 or above.

Minoso had a lifetime average of .298 with 186 home runs, 1,963 hits, 1,023 RBI and 1,136 runs scored during a career that went from 1949 to 1964 (as a publicity stunt, he batted eight times in 1976 and twice in 1980, thereby becoming the only player ever to perform in five decades).

Although the record book says he was born in 1922, there was always some question about Minnie's actual age. But even though he is well over 60, he might still be playing if they'd let him. He is in extremely good condition, and in old-timers' games still swings the bat with considerable gusto.

"After I stopped playing in the big leagues in 1964, I played and managed another 10 years in Mexico," Minoso says. "I got a hit my first time up when I came to bat for the White Sox in 1976 at the age of 53.

"But I guess I have to accept the truth. I've never seen anyone play forever, even if you're in good physical condition."

Minoso works hard at staying in shape. It pays dividends because he might be the fittest-looking over 65-year-old ex-ballplayer alive.

"I work out every day," he says. "And I dance a lot. I like to dance. I never was drunk in my life. And I don't fool around with the law. I never did that as a player, and I don't do it now that I'm older."

A resident of Chicago, Minnie performs public relations duties for the

White Sox and for a local beer company. He also works with White Sox hitters.

"I like doing that," he says. "It's part of my life. When I can't do it anymore, I'm really going to miss it."

Minoso also wrote a book called *Extra Innings, My Life in Baseball*, which was published by a Chicago firm and released in 1984.

Minnie is still the flashy sprite he was as a player when he wore fancy clothes and was credited with owning a car in every city in which he spent any length of time.

In those days, Minoso could produce electricity just by making an appearance.

That was especially the case on the playing field where Minnie could not only lace line drives all over the lot, but with his speed and daring was always an exciting base-runner.

Minoso came to the big leagues after serving a varied apprenticeship. As a teenager, he had become one of the top players in Cuba. He then came to the United States and in 1946 led the New York Cubans to the Negro League championship over the Cleveland Buckeyes.

In 1948, Minoso was signed by the Cleveland Indians, becoming one of the first black players in professional baseball. He spent a little over two years in the minors, hitting .339 in 1950 in his second full year in San Diego.

As a young player, Minoso played every position except pitcher and catcher. But once he reached the majors, he played mostly in the outfield where at first he was a defensive liability. Although he never really became an accomplished fielder, Minnie did win a Gold Glove award in 1957 as a left fielder.

After a brief trip to Cleveland in 1949, Minoso came to the majors for good in 1951. But before the first month of the season was over, Minnie had become part of one of the biggest trades of the era.

In a three-team trade, the Indians sent Minoso to the White Sox and Sam Zoldak and Ray Murray to the Philadelphia Athletics while the A's got Gus Zernial and Dave Philley from Chicago. The A's shipped Lou Brissie to the Indians and Paul Lehner to the White Sox.

Chicago was just what Minnie needed. Hitting a 430-foot home run in his first at-bat with the White Sox, Minoso quickly became a favorite of Chicago fans with his uninhibited style of play.

Minnie hit .326 in his rookie season while leading the league in triples with 14 and stolen bases with 31. With Minnie's dazzling play combining with Nellie Fox and Chico Carrasquel to set a fast pace, the rejuvenated White Sox quickly went from a second division team to a pennant contender. The fleet Chisox became known as the "Go-Go Sox."

Minoso led the league in triples twice more (1954 and 1956), in doubles in 1957 and in stolen bases in 1952 and 1953.

In 1953, Minoso hit .313 with 104 RBI and 104 runs scored. The following year, he recorded a .320 average with 116 RBI and 119 runs. By then, Minoso had become one of the premier players in the American League.

Minnie Minoso.

Minoso, who ultimately was named to seven American League All-Star teams, continued to spark the White Sox until 1957 when he was involved in another major trade. This time, Chicago sent him back to Cleveland with Fred Hatfield in exchange for Early Wynn and Al Smith.

The 5' 10", 175-pounder played with the Indians for two years before the White Sox got him back in another trade. Unfortunately for Minnie, his return to Chicago came the season after the White Sox had won the American League pennant. Thus, Minoso missed his only chance to play in a World Series.

It didn't seem to matter. In 1960, Minnie had one of the best seasons of his career, hitting .311 and leading the league in hits with 184. It was to be, however, his last big year in the majors.

In 1962, Minoso was waived to the St. Louis Cardinals. He played one season in St. Louis, then one season with the Washington Senators before returning to the White Sox for his final campaign in 1964.

As colorful a player as anybody in his era, Minoso takes a humble view of his outstanding baseball record.

"I am satisfied with everything I did," he says. "I learned so many things. Being in baseball all my life has been a great opportunity.

"What more could I ask of life? I came from nowhere. I worked in the sugar fields as a boy. It was a tough life. I had one pair of shoes and one pair of pants.

"But I always had a smile on my face. I followed the directions that my mother and father gave me. They taught me to be a good citizen, a good human being, and to love life."

In 1984, the White Sox retired Minnie's number nine. Among the accolades that followed the presentation was a letter from President Reagan, "A beautiful letter," as Minoso recalls it.

"It made me realize," says Minnie, "how fortunate I've been to have played baseball in this country."

Andy Pafko—
Solid as a Rock

If there is one symbol that could characterize the play of Andy Pafko during his 17-year major league career, it would have to be the Rock of Gibraltar.

Andy wasn't sensational and he didn't make a lot of noise. He was just a quiet guy with an unshakable foundation who performed his job with strength and endurance.

Pafko was dependable, efficient and, most of all, solid. Modern coaches call the quality that Andy displayed, "character." By any name, it was an attribute that players, managers and fans appreciated, and that made Pafko a workingman's favorite in the three cities in which he played.

He spent his time with the Chicago Cubs, Brooklyn Dodgers and Milwaukee Braves, breaking into the big leagues in 1943 and retiring in 1959. Pafko finished his career with a .285 batting average, accumulating 1,796 hits, 213 home runs and 976 runs-batted-in.

Andy was a member of four National League All-Star teams (1947–48–49–50), and he played in four World Series' with three different clubs: 1945 with the Cubs, 1952 with the Dodgers and 1957–58 with the Braves.

His willingness to play wherever his club needed him made Pafko a valuable man to have on the team. He was a center fielder for the Cubs, with the exception of 1948 when Chicago needed a third baseman and put him there. Andy played left field for the Dodgers and right field for the Braves.

Regardless of which position he played, Pafko's strong arm and sure hands were always precious resources.

Now retired and living in the Chicago suburb of Mt. Prospect, Pafko keeps busy by playing a lot of golf. When he's not playing, he works two days a week as a starter at the local club.

An eight to 10 handicap player, Pafko learned to play golf when his playing days were over. "It's a good way to stay in shape," he says. One of his frequent partners is former Cub, Ernie Banks.

Pafko also gets together on occasion with several other ex-players who live in the area, including Lou Boudreau, Bill Skowron and Johnny Klippstein. He also sees some of his old friends and opponents by attending two or three old-timers games each year.

"I really enjoy playing in those old-timers games," says Andy, who is still trim and close to his playing weight. "Unfortunately, the spirit is willing, but the flesh is weak. Every time I go to one of those games, my wife says, 'Don't try to be a hero. Act your age.' It's fun to reminisce, to talk about the old days with the other ex-players."

Andy has some special mementoes at home. His most cherished items are a glove, uniform and shoes he wore in his final World Series in 1958. "I'll never part with them," he says. "They mean quite a bit to me."

Another item that Pafko values is a baseball. It's the one he caught to save Warren Spahn's 300th career victory.

While that was one of Andy's most thrilling catches, a catch that he didn't make in 1951 ranks as one of his biggest letdowns.

Every baseball fan has at least heard of Bobby Thomson's dramatic Polo Grounds home run that gave the New York Giants the playoff victory over the Brooklyn Dodgers and the National League pennant. But who remembers the name of the left fielder over whose head that heroic blow sailed?

His name was Pafko. "Talk about disappointments," Andy says. "All I could do was stand there and watch the ball go into the stands. I felt so helpless. That home run was the biggest disappointment of my life. And it cost me an awful lot of money (nearly $7,000 was the winner's individual Series share).

"My wife wanted to come to Brooklyn for the World Series that year," Andy adds. "I told her to stay home until we clinched the pennant. It's a good thing she didn't come."

During his long career, though, Pafko had plenty of satisfying experiences to offset that one, big disappointment. "It was a thrill to me to have just been able to play," he says. "Baseball is a great game. I met a lot of nice people, and some important people. I did a lot of traveling. I wouldn't have done anything else. I'd rather have played baseball than eaten.

"I was quite fortunate to have played so long and in such a good era," he continues. "There are many good players today, but I don't think the caliber of player is as good, generally, as it was when I played.

"Today's players also have no identity," Pafko says, suggesting that the average modern pro is a nameless, faceless figure despite the fact that his visage is plastered all over the country.

Identity was never a problem with Pafko. He had large followings everywhere he played, and he could never walk down a street without being recognized.

Andy broke into organized ball in 1940 with Eau Clair (Wisconsin) of the Class D Northern League. A native of Boyceville, Wisconsin, where he was raised on a farm, Pafko wasn't showered with riches in his first professional assignment.

Andy Pafko.

"When I signed, I didn't get a bonus or anything like it," he recalls. "I was just happy to get a job. I got $75 a month, and I was darned glad to get it."

Pafko played three years in the minors. In his third year, while playing for Los Angeles, he tore apart the Pacific Coast League, leading the loop in batting average (.356), hits (215) and RBI (118).

Near the end of the 1943 season, Pafko was called up to the Cubs. He hit .379 for the remainder of the season. The following year, he took over as the Bruins' regular center fielder, joining a redoubtable group of sluggers that included Phil Cavarretta, Bill Nicholson and Stan Hack.

Andy was a regular for the Cubs for seven years. He was one of the most popular players ever to perform at Wrigley Field. Even today, his name evokes feelings of excitement and special memories among Chicago fans of the 1940s.

Pafko had many fine seasons in Chicago, not the least of which occurred in 1945 when he helped the Cubs win their last National League pennant. Andy hit .298 that season while collecting 110 RBI. He led National League outfielders in fielding average, making only two errors all year, and in assists with 26. At the end of the year, *The Sporting News* named him as outfielder on its major league All-Star team.

The muscular slugger hit only .214 in the World Series as the Cubs lost in seven games to the Detroit Tigers.

After suffering both a broken leg and a broken arm and playing only part of the season in 1946, Pafko came back in 1947 to hit .302. In 1948, he hit .312 with 26 home runs. His best all-around season was in 1950 when he hit .304 with a career high 36 home runs. That year, Andy ranked second in the league to Ralph Kiner in home runs and second to Stan Musial in slugging percentage.

In June, 1951, the Cubs stunned both Pafko and his fans by shipping Andy, pitcher Johnny Schmitz, catcher Al Walker and second baseman Wayne Terwilliger in a lopsided trade to the Dodgers for a quartet of second-line players, pitcher Joe Hatten, catcher Bruce Edwards, infielder Eddie Miksis and outfielder Gene Hermanski.

In Brooklyn, Pafko teamed with Duke Snider and Carl Furillo to form one of the finest outfields ever to set foot on a major league diamond.

"That was not only one of the greatest outfields," Andy concedes, "but I think that team was one of the greatest clubs ever put together."

The Dodgers, with Jackie Robinson, Pee Wee Reese, Gil Hodges, Roy Campanella and the aforementioned outfielders forming a modern Murderer's Row, won the National League pennant in 1952. That year, Andy hit .287.

The following winter, Brooklyn swapped Pafko to the Braves for second baseman Roy Hartsfield and $50,000. Again, Andy was in the company of some formidable swingers, notably Eddie Mathews, Joe Adcock and before long, Hank Aaron.

In 1957, Pafko got to collect his first World Series winners' check as the Braves, behind pitcher Lew Burdette, laced the New York Yankees in a spectacular seven-game set. By that time, though, Andy had yielded his regular position to the up and coming youngster named Aaron, the future all-time major league home run king.

Pafko retired as a player after the 1959 season. But he stayed in baseball, spending the next three years as a coach with the Braves, and the next six as a minor league manager. He also scouted for the Montreal Expos for three years before leaving the game altogether.

Andy says the toughest pitcher he faced was the Cincinnati Reds' side-arming righthander, Ewell Blackwell. "He was really hard to hit," Pafko says. "He was also very mean-looking, standing out there on the mound.

"Sal Maglie was tough, too," he adds, "although I did hit three home runs off of him one time in the Polo Grounds."

Pafko rates playing in his first World Series in 1945 as one of his most memorable experiences in baseball.

"I guess the biggest thrill of all, though," he says, "was when my mother came to see me play for the first time. It was in 1945, and we were playing the Pittsburgh Pirates. It was Andy Pafko Day, the first time I'd been honored. At one point, I came up with the bases loaded and two outs. I went to a 3–2 count and struck out.

"Later in the game, the same situation happened. But this time, I hit a grand slam off of Preacher Roe. My poor mother was beside herself. She didn't know baseball, and couldn't understand what was going on. As it turned out, it was the only game she ever saw. It was a big thrill for me that she saw that particular game."

Elmer Valo—
Fearless Flychaser

It was a scene that no follower of the Philadelphia Athletics could ever forget.

The ball would leap from the bat of an opposing hitter, and rocket toward an uncharted spot in right field, a certain extra base hit.

The crowd would roar in anticipation.

And the right fielder, his eyes glued to the ball and his legs pumping like frenzied pistons, would streak across the outfield, heading with utmost determination to the spot where the ball might land.

Sometimes Elmer Valo would crash with a dull thud into the outfield wall. Sometimes he would tumble violently into the stands. Sometimes he would dive headlong across the grass.

But almost always, if the ball could be reached, Elmer Valo would catch it.

It didn't matter how. It didn't matter where. A fly ball was never without company when it ventured near the territory patrolled by the stocky outfielder from Ribnik, Czechoslovakia.

Valo pursued fly balls like a hungry hound going after a piece of beefsteak. To Valo, snaring a ball in flight was like going to church. It was something that had to be done, no matter how hard it was sometimes.

And sometimes it was quite hard. Few walls or fences in the big leagues did not bear the brunt of the 5' 10", 190-pound Valo charging full speed into them during the fearless flychaser's 20 years in the majors.

Elmer had the scars to prove it. He always seemed to be crashing into a wall, and getting helped or carried off the field. Valo had an amazing disregard for both his own safety and the obstacles that stood in his way.

"Anytime a game was close, I'd take a chance," Valo says. "If the game wasn't close, I wouldn't be as aggressive. But if I could help the pitcher out by making a good catch, I would.

"I used to judge my distance," he adds. "I had a pretty good idea if I could catch a ball or not. I usually knew where I was in relation to the wall. Of course, we didn't have warning tracks when I played. I think Connie Mack put in the first one at Shibe Park.

Elmer Valo.

"I ran into some walls. But the only times I really got hurt were at the parks that had low fences like Yankee Stadium. Once, I went through a fence at Shibe Park, too. I tripped over the bullpen mound in right field. Grazed my head on the rail and went into the seats. It knocked me out."

Valo was knocked out more than once. There was the time he ran into the wall at Yankee Stadium to rob Yogi Berra of a home run and save a game for the A's and Joe Coleman. Elmer fell into a crumpled heap, as it turned out with three broken ribs, and with center fielder Sam Chapman desperately trying to pry the ball loose from Valo's glove to show the umpire that the catch had been made.

Another time he dove for a low line drive, knocking the wind out of himself as he landed heavily on his stomach while catching a ball that helped to preserve a no-hitter for the A's Bill McCahan.

"It was the seventh or eighth inning," Valo recalls. "I had to go for it. It was a do or die situation. I gambled and it went into the glove. I knew if I missed it, Chapman was there to back me up. He and I were always talking to each other, always backing each other up."

Elmer, of course, could do more than catch a ball. He was an excellent hitter and base-runner. A lefthanded hitter, he had a career batting average of .282 with 1,420 hits in 1,806 games. Valo hit over .300 four times as a regular. Four other times he hit in the .280s. He had 601 career RBI and 768 runs scored.

Although the best years of his career were spent with the A's, Valo had the unusual distinction of having played for three different teams when their franchises were shifted. He was with the A's when they moved to Kansas City, the Brooklyn Dodgers when they shifted to Los Angeles and the Washington Senators when they became the Minnesota Twins.

"They were all somewhat similar," Valo says of the three moves. "In each case, we were leaving places where the interest in our club had decreased and going to places that really wanted major league clubs. The people in those cities really treated us well. They gave us beautiful receptions and always made us feel welcome."

Valo can also claim the distinction of being the only Czechoslovakian native to play in the big leagues. He moved with his parents to the United States when he was six years old.

"Before that, I didn't even know what baseball was," he says. "I didn't know what sports were. At that age, I just knew how to herd ducks and geese."

Valo's parents settled in Palmerton, Pennsylvania, a town in northeastern Pennsylvania that also gave the sports world an All-American basketball player named Bill Mlkvy, the famed "Owl Without a Vowel" from Temple University.

Valo still lives in Palmerton, just a few line drives away from the field where he first attracted the attention of baseball scouts.

"I began playing baseball as a little kid," Elmer remembers. "First, it was pickup games. Then we formed teams. Finally, I played high school and American Legion ball."

At 16, Valo was good enough to earn a spot on a local semipro team. By then, he had created such a stir that one of his teachers, a local baseball enthusiast, wrote to Connie Mack, telling him of the talents of the young player.

"Roy Mack, Connie's son, came up to watch me, and then a couple of A's scouts, Ira Thomas and Jack Coombs, scouted me," Valo says. "Then they invited me to Philadelphia. They asked my dad to come along, too."

Since the Valos didn't have a car, the teacher who had written the letter drove them to Shibe Park. The A's gave him $10 for transportation expenses.

Although he had not yet entered his senior year in high school, Valo signed a contract with the A's, who then got him a spot on a local semipro team. Max Patkin, later to win fame as the "Clown Prince of Baseball," was also a member of that team.

"They had my name on a contract, but I didn't get any money," Valo says. "They desked (put it away in a drawer) the contract until I was out of high school. But I hung around the A's a lot, and they taught me things about the game. Mr. Mack took care of my expenses."

Finally eligible to play professionally, Valo was assigned in 1939 to the low minors. He hit .374 at Federalsburg in the Eastern Shore League. The following year, he led the Inter-State League in hitting with a .364 average at Wilmington. That got Valo a promotion to the A's, and he finished the 1940 season in Philadelphia, hitting .348 in six games.

Back in Wilmington the next year where he hit .324, Valo again returned to the A's at the end of the season. This time, after hitting .420 in 15 games, he stayed in Philadelphia.

Valo broke into the starting lineup the following year and hit .251 as a 21-year-old rookie in 1942. But less than one year later, he joined the Army. Elmer, who rose to the rank of lieutenant, missed two full seasons before returning to the A's in 1946.

By then, the A's had pulled themselves up from being perennial door-mats over the last decade to respectability.

"We had gone out and picked up Ferris Fain, Eddie Joost, Hank Majeski, Buddy Rosar and Barney McCoskey," Valo says. "Mr. Mack put together a pretty good team."

Valo celebrated his return from the war with a .307 average in 1946. Over the next six years, he went .300, .305, .283, .280, .302 and .281.

"I was mostly a line drive hitter," he states. "My idols had been Jimmie Foxx and Babe Ruth, both long ball hitters, but I didn't try to hit the long ball at Shibe Park. It made no sense with that high wall in right field. So I concentrated on hitting line drives, getting a lot of doubles."

Valo hit double figures in doubles 12 times, ranking among the league leaders in 1949, 1951 and 1952 when he hit 27 two-baggers twice and 26 once.

The A's, meanwhile, had climbed from eighth place in 1946 to fifth in

1947 to a contending position in 1948, the club gradually developing into a team that could compete nearly on a par with the New York Yankees, Boston Red Sox and Cleveland Indians.

The '48 team had a strong starting lineup, an excellent pitching staff and was in first place as late as August 12. But injuries and the Cleveland Indians eventually beat the A's back to fourth place where they finished 12 1/2 games out of first in what had been one of the tightest four-team pennant races in major league history.

"That was a very exciting year," Valo recalls. "I think we were on a par with the other contenders, except we had no depth and only one left-handed pitcher, Lou Brissie. If we'd have had Bobby Shantz or Alex Kellner, who came the following year, I think we could've won the pennant.

"We had a lot of pitchers with sore arms. Phil Marchildon had one. Coleman had one, McCahan had one. Then when Joost, our shortstop, injured his ankle, everything started to come apart."

The A's would never have another year like 1948, but they continued to field mostly respectable teams under Connie Mack and Dykes, his successor.

"It was great playing for Connie Mack," Valo says. "He never bothered you much. Toward the end, he couldn't see too well, so they had to tell him what was going on. Sometimes, that made communications a little slow. But Al Simmons and Dykes used to tell me that he was the greatest manager they ever saw when he was younger."

Valo, by then, was one of Philadelphia's most popular players. He had been given the nickname, Mr. Hustle, and the fans loved his hell-bent style of play.

"I just liked to play," he says. "And I liked to win. I enjoyed playing. I really did. If I could steal a base, get a basehit or make a good catch, I was happy.

"The greatest thrill I had in baseball," Valo continues, "was simply playing the game itself; playing in the major leagues and making a living out of it. It wasn't an exceptional living, but it was a good one.

"I would have been glad to have played anytime. But it was especially good to play in that era. We had some great players like (Ted) Williams and (Joe) DiMaggio. I have a lot of fond memories, especially of the players. Pete Suder. He was my roommate. What a great guy.

"And some of the pitchers. Every team had two or three tough ones. Bob Feller, Hal Newhouser, Bob Lemon; boy, were they tough. Probably the toughest pitcher on me, though, was a lefthanded named Maury McDermott. When he wasn't wild, his curve was very sharp and the ball sank really well. I always just hoped I'd get one hit and walk twice off him.

"Newhouser, when he was on, was really tough, too. He would pitch you high. Feller had a great fastball. His balls always had a lot of action on them, and they tailed in on you. Virgil Trucks and Dizzy Trout also threw very hard, but their balls didn't move as much as Feller's."

When it came to facing the American League hurlers, though, Valo was no slouch. And he had some big games with the bat, including two bases-loaded triples in one game in 1949. In 1950, he hit for the cycle.

Also in 1949, he set a career high with 85 RBI. A year later, he reached a career high in home runs with 10.

In the early 1950s, Valo had several serious injuries that cut into his playing time. Then the A's moved from Philadelphia after the 1954 season. Elmer played a little more than one season in Kansas City before returning to Philadelphia to play with the Phillies.

He became the Phillies' regular right fielder shortly after joining the club. A few weeks later, he led the team to a 4–2 win over the Pittsburgh Pirates in the first game of a Fourth of July doubleheader at Forbes Field with two home runs and three RBI.

After batting .289 for the Phillies in 1956, Valo was traded to the Dodgers. He played one year in Brooklyn and one year in LA. Then he spent a year with the Indians before dividing the next year between the Yankees and Senators.

Along with his frequent crashes into outfield walls, Elmer Valo was also a fine hitter. Here he's greeted by Wally Moses after belting a home run in 1949.

In 1961, the Twins released Valo, and he was picked up for the second time by the Phillies. He ended his big league career that season as a pinch-hitter.

Valo, who for a number of years refereed high school, college and Eastern League basketball during the off-season, attributes his long career to conditioning.

''I kept in shape during the season and worked out all winter,'' he says.

Valo spent one year as a scout for the New York Mets. He was a coach for two years with the Indians and a manager for two more years in Cleveland's farm system.

In 1966, he returned once again to the Phillies, this time joining the club in the front office. After spending some time in public relations, he became a scout and instructor with the club. Although he retired in 1982, Valo still goes to spring training with the Phillies, and works with the young hitters and outfielders.

Valo spent nearly 50 years in professional baseball. During that period, especially during his 20 years as a major league player, Elmer left an indelible mark on the game as a fearless, hustling player. He left his mark on a few outfield walls, too.

Gene Woodling—
A Certified Winner

In a career in which he curried the favor of good fortune, Gene Woodling was described by many words.

Sometimes belligerent, always competitive, intelligent, skillful, diligent and persistent, Woodling was the perfect embodiment of all the characteristics that go into the make-up of a good major league player.

He had one other characteristic, though, that eluded some good players. He was a winner.

Woodling was a winner, not merely because he was a key member of five straight New York Yankees world championship teams. He was a winner, not just because he was one of the premier clutch hitters of his day, or because he hustled every minute he was on the field, or because he was an excellent left fielder. Woodling was a winner, most of all, because he took what he had and made it work—turning a latent baseball talent into a highly successful 17-year career in the big leagues, and then applying the same principles to construct a prosperous life after baseball.

It wasn't easy. Woodling had an early background in swimming that precluded giving any attention to baseball. And even after he did discover the pleasures of the diamond, he had to overcome failure and the eventual reconstruction of his game before he was able to take a place among the redwoods of baseball's forest.

In the end, Woodling was the winner, posting a career batting average of .284 with 1,585 hits, 147 home runs and 830 RBI in 1,796 games with six major league teams, including two terms with two of them.

It would not be accurate to say that Woodling was the heart of the Yankees because names such as DiMaggio, Berra, Henrich and later Mantle satisfied that definition. But there was no less valuable cog in the well-oiled machine of the New Yorkers as they marched to five straight pennants and World Series triumphs.

From 1949 to 1953, Woodling hit .270, .283, .281, .309 and .306 while averaging 59 runs batted in and 66 runs scored a year. Three times his home run totals were in double figures, the high being 15, and he averaged 19 doubles a season while three times leading the Yankees in triples during that period.

It wasn't only as a hitter that the 5' 9 1/2", 195-pound lefthanded batter excelled. Three times (1951-53) he led American League outfielders in fielding percentage (tying for first in 1951). He committed just one error in each of the 1952 and 1953 seasons. And his .989 lifetime fielding average ranks as the ninth-highest in major league history.

Woodling, who became a master at playing the treacherous left field wall at Yankee Stadium, resides in Medina, Ohio, not far from his birthplace in Akron. He lives comfortably, having put his five World Series checks to good use.

"I made some good investments," he says. "I put the money into some fine companies, and I've done pretty well. I just wish every player could end up like this."

Woodling has a farm in Ohio and a condominium in Florida. Six years ago, he retired, and is now a gentleman of leisure. "I'm not ashamed," he says. "I've traveled all over the world. I spend my winters in Florida. Life has been good to me."

It's all because he learned to hit.

"I just can't get over the fact that I made a living hitting a baseball," he marvels. "How lucky can you be?

"I never really dreamed of being a big league player. I just lucked out. The good Lord gave me the ability to hit a baseball. Everything worked out perfectly for me."

In Akron, Woodling grew up in a family of championship swimmers. Baseball was regarded as a sport that other people played, but not the Woodlings.

"The whole family swam," Woodling recalls. "We were all good athletes, but swimming was our sport. My brother was a state champion."

Gene made his high school's hall of fame for swimming. He played "a little baseball," he says, "but was always better in basketball."

After high school, though, Woodling edged toward baseball. "I never had a thought about signing," he says, "but the scouts found me, and I finally signed with the Cleveland Indians. It was better than working for $15 a week at Goodyear.

"The scout who found me had to be a super scout," Woodling jests. "His name was Bill Bradley. To find me, he really had to beat the bushes."

Woodling entered organized baseball in 1940, and in his first year hit .398 at Mansfield to win the Class D Ohio State League batting title. The following year, he hit .394 at Flint to win the Michigan State League batting crown. Two years later, he won the Eastern League title at Wilkes-Barre with a .344 mark.

That was enough to get him called up to Cleveland for the final weeks of the 1943 season. Woodling hit .320 in eight games, then left to spend two years in the armed forces.

Gene Woodling.

After returning in 1946, Woodling was a dismal failure at Cleveland, and the Indians traded him to the Pittsburgh Pirates for catcher Al Lopez. Woodling wasn't much better with the Bucs, and after 22 games in 1947, they shipped him to Newark of the International League.

By 1948, Woodling had been a two-time loser in major league tryouts, and appeared headed back down the baseball ladder. Winding up with the San Francisco Seals of the Pacific Coast League against his wishes, the disappointed outfielder came under manager Frank O'Doul, a two-time National League batting champion and an outstanding hitting instructor.

"Until then, I had always stood straight up to hit," Woodling recalls. "I hit to all fields, often long flies to center that turned into big outs. Lefty O'Doul got me to hit from a crouch and to pull the ball."

The results were sensational. Woodling peppered PCL pitching for a .385 average to capture his fourth minor league batting title while setting career highs in home runs (22), hits (212) and RBI (107).

At the end of the season, Woodling was named Minor League Player of the Year by *The Sporting News*. More important, his hitting and fiery competitive spirit had caught the eye of a rival manager, the pilot of the Oakland Oaks whose name was Casey Stengel.

When Stengel was appointed manager of the Yankees soon afterward, one of his first orders of business was to instruct general manager George Weiss to get "that feller" Woodling from the Seals.

Woodling was purchased for $17,500, and the following season embarked on a full-time big league career that would last until the end of 1962.

At first, Stengel platooned the 26-year-old slugger in left, alternating him primarily with the righthanded-hitting Johnny Lindell. Woodling didn't like sitting on the bench, but he never let his displeasure jeopardize his chances of staying with the Yankees.

"What could I say," he shrugs, "when every year they'd win the pennant? I wanted to play every day, of course, but we just kept winning, and there's nothing that can beat that."

Gradually, Stengel played Woodling on more of an everyday basis, and Gene eventually gained the reputation as one of the smartest and best pure hitters in the league.

His best year with the Yankees came in 1952 when he hit a major league career high .309, placing fifth in the league. For a while, Gene was battling the Philadelphia A's Ferris Fain for the title, but a painful groin injury late in the year helped to drop the New York belter's average from .320 to its final level.

Throughout his years with the Yankees, Woodling was known for his clutch hits. He never had great numbers of RBI (his career high was 71 in 1951), but he always seemed to come through at the right time. Three times he won 1-0 games with home runs, once breaking up a pitching duel between Allie Reynolds and Bob Feller in which the former hurled a no-hitter.

"That game gave me one of my biggest thrills," Woodling says of the 1951 encounter. "It not only won the game for us, it also came in front of my hometown fans in Cleveland."

Woodling saved some of his best moments for the World Series. He hit .400 in the 1949 Series, .429 in the 1950 classic and .348 in 1952, winding up with a .318 batting average in 26 World Series games. His home run in the seventh game of the '52 Series helped the Yankees beat the Dodgers, 4–2.

Gene also had a rare miscue in the field in a Series. In 1950, he lost a two-out fly ball hit by the Philadelphia Phillies' Andy Seminick in the ninth inning of the final game. The error let in two runs and lost a shutout for Whitey Ford.

Woodling was one of 12 Yankees to be a member of all five consecutive World Series winners. Although each team was a powerhouse of heavy hitters and strong pitchers, Gene says each one was different.

"There were changes every year, so they weren't really the same teams," Woodling says. "I don't think one team was any better than another. They were a great bunch of guys. All the players were very close—and still are. I'll guarantee, if anybody ever got into trouble, the others would be there to help him out.

"I idolized Joe DiMaggio," Woodling adds. "Just playing alongside of him was to me one of the greatest thrills."

Woodling got another thrill of sorts after the 1954 season when the Yankees made him part of the biggest trade in baseball history in an 18-player deal with the Baltimore Orioles. Among others, New York received pitchers Bob Turley and Don Larsen and Baltimore landed catcher Gus Triandos, shortstop Willie Miranda and Woodling.

"The Orioles were really a raggedy team," Woodling remembers. "Of course, to the fans, I was still a Yankee. I did very badly, and they booed me constantly."

Woodling spent only 47 games with the Orioles before they packed him off to the Indians. Gene played for his original team for two and one-half seasons. After hitting .321 in 1957, he was shipped back to Baltimore in a trade that also sent Dick Williams to the Birds and Lary Doby back to Cleveland.

"It was kind of strange," Woodling remembers. "Here I was, 36 years old, traded back to the town that didn't like me. But Paul Richards said he wanted me, and so I went and gave 150 percent. This time, the fans got on my side.

"In fact," he continues, "I was the first guy ever given a day in Baltimore. As it turned out, the town was really good to me."

Woodling played three seasons as a regular with Baltimore, hitting .276, .300 and .283. On an Orioles team that was an odd blend of fuzzy-cheeked youth and grizzled veterans, Woodling was one of the steadying forces that helped to get the team out of the American League doldrums and propel it all the way to second place by 1960.

Woodling went in the expansion draft to the new Washington Senators in 1961, the year the old Senators took up residence in Minnesota. He hit .313. The following year, Washington dealt him to the New York Mets in mid-season, and in 1962, at the age of 40, Woodling finished his career with a .276 batting average for the season.

The southpaw swinger rejoined the Yankees as a scout, and during the 1960s and 1970s, he bird-dogged for the Yankees. His biggest find was catcher Thurman Munson, a fellow native of Akron. Gene later scouted for the Indians before bowing out of baseball.

"I never set any records," he says, "but I could hit and I was a good, steady ballplayer. I had a helluva reputation for winning ball games in the late innings, and I never struck out much.

"I never had a serious injury. I just came to play. That's all that mattered."

About the Author

Rich Westcott is publisher and editor of *Phillies Report* in Philadelphia. He is also a columnist for *Baseball Hobby News,* and is co-author of *The Phillies Encyclopedia.*

A former pitcher of no particular note who decided long ago that writing was a more appropriate use of his fingers than throwing baseballs, he has served on a number of newspaper and magazine staffs during a 25-year career as a journalist.

The author is a graduate of Drexel University in Philadelphia and Johns Hopkins University in Baltimore. He lives with his wife and four children in Springfield, Pa.